DATE DUE

			PRINTED IN U.S.A.

Authors & Artists for Young Adults

ISSN 1040-5682

R

Authors & Artists for Young Adults

VOLUME 25

Thomas McMahon
Editor

GALE

DETROIT · LONDON

Thomas McMahon, *Editor*

Joyce Nakamura, *Managing Editor*
Hal May, *Publisher*

...nna Brod, Ken Cuthbertson, Kelly Druckenbroad, R. Garcia-
Johnson, Marian C. Gonsior, J. Sydney Jones, Irene Durham, Nancy Rampson,
C. M. Ratner, Jon Saari, Peggy Saari, Pamela L. Shelton, Kathleen Witman,
Sketchwriters/Contributing Editors

Victoria B. Cariappa, *Research Manager*
Cheryl L. Warnock, *Project Coordinator*
Michael P. LaMeau, Andrew Guy Malonis, Barbara McNeil, *Research Specialists*
Jeffrey D. Daniels, Norma Sawaya, *Research Associates*
Phyllis Blackman, Talitha A. Jean, Corrine A. Stocker, *Research Assistants*

Susan M. Trosky, *Permissions Manager*
Maria L. Franklin, *Permissions Specialist*
Edna Hedblad, Michele Lonoconus, *Permissions Associate*

Mary Beth Trimper, *Production Director*
Carolyn Fischer, *Production Assistant*

Randy Bassett, *Image Database Supervisor*
Gary Leach, *Graphic Artist*
Robert Duncan, Michael Logusz, *Imaging Specialists*
Pamela A. Reed, *Photography Coordinator*

Library of Congress Catalog Card Number 89-641100
ISBN 0-7876-1972-8
ISSN 1040-5682

10 9 8 7 6 5 4 3 2 1

Printed in the United States of America

Authors and Artists for Young Adults

TEEN BOARD

The staff of *Authors and Artists for Young Adults* wishes to thank the following young adult readers for their teen board participation:

Michael Arawy
Rebecca Athan
Andrew Bagley
Catharine Banasiak
Melissa Barnaby
Allison Barrett
Devin Barry
Amy Becker
Melanie Beene
Dara Bonetti
Jesse Bonware
Jessica Buchser
Emily Burleson
Dylan Burns
Annie Burton
Rachel Campominos
Abby Conover
Christy Cook
Teresa Copeland
Jordan Copes
Heather Lee Cordeira
Lin Costello
Kate Cottrell
John Crower
Jennifer Dennis
Joanne M. Dimenno
Alison Dougherty
Josh Dukelow
Joe Eckert
Ellis Farmer
Kylin Follenweider
Alda Fox
Michelle Gagnon
Sarah Gangstad
Mary Genest
Eric Gilbert
Kate Gunther

Grant Hamilton
Alice Harnisch
Mark Haseltine
Allen Heinecke
Erin Hooley
Laura Huber
Maeghan Hurley
Kristin Hursh
Kristina Ivanisin
Tom Ivers
Adam James
Amanda Joy
Austin Joy
Ian Kelly
Alysia Kulas
Sarah Kulik
Dana-Jean LaHaie
Rolland LaHaie
Sarah Lairy
Aaron Landini
Sarah Lawhead
Erin Lewis
Nisha Low-Nam
Jamie Luna
Chenda Ly
Lauren Makowski
Jaimie Mantie
Kimberly Marie Rutkauski
Jen Mathiason
Megan McDonald
Niamh McGuigan
Allison C. Mikkalo
Jocelyn Miller
Glynn Miller II
Neal Mody
Shannon Murphy
Jason Nealy

Pablo Nevares
Brittany Pagella
Carlene Palmer
Krista Paradiso
Daniel Pereira
Eric Peters
Brian Petersen
Leah M. Pickren
Anne Pizzi
Mike Quilligan
Jessi Quizar
Christina Rampelli
Matthew R. Reese
Eric Rice
Benjamin Rockey
Meghan E. Rozarie
Tony Ruggiero
Peter Ryan
Erica Sebeok
Amee Shelley
Elizabeth Shouse
Kersten Stevens
Erin Stick
Mark Strauss
Avery Thatcher
Adam Tierney
Dan Uznanski
Melissa Vosburg
Rebecca Weide
Jonathan Weinberg
Lynn Weisee
Joe Wenzel
Kenyon Whitehead
Alisson Wood
Brandon C. Wood
Ally Wright
Josh Yorke

Contents

Introduction

Authors and Artists for Young Adults is a reference series designed to serve the needs of middle school, junior high, and high school students interested in creative artists. Originally inspired by the need to bridge the gap between Gale's *Something about the Author,* created for children, and *Contemporary Authors,* intended for older students and adults, *Authors and Artists for Young Adults* has been expanded to cover not only an international scope of authors, but also a wide variety of other artists.

Although the emphasis of the series remains on the writer for young adults, we recognize that these readers have diverse interests covering a wide range of reading levels. The series therefore contains not only those creative artists who are of high interest to young adults, including cartoonists, photographers, music composers, bestselling authors of adult novels, media directors, producers, and performers, but also literary and artistic figures studied in academic curricula, such as influential novelists, playwrights, poets, and painters. The goal of *Authors and Artists for Young Adults* is to present this great diversity of creative artists in a format that is entertaining, informative, and understandable to the young adult reader.

Entry Format

Each volume of *Authors and Artists for Young Adults* will furnish in-depth coverage of twenty to twenty-five authors and artists. The typical entry consists of:

—A detailed biographical section that includes date of birth, marriage, children, education, and addresses.

—A comprehensive bibliography or filmography including publishers, producers, and years.

—Adaptations into other media forms.

—Works in progress.

—A distinctive essay featuring comments on an artist's life, career, artistic intentions, world views, and controversies.

—References for further reading.

—Extensive illustrations, photographs, movie stills, cartoons, book covers, and other relevant visual material.

A cumulative index to featured authors and artists appears in each volume.

Compilation Methods

The editors of *Authors and Artists for Young Adults* make every effort to secure information directly from the authors and artists through personal correspondence and interviews. Sketches on living authors and artists are sent to the biographee for review prior to publication. Any sketches not personally reviewed by biographees or their representatives are marked with an asterisk (*).

Highlights of Forthcoming Volumes

Among the authors and artists planned for future volumes are:

Nathan Aaseng	Ian Fleming	Larry Niven
Scott Adams	Terry Goodkind	Alan Paton
Lloyd Alexander	Stephen Jay Gould	Tamora Pierce
James W. Bennett	Alex Haley	Erich Maria Remarque
Judy Blume	Robert Jordan	Kim Stanley Robinson
Ken Burns	Charles Keeping	Graham Salisbury
Bebe Moore Campbell	David Klass	Barry Sonnenfeld
Aidan Chambers	Annette Curtis Klause	Suzanne Fisher Staples
Joseph Conrad	Susan Kuklin	Joyce Sweeney
Daniel Defoe	Mary E. Lyons	Laura Ingalls Wilder
Carl Deuker	Sharyn McCrumb	Margaret Willey
Nancy Farmer	Michael Moorcock	Virginia Euwer Wolff

Contact the Editor

We encourage our readers to examine the entire *AAYA* series. Please write and tell us if we can make AAYA even more helpful to you. Give your comments and suggestions to the editor:

BY MAIL: The Editor, *Authors and Artists for Young Adults*, Gale Research, 835 Penobscot Building, 645 Griswold St., Detroit, MI 48226-4094. **Note:** New address, effective September 15, 1998: 27500 Drake Rd., Farmington Hills, MI 48331-3535.

BY TELEPHONE: (800) 347-GALE

BY FAX: (313) 961-6599

Authors & Artists for Young Adults

Joan Aiken

■ Personal

Born September 4, 1924, in Rye, Sussex, England; daughter of Conrad Potter (a poet) and Jessie (McDonald) Aiken; married Ronald George Brown (a journalist), July 7, 1945 (deceased, 1955); married Julius Goldstein (a painter and teacher), September 2, 1976; children: (first marriage) John Sebastian, Elizabeth Delano. *Education:* Attended schools in Oxford, England. *Politics:* Liberal. *Religion:* Agnostic.

■ Addresses

Home—The Hermitage, East St., Petworth, West Sussex GU28 0AB, England; New York, NY. *Agent*—A. M. Heath, 40-42 William IV St., London WC2N 4DD, England; Brandt & Brandt, 1501 Broadway, New York, NY 10036.

■ Career

British Broadcasting Corp., BBC Registry Department, Goring-on-Thames, Berkshire, England, clerk, 1941-43; United Nations Information Office, London, England, secretary and librarian, 1943-49; worked at St. Thomas' Hospital, London, 1943; *Argosy* (magazine), London, features editor, 1955-60; J. Walter Thompson Advertising Agency, London, advertising copywriter, 1961; full-time writer, 1961—. Writer in residence, Lynchburg College, 1988. *Member:* Authors Society, Writers Guild, Mystery Writers Circle.

■ Awards, Honors

Lewis Carroll Shelf Award, 1965, for *The Wolves of Willoughby Chase;* Guardian Award for Children's Fiction, and Carnegie Award runner-up, both 1969, both for *The Whispering Mountain;* Edgar Allan Poe Award, best juvenile mystery, Mystery Writers of America, 1972, for *Night Fall; Midnight Is a Place* was selected one of the *New York Times* Outstanding Books, 1974; *The Skin Spinners* was included in the American Institute of Graphic Arts Book Show, 1975.

■ Writings

FOR CHILDREN

All You've Ever Wanted and Other Stories, illustrated by Pat Marriott, J. Cape, 1953.
More Than You Bargained For and Other Stories, illustrated by Pat Marriott, J. Cape, 1955, Abelard, 1957.

The Kingdom and the Cave, illustrated by Dick Hart, Abelard, 1960, new edition, illustrated by Victor Ambrus, Doubleday, 1974.

The Wolves of Willoughby Chase, Doubleday, 1962.

Black Hearts in Battersea (sequel to *The Wolves of Willoughby Chase*), illustrated by Robin Jacques, Doubleday, 1964, British edition, illustrated by Pat Marriott, J. Cape, 1964.

Night Birds on Nantucket, illustrated by Robin Jacques, Doubleday, 1966, British edition published as *Nightbirds on Nantucket,* illustrated by Pat Marriott, J. Cape, 1966.

Armitage, Armitage, Fly Away Home, illustrated by Betty Fraser, Doubleday, 1968.

The Whispering Mountain, illustrated by Frank Bozzo, J. Cape, 1968, Doubleday, 1969.

A Necklace of Raindrops and Other Stories, illustrated by Jan Pienkowski, J. Cape, 1968, Doubleday, 1969.

A Small Pinch of Weather and Other Stories, illustrated by Pat Marriott, J. Cape, 1969.

Night Fall, Macmillan (England), 1969, Holt, 1970.

Smoke from Cromwell's Time and Other Stories, Doubleday, 1970.

Winterthing: A Child's Play (first produced in London, England, at the Young Vic Theatre, 1970, and in the United States in Albany, NY, 1977, music by John Sebastian Brown), illustrated by Arvis Stewart, Holt, 1972, published in England with *The Mooncusser's Daughter,* J. Cape, 1973.

The Cuckoo Tree, illustrated by Susan Obrant, Doubleday, 1971, British edition, illustrated by Pat Marriott, J. Cape, 1971.

The Kingdom under the Sea and Other Stories, illustrated by Jan Pienkowski, J. Cape, 1971.

All and More (stories; originally published as *All You've Ever Wanted* and *More Than You Bargained For*), J. Cape, 1971.

A Harp of Fishbones and Other Stories, illustrated by Pat Marriott, J. Cape, 1972.

The Escaped Black Mamba, (produced on BBC-TV), illustrated by Quentin Blake, BBC Books, 1973, published as *Arabel and the Escaped Mamba,* Knight, 1984.

The Mooncusser's Daughter (play; first produced in London at the Unicorn Theatre, 1973, music by John Sebastian Brown), Viking, 1973, published in England with *Winterthing,* J. Cape, 1973.

The Bread Bin (produced on BBC-TV), illustrated by Quentin Blake, BBC Books, 1974.

All but a Few, Penguin, 1974.

Midnight Is a Place, illustrated by Pat Marriott, Viking, 1974.

Tales of Arabel's Raven (produced on BBC-TV), illustrated by Quentin Blake, J. Cape, 1974, published as *Arabel's Raven,* Doubleday, 1974.

Not What You Expected: A Collection of Short Stories, Doubleday, 1974.

The Skin Spinners: Poems, illustrated by Ken Rinciari, Viking, 1976.

A Bundle of Nerves: Stories of Horror, Suspense, and Fantasy, Gollancz, 1976.

Mortimer's Tie (produced on BBC-TV, 1976), illustrated by Quentin Blake, BBC Books, 1976.

(Translator from the French) Sophie de Segur, *The Angel Inn,* illustrated by Pat Marriott, J. Cape, 1976, Stemmer House, 1978.

Go Saddle the Sea, illustrated by Pat Marriott, Doubleday, 1977.

The Far Forests: Tales of Romance, Fantasy, and Suspense, Viking, 1977.

The Faithless Lollybird and Other Stories, illustrated by Pat Marriott, J. Cape, 1977, United States edition, illustrated by Eros Keith, Doubleday, 1978.

Street (play; first produced at the Unicorn Theatre, 1977, music by John Sebastian Brown), illustrated by Arvis Stewart, Viking, 1978.

Tale of a One-Way Street and Other Stories, illustrated by Jan Pienkowski, J. Cape, 1978, Doubleday, 1980.

Mice and Mendelson, illustrated by Babette Cole, published with music by John Sebastian Brown, J. Cape, 1978.

Mortimer and the Sword Excalibur, (produced on BBC-TV), illustrated by Quentin Blake, BBC Books, 1979.

The Spiral Stair, illustrated by Quentin Blake, BBC Books, 1979.

A Touch of Chill, Gollancz, 1979, Delacorte, 1980.

Arabel and Mortimer (includes *Mortimer's Tie, The Spiral Stair,* and *Mortimer and the Sword Excalibur*), illustrated by Quentin Blake, J. Cape/ BBC Books, 1980, Doubleday, 1981.

The Shadow Guests, Delacorte, 1980.

The Stolen Lake, illustrated by Pat Marriott, Delacorte, 1981.

Mortimer's Portrait on Glass (produced on BBC-TV), illustrated by Quentin Blake, BBC Books, 1982.

The Mystery of Mr. Jones's Disappearing Taxi (produced on BBC-TV), illustrated by Quentin Blake, BBC Books, 1982.

A Whisper in the Night (horror stories), Gollancz, 1982, Delacorte, 1984.

Moon Hill (play), first produced at the Unicorn Theatre, 1982.

Bridle the Wind (sequel to *Go Saddle the Sea*), illustrated by Pat Marriott, Delacorte, 1983.

The Kitchen Warriors, illustrated by Jo Worth, BBC Books/Knight Books, 1983.

Mortimer's Cross (includes *The Mystery of Mr. Jones's Disappearing Taxi* and *Mortimer's Portrait on Glass*), illustrated by Quentin Blake, J. Cape/BBC Books, 1983, Harper, 1984.

Fog Hounds, Wind Cat, Sea Mice (stories), Macmillan, 1984.

Up the Chimney Down and Other Stories, illustrated by Pat Marriott, J. Cape, 1984, Harper, 1985.

Mortimer Says Nothing (stories), illustrated by Quentin Blake, J. Cape, 1985, Harper, 1986.

The Last Slice of Rainbow, illustrated by Margaret Walty, J. Cape, 1985, illustrated by Alix Berenzy, Harper, 1988.

Past Eight O'Clock (stories), illustrated by Jan Pienkowski, Cape, 1986, Viking, 1987.

Dido and Pa, J. Cape, 1986, Delacorte, 1987.

The Moon's Revenge, illustrated by Lee Alan, Knopf, 1987.

The Teeth of the Gale, Harper, 1988.

The Erl King's Daughter, Heinemann, 1988.

Give Yourself a Fright, Delacorte, 1989.

Return to Harken House, Delacorte, 1990.

A Fit of Shivers: Tales for Late at Night, Gollancz, 1990, Delacorte, 1992.

The Shoemaker's Boy, Simon & Schuster, 1991.

Mortimer and Arabel, BBC Books, 1992.

A Foot in the Grave, illustrated by Jan Pienkowski, Viking, 1992.

Is, Cape, 1992, published as *Is Underground*, Delacorte, 1993.

A Creepy Company, Gollancz, 1993, Dell, 1995.

The Midnight Moropus, Simon & Schuster, 1993.

Cold Shoulder Road, Delacorte, 1996.

Contributor to anthology *Sixteen: Short Stories by Outstanding Writers for Young Adults*, edited by Donald R. Gallo, Dell, 1984; *A Treasury of Pony Stories*, edited by Linda Jenning and illustrated by Anthony Lewis, Kingfisher, 1996; *Night Terrors: Stories of Shadow and Substance*, edited by Lois Duncan, Simon & Schuster, 1996; *Breaking the Spell: Tales of Enchantment*, edited by Sally Grindley and illustrated by Susan Field, Kingfisher, 1997. Also author of a television play, *The Dark Streets of Kimballs Green*.

FOR ADULTS

The Silence of Herondale, Doubleday, 1964.

The Fortune Hunters, Doubleday, 1965.

Beware of the Bouquet, Doubleday, 1966, published in England as *Trouble with Product X*, Gollancz, 1966.

Dark Interval, Doubleday, 1967, published in England as *Hate Begins at Home*, Gollancz, 1967.

The Ribs of Death, Gollancz, 1967, published as *The Crystal Crow*, Doubleday, 1968.

The Windscreen Weepers and Other Tales of Horror and Suspense, Gollancz, 1969, published as *Green Flash and Other Tales of Horror, Suspense, and Fantasy*, Holt, 1971.

The Embroidered Sunset, Doubleday, 1970.

The Butterfly Picnic, Gollancz, 1970, published as *A Cluster of Separate Sparks*, Doubleday, 1972.

Died on a Rainy Sunday, Holt, 1972.

Voices in an Empty House, Doubleday, 1975.

Castle Barebane, Viking, 1976.

The Five-Minute Marriage, Gollancz, 1977, Doubleday, 1978.

Last Movement, Doubleday, 1977.

The Smile of the Stranger, Doubleday, 1978.

The Lightning Tree, Gollancz, 1980, published as *The Weeping Ash*, Doubleday, 1980.

The Young Lady from Paris, Gollancz, 1982, published as *The Girl from Paris*, Doubleday, 1982.

The Way to Write for Children, St. Martin's, 1982.

Foul Matter, Doubleday, 1983.

Mansfield Revisited (a sequel to *Mansfield Park* by Jane Austen), Gollancz, 1984, Doubleday, 1985.

Deception, Gollancz, 1987, published as *If I Were You*, Doubleday, 1987.

Blackground, Doubleday, 1989.

Jane Fairfax (a sequel to *Emma* by Jane Austen), Gollancz, 1990, St. Martin's, 1991.

The Haunting of Lamb House, Cape, 1991, St. Martin's, 1993.

Morningquest, Gollancz, 1992, St. Martin's, 1993.

Eliza's Daughter (a sequel to *Sense and Sensibility* by Jane Austen), St. Martin's Press, 1994.

The Winter Sleepwalker, Cape, 1994.

Emma Watson (a completion of an unfinished manuscript by Jane Austen), St. Martin's, 1996.

The Cockatrice Boys, Tor, 1996.

Also contributor of short stories to *Abinger Chronicle, Argosy, Everywoman, John Bull, Vogue, Good Housekeeping, Housewife, Vanity Fair, New Statesman, Woman's Own, Woman's Journal*, and of reviews to *History Today* and *Washington Post*.

■ Adaptations

Midnight Is a Place was adapted as a thirteen-part serial and broadcast on Southern Television in

England, 1977; *Armitage, Armitage, Fly Away Home* was adapted for broadcast on BBC-TV, 1978; *The Wolves of Willoughby Chase* was adapted for film by Atlantic/Zenith, 1988; *Apple of Discord* and *The Rose of Puddle Fratrum* were adapted from Aiken's short stories and broadcast on BBC-TV. *The Wolves of Willoughby Chase* and *A Necklace of Raindrops and Other Stories* were released on audiocassette by Caedmon, 1978.

■ Overview

Joan Aiken comes from a literary family—her father, Conrad Aiken, was a distinguished American poet, and her stepfather, Martin Armstrong, was a novelist. It was no surprise that at the age of five, Aiken bought a notebook and decided that she would be a writer when she grew up. Using the haunting country settings that she experienced as a youth, Aiken has written many well-received children's stories and several books for adults. She has legions of fans around the world who, after reading her books, have become hooked on her many mysterious and fantastical tales.

"A happy childhood is supposed to lead to neurosis in middle age. By which criterion I should be a hundred percent neurotic, for my childhood was, in most ways, extremely happy," Joan Aiken wrote in an essay in *Something About the Author Autobiography Series* (*SAAS*). However, her young life was not without incident. Aiken's early years were spent in the village of Rye, England, in an ancient dwelling called Yeake's House. Despite the inconveniences of the building—steep staircases, no central heating, ancient plumbing, and insufficient lighting—it was a place that would inspire a young writer.

Aiken's early memories of her father were shadowy; when she was young, he left the family, later deciding to divorce her mother. The divorce caused a family crisis. Her mother was Canadian, and she would now be alone in a foreign country trying to raise three children. Instead, she decided to marry her husband's best friend, Martin Armstrong, and settle down in a small village in a house called Farrs. Armstrong made it clear that he was not the fatherly type; Aiken's older siblings were then sent to boarding schools that did not suit them. Aiken had lost a father and her mother was becoming distant also.

Because she was the youngest child, Aiken was schooled at home "because of lack of money," she told Catherine Courtney in an interview for *Authors and Artists for Young Adults* (*AAYA*). "When she and my father divorced, he never sent us any money because he was only just making a living as poet. My mother had lost most of what little money she had in the 1929 slump; her brothers had invested it in Canadian paper. So I couldn't start going to boarding school until my sister finished." Aiken's mother was a worthy teacher. She had been received degrees in North America at McGill and Radcliffe and taught Aiken languages and history exceptionally well. "Things like math we fell down on, however, because I was naturally bad at it, and I expect it wasn't her 'thing,'" she related in *AAYA*.

Despite some of the difficulties of changing homes and getting a new father figure in her life, Aiken remembers the place as a happy one. "I think of the house always in sunshine; as one came in the glass-paned front door there would be warmth, a smell of apples and woodsmoke, the contented sound of a house where quiet, busy activities are proceeding, the sound of a typewriter or sewing machine, cooking noises, Scarlatti from the piano, the rustle of a log fire," she wrote in *SAAS*. The garden was another top feature—there were grass lawns where she could play, and many different types of flowers.

Aiken often went out exploring in their small village with their maid, Lily. "On these walks we developed our private mythology, woven across the framework of the films Lily had seen, the books I had read," she wrote in *SAAS*. They toured the local places that were wrapped in mist and mystery; many of these became inspiration for her later writings. They included "Sutton 'Ollow, the deep-banked road that climbed to our village, haunted by a ghost who sat on a leaning tree; Crouch Cave, an underground brick vault in the wood, really an old icehouse; The Decoy, another haunted path (by the ghost of a shot gamekeeper); the Slipes . . . where we picked young beech sprays to decorate the May Queen's Throne best of all, Burton waterfall, a twenty-foot artificial cascade, underneath which a damp and drippy tunnel ran clean through from one side to the other," she related in *SAAS*.

Aiken chronicled her experiences using the notebook she had purchased when she was five. In addition, she was an avid reader. However, her stepfather was extremely critical of all reading material in her house, so that she often felt she was not living up to his exacting standards. "My stepfather's opinions occupied a very distinct place in my early life; I was conscious all the time of living by a double standard, his and mine," she related in *SAAS*.

When she was seven, she began to have more encounters with her birth father, going to visit him and his new wife several times a year. Although her interactions with him were often difficult and uncomfortable, she looked up to him and admired him greatly. She also dreamt of having he and her mother married again. "I developed a great romantic devotion to Conrad and used to invent

The first in a series of books set in an alternate-history Britain, Aiken's Lewis Carroll Shelf Award-winner finds two cousins threatened by frightening wolves and a cruel governess.

tales of how he and Jessie made up their differences and came together again," she wrote in *SAAS*. Still, her father became a positive literary influence, encouraging her writing and giving her many books to read.

Aiken's parents had decided that she would go away to a boarding school when she was twelve and her older siblings were at university. This was the only way the family could afford to send her away. Although her mother went out of her way to make Aiken feel comfortable at the school, the changes were severe. "The contrast between our small, orderly, quiet house, filled with ancient, beautiful objects and civilised practises—and this noisy, bare, crowded, ugly barrack, and its bleak, trampled garden, both filled with girls in uniform, came as an inconceivable shock," she related in *SAAS*. Furthermore, there were other difficulties to encounter: "It was incredible the amount of clothes they piled on us—gym tunics and blazers," she confided in *AAYA*. "I had been used to wearing shorts and a jersey, and then suddenly I was in stockings and a suspender belt, combinations and a liberty bodice."

Although adjusting to the school experience was difficult, after a time, Aiken began to enjoy the learning and competitive aspects. "In no time I was devoting all my energy to getting the highest marks in class, getting parts in school plays, getting poems into the school magazine, being elected Form Representative, and so on," she related in *SAAS*. However, she felt that she never really fit in—she was too used to belonging in an adult world. Towards the end of her career there, she had become too much of a dissident to be accepted by the staff. In addition, World War II had started, the school was in disarray, then bankrupt, and had to be conjoined with a larger school. This upset Aiken so much that she got sick, had to spend an entire term in bed, and her much prized grades dropped. When she tried to gain entrance to Oxford University, she failed, to the dismay of her family.

Dreams of Literary Career

Once out of school, Aiken took a job at the British Broadcasting Corporation, hoping to find a career there that might involve writing and editing. However, deep down inside she was longing to find a very rich man to marry so she could live once again in the countryside she found so idyllic. She did get a job at the BBC, but instead of a pleasant job editing poetry, she became a file clerk. Since it was during the worst part of the war, she commented in *SAAS* that "their filing system had been evacuated from London to a mansion in the Thames valley near Reading. Here dwelt thirty women, all ages and classes, sleeping in bunks, filing and indexing the corporation's written matter, scripts and letters, which arrived daily in sacks. My first duties were to open the mail, cycle to the post office four miles distant for more stamps, and (because of the national paper shortage) rule lines on the back of used index cards, so that they could be used again."

Aiken realized that this job was leading nowhere, so she enrolled in a secretarial course, learning typing and other skills. She got a well-paying job at the United Nations Information Office but disliked living in London, especially during the bombing raids. She had been writing children's stories for the BBC show "Children's Hour" and also trying her hand at writing adult short stories, with little success. In 1945 she married her boss from the United Nations office, journalist Ron Brown.

The couple moved out to the country, near to her early childhood home. The country setting enhanced her creativity, and she wrote short stories and fantasies for children. Soon after their first child was born, they moved to a plot of land closer to London that had a brook running through it. Defying the local culture, they bought a bus, parked it on the land, and used it as their house. "We lived in the bus for about eighteen months with the children," she told *AAYA*. "There was remarkably little housework. An enormous piece of carpet was laid all the way up to the windows. We had water and electricity. . . . The bus was a terribly unsightly object, however, and the neighbors objected to it strongly." Soon after, they built a house on the land and had a second child. But the resulting bills they amassed were very stressful to the couple. Aiken focused more and more on getting her writing published. Her first book, *All You've Ever Wanted and Other Stories*, saw print in 1953.

Tragedy struck when her husband was diagnosed with tuberculosis and fired from his job. With no other resources, they moved into a relative's house in the country, then found a guesthouse in rural

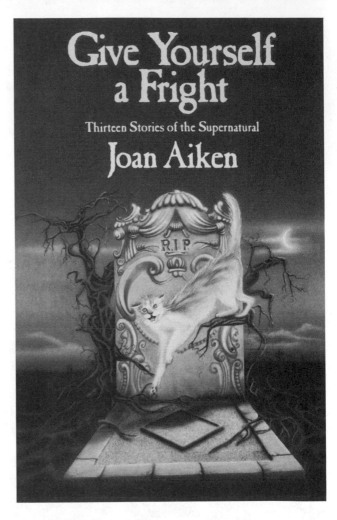

The author creates fantasy worlds inhabited by mischievous ghosts in this 1989 work.

Cornwall where they would take in tourists. Aiken honed her writing skills while there, but unfortunately, her husband became sicker. He was diagnosed with lung cancer and muscular dystrophy and died in 1955. "Ron's death made me grow up," she told *AAYA*. "Looking back at myself in my twenties, it seems to me now that I was terribly callow and self-centered. After his death, my main aim was to get a house where my children and I could all be together." (Aiken eventually remarried in 1976.)

Towards this end, she became even more intent on publishing her writing. "I was living in a one-room flat in Wimbledon and my children were living with an ex-sister-in-law who ran a small school in south London for children. . . . This was a miserable situation for all of us and I was resolved to change it as soon as I could scrape up enough money to buy a dwelling—Ron had left me with nothing but debts. So I worked like a beaver, selling stories to . . . any magazine that would take fiction other than the woman's sob-type," she wrote in *SAAS*. She got a job at the short story magazine *Argosy* and eventually made enough money to buy a small house in Petworth, West Sussex. "We stayed in it twenty years and I must have written nearly forty books there," she told *SAAS*.

Successful with Wolves

The Wolves of Willoughby Chase (1962) was to become the first in a series of books following a set of characters in an alternative nineteenth-century Britain. In Aiken's Britain, a tunnel between Europe and England has introduced hungry wolves to the terrain. Additionally, King James III reigns instead of Prince George of Hanover, whose supporters look to overthrow the crown. Against this backdrop, *The Wolves of Willoughby Chase* opens in 1832. Two girls, Sylvia Green and her cousin Bonnie, must deal with their evil governess Miss Slighcarp, who takes over the family home when Bonnie's parents leave for an extended cruise. Slighcarp eventually puts the girls in a horrible industrial school in Blastburn. They befriend an orphaned local lad, Simon, who helps them in their time of need. Sarah V. Clere, writing in the *Dictionary of Literary Biography*, stated, "Like many melodramas, the book sounds improbable and is cliche-ridden in plot summary, but Aiken's deft style sketches the admittedly flat characters quickly and satisfyingly. The book . . . gives a new twist to an old form."

"*The Wolves* . . . had been such a pleasure that I started writing its sequel *Black Hearts in Battersea* (1964)," wrote Aiken in *AAYA*. Simon, now age fifteen, is studying art in London where he befriends the cockney Twite family, including Pa and Ma Twite and their daughters, Penelope and the lively Dido. Simon discovers a Hanoverian plot to kill the king of England, and the Twites are prime suspects. When Mr. Twite kidnaps Simon and takes him aboard a ship bound for Hanover, Dido and a friend stow away, only to be abandoned at sea.

It was Aiken's intention with *Black Hearts* to kill off Dido, but a letter from an American child made her change her mind. "I was so touched

and appalled by this letter that the only thing I could do was to write another book in which Dido was rescued from the sea," she wrote in *AAYA*. *Nightbirds on Nantucket* (1966) features Dido being rescued by an American whaling ship whose captain is searching for a pink whale. Dido is left on Nantucket with the captain's sister, Aunt Tribulation, who subjects her to terrible treatment. The aunt turns out to be the evil Mrs. Slighcarp, who is involved in a plot to launch a cannonball across the Atlantic which will kill King James. Dido manages to have the pink whale tow the cannon—and Mrs. Slighcarp—out to the ocean. Critical reception to the book was generally positive. A *Times Literary Supplement* reviewer wrote that it is "altogether an invigorating book, in which the wit and the nonsense make such a sparkling fizz together that it is hard to tell one from the other." The fourth book in the series, *The Whispering Mountain* (1968) follows a series of characters through a fantastical romp in Wales. *The Cuckoo Tree* (1971) features Dido Twite again, this time trying to save the soon-to-be King, Richard IV, from a plot to roll St. Paul's Cathedral into the Thames river during his coronation.

The Stolen Lake (1981) takes Dido to South America, where she travels to the Andean mountain city of Bath Regis, where Queen Genevra waits for her husband, King Arthur, to reappear after an absence of thirteen centuries—an absence that coincides with the disappearance of Lake Arianrod. Dido must impersonate a missing princess to help solve the mystery. In 1986 Aiken published *Dido and Pa*. The book begins with a happy reunion between Dido and Simon, but Dido's scheming father, in disguise, soon takes her away, telling her that her older sister is very ill. They travel to London where he unveils his latest plot: Pa Twite plans to murder the King Richard and replace him with a look-alike.

"For those who love thick books with clever young protagonists, this is a delight," stated Janice Toomajian in *Voice of Youth Advocates*. "Aiken is worth knowing." Writing in the *Junior Bookshelf*, Daphne J. Stroud praised the main character Dido Twite, "who steadily grows in stature throughout the series. Behind the gamin exterior and gutter patois of this streetwise Cockney urchin lies real nobility of spirit. Dido is both courageous and loyal, even towards a parent who has never demonstrated the slightest genuine feeling for her, and sought only to use her for his own ends."

■ Update

Is Underground (1993) introduces another spunky female character from the Twite family. Is (short for Isabett) is Dido's equally capable younger sister. After making friends with an older traveler, Is finds out he is really her uncle who is desperately searching for his son, Arun. Arun and many other English children have been mysteriously disappearing, and her uncle makes it his deathbed wish that Is find Arun and bring him back home. Is agrees, knowing also that the King of England's son is missing. She has heard talk about a train that takes children to a mythical "Playland." Soon, she is aboard that train and realizes that the children are being kidnapped to work in the coal mines.

Critics generally praised the work for its realistic details about what life in the mines was really like for children in the 1900s. "The picture of life in 19th century industrial England is a grim one, showing the dirt, the daily grind and the despair of those condemned to a life in the mines," Bonnie Kunzel commented in *Voice of Youth Advocates.* Bruce Anne Shook in *School Library Journal* noted that "the story is an exciting Dickensian adventure with clear-cut good and evil characters that are easy to love or hate." Faren Miller, writing in *Locus,* found delight in the latest generation of Twite heroines: "Young Is herself makes an indomitable and attractive heroine, and the bleakness of her quest is mitigated by moments of homely (yet bizarre) family interaction." A *Publishers Weekly* reviewer concluded that the book is "sad and frightening and defiantly hopeful all at once."

Is Twite returns with her newly-rescued cousin Arun in *Cold Shoulder Road* (1996). The duo return to Arun's home to search for his mother. When they arrive there, they find she has disappeared, along with a young mute child. Neighbors accuse Arun's mother of being a witch, so Arun and Is flee to a nearby cave where they find treasure—along with smugglers intent on stealing it. "This is an adventurous yarn filled with humor, chills, and melodrama," declared Susan Dove Lempke in *Booklist.* Noting the pacing, dialogue, and characters, a *Kirkus Reviews* critic remarked that "evil receives its just desserts while virtue gets a handsome reward. What could be more satisfying?" Lisa Dennis also praised the volume, writing in *School Library Journal* that "it should

find an appreciative audience among those who enjoy sophisticated storytelling, inventive adventure, and distinctive characters."

Aiken's "Wolves Chronicles" have been a pinnacle achievement. Because of the detailed settings combined with inventive fantasy, and her enchanting characters, they have become popular worldwide. John Rowe Townsend, in *A Sense of Story: Essays on Contemporary Writing for Children,* believed that Aiken's "appeal is primarily as a storyteller of great pace and resource."

Aiken Tackles Austen

Aiken doesn't write only for younger readers; in fact, she began writing for adults as early in her career as she was writing for children. She had a formula then: to complete one adult novel for each children's novel she wrote. Her first adult works were thrillers; however, she decided later—almost on a whim—that she would write sequels to books by the renowned British author Jane Austen. Her first attempt was *Mansfield Revisited* (1984), a sequel to *Mansfield Park.* "I wrote *Mansfield Revisited* to pass the time. I was doing a series of plays for the BBC just then. They had asked me to do some educational plays about the plantations of Virginia. I would send in my script, and weeks would go by when I was just kicking my heels and biting my nails. One night lying in bed I thought I would write a sequel to Austen's *Mansfield Park* to fill in the time," she related in *AAYA.*

Aiken was very careful with her subject matter. She had loved Austen's works since she came of reading age. "It was different from writing any of the others. I did it very carefully with a copy of Johnson's dictionary to make sure I wasn't using words that weren't in use during that time. I re-read Jane Austen at least once a year, so her style is very much in my ear. I read all the biographies of her that I could lay my hands on," she told *AAYA.*

Aiken's book takes up the action of *Mansfield Park,* focusing again on the Bertram family, and especially on Fanny's younger sister, Susan. However, many critics felt that she had taken liberties with character development and plotting. "*Mansfield Revisited* is agreeably written and at times decidedly ingenious. . .," observed Patricia Beer in the

New York Times Book Review. "But . . . there is something puzzling about Joan Aiken's motivation. She claims that the book is inspired by love and admiration for Jane Austen, yet it so absolutely flouts Austen's deeply held beliefs that it suggests something between a bold act of iconoclasm and a mildly naughty joke." Lindsay Duguid, writing in the *Times Literary Supplement,* claimed that "it is not incongruity but artificiality that makes Joan Aiken's *Mansfield Revisited* so unsatisfactory."

Aiken was nonplussed by the criticism the book received. She commented to *AAYA* that "the book shocked Americans on the whole—they're all such experts. They said, for instance, in Austen's novels the servants never speak, whereas in Aiken's they spoke continually. Things like that. Technical points. It didn't worry me particularly." This coincides with her overall feeling of literary criticism: "I write as I please and get a great deal of pleasure from reactions to my books. I used to mind the fact that I wasn't reviewed on book pages more than I was. Nowadays, I'm hardly

reviewed at all, but I don't really think about it much. There seems to be a slide away from English authors in American review pages. In the fifties there was a fashion of pro-English."

In 1990 Aiken published *Jane Fairfax,* a continuation of *Emma.* Austen's novel centers on Emma Woodhouse, the daughter of a rich landowner. She dotes on her father, spurns suitors, and plays matchmaker with her friends. She also tries to make herself the highlight of the Highbury social scene. She has problems when her childhood friend and rival, Jane Fairfax, is sought after by one of the most eligible bachelors in the area. Aiken's novel follows the life of Fairfax, who, though talented in art and other areas, is incurably poor. The rivalry between Emma and Jane starts early, when Emma ridicules Jane during their school years. Jane is sent to the house of the Campbells, who agree to raise her in London. There, she is exposed to a more sophisticated lifestyle. When Jane returns to Highbury as a young woman, she is a threat to Emma's social dominance. To make matters worse, the dashing Frank Churchill, who flirts with Emma, only has eyes for Jane.

Critics generally were appreciative of this work. A *Kirkus Reviews* critic applauded Aiken's tone, calling the book "an agreeable tribute to Austen rather than an imitation; the style approximates, never parrots that of the Mighty Jane." Cynthia Johnson Whealler, writing in *Library Journal,* acknowledged that the novel doesn't contain some of Austen's touches of humor and irony, but it is "extraordinarily well done." *Booklist* reviewer Mary Banas declared that "with the highly stylized *Jane Fairfax,* . . . Aiken reaches the height of her craft."

Sixth Sense

Aiken also penned a sequel to Austen's classic work *Sense and Sensibility,* the 1994 offering *Eliza's Daughter,* which depicts the life of Eliza Williams, the illegitimate offspring of the philandering John Willoughby and Colonel Brandon's ward. Eliza, raised in Bylow Bottom, a village for foster children, goes out in the world to try to discover her real parents, and finds all manners of adventures in England, Portugal, and Spain. A *Publishers Weekly* reviewer enjoyed the work, indicating that "others may try, but nobody comes close to Aiken . . . in writing sequels to Jane Austen."

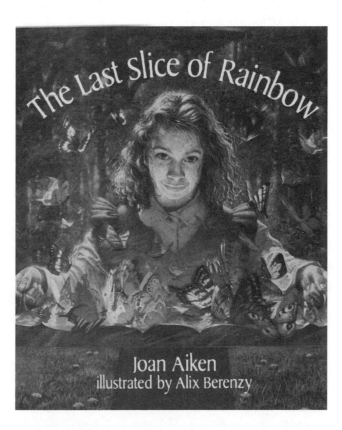

The Last Slice of Rainbow

Joan Aiken
illustrated by Alix Berenzy

Rainbows, dreams, and trees come alive in these nine fairy tales offering enchanted views of the everyday world.

If you enjoy the works of Joan Aiken, you may also want to check out the following books and films:

Antonia Fraser, *The Cavalier Case,* 1991.
Barbara Pym, *Some Tame Gazelle,* 1983.
Mary Stewart, *Thornyhold,* 1988.
Emma, starring Gwyneth Paltrow, Miramax, 1996.

Peter Kemp, writing in the *Times Literary Supplement* expounded on the chances Aiken takes with the characters and settings. The novel takes place during the bloody Napoleonic Wars, which Austen had left out of her books. Aiken spares no feelings here, including having Colonel Brandon killed during one of the battles. Also, many of the characters from Austen's novel have taken a hard turn, suffering with everything from senile dementia to cancer. Kemp remarked that "In *Eliza's Daughter,* a lively profusion of fresh characters and vigorously recounted new turns of events coexists curiously with an impulsion to kill off or devitalize Austen's creations." Kemp, however, praised Aiken's use of a first person narrative for the strong main character, and also indicated that Aiken is much more adept than Austen at delving into the sensuality of the characters.

In *Emma Watson* (1996) Aiken took on the challenge of completing an unfinished manuscript by Austen entitled "The Watsons." Emma Watson, raised by an aunt for most of her childhood, returns to her family home as a young woman. Subsequently her father dies. Her brother and his wife, who are to become the heads of the household, are horrid and unsympathetic. Emma decides to move away and become a music teacher, and within a short time she is being pursued by two suitors. A *Publishers Weekly* reviewer concluded, "Aiken is no Austen, but she's at the top of the class of disciples." A critic in *Kirkus Reviews* stated that *Emma Watson* is "as always, for those attuned to Austen and to Aiken's imaginative, respectful variations, simply charming."

Monstrous Invaders

In 1996, Aiken published *The Cockatrice Boys,* a fantasy novel marketed for adults but equally enjoyable to young adults. Taking place in con-

temporary times, the work is set in the British Isles after a global climactic holocaust has taken place. There is an enormous hole in the ozone layer, through which strange monsters have invaded Britain. The monsters, who are collectively called Cockatrices, have forced most of the inhabitants into squalid underground villages. The hero of the story, Dakin Preswick, joins the monster-fighting Cockatrice Corps as the drummer. Dakin, along with a rag-tag troop of monster-fighters, go to Scotland to locate a medieval alchemist's papers that will help them win the battle.

Reviewers had mixed feelings about Aiken's work. A *Kirkus Reviews* critic observed that the book is "whimsical and sprightly, but not even half worked-out—and the ending just fizzes." A *Publishers Weekly* contributor pointed out that Aiken seems not to have found the most effective voice for the novel: "She adopts a hybrid tone that mixes whimsy with menace, resulting in a murky morality tale that is awkwardly poised between adult and childlike sensibilities." Jamie S. Hansen, writing in *Voice of Youth Advocates,* had a different take on the story, likening the main characters to *The Hobbit*'s Bilbo Baggins. Hansen remarked that the book "is alternately chilling and charming. . . . Many pleasing and surprising threads are woven into this little tapestry."

With the dozens of books Aiken has written, she is now permanently etched into the pantheon of popular children's writers. She once commented, "I know that my books vary. Some I am proud of; some are mere jobs of work, money-earners; a couple now fill me with slight embarrassment." Clere admitted in *Dictionary of Literary Biography* that the large number of Aiken's books "has hindered an appreciation of her full stature as a serious writer." However, Clere also noted that "Her children's novels especially show that fast-paced entertainment is compatible with serious thematic development, for undergirding the high-spirited adventure of her best fiction is a bedrock of humane values."

■ Works Cited

Aiken, Joan, essay in *Something about the Author Autobiography Series,* Volume 1, Gale, 1986, pp. 17-37.
Banas, Mary, review of *Jane Fairfax, Booklist,* May 15, 1991, p. 1778.

Beer, Patricia, review of *Mansfield Revisited, New York Times Book Review,* July 21, 1985, section 7, p. 12.

Clere, Sarah V., "Joan Aiken," *Dictionary of Literary Biography,* Volume 161: *British Children's Writers since 1960, First Series,* Gale, 1996, pp. 3-11.

Review of *The Cockatrice Boys, Kirkus Reviews,* July 15, 1996.

Review of *The Cockatrice Boys, Publishers Weekly,* August 19, 1996.

Review of *Cold Shoulder Road, Kirkus Reviews,* December 15, 1995.

Courtney, Catherine, interview with Joan Aiken in *Authors and Artists for Young Adults,* Volume 1, Gale, 1989, pp. 1-14.

Dennis, Lisa, review of *Cold Shoulder Road, School Library Journal,* March, 1996.

Duguid, Lindsay, review of *Mansfield Revisited, Times Literary Supplement,* October 26, 1984, p. 1224.

Review of *Eliza's Daughter, Publishers Weekly,* May 16, 1994, p. 49.

Review of *Emma Watson, Kirkus Reviews,* July 15, 1996.

Review of *Emma Watson, Publishers Weekly,* August 12, 1996.

Hansen, Jamie S., review of *The Cockatrice Boys, Voice of Youth Advocates,* February, 1997.

Review of *Is Underground, Publishers Weekly,* May 17, 1993, pp. 80-81.

Review of *Jane Fairfax, Kirkus Reviews,* April 1, 1991, p. 410.

Kemp, Peter, review of *Eliza's Daughter, Times Literary Supplement,* August 5, 1994, p. 17.

Kunzel, Bonnie, review of *Is Underground, Voice of Youth Advocates,* June, 1993, p. 85.

Lempke, Susan Dove, review of *Cold Shoulder Road, Booklist,* April 1, 1996.

Miller, Faren, review of *Is Underground, Locus,* October, 1993, p. 59.

Review of *Nightbirds on Nantucket, Times Literary Supplement,* November 24, 1966, p. 1071.

Shook, Bruce Anne, review of *Is Underground, School Library Journal,* March, 1993, p. 218.

Stroud, Daphne J., "Aiken's England," *Junior Bookshelf,* April 15, 1991, pp. 3-8.

Toomajian, Janice, review of *Dido and Pa, Voice of Youth Advocates,* February, 1987, p. 282.

Townsend, John Rowe, *A Sense of Story: Essays on Contemporary Writers for Children,* Lippincott, 1971.

Whealler, Cynthia Johnson, review of *Jane Fairfax, Library Journal,* April 15, 1991, p. 123.

■ For More Information See

BOOKS

Cadogan, Mary, and Patricia Craig, *You're A Brick, Angela! A New Look at Girls' Fiction From 1839-1975,* Gollancz, 1976.

Chevalier, Tracy, editor, *Twentieth-Century Children's Writers,* third edition, St. James, 1989.

Children's Literature Review, Gale, Volume 1, 1976, Volume 19, 1990.

Contemporary Literary Criticism, Volume 35, Gale, 1985.

De Montreville, Doris, and Donna Hill, editors, *Third Book of Junior Authors and Illustrators,* Wilson, 1972.

Egoff, Sheila A., *Thursday's Child: Trends and Patterns in Contemporary Children's Literature,* American Library Association, 1981.

Silvey, Anita, editor, *Children's Books and Their Creators,* Houghton Mifflin, 1995.

Something about the Author, Gale, Volume 2, 1971, Volume 30, 1983.

PERIODICALS

Best Sellers, April, 1978.

Booklist, March 15, 1993, p. 1274.

Books for Keeps, January, 1990, p. 10; July, 1995, p. 12; March, 1996, p. 11.

British Book News, August, 1982.

Bulletin of the Center for Children's Books, April, 1992, p. 197.

Calendar, March-October, 1979.

Chicago Tribune, November 9, 1980.

Children's Books, December 15, 1995, p. 1766.

Children's Literature Association Quarterly, fall, 1980.

Children's Literature in Education, spring, 1988.

Growing Point, July, 1978; July, 1981; November, 1983; March, 1988.

Horn Book, October, 1970; October, 1973; April, 1974; August, 1976; December, 1976; April, 1978; December, 1983; March/April, 1986; November/December, 1986; July/August, 1992, p. 449; September/October, 1993, p. 595; May/June, 1996, p. 334.

Junior Bookshelf, February, 1972; August, 1974; June, 1976; October, 1977; August, 1978; February, 1979; August, 1980; October, 1982; February, 1984; December, 1984; February, 1986; April, 1987; August, 1987; August, 1993, p. 147; December, 1994, p. 210; April, 1996, p. 65.

Kirkus Reviews, March 15, 1993, p. 313; April 15, 1994, p. 490.

Library Journal, May 15, 1994, p. 96; August, 1996, p. 120.

London Review of Books, September 27, 1990, p. 20.

Magpies, July, 1994, p. 30.

National Observer, September 23, 1968.

New Statesman, December 4, 1981.

New Yorker, May 27, 1991, p. 100.

New York Times, December 3, 1987.

New York Times Book Review, July 23, 1967; March 24, 1968; July 23, 1972; May 5, 1974; May 2, 1976; April 27, 1980; February 14, 1982.

Observer, April 18, 1982.

Publishers Weekly, March 22, 1991, p. 72; March 16, 1992, p. 80; September 14, 1992, p. 126; November 9, 1992, p. 74; March 15, 1993, p. 69; May 9, 1994, p. 73.

Punch, August 15, 1984.

Saturday Review, April 18, 1970; April 17, 1971; May 20, 1972.

School Librarian, February, 1995, p. 20.

School Library Journal, May, 1992, p. 130; November, 1992, p. 116; May, 1993, p. 141; June, 1994, p. 94.

Science Fiction and Fantasy, July 15, 1996, p. 1011.

Spectator, December 10, 1994, p. 46.

Times (London), March 5, 1980; February 8, 1982; August 25, 1983; December 27, 1984; October 22, 1988; February 3, 1990; November 15, 1990.

Times Educational Supplement, June 5, 1981; March 6, 1987.

Times Literary Supplement, June 15, 1967; July 2, 1971; December 3, 1971; July 15, 1977; April 7, 1978; March 28, 1980; July 24, 1981; November 28, 1986; February 13, 1987; July 10, 1987; July 31, 1987; May 6, 1988; July 12, 1991, p. 20; January 26, 1996, p. 19; August 5, 1996, p. 17.

Tribune Books (Chicago), July 10, 1988; June 26, 1994, p. 6.

Voice of Youth Advocates, October, 1992, p. 235.

Washington Post, July 17, 1987.

Washington Post Book World, January 8, 1978; May 22, 1980; July 13, 1980; January 13, 1985; June 9, 1985; November 4, 1986; August 14, 1988; October 9, 1988; February 11, 1990; May 9, 1993, p. 15.

Writer, March, 1980; May, 1982; February, 1994, p. 9.*

—Sketch by Nancy Rampson

Julia Alvarez

■ Personal

Born March 27, 1950, in New York, NY; married Bill Eichner (a doctor), June 3, 1989. *Education:* Attended Connecticut College, 1967-69; Middlebury College, B.A. (summa cum laude), 1971; Syracuse University, M.F.A., 1975; attended Bread Loaf School of English, 1979-80; has earned a Ph.D in literature.

■ Addresses

Agent—Susan Bergholz Literary Services, 17 West 10th St., No. 5, New York, NY 10011-8769.

■ Career

Writer. Kentucky, Delaware, and North Carolina, poet-in-residence, 1975-78; Phillips Andover Academy, Andover, MA, instructor in English, 1979-81; University of Vermont, Burlington, visiting assistant professor of creative writing, 1981-83; George Washington University, Washington, DC, Jenny McKean Moore Visiting Writer, 1984-85; University of Illinois, Urbana, assistant professor of English, 1985-88; Middlebury College, Middlebury, VT, associate professor of English, 1988—.

■ Awards, Honors

Benjamin T. Marshall Poetry Prize, Connecticut College, 1968-69; prize, Academy of American Poetry, 1974; creative writing fellowship, Syracuse University, 1974-75; Kenan Grant, Phillips Andover Academy, 1980; poetry award, La Reina Press, 1982; exhibition grant, Vermont Arts Council, 1984-85; Robert Frost Poetry Fellowship, Bread Loaf Writers' Conference, 1986; first prize in narrative award, Third Woman Press, 1986; award for younger writers, General Electric Foundation, 1986; grant, National Endowment for the Arts, 1987-88; syndicated fiction prize, PEN, for "Snow"; grant, Engram Merrill Foundation, 1990; Josephine Miles Award, PEN, Oakland, 1991, and notable book selection, American Library Association, 1992, both for *How the Garcia Girls Lost Their Accents.*

■ Writings

NOVELS

How the Garcia Girls Lost Their Accents, Algonquin Books of Chapel Hill, 1991.
In the Time of the Butterflies, Algonquin Books of Chapel Hill, 1994.
¡Yo!, Algonquin Books of Chapel Hill, 1997.

Contributor to anthologies, including *The One You Call Sister: New Women's Fiction*, edited by Paula Martinac, Cleis Press, 1989; *Mondo Barbie*, edited by Lucinda Ebersole and Richard Peabody, St. Martin's, 1993; *Growing up Female: Short Stories by Women Writers from the American Mosaic*, edited by Susan Cahill, Penguin, 1993; *New Writing from the Caribbean*, Macmillan, 1994. Contributor to periodicals, including *Caribbean Writer, Commonwoman, Greensboro Review, New Mexico Humanities Review, Story*, and *Syracuse Magazine*.

POETRY

(Editor) *Old Age Ain't for Sissies*, Crane Creek Press, 1979.
The Housekeeping Book, illustrations by Carol MacDonald and Rene Schall, Burlington, 1984.
Homecoming, Grove Press, 1984, revised edition, Dutton, 1995, published as *Homecoming: New and Collected Poems*, Plume, 1996.
The Other Side/El Otro Lado, Dutton, 1995.

Contributor to anthologies, including *The Best American Poetry 1991*, edited by David Lehman, Scribner's, 1991; *Poems for a Small Planet: Contemporary American Nature Poetry*, edited by Robert Pack and Jay Parini, Middlebury College Press, 1993; *A Formal Feeling Comes: Poems in Form by Contemporary Women*, edited by Annie Finchory Line Press, 1994. Contributor to periodicals, including *Barataria Review, Burlington Review, Caribbean Writer, Florilegia, George Washington Review, Green Mountain Review, Helicon Nine, Jar, Kentucky Poetry Review, Kenyon Review, Latinos in the U. S. Review, Poetry, Poetry Miscellany, Wind*, and *Womanspirit*.

OTHER

Contributor of translations to *Barataria Review, Bitter Oleander, Pan American Review, Pulse: The Lamar Review*, and *Tower*. Editor of *Special Reports/Ecology*, 1971.

■ **Adaptations**

Plans were made to film *In the Time of the Butterflies* by the Helen Bartlett/Tony Bill company, Barnstorm Films and Phoenix Pictures.

■ **Sidelights**

As Julia Alvarez stepped up to give a talk about her first novel, based on her Dominican family's immigration to the United States, a Dominican girl in the audience turned to her friend and said, "What she got to say to us? She's a white girl." Nevertheless, by the time Alvarez finished her speech, the girls were laughing along with her. Alvarez, who related this story in *Essence*, may not appear to be a Dominican. She writes in English, not Spanish. In addition, she is an American citizen by birth. Yet, in her work, Alvarez has pulled together her Dominican roots and her experience as a young woman growing up in the United States to the delight of people of Latin American descent, other immigrants, and Americans of all backgrounds. Doing so with intellectual rigor and passion, Alvarez is not just considered to be one of the most important contributors to Hispanic American literature—she is counted among the

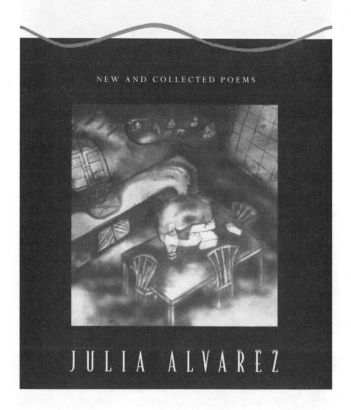

An accomplished poet, Alvarez published this collection in 1996.

most talented young writers in the United States. Although she began her career as a poet, Alvarez is increasingly known for her novels, which treat immigration, alienation, heritage, and identity all in the context of family relations.

Alvarez's parents met in the United States, where her father ran a hospital and her mother was a student. Alvarez was born in the United States and was encouraged to identify herself as an American, but she spent her early years on her mother's family compound in the Dominican Republic. Along with her three sisters, Alvarez grew up surrounded by numerous cousins and was supervised by maids and the women of the family. As Alvarez once explained in the *American Scholar*, her family's life changed when her father joined a group which planned to fight the dictator of the Dominican Republic, Rafael Leonidas Trujillo Molina. Though Alvarez's family on her mother's side had many American ties (her grandfather served as a cultural attaché to the United Nations), Alvarez's father was not safe from the dictator's police. Just before he was to be apprehended, a tip from an American agent prompted him to leave the country with his wife and daughters in a plane bound for the United States.

Alvarez wrote about her expectations in *American Scholar*: "All my childhood I had dressed like an American, eaten American foods, and befriended American children. I had gone to an American school and spent most of the day speaking and reading English. At night, my prayers were full of blond hair and blue eyes and snow. . . . All my childhood I had longed for this moment of arrival. And here I was, an American girl, coming home at last." Life in New York was not as sweet as the ten-year-old had imagined it would be, however. Instead of feeling like home, the Bronx alienated Alvarez. She turned to the world of books, and spent a great deal of time reading and writing.

Alvarez once elaborated for *Contemporary Authors*, "I found myself turning more and more to writing as the one place where I felt I belonged and could make sense of myself, my life, all that was happening to me. I realized that I had lost the island we had come from, but with the words and encouragement of my teacher, I had discovered an even better world: the one words can create in a story or poem."

This 1991 book, a series of fifteen interconnected stories about a Dominican family, is Alvarez's best known work.

As Alvarez explained to Jonathan Bing in *Publishers Weekly*, she left home at the age of thirteen to attend boarding school and never lived at home again. Alvarez attended Connecticut College in New England, where she earned a poetry prize. In 1971, she received a bachelor's degree with highest honors from Middlebury College. She won a poetry prize from the Academy of American Poetry in 1974 and a creative writing fellowship from Syracuse University, where she graduated with an M.F.A. in 1975. Alvarez then worked as a poet-in-residence in Kentucky, Delaware, and North Carolina. Later, she taught English at Phillips Andover Academy in Andover, Massachusetts. "I was a migrant poet," she remarked in her conversation with Bing. "I would go anywhere."

Alvarez then worked at the University of Vermont, where she taught as a visiting assistant professor of creative writing in 1981, and then at George Washington University, as the Jenny McKean Moore Visiting Writer, in 1984. It was during these years that Alvarez put together her first poetry collection, called *Homecomings*, which was published by Grove in 1984. According to Fred Muratori, writing in the *New England Review and Bread Loaf Quarterly*, "33," a sequence of sonnets that "fills half the volume" is a "diary-like assemblage of meditations, stories, and confessions." While Alvarez's reputation as a writer grew, she continued her career in academia. Alvarez taught at the University of Illinois, Urbana, as assistant professor of English from 1985 to 1988, and then moved to Middlebury College as an associate professor of English. By the end of the decade, she had received several awards for her poetry.

Coming of Age

During her early years as a writer, Alvarez revealed to Bing, she had not enthusiastically considered the prospect of "writing something bigger than a poem." Yet "Homecoming," according to Alvarez, is "a narrative poem, longer than the others. It's almost as if it's the beginning of a story." As she told Catherine Wiley in an interview published in the *Bloomsbury Review*, she "started writing stories, thinking that" she "would just write a few." Alvarez recalled for Bing that she was approached by an agent after accepting the 1986 G.E. Foundation Award for Younger Writers, and was placed with editor Shannon Ravenal of Algonquin books. Ravenal promoted Alvarez's work, encouraged her, and guided her in the organization of various stories. In 1991, Algonquin published the resulting work, Alvarez's first novel, *How the García Girls Lost Their Accents*.

How the García Girls Lost Their Accents is a series of fifteen stories about a Dominican family which has moved to the United States. Like Alvarez and her siblings, the four sisters in the family, Carla, Sandra, Yolanda, and Sofia, must work hard to make a place in their new home. The book, in the words of Cecilia Rodríguez Milanés, writing in the *Women's Review of Books*, "is not simply about adjustment and acculturation. It is about its protagonists' precarious coming of age as Latinas in the United States and gringas in Santo Domingo."

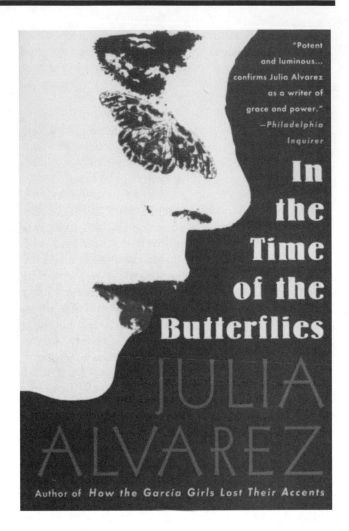

Four sisters dedicated their lives to freedom during the reign of Dominican dictator Trujillo in this 1994 novel.

"Made of fifteen self-contained chapters collected in three symmetrical parts, more than a novel the volume ought to be read as a collection of inter-related stories," observed Ilan Stavans in the *Commonweal*. The book begins with stories from "1989-1972," and includes tales of Yolanda's return to the Dominican Republic; Sofia's unwillingness to obey her father; and Mamita's troubles with her daughters. The second part of the novel, titled "1960-1970," returns to a time when the girls were newcomers to the United States. The stories reveal how Carla is exposed to a pervert; how Yolanda, seeing snow for the first time, worries she is witnessing the fall-out from an atom bomb; and how Sandi is shocked when the American wife of another man kisses her father. The final section, "1960-1956," portrays the García family's life in the Dominican Republic in reverse order—from their dramatic getaway from the country to Yolanda's earlier theft of a kitten from its mother.

How the García Girls Lost Their Accents won praise from critics. Stavans wrote that, while the book is "imperfect and at times unbalanced, this is a brilliant debut—an important addition to the canon of Hispanic letters in the U.S." In a review of *How the García Girls Lost Their Accents* in *World Literature Today*, Bruce-Novoa offered that "possibly the best novel in" U.S. Latino literature "comes from a Dominican American woman." Elizabeth Starcevic, writing in the *American Book Review*, concluded, "We enjoy what we learn, we enjoy the music of the chorus, we feel included in their lively, passionate world, and we want more."

Although *How the García Girls Lost Their Accents* was generally well received, some critics found flaws in the work. Donna Rifkind of the *New York Times Book Review* believed the section of the book devoted to the stories of the girls as adults to be "by far the book's weaker half" because their concerns "are by now such cliches—the staples of women's magazines and pop fiction. . . . Much more powerful are the rich descriptions of island life and the poignant stories detailing the Garcias' first year in the United States. . . . Ms. Alvarez has . . . beautifully captured the threshold experience of the new immigrant, where the past is not yet a memory and the future remains an anxious dream."

Alvarez's family also reacted to the novel. Alvarez explained to Wiley that "the person I thought would give me the hardest time—my father—not at all. He called up after he read it, weeping, saying that he was so proud of me. My sisters were a little taken aback. . . . Each one reacted differently, and they all have come around. One of them said that it was really hard for her, but she really felt that it was for her to deal with. But they're also very proud of me and feeling kind of mixed." Alvarez's mother was less enthusiastic about the publication of a work so similar to the Alvarez family's story.

Alvarez published her second novel, *In the Time of the Butterflies*, in 1994. As the author explained in her conversations with Bing, the book contains a story that she had wanted to tell for some time,

If you enjoy the works of Julia Alvarez, you may also want to check out the following books and films:

Rudolfo Anaya, *Bless Me, Ultima*, 1976.
Oscar Hijuelos, *Our House in the Last World*, 1983.
Gary Soto, *Baseball in April: And Other Stories*, 1990.
El Norte, starring David Villalpando, 1983.

"but I didn't know how to do it." The resulting work is historical fiction, a recreation of the lives of three Dominican sisters—Patria, Minerva, and Maria Teresa Mirabal—who were murdered for their work to overthrow Trujillo the same year Alvarez's family fled to the United States. Known as "Las Mariposas," or "The Butterflies," the womens' political struggle is celebrated in parts of Latin America. The book is also about the fourth sister, Dedé, who survived because she stayed home the night her sisters were killed, and to whom Alvarez dedicated her work.

"*In the Time of the Butterflies* opens with a thinly disguised version of Ms. Alvarez, an Americanized Dominican woman who wants to write something about the Mirabals and is looking for information. She visits the family home, now a kind of shrine, run by Dedé. . . . Dedé's recollections and musings open and close the novel, nicely framing the action," related Roberto González Echevarría in the *New York Times Book Review*. "The story is related through first-person accounts of each sister, resulting in multiple perspectives of central events," explained Janet Jones Hampton in *Belles Lettres*. The novel concludes with what Susan Miller of *Newsweek* described as a "gut-wrenching climax." "In a brief 'real life' postscript, Alvarez claims that only through fiction's transformations is it possible to understand a history as complex as that surrounding the Mirabal sisters," related Ruth Behar in the *Women's Review of Books*. "The novel's 300-plus pages are full of pathos and passion, with beautifully crafted anecdotes interstitched to create a patchwork quilt of memory and ideology," asserted Stavans in the *Nation*. The critic also stated that this "haunting second novel easily surpasses her earlier achievement. . . . *In the Time of the Butterflies* is enchanting, a novel only a female, English-speaking Hispanic could have written. By inserting herself in the cast as *la gringa norteamericana*, Alvarez links the old and the new."

Though Dwight Garner of *Hungry Mind Review* proclaimed Alvarez to be "among America's finest young writers," with her "remarkable ability to climb in side the heads of her characters and distill complicated emotions into a sharp sentence or two," Garner found the portrayal of the sisters when they become politically active "less than convincing," adding, "One minute they [the sisters] are kissing boys behind shrubs; the next, they're whipping up Molotov cocktails." Echevarría, writing in the *New York Times Book Review*, complained that Alvarez "clutters her novel with far too many misdeeds and misfortunes: rape, harassment, miscarriage, separation, abuse, breast cancer. . . . There is indeed much too much crying in this novel." He also found "no connection between the specific dates Ms. Alvarez gives to mark periods in the Mirabals' lives and either Dominican or broader Latin American history. Serious historical fiction establishes links between individual destiny and pivotal political events . . . in this novel the reader is not made aware of a broader, more encompassing political world."

¡Yo!, the sequel to *How the Garcia Girls Lost Their Accents*, finds the four adult Garcia sisters arguing about Yo's portrayal of them in her books. The novel begins with what a *Publishers Weekly* critic called an "exuberant and funny" first chapter. The book, divided in three parts, focuses on the life of Yo through the perspectives of various narrators—people who have known Yo at different times in her life, from her childhood and college years to her early thirties. The daughter of the family maid, a farmer, an abused wife, Yo's college professor, and a boyfriend all make appearances.

"Because of the shifting perspectives, the reader doesn't get a clear enough idea of what makes Yo tick," argued Clare McHugh of *People*. In the *New York Times Book Review*, Abby Frucht stated, "Perhaps it's the neatness, the summing-up of a tidy sequence of Yo-induced epiphanies, that makes this book more quaint than complex, more an assemblage of inspirations than the satisfying novel it could have been." "This is an entrancing novel, at once an evocation of a complex heroine and a wise and compassionate view of life's vi-

cissitudes and the chances for redemption," concluded a *Publishers Weekly* reviewer.

With the publication of *The Other Side/El Otro Lado* in 1995, Alvarez brought her talents as a poet to the attention of those who only knew her fiction. Some critics, including Rochelle Ratner of *Library Journal*, were charmed by Alvarez's poems. "Alvarez . . . writes poems as impressive as her fiction." The poems, declared a *Publishers Weekly* critic, are "direct, reflective, and often sensuous." "The book's tour de force is the 21-canto title poem about her residency at a Dominican artists' colony," wrote Philip Gambone in the *New York Times Book Review*. In 1996, Alvarez's first poetry collection was republished in *Homecoming: New and Collected Poems*. This volume contains forty-six sonnets and a number of separate poems. Christine Stenstrom of *Library Journal* found the collection "vivid and engaging," and most appreciated the poems in the "Housekeeping" series.

Alvarez continues to teach as a professor at Middlebury College, and to write. Regarding her perspective as an immigrant, she told Miller in *Newsweek*: "We travel on that border between two worlds and we can see both points of view." According to her fans and critics, Alvarez does so successfully. As Bing stated in *Publishers Weekly*, "Once an author without an address, a language or a homeland to call her own, Alvarez now has a loyal readership that in years to come will undoubtedly only grow larger."

■ Works Cited

Alvarez, Julia, *American Scholar*, Winter, 1987, pp. 71-85.

Alvarez, Julia, interview with Catherine Wiley, *Bloomsbury Review*, March, 1992, pp. 9-10.

Alvarez, Julia, "Black behind the Ears," *Essence*, February, 1993, pp. 42, 129, 132.

Alvarez, Julia, comments in *Contemporary Authors*, Volume 147, Gale, 1995, pp. 15-17.

Behar, Ruth, "Revolutions of the Heart," *Women's Review of Books*, May, 1995, pp. 6-7.

Bing, Jonathan, "Julia Alvarez: Books That Cross Borders," *Publishers Weekly*, December 16, 1996, pp. 38-39.

Bruce-Novoa, review of *How the García Girls Lost Their Accents*, *World Literature Today*, Summer, 1992, p. 516.

Echevarría, Roberto González, "Sisters in Death," *New York Times Book Review*, December 18, 1994, p. 28.

Frucht, Abby, "That García Girl," *New York Times Book Review*, February 9, 1997, p. 19.

Gambone, Philip, review of *The Other Side/El Otro Lado*, *New York Times Book Review*, July 16, 1995, p. 20.

Garner, Dwight, "A Writer's Revolution," *Hungry Mind Review*, Winter, 1994, p. 23.

Hampton, Janet Jones, "The Time of the Tyrants," *Belles Lettres*, Spring, 1995, pp. 6-7.

McHugh, Clare, review of *¡Yo!*, *People*, January 20, 1997, p. 33.

Milanés, Cecilia Rodríguez, "No Place like Home," *Women's Review of Books*, July, 1991, p. 39.

Miller, Susan, "Family Spats, Urgent Prayers," *Newsweek*, October 17, 1994, p. 77.

Muratori, Fred, review of *Homecoming*, *New England Review and Bread loaf Quarterly*, Winter, 1986, pp. 231-32.

Ratner, Rochelle, review of *The Other Side/El Otro Lado*, *Library Journal*, April 15, 1995, p. 80.

Rifkind, Donna, "Speaking American," *New York Times Book Review*, October 6, 1991, p. 14.

Starcevic, Elizabeth, "Talking about Language," *American Book Review*, August-September, 1992, p. 15.

Stavans, Ilan, "Daughters of Invention," *Commonweal*, April 10, 1992, pp. 23-25.

Stenstrom, Christine, review of *Homecoming: New and Collected Poems*, *Library Journal*, April 1, 1996, p. 84.

Review of *¡Yo!*, *Publishers Weekly*, October 14, 1996, p. 62.

■ **For More Information See**

PERIODICALS

Booklist, March 15, 1992, p. 1361.
Glamour, October, 1994, p. 176.
Globe and Mail (Toronto), August 31, 1991, p. C6.
Hispanic, June, 1991, p. 55.
Kirkus Reviews, March 15, 1991, p. 336.
Library Journal, August, 1994, p. 123.
Los Angeles Times Book Review, February 26, 1995, p. 8.
School Library Journal, September, 1991, p. 292.*

—Sketch by R. Garcia-Johnson

Allan Baillie

■ Personal

Born January 29, 1943, in Prestwick, Scotland; moved to Australia, 1950; son of Alistair (a bank teller) and Anne (a hotel manager; maiden name, McEwan) Baillie; married Ngan Yeok "Agnes" (a librarian), January 14, 1972; children: Lynne, Peter. *Education:* Attended University of Melbourne, 1962-63. *Politics:* Australian Labour Party. *Religion:* None.

■ Addresses

Home—197 Riverview Rd., Clareville, New South Wales 2107, Australia.

■ Career

Full-time writer, 1987—. *Herald/Sun,* Melbourne, Australia, reporter and subeditor, 1961-64; *Middlesex Advertiser,* London, England, subeditor, 1966-67; Australian Associated Press, Sydney, Australia, subeditor, 1968-69; freelance writer, Cambodia and Laos, 1969; *Sunday Telegraph,* Sydney, subeditor, 1970-73; *Daily Telegraph,* Sydney, subeditor, 1973-74; Australian Broadcasting Commission, Sydney, subeditor, 1974-78; *Women's Weekly,* Sydney, subeditor, 1978-80; *Sun,* Sydney, casual subeditor, 1980-87. *Member:* Australian Society of Authors.

■ Awards, Honors

Captain Cook Literature Award, 1970, for short story "Chuck's Town"; Warana Short Story Award, 1973, for "Empty House"; Kathleen Fidler Award, National Book League, 1982, for "The Pirate's Last Voyage" (published as *Adrift*); Arts Council Special Purpose Grants, 1983, for *Riverman,* and 1984, for *Eagle Island;* Australian Children's Book Award, Book of the Year Highly Commended citation, 1986, for *Little Brother;* Arts Council fellowship, 1988, for *The China Coin;* International Board on Books for Young People Honour Diploma, 1988, for *Riverman;* Children's Book Council of Australia Picture Book of the Year, 1989, for *Drac and the Gremlin;* Peace and Friendship Prize for Children's Literature of the World, *Children's Literary Monthly* (Beijing), 1990, for "The Sorcerers"; Multicultural Children's Book Award, 1992, for *The China Coin;* Diabetes Australia Alan Marshall Prize for children's literature, and 1995 Victorian Premier's Literary Award in Children's Books, both for *Songman.*

■ Writings

JUVENILE FICTION

Adrift, Blackie, 1983, Viking Penguin, 1992.

Little Brother, Blackie, 1985, Viking Penguin, 1992.

Riverman, Blackie, 1986.

Eagle Island, Blackie, 1987.

Drac and the Gremlin, illustrated by Jane Tanner, Dial, 1988.

Megan's Star, Blackie, 1988.

Mates, Omnibus (Adelaide, Australia), 1989.

Hero, Blackie, 1990.

(With Chun-Chan Yeh) *Bawshou Rescues the Sun: A Han Folktale*, illustrated by Michelle Powell, Scholastic, 1991.

The China Coin, Blackie, 1991.

Little Monster, illustrated by David Cox, Omnibus, 1991.

The Boss, illustrated by Fiona O'Bierne, Scholastic, 1992.

The Bad Boys, Scholastic, 1993, published in Australia as *The Bad Guys*, illustrated by David Cox, Omnibus, 1993.

Magician, Viking O'Neil (Melbourne, Australia), 1993.

Rebel!, illustrated by Di Wu, Ashton, 1994, Ticknor & Fields, 1994.

Songman, Viking O'Neil, 1994.

The Dream Catcher, Omnibus/Scholastic (Sydney, Australia), 1995.

Secrets of Walden Rising, Penguin, 1996, Viking, 1997.

Old Magic, illustrated by Di Wu, Random House, 1996.

DragonQuest, illustrated by Wayne Harris, Scholastic, 1996.

Wreck!, Puffin, 1997.

The Excuse, illustrated by Ned Culic, Puffin, 1997.

The Last Shot, Omnibus, 1997.

Star Navigator, illustrated by Wayne Harris, ABC Books for the Australian Broadcasting Corporation, 1997.

OTHER

Mask Maker (adult novel), Macmillan (London), 1975.

(Contributor) Susan Lehr, editor, *Battling Dragons—Issues and Controversy in Children's Literature*, Academic Press, 1994.

Contributor of short stories to anthologies (including *Under Twenty-Five*, *Transition*, and *Bad Deeds Gang*) and magazines (including *Child Life*, *Pursuit*, *School Magazine*, and *Meanjin*) in Australia, Britain, the United States, and China. A number of Baillie's books are available in Braille or on audio tape; some have also been translated and published in Japan, South Africa, and several European countries.

■ Sidelights

"I had finally learned that my imagination, was never as good as the real thing," wrote Australian author Allan Baillie, explaining his first success as an author of young-adult fiction in an essay for *Something about the Author Autobiography Series* (*SAAS*). "The real thing" has remained important in Baillie's work—from that first attempt to his most recent effort. Baillie excels at what *Times Literary Supplement* contributor Elizabeth Barry called tales of "high adventure." His books are filled with concrete details that vividly connect the reader with a time in history and a geographic place, usually one the author knows intimately. Baillie's love of adventure—including trips to Cambodia, China, and India—has given him enough material for more than a dozen books, with many award-winners among them. "Baillie has a splendid prose," wrote Alf Mappin in *Twentieth-Century Young Adult Writers*, "especially when he describes the things he knows at first-hand."

Baillie received an early dose of adventure when his family moved from Scotland, where he was born, to Australia when he was seven. In his autobiographical essay, he recalled the move as one of the important events in his life that influenced him to become a writer. The family's voyage to Australia included an angry confrontation between Arabian boat merchants and the ship's crew at Port Said, Saudi Arabia, that both frightened and inspired the young boy. Once in Australia, more adventure awaited Baillie as he and his family relocated time and again, due to his stepfather's (his father died in combat during World War II) occupation as a traveling salesman. By the time he was thirteen, the family had moved five times.

Even as a child Baillie was interest in writing. He wrote a poem published in the Melbourne *Sun*'s Children's Supplement and a puppet play based on *Treasure Island* for a school project. In his early teens, he wrote his first book, a science-fiction tale titled "The Silver Streak." Two more futuristic titles followed: "The Planet of Horror" and "Destination Universe." He also entered a short-story contest sponsored by Bond Athletics to promote their comic strip hero, Chesty Bond. He was pleased to learn he had won first prize. As a high school senior, he purchased a typewriter, determined to make money off his writing. Discouragement quickly set in, however, when two publishers in a row rejected his manuscript, "The Voyage of the Lady Jane."

The Accident

Baillie eventually landed a position at the *Sun* as a reporter, a first step in what would become a career in journalism. Meanwhile, his love for fiction continued, and he marked his first sale as a fiction writer when a farming newspaper paid him for "Stranger on the Shore," a short story. Just as the future was looking bright for the young author, tragedy stuck. At twenty-one, his love for adventure caught up to him, when he and a school chum decided to have a fencing duel, without masks, in imitation of swashbuckling film star Errol Flynn. Baillie's friend accidentally hit him between the left eye and the bridge of his nose. Baillie ended up in the hospital unable to speak and paralyzed on one side. His hospital stay stretched on to eleven months. When he left, he was still not completely healed; a limp, an awkward right hand, and a slowness with speech remained as reminders of the accident.

Like his family's move from Great Britain to Australia, "the accident" became another defining moment in his life as a writer. "Something had happened to me since the accident," the author recalled in his *SAAS* entry. "The most obvious part of that was an obsession with pushing out my personal envelope, the hell with anything else. I learned to drive my way, to swim, to write." After the accident, the *Sun* promoted Baillie to subeditor, a position he held for about a year. Having narrowly missed death, he felt he had to live life to the fullest, and that did not include sitting in an office. He soon left his newspaper position to make an extended trip that would take him to Asia, Europe, Mexico, and Central America.

Baillie's many adventures along the way included getting arrested for being a Pakistani spy in India, accidentally insulting a group of Iranian men by wearing shorts inside the holy city of Meshed, and narrowly escaping being driven off a high mountain road outside Mexico City. During his trip he didn't forget his writing; he spent several month working at the *Middlesex Advertiser* in Uxbridge, outside of London, and attempted to write a novel as well as a picture book. Shortly after returning home, he found himself once again traveling. In 1969 he headed for Cambodia and Laos in Southeast Asia. While there he planned to gather material for various writing projects, including books on the area for tourists and students.

After his return to Australia, Baillie held a series of newspaper jobs. In 1972 he married a Chinese librarian, Ngan Yeok (which means "Silver Jade"), who had been given the name Agnes when she attended a convent school as a girl in Penang, Malaysia. She had helped him with the research he had done to prepare himself for his trip to Southeast Asia. In 1975 his first novel, *Mask Maker*, an adult novel based on his experiences in Laos, was published. Several years later, Baillie and his wife decide to return to Southeast Asia. By that time they had a daughter, Lynn, and Agnes wanted to introduce the child to her relatives in Singapore and Penang. Baillie planned to go to Thailand to interview the Cambodian refugees who had flocked there following the takeover of their country by a brutal communist guerrilla group called the Khmer Rouge. Through these interviews, he hoped to be able to write a book about the plight of the Cambodian people.

When Baillie and his family returned home to Australia, however, the proposed novel on Cambodia was put on hold. Baillie's wife had shown him a newspaper clipping about four Lebanese boys and their dog who had accidentally drifted out into the Mediterranean on a crate. Suddenly, Baillie had a plan for a novel for young adults. It would be based on the true tale, but changed just enough to make a more workable story. When the manuscript, which he called "The Pirate's Last Voyage" was finished, he sent it to an Australian publisher and entered it in the competition for Scotland's newly established Kathleen Fidler Award. This award was to be given to the best manuscript for young adults received from aspiring Commonwealth authors. Baillie soon learned that the manuscript, with some changes, had been both accepted by the publisher and won the first ever Fedler Award.

Two Kids, a Cat, and a Crate

Baillie's revised manuscript was published in 1983 as *Adrift*, his first book for young adults. The novel tells the story of Flynn, a young boy, who is stuck watching his pesky little sister on the beach while his parents visit relatives in the Australian coastal town of Avalon. As the two play pirates in an old crate they find on the beach, they suddenly discover that they, and their cat, Nebuchadnezzar, have drifted out to sea. In *SAAS* Baillie recalled basing the little sister character on his daughter. "Why not put Lynne, age five now, on the crate?" he wrote. "She was giving me no end of trouble, including a demand that she be given a new name, Sally. So Sally is going to be stuck on a crate in the Pacific—with her arrogant and irksome black cat."

Reviewers of Baillie's novel recognized the book as an adventure story that would appeal to young readers. In the *Bulletin of the Center for Children's Books*, Roger Sutton recommended it especially to those "who like to imagine themselves in perilous circumstances." *Growing Point*'s Margery Fisher and a *Publishers Weekly* contributor both admired Baillie's successful development of his young male protagonist. "Baillie has been alert to suggest the ebb and flow of courage," Fisher wrote, "the moments of resentment and despair which direct the actions of schoolboy Flynn." "The novel," noted the *Publishers Weekly* reviewer, "offers a harrowing look at survival without losing sight of the protagonist's character."

During the writing of *Adrift*, Baillie was inspired to write another book for young people. This time his focus would be Cambodia, his inspiration coming from a boy named Vuthy whose story he had heard in a Thai refugee camp in 1980. In an essay appearing in *Reading Time*, Baillie wrote about the origin of what would become *Little Brother*. "Two years after speaking to Vuthy I began to realise what he had given me," Baillie commented. "It was a good story, why not tell it? More, why not use it to tell the story of Cambodia? Tell the Cambodia story through the eyes of a child." His purpose was not merely to elicit sympathy for the young Cambodians, but rather "to make a boy from Utah feel he could *be* the boy in Cambodia. By a casual spin of the coin."

Little Brother was runner-up for the Children's Book Council of Australia Award and widely praised by critics. For the novel, Baillie changed the name of the real boy he had met to Vithy and made him a few years younger, eleven years old. Baillie also set part of the novel in the Cambodian city of Angkor, choosing it because he was more familiar with it than the area in which Vuthy had been. *Little Brother* tells how Vithy and his older brother, Mang, escape from a Cambodian prison camp with hopes of traveling to the refugee camps in Thailand. Unfortunately, when Mang saves his little brother by drawing Khmer Rouge troops away from him, the two become separated. Vithy spends the rest of the novel trying to locate Mang.

Reviewers found *Little Brother* a moving introduction to another culture for young readers. *Booklist* contributor Carolyn Phelan described the book as a "historical novel, adventure, and character study" and noted it "takes readers to another place and time." In *Voice of Youth Advocates*, Barbara Flottmeier called it a "rare" example of a young adult novel that encourages "an understanding of another culture and history." Reviewers Nancy Vasilakis and Margery Fisher both found lots to praise in the novel. In *Horn Book*, Vasilakis applauded the novel's construction as well as the characterizations, while in *Growing Point* Fisher noted that the many features of the Cambodian countryside "appear vividly before our eyes." Baillie also seemed pleased with his work, as he explained in *SAAS*, "When [*Little Brother*] was finished, I had become completely sold on writing for children."

Commits to Career as Children's Book Author

The idea for *Riverman*, grew from a story about a three-thousand-year-old Huon pine the author first heard on his honeymoon on the island of Tasmania, off Australia's southern coast. As the novel begins, ten-year-old Brian Walker is visiting his great uncle Tim to find out more about his family history for a school assignment. During Brian's research, Great Uncle Tim reminisces about events from his own boyhood. Brian learns that Tim's father was killed in the Tasmanian mining disaster of 1912. To help Tim forget his loss, his Uncle Larry takes him on a tortuous ride up the island's Franklin River with a group of loggers. During the journey the boy learns about the Huon Pine— which they name Walker's Pine—and the importance of self-reliance. Humankind's peaceful co-existence with nature is one of the many themes Baillie examines in *Riverman*.

Every facet of the book was backed by careful research that Baillie had returned to Tasmania to complete. In preparation for the writing of the book, the author spoke with one of the miners that had actually been trapped underground in the original disaster, and to one of the drivers of the steam locomotive that brought experts to the area trying to save those underground. His efforts were rewarded when *Riverman* received several honors, including being nominated for the Australian Children's Book of the Year award and the *Guardian* Children's Fiction award, and receiving the International Board on Books for Young People Honour Diploma. In the *Times Literary Supplement,* Elizabeth Barry remarked on how Baillie's skillful descriptions enlivened many of the novel's scenes. "The details of Tim's steam-propelled ride . . . ," she comments, "are clear and, presumably, historically accurate, but the sweep of the train through the dramatic landscape is never slowed."

With the success of *Riverman*, Baillie was able to become a full-time writer. An idea for a book came to him while on a family vacation to the islands and reefs off Australia's eastern coast that make up the Great Barrier Reef. Baillie was impressed enough with the area to make a return trip to do research for the book. *Eagle Island* features a deaf boy named Lew and is set on an island in the Great Barrier Reef. Lew's great love is his catamaran, which he sails despite his parents' misgivings. In the novel, Lew sails to the Great Barrier Reef area to escape the taunting of Col, a schoolmate who makes fun of the way he talks. Baillie strikingly describes the teeming wildlife the boy encounters as he enters the area of the reef. Lew's enjoyment of his tropical paradise is interrupted by the arrival of Col and two unsavory characters. "*Eagle Island* should be lapped up by older readers," Val Bierman claimed in *Books for Keeps.*

Baillie, whose family had by now grown to include a son, Peter, also used his extra time to explore new forms of writing. He wrote a picture book, *Drac and the Gremlin*, which the Children's Book Council of Australia named Picture Book of the Year in 1989. He also wrote the futuristic *Megan's Star,* set in a twenty-first century suburb of Sydney, Australia. It marks the first time Baillie centered his novel on a female character. Megan's problems include being teased at school for being a witch, having a father who left her mother for a younger woman, and having to look after her annoying little brother. Megan meets Kel, a boy with psychic abilities, and the two take a voyage

---

If you enjoy the works of Allan Baillie, you may also want to check out the following books and films:

Gary Crew, *Strange Objects,* 1993.
Will Hobbs, *Downriver,* 1991.
William Sleator, *Dangerous Wishes,* 1995.
The Killing Fields, an Academy Award-winning film, 1984.

---

to the Moon and beyond, using a power called Distant Vision. Kel decides to stay on a planet where they discover intelligent life, but Megan opts to return to her home despite the disappointment waiting there. *Growing Point*'s Margery Fisher praised the novel, commenting: "The idea of a girl trying to break out of a lonely, constricting life is deepened by superb descriptions of movement in space."

For *Hero*, published in 1990, Baillie chose to again return to Australia's history for the basis of his story. This time the action takes place during the terrible flooding that occurred in Sydney and its suburbs in 1986. As their lives are threatened by the rising waters, three teens—Pam, Darcy, and Barney—are forced to work together. Each successive chapter is narrated by a different child, so we see the same situation through the eyes of Pam, the rich girl; Darcy, the rebellious one; or the serious-minded Barney. In *Horn Book*, Karen Jameyson suggested that, while difficult, Baillie's innovative use of narration is successful. "While Baillie demands a lot of his readers with such a technique," she wrote, "the structure is a remarkably effective one for conveying character." Fisher was equally impressed with the book and observed in *Growing Point* that "of Allan Baillie's adventures setting problems for the inexperienced young to solve [*Hero*] is perhaps his most powerful tale so far."

Tragedy in China

In 1988 Baillie toured China as a member of a delegation sponsored by the Children's Book Council of Australia. As his trip suggested several book ideas, he decided to explore the country further on a return trip with his family the following year. Although he didn't know it at the time, Baillie had chosen a pivotal year in China's history for his trip. After touring through the mainland, he decided to remain in China for a short while after his family returned home. Baillie ended up being in Beijing on June 3 and 4, 1989, when the Chinese Army brought a violent end to the student-led pro-democracy movement that had its center of protest in Tiananmen Square. When Baillie left the country two days later, he knew he had to include the events he had witnessed in his novel, *The China Coin*. Baillie once told *Contemporary Authors* that like *Little Brother*, "The book *China Coin* also *had* to be written."

The China Coin follows eleven-year-old Leah Waters, a half-Chinese, half-Australian girl, on her trip to China with her mother. Leah brings with her the half of a golden coin that had belonged to her grandfather and the hope of finding the coin's other half. Her search leads them to a remote village where they meet Ke, a student whom they follow to Beijing where he joins the other protesters. Although the other half of the coin is found, Leah sadly realizes the many conflicts the divided coin has come to symbolize. Reviewers were pleased with Baillie's ability to explore a historical situation while keeping the action of his story in balance. "This is strong stuff and at times bitter stuff," observed a *Junior Bookshelf* critic, "but *The China Coin* is rich too in humour, in sharp observation, and with an abundance of loving warmth." *Magpies* contributor Kevin Steinberger found the book "superbly constructed" and commented, "the revolution is deep and complex, [but Baillie] manages to weave essential details into the story without congestion."

Three other books that Baillie wrote in the early 1990s contain traces of his China experience. *The Boss*, a picture book set in a Chinese village, was based on all the little boys wearing general's hats that Baillie saw in Beijing. *The Magician*, a science-fiction fantasy set in a future Australia, tells of the struggle between the people of Howling Gap and the Darkness which threatens them. As Baillie related in his *SAAS* entry, "The mindless soldiers of Tiananmen popped up in the science fiction of *Magician*, and that was not planned." *Rebel!*, published in 1994, is a picture book that has implications for Baillie's older readers. Based on an actual event, it tells the story of a small village in Burma that is taken over by a General and his army. As the General stands in front of the villagers, a tiny sandal is flung out of the window

of the village school and knocks off the general's hat. When the general orders everyone out of the school, hoping to punish the one with one sandal, he discovers that teachers and students alike stand barefoot before him. In recommending the book, *Five Owls* reviewer Lynne T. Burke noted, "At its heart is a plea to every person who sees evil in the world to have the courage to be a witness, to stand up for truth and justice."

After exploring life in Cambodia and China, Baillie turned his attention to a forgotten piece of Australian history. He wanted to write about the life of the Australian Aborigines in the early 1700s, before Australia was known to the rest of the world. In particular, he hoped to tell the story of the trading that took place between the Aborigines and the people of Madagascar. It took Baillie two years of research and writing, as well as eight drafts, before *Riverman* was ready for publication. To make the book as realistic as possible, he went to the Yolgnu Aboriginal settlement Yirrkala in Arnhem Land on Australia's northern coast and lived among the native people there for six weeks. He also spent three weeks strengthening his understanding of the area around the city of Ujung Pandang (formerly Macassar) in Indonesia.

The story he put together tells of Dawu, an Yolngu elder, and Yukawa, his spiritual son. After Yukawa saves Dawu from a shark attack, the two leave their home in Australia to visit their trading partners in the Dutch colony at Macassar. Yukawa becomes friends with Jago, a Macassan boy. Dawu is impressed by the beautiful boats made by the Macassans and decides to stay with them. Yukawa returns to his village to become a keeper of the tribe's history, or a songman. Calling *Songman* Baillie's "best book yet," *Magpies* contributor Agnes Nieuwenhuizen further remarked: "*Songman* is ambitious in its scope, courageous in its stance and masterly in its execution." In his *SAAS* entry Baillie called the book "a culmination of my moving about and the books I have done." The novel was awarded both the Diabetes Australia Alan Marshall Prize for children's literature, and the Victorian Premier's Literary Award in Children's Books.

In *Secrets of Walden Rising* Baillie reworks a bit of his own autobiography while writing the story of Brendan, a boy who—like Baillie—moves to Australia from the United Kingdom. Because of his "foreign" accent, Brendan is rejected by his classmates, especially the class bully, Bago. To pass time, Brendan likes to explore the area around Fedder Lake, a nearby reservoir. When a severe drought lowers the water level in the reservoir, he realizes that the ruins of Walden, an abandoned gold mining town, appear to be rising from the water. Discovering rumors about a bandit named Captain Thunderbolt hiding a treasure in the city, Brendan decides to search for the gold. Although Brendan is accompanied by Bago, who has become his ally, he is soon confronted by two adult treasure-seekers, and his previous boredom is quickly forgotten.

Wendy D. Caldiero applauded *Secrets of Walden Rising* in *School Library Journal*, calling it a "powerfully written, gripping novel." In the *Bulletin of the Center for Children's Books* Deborah Stevenson found the book difficult reading but conceded "the fascination of Brendan's private (or so he thinks) world and an exciting climax will reward those readers who persevere." *Secrets of Walden Rising* is another successful novel to add to the many Baillie has written in his more than a decade writing books for young adults. In *Secrets of Walden Rising*, as in all his books, Baillie's young characters face major challenges and overcome them, just as Baillie faced the challenges of his move to Australia and his accident. Explaining his technique, Baillie told Nieuwenhuizen, "The event, perhaps a disaster, will bring out special qualities in the character . . . all my books have the same element. Give 'em hell."

■ Works Cited

Review of *Adrift, Publishers Weekly*, May 4, 1992, p. 57.

Baillie, Allan, "Allan Baillie," *Contemporary Authors, New Revisions Series*, Volume 42, Gale, 1993.

Baillie, Allan, essay in *Something about the Author Autobiography Series*, Volume 21, Gale, 1995, pp. 1-22.

Baillie, Allan, "Allan Baillie's Cambodia," *Reading Time*, Volume 41, number 4, 1996, pp. 6-9.

Barry, Elizabeth, "Pining among the Piners," *Times Literary Supplement*, February 6, 1987, p. 145.

Bierman, Val, "May We Recommend: Allan Baillie," *Books for Keeps*, July, 1988, p. 17.

Burke, Lynne T., review of *Rebel!*, *Five Owls*, March/April, 1994, p. 85.

Caldiero, Wendy D., review of *Secrets of Walden Rising*, *School Library Journal*, May, 1997.

Review of *The China Coin, Junior Bookshelf*, December, 1991, p. 257.

Fisher, Margery, "Boys in Trouble," *Growing Point*, September, 1983, pp. 4131-33.

Fisher, Margery, "Scenes of Adventure," *Growing Point*, September, 1985, p. 4490-92.

Fisher, Margery, "Believe It or Not," *Growing Point*, January, 1989, pp. 5087-89.

Fisher, Margery, "Motives for Action," *Growing Point*, July, 1990, pp. 5364-70.

Flottmeier, Barbara, review of *Little Brother, Voice of Youth Advocates*, August, 1992, p. 166.

Jameyson, Karen, "News from Down Under," *Horn Book*, July, 1991, pp. 493-95.

Mappin, Alf, "Allan Baillie," *Twentieth-Century Young Adult Writers*, edited by Laura Standley Berger, St. James Press, 1994, pp. 44-45.

Nieuwenhuizen, Agnes, "Know the Author: Allan Baillie," *Magpies*, March, 1995, pp. 16-18.

Phelan, Carolyn, review of *Little Brother, Booklist*, January 15, 1992, p. 939.

Steinberger, Kevin, review of *The China Coin, Magpies*, November, 1991, p. 32.

Stevenson, Deborah, review of *Secrets of Walden Rising, Bulletin of the Center for Children's Books*, May, 1997, p. 312.

Sutton, Roger, review of *Adrift, Bulletin of the Center for Children's Books*, September, 1992, pp. 5-6.

Vasilakis, Nancy, review of *Little Brother, Horn Book*, March/April, 1992, pp. 201-2.

■ For More Information See

PERIODICALS

Australian Book Review, December, 1994, p. 56; November, 1995, p. 60; September, 1996, p. 58; November, 1996, p. 63; February, 1997, p. 54; May, 1997, p. 312.

Books for Keeps, May, 1993, p. 17; May, 1995, p. 13.

Horn Book, September/October, 1992, p. 584.

Junior Bookshelf, December, 1983, p. 253; June, 1987, p. 129; June, 1990, p. 139; December, 1993, p. 238; August, 1995, pp. 141-42.

Kirkus Reviews, January 15, 1989, p. 119.

Publishers Weekly, January 24, 1994, p. 54.

Reading Time, Volume 36, number 1, 1991, p. 28.

School Librarian, February, 1992, p. 30; November, 1993, p. 164; August, 1995, p. 116.

School Library Journal, August, 1989, p. 114.*

—Sketch by Marian C. Gonsior

Anthony Burgess

■ Personal

Full name, John Anthony Burgess Wilson, February 25, 1917, in Manchester, England; died of cancer, November 25, 1993, in London, England; son of Joseph and Elizabeth (maiden name, Burgess) Wilson; married Llewela (Lynne) Isherwood Jones, January 23, 1942 (died, 1968); married Liliana Macellari (a translator), 1968; children: (second marriage) Andreas. *Education:* Attended Bishop Bilsborrow School, Xaverian College; Manchester University, B.A. (honors), 1940.

■ Career

Writer. Lecturer, Central Advisory Council for Adult Education in the Forces, 1946-48; lecturer in phonetics, Ministry of Education, 1948-50; Banbury Grammar School, Oxfordshire, England, master, 1950-54; Colonial Service, education officer in Malaya and Brunei, 1954-59. Visiting professor, Columbia University, 1970-71, and City University of New York, 1972-73. Visiting fellow, Princeton University, 1970-71. Literary adviser, Guthrie Theater, 1972-93. Composer. *Military Service:* British Army, Education Corps, 1940-46; became sergeant-major. *Member:* Royal Society of Literature (fellow).

■ Awards, Honors

National Arts Club Award, 1973; Prix du Meilleur Livre Etranger, 1981, for *Earthly Powers; Sunday Times* Mont Blanc award, 1987; D. Litt., Manchester University, 1978, and University of Birmingham, 1986; Commandeur de Merite Culturel (Monaco), 1986; Commandeur des Arts et des Lettres (France), 1986.

■ Writings

FICTION; UNDER PSEUDONYM ANTHONY BURGESS, EXCEPT AS INDICATED

The Right to an Answer, Norton, 1960.
The Doctor Is Sick, Heinemann, 1960, Norton, 1966.
The Worm and the Ring, Heinemann, 1961, revised edition, 1970.
Devil of a State, Heinemann, 1961, Norton, 1962.
(Under pseudonym Joseph Kell) *One Hand Clapping,* P. Davies, 1961, published under pseudonym Anthony Burgess, Knopf, 1972.
A Clockwork Orange (also see below), Heinemann, 1962, published in the United States with last chapter omitted, Norton, 1963, reprinted with final chapter, 1987.
The Wanting Seed, Heinemann, 1962, Norton, 1963.

Honey for the Bears (also see below), Heinemann, 1963, Norton, 1964.

Nothing Like the Sun: A Story of Shakespeare's Love Life, Norton, 1964.

The Eve of Saint Venus, Sidgwick & Jackson, 1964, Norton, 1970.

A Vision of Battlements, Sidgwick & Jackson, 1965, Norton, 1966.

A Clockwork Orange and Honey for the Bears, Modern Library, 1968.

MF, Knopf, 1971.

Tremor of Intent, Penguin, 1972.

Napoleon Symphony, Knopf, 1974.

Beard's Roman Women, McGraw, 1976.

A Long Trip to Tea Time, Stonehill Publishing, 1976.

Moses the Lawgiver (based on Burgess' screenplay of the same title; also see below), Stonehill Publishing, 1976.

Abba, Abba, Faber, 1977.

Nineteen Eighty-Five, Little, Brown, 1978.

Man of Nazareth (based on Burgess' teleplay *Jesus of Nazareth*; also see below), McGraw, 1979.

The Land Where the Ice Cream Grows, Doubleday, 1979.

Earthly Powers, Simon & Schuster, 1980.

On Going to Bed, Abbeville Press, 1982.

The End of the World News: An Entertainment, Hutchinson, 1982, McGraw, 1983.

This Man and Music, McGraw, 1983.

The Kingdom of the Wicked (also see below), Arbor House, 1985.

The Pianoplayers, Arbor House, 1986.

The Devil's Mode (short stories), Random House, 1989.

Any Old Iron, Random House, 1989.

A Dead Man in Deptford, Hutchinson, 1993.

Byrne, Carroll and Graf, 1997.

THE MALAYAN TRILOGY; UNDER PSEUDONYM ANTHONY BURGESS

Time for a Tiger (also see below), Heinemann, 1956.

The Enemy in the Blanket (also see below), Heinemann, 1958.

Beds in the East (also see below), Heinemann, 1959.

The Long Day Wanes: A Malayan Trilogy (includes *Time for a Tiger*, *The Enemy in the Blanket*, and *Beds in the East*; published in England as *Malayan Trilogy*, Penguin, 1972), Norton, 1965.

THE "ENDERBY" SERIES; UNDER PSEUDONYM ANTHONY BURGESS, EXCEPT AS INDICATED

(Under pseudonym Joseph Kell) *Inside Mr. Enderby* (also see below), Heinemann, 1963.

Enderby Outside (also see below), Heinemann, 1968.

Enderby (includes *Inside Mr. Enderby* and *Enderby Outside*), Norton, 1968.

The Clockwork Testament, or Enderby's End, Hart-Davis, 1974, Knopf, 1975.

Enderby's Dark Lady, or No End to Enderby, McGraw, 1984.

NONFICTION; UNDER PSEUDONYM ANTHONY BURGESS, EXCEPT AS INDICATED

(Under name John Burgess Wilson) *English Literature: A Survey for Students*, Longmans, 1958, revised edition published under pseudonym Anthony Burgess, 1974.

The Novel Today, British Council, 1963.

Language Made Plain, English Universities Press, 1964, Crowell, 1965, revised edition, Fontana, 1975.

Re Joyce (published in England as *Here Comes Everybody*, Faber, 1965), Norton, 1965.

The Novel Now: A Guide to Contemporary Fiction (published in England as *The Novel Now: A Student's Guide to Contemporary Fiction*, Faber, 1967, revised edition, 1971), Norton, 1967.

Urgent Copy: Literary Studies (essays), J. Cape, 1968, Norton, 1969.

Shakespeare, J. Cape, 1970, Knopf, 1971.

Joysprick: An Introduction to the Language of James Joyce, Deutsch, 1973, Harcourt, 1975.

Ernest Hemingway and His World, Scribner, 1978.

Ninety-Nine Novels: The Best in English since 1939, Summit, 1984.

D. H. Lawrence in Italy, Penguin, 1985.

Flame into Being: The Life and Work of D. H. Lawrence, Arbor House, 1985.

But Do Blondes Prefer Gentlemen? Homage to QWERTYUIOP: Selected Journalism, 1978-1985, McGraw, 1986.

Little Wilson and Big God (autobiography), Weidenfeld & Nicolson, 1987.

You've Had Your Time: Being the Second Part of the Confessions of Anthony Burgess (autobiography), Heinemann, 1990, Grove Weidenfeld, 1991.

On Mozart: A Paean for Wolfgang, Ticknor and Fields, 1991, published as *Mozart and the WolfGang*, Hutchinson, 1991.

A Mouthful of Air: Languages, Languages—Especially English, Morrow, 1993.

Contributor to *Partisan Review, Hudson Review, Times Literary Supplement, New York Times Book Review,* and other periodicals.

TRANSLATOR; UNDER PSEUDONYM ANTHONY BURGESS

(With first wife, Lynne Burgess) Michel de Saint-Pierre, *The New Aristocrats*, Gollancz, 1962.

(With Lynne Burgess) Jean Pelegri, *The Olive Trees of Justice*, Sidgwick & Jackson, 1962.

Jean Sewin, *The Man Who Robbed Poor Boxes*, Gollancz, 1965.

(And adaptor) Edmond de Rostand, *Cyrano de Bergerac* (play; produced on Broadway as *Cyrano*, 1973), Knopf, 1971.

(And adaptor) Sophocles, *Oedipus the King* (play; produced in Minneapolis, MN, 1972), University of Minnesota Press, 1972.

Also translator of librettos for *Carmen* and *Oberon*.

OTHER; UNDER PSEUDONYM ANTHONY BURGESS

(Editor) Daniel Defoe, *A Journal of the Plague Year*, Penguin, 1966.

(Editor) James Joyce, *A Shorter Finnegan's Wake*, Faber, 1966, Viking, 1967.

(Author of introduction) Francis Haskell, editor, *The Age of the Grand Tour*, Crown, 1967.

(Author of commentary) Paul Elek and Elizabeth Elek, editors, *Coaching Days of England*, Time-Life, 1967.

(Author of introduction) G. K. Chesterton, *Autobiography*, Hutchinson, 1969.

(Author of introduction) G. V. Desani, *All about H. Hatten*, Bodley Head, 1970.

A Clockwork Orange (audiocassette), Caedmon, 1973.

Anthony Burgess Reads from "The Eve of Saint Venus" and "Nothing Like the Sun" (audiocassette), Caedmon, 1974.

Anthony Burgess Reads from "A Clockwork Orange" and "Enderby" (audiocassette), Spoken Arts, 1974.

Moses the Lawgiver (screenplay), ITC/RAI, 1976.

Jesus of Nazareth (teleplay), National Broadcasting Company, 1977.

(Editor) *New York*, Time-Life, 1977.

(Author of preface) Benjamin Forkner, editor, *More Irish Short Stories*, Viking, 1980.

(Contributor) *Quest for Fire* (screenplay), Twentieth Century-Fox, 1982.

(Author of introduction) Rex Warner, *The Aerodrome: A Love Story*, Oxford University Press, 1982.

(Author of introduction) Henry Yule, *Hobson-Jobson: A Glossary of Anglo-Indian Colloquial Words and Phrases*, Routledge, 1986.

(Author of foreword) Alison Armstrong, *The Joyce of Cooking: Food and Drink in James Joyce's Dublin*, illustrated by John Digby, Station Hill, 1986, second edition, 1989.

The Rage of D. H. Lawrence (teleplay), TV Ontario, 1986.

(Author of introduction) H. E. Bates, *A Month by the Lake and Other Stories*, New Directions, 1987.

(Author of introduction) Budd Schulberg, *The Disenchanted*, Donald I. Fine, 1987.

(Author of introduction) Dieter Hildebrandt, *Pianoforte: A Social History of the Piano*, Braziller, 1988.

(Author of introduction) Mervyn Peake, *The Gormenghast Trilogy*, Overlook Press, 1988.

A Clockwork Orange 2004 (stage play; adapted from Burgess's novel *A Clockwork Orange*), produced at Barbican Theater, London, 1990.

(Contributor) Mervyn Peake, *The Gormenghast Trilogy, Volume 2: Gormenghast*, Overlook Press, 1991.

(Author of preface) David W. Barber, *If It Ain't Baroque: More Music History As It Ought to Be Taught*, Firefly Books, 1992.

(Author of introduction) Greg Vitiello, editor, *Joyce Images*, Norton, 1994.

Also author of the stage play *Morning in His Eyes*, 1968, and of the television miniseries *A.D.*, based on Burgess's novel *The Kingdom of the Wicked*. Burgess was also a prolific composer, with sixty-five original compositions to his credit, in forms from the symphony to opera.

■ **Adaptations**

A Clockwork Orange was adapted for film and directed by Stanley Kubrick, Warner Bros., 1971.

■ **Sidelights**

Anthony Burgess was a British writer of enormous powers and capacity. Starting his writing career at age forty-two, he was still able to create over fifty books of fiction, criticism, essays, and translation, including the novel, *A Clockwork Orange*, for which he is perhaps best known, and from whose shadow he was never fully able to escape. Burgess dealt with large themes: mortality, the decline of the West, sex, religion, art, the nature of violence, and the juxtaposition of two opposing world views—one which assumes the best in mankind and one which assumes the worst. Both extremes, Burgess eventually rejected. Often connected to the bleak satiric tone of his dystopian novel, *A Clockwork Orange*, Burgess also looked at the world humorously, especially in his comic creation, Enderby, the constipated poet who wrote his verses in the bathroom. A composer of note, Burgess delighted in employing musical forms to his literary creations, his *Napoleon Symphony* only one case in point. "Burgess, one would swear, has it all," noted Reid Buckley in the *American Spectator*. "He is fecund and prolific (dear God, *is* he!) and a master of language. There seems to be almost nothing that he cannot *say*, and so say it that it sticks to the tastebuds deliciously long after." Language for Burgess was not only a tool of the craft, it was a reigning passion. He was a master of several languages and invented private vocabularies for more than one of his books, the best known being his blending of Cockney slang and Russian for *A Clockwork Orange*.

Critical assessment of Burgess ranges from the ecstatic to the offended, for as a writer Burgess pulled few punches. The American author Gore Vidal observed in the *New York Review of Books* that Burgess was "easily the most interesting English writer of the last half century." In a review of a later collection of essays, critic Michael Dirda observed in the *Washington Post Book World* that Burgess's "knowledge of literary, linguistic and musical arcana rivals that of any Oxford don; he writes with a lyrical verve; and he seems willing to turn his hand to anything whatever." Yet perhaps the most balanced view of his work came in a review of his final book, the posthumously published verse-novel, *Byrne*. Writing about that work in the *New York Times Book Review*, Dana Gioia noted that "Anthony Burgess was a novelist of indisputable genius who never published an indisputably great novel. . . . Burgess lavishly spread his gifts across 33 novels of startling diversity. He left no magnum opus but scored nearly a dozen brilliant near misses."

Jack Wilson's Catholic Upbringing

Burgess was born John Burgess Wilson in Manchester, England, on February 25, 1917, the son of Joseph and Elizabeth Wilson. The Wilsons had a long heritage of Catholicism, one of the forebears being martyred during the reign of Elizabeth I. Though Burgess, nicknamed Jack, rejected Catholicism when still a teenager, his early religious training never fully left the adult man. Cen-

tral themes of his work revolve around the questions of good and evil, the question of original sin and of man's free will. Later, when he began writing, he chose as a nom de plume his confirmation name and his mother's maiden name.

Burgess was a product of the north of England. In the first part of his autobiography, *Little Wilson and Big God*, he described his lineage: "Whatever land the Wilsons originally had they lost. Having no land, achieving no distinction in the public life which was barred to them, they merit the silence of history. All we have is shaky myths told by the fire. They did odd jobs, sang and danced, joined foreign armies and disappeared into Belgium, migrated to Dublin, came back again

Burgess's daring classic set in the future explores the world of violent criminals and the manner in which society deals with them.

with Irish wives." But these "shaky myths" informed much of Burgess's childhood, and the rich Lancashire dialect was used by his relatives to relate stories of pub life and neighbors—humorous tales that stuck with him all his life.

Burgess's grandfather, Jack Wilson, after whom he was named, ran a pub in Manchester, and his father, Joseph, a would-be musician, never had an occupation to mention, though he worked variously in accountancy, and helped to run a pub, tobacco shop, and a liquor store. Joseph married a dancer from one of the theaters in which he was playing, and the couple had a daughter, Muriel, and then the son who became Anthony Burgess. Both the mother and daughter died in an influenza epidemic following the First World War. Burgess, or Jack Wilson as he was then called, was still a baby, and was shunted off to an aunt for the next few years until his father remarried. The new stepmother was a widow with two grown daughters who ran a pub, and Burgess was largely ignored by these parents as a child growing up, turning to drawing, music, and books as a refuge. An early flirtation with becoming a painter came to nothing when the young Burgess discovered he was color blind. But from his father, he did learn a love for music and for composition. As Burt A. Folkart mentioned in his obituary of Burgess in the *Los Angeles Times*, this early upbringing effected his later literary slant: "After [Burgess] became a successful novelist, he was criticized for his aloof characters that are bereft of emotion. He admitted that he found it difficult to imbue his work with affection when he had received so little himself."

Attending the University of Manchester, Burgess intended to pursue his other childhood ambition of becoming a composer. This pursuit was temporarily thwarted, however, when he discovered that the university required mathematics courses as a preparation to the study of music, classes for which he was ill prepared. Instead, Burgess studied English literature, falling under the influence of such important textual critics as F. R. Leavis and I. A. Richards. According to Geoffrey Aggeler in *Dictionary of Literary Biography*, Burgess "was struck by their method, which enabled one to assess a novel critically by close analysis and explication of the text." Burgess concentrated on his English studies, coasting through other required courses with a minimum of effort. He also edited the university magazine, *The Serpent*, and was involved with the dramatic society. During this intensely political time at university when most students were fervently leftist or rightist, Burgess maintained an apolitical stance, as he would for the rest of his life, remaining something of a cynic about either extremes of the political spectrum.

During his years at the university, Burgess met a young economics major, four years his junior. Burgess and Llewela Isherwood Jones—a distant cousin of the writer Christopher Isherwood—were married in 1942, when Burgess was already on active duty in the British Army, assigned initially to the Royal Army Medical Corps. He was dispatched as a pianist with a small entertainment group, giving concerts at army camps. In 1943 Burgess was transferred to the Army Education Corps, lecturing on foreign languages at Gibraltar. He was also involved in Army Intelligence, and during his six years in the service, he continued composing music. In his first year on Gibraltar, Burgess received startling news from home: His pregnant wife had been attacked by deserting American GIs and so badly injured that she lost the child she was carrying. This incident—later employed in a different guise in *A Clockwork Orange*—not only was seminal in Burgess's growing sense of horror at violence toward women, but also initiated a distrust and sometimes active dislike for things American. Burgess felt a lasting personal guilt that he had not been home in this hour of need.

Upon discharge from the army, Burgess returned to England and worked as a pianist with a jazz combo, a civilian instructor for the army, and as a senior master in a grammar school. Low pay eventually drove him from the latter position, and on a whim he applied for a teaching post in Malaya. In 1954, he and his wife departed for Kuala Kangsar in Malaya, as an instructor of English literature for the British Colonial Service.

Anthony Burgess—Writer

It was in Malaya that Burgess first began his writing career. Initially inspired by the amazing mixture of cultures and languages he discovered there, he attempted to put some artistic order to it by composing a symphony. After the symphony's poor reception, he attacked this material from a literary angle. The resulting work is known as the *Malayan Trilogy*, including the novels *Time for a Tiger, The Enemy in the Blanket,* and *Beds in the East.* As Aggeler noted in *Dictionary of Literary Biography,* the "resultant oeuvre . . . may be likened to a giant canvas upon which Burgess has painted portraits representing most of the generic types he knew. He introduces Malays, Tamils, Sikhs, and Eurasians, as well as a collection of largely maladapted British colonials." Burgess's love for languages also gets full play in these early novels, as the author included terms and expressions in Malay, Urdu, Arabic, Tamil, and Chinese into the English text. The trio of novels is unified by the central character, Victor Crabbe, a young school teacher who has come to the Far East to start a new life. Much like Burgess himself, Crabbe is plagued by guilt over his wife. In Crabbe's case, however, the wife has drowned. Crabbe was the first of many narrators to stand in for Burgess as spokesperson in his novels, and more than one critic has noted the fact that Burgess wrote closely from his own experiences, employing large dollops of autobiography in his writings.

With these three early novels, Burgess still looked on the craft of fiction as little more than a hobby. Writing had not yet become for him the all-encompassing activity it would. Also, Burgess created a new persona as author. As it was not thought correct for an officer of the Colonial Service to be publishing novels, he chose as a pen name Anthony Burgess, largely giving up his former identity of Jack Wilson in the process. Favorable reception of the *Malayan Trilogy* was not enough to make Burgess quit his day job; he considered himself first and foremost an educator. Yet evident in these works are many of the themes and techniques Burgess would perfect over the years: the play of language, the juxtaposition of culture against culture, the heavy use of autobiographical materials, and the employment of musical forms to determine literary structure. As the critic Robert K. Morris noted in his *Continuance and Change: The Contemporary British Novel Sequence,* Burgess "set about to show the twilight of British rule in Malaya and the dawn of freedom for the Malay states" in his trilogy, entitled *The Long Day Wanes* in its American edition. According to Morris, Burgess came up with a "tragicomic view of imperialism and an anatomy of the heart of Malaya. In technique Burgess is close to Waugh, but in sensibility he is closer to Orwell." In addition to those two writers, Morris might have also mentioned James Joyce and Shakespeare,

both of whose work deeply influenced Burgess, and about whom he would later write. Aggeler observed the powerful influence that the writing of these first three novels had on Burgess: "His success in capturing so much of Malaya's cultural variety in an extended piece of fiction seems to have been a tremendous impetus for him toward writing other fiction dealing with worlds he either knew or imagined."

After Malaya gained independence in 1957, Burgess moved on to Borneo, where he continued teaching. More interested in the local culture than he was in cultivating connections amongst the British colonials, Burgess was considered an outsider, dubbed a "bolshy" or Bolshevik, because of his antisocial behavior. At one point he was even asked to lead the local Freedom Party, but refused. One day, however, Burgess's life took a profound new direction. Lecturing a group of students on phonetics, he suddenly collapsed. Sent back to England, he was diagnosed with an inoperable brain tumor and given one year to live.

A Crucible Year

Back in England, Burgess hunkered down to his writing with a renewed fervor. He was determined to leave his wife with some sort of financial security when he was gone. In the next fourteen months, financed by the savings which his wife had wisely invested, Burgess produced five novels: *The Doctor Is Sick, One Hand Clapping, The Worm and the Ring, The Wanting Seed,* and *Inside Mr. Enderby.* In the event, the terminal diagnosis proved wrong. Burgess's death sentence became a life-shaper: For the remaining years of his life, Burgess would turn out an enormous annual word count in a variety of literary forms. In book reviews alone, it is estimated he wrote 150,000 words per year. The books Burgess wrote in his so-called "terminal" year introduced, according to Aggeler in *Dictionary of Literary Biography,* "themes to which [Burgess] was to develop again and again . . . the role and situation of the artist vis-a-vis an impinging world, love and decay in the West, the quest for a darker culture, and his view of history as a perpetual oscillation or 'waltz' between 'Pelagian' [or liberal] and 'Augustinian' [conservative] phases." So prolific was Burgess in this year, in fact, that his publishers brought out two of the books under a second pen name, Joseph Kell, and spread their publication dates out

Stanley Kubrick directed this dark, chilling 1971 film version of *A Clockwork Orange.*

over the next three years. By the time the "Kell" books were published, Burgess was established as a book reviewer, and in fact was asked—and agreed—to review one of his own books.

Of particular note are two of these novels—*Inside Mr. Enderby* and *The Wanting Seed.* Enderby introduces the comic side to Burgess, and the four novels that ultimately form that sequence have created something of a cult following. F. X. Enderby is a middle-aged poet who composes in the bathroom; his poetry is read by a mere handful of people who still appreciate poetry. Burgess returned to this comic turn in *Enderby Outside, The Clockwork Testament, or Enderby's End,* and in a curtain-call book, *Enderby's Dark Lady, or No End to Enderby.* Reviewing the first three books in the series, J. D. O'Hara in the *New York Times Book Review* called Enderby "an Englished 'Portrait of the Artist,' with its middle-aged Blooming poet struggling against church, state, and his dead but unforgotten mother." Paul Theroux observed in the

Washington Post Book World that he had read *Inside Mr. Enderby* twelve times. "Few novels have given me such pleasure," he noted, concluding that "Burgess's deftness with language is a delight, but it is underpinned by sustained thought and a great satirical gift."

The Wanting Seed is the first of Burgess's "Orwellian proleptic nightmare" novels, according to Aggeler. It is an extrapolation of the Malthusian dilemma, presenting a future England vastly over-crowded, one in which homosexuality, castration, abortion, and infanticide are all encouraged by a government desperate to curb population growth. The protagonist, Tristram Foxe, is denied a promotion at his work because he fathered a child. With this novel, Burgess introduced his theory of the cycles of history alternating between liberal and conservative: between the view that mankind is perfectible and with the proper nurturing will lead to the best for all, and the belief that mankind's nature is red in tooth and claw and needs a strong hand to control its appetites. For Burgess, the history of governments is the ping-pong back and forth between these two extremes. Though *The Wanting Seed* stands on its own merits, it is more often looked at from the critical standpoint as a precursor to Burgess's best known novel.

A Clockwork Orange

In 1961, Burgess and his wife traveled to the then Soviet Union to visit Leningrad and gather research for future novels. Before the trip, he worked on his Russian so that he would not be dependent on a guide for his insights. One of the books resulting from this trip was the comedy, *Honey for the Bears,* about an antiques dealer who goes to Russia to deal in smuggled goods and loses his wife to another woman in the process. The other creative result of the Russian trip was *A Clockwork Orange,* in part inspired by the gangs of young toughs or "stilyagi" whom he encountered in Leningrad. The title comes, as Burgess explained in the *Listener,* from a remark once overheard in a pub. An old Cockney described someone as being as crazy as "a clockwork orange," a phrase that Burgess found at once "demotic and surrealistic." He knew he had to use it for a title some day, but it was nearly twenty years before he found the right place for it. Burgess's experiences with the youth gangs of Russia and England's own "teddy boys," along with society's reactions to these growing forms of criminality—the use of B. F. Skinner's behavior modification in prisons, for example—formed the nexus out of which Burgess created *A Clockwork Orange.* The novel, as he explained in the *Listener,* "was intended to be a sort of tract, even a sermon, on the importance of the power of choice."

Burgess's protagonist in the novel is Alex, a teenage anti-hero, an addict of "ultra-violence," in the terms of the novel. The very name of the protagonist sets the theme of the book: 'a-lex', without words or more to the point, without law, for Alex has his own eloquent if bizarre patois. Burgess invented a language for the book, "nadsat," an amalgam of Cockney English and Russian, with some German and French thrown in for good measure. One critic estimated that some three per cent of the novel is written in the invented language of nadsat, and foreign words pepper each page. The U. S. edition of the book included a glossary at the end to aid in understanding, though most reviewers and readers agree that the neologisms can be understood from context without need for direct translation. An excerpt from the opening of the novel gives a small taste for Burgess's language play:

"'What's it going to be then, eh?'

"There was me, that is Alex, and my three droogs, that is Pete, Georgie, and Dim, Dim being really dim, and we sat in the Korova Milkbar making up our rassoodocks what to do with the evening. . . . Our pockets were full of deng, so there was no real need from the point of view of crasting any more pretty polly to tolchock some old veck in an alley and viddy him swim in his blood while we counted the takings and divided by four . . . "

Alex is the leader of a group of thugs who inhabit the mean streets of a futuristic Western industrial city. Under the influence of hallucinogenic milk, Alex and his "droogs" or mates, go on a violent spree, beating up an old man and smashing his false teeth, robbing a shop, and fighting another gang which is in the process of raping a young girl. To cap off their evening, they steal a car and drive to the suburban edges of their city, invading a home and beating senseless the owner—a writer named F. Alexander—destroying his work (titled *A Clockwork Orange*) and raping his wife before his eyes. The next day, Alex continues his violent ways, staying home from school and picking up two young girls in a record shop. Bringing these girls home, he puts on his favorite music, Beethoven's Ninth Symphony, and proceeds to rape these girls, as well. That night he is challenged by two members of his gang, Dim and Georgie, and retaliates by slashing them with his razor. Finally, Alex's rampage ends with the murder of an old woman in the furtherance of a burglary. Dim gets his revenge, beating Alex with a chain while he is attempting to escape, and Alex is captured by the police, the "milicents" in the language of nadsat.

In prison, Alex comes up to the chaplain and takes great delight in reading the Bible for its violent parts. After he kills another prisoner who has made sexual advances toward him, Alex is chosen as a candidate for a new form of behavior conditioning known as the "Ludovico Treatment." A new government is attempting to deal with the lawlessness in society by conditioning violent behavior out of criminals. Alex is injected with drugs that make him ill when he witnesses scenes of violence. Strapped in place, he is forced to watch horrifying films that ultimately "cure" him. One side effect is that his love for music is also destroyed, for Beethoven is used as background music for many of the films.

Now that he no longer can commit acts of violence, Alex is released from prison, only to find that his place at home has been usurped by another. Defenseless and alone, Alex runs into Dim and an old rival from another gang, Billyboy. These two have now become policemen and take him to a remote spot, beat him savagely, and

Considered by many to be Burgess's masterpiece, this autobiography of a fictional playwright deals with inherent goodness versus inherent evil in mankind.

leave him for dead. Recovering, Alex stumbles to the nearest home, that of F. Alexander whom he had earlier attacked. The writer Alexander at first does not recognize Alex and takes him in, intending to use him as a pawn in his fight against the authoritarian excesses of the new government. Alexander and his friends plan to use Alex as a terrible example of the government's conditioning program, a human stripped bare of free choice. Alex's suicide will create a scandal. To that end, he is imprisoned in a room with Beethoven piped in, enough to drive him to madness. Alex jumps out of the window, but does not die. Instead, his "fall" has knocked the conditioning out of him, and he is free once again to contemplate violent acts.

So ends the American edition of *A Clockwork Orange,* as well as the later film version by Stanley Kubrick. Burgess's original English edition, however, had a final chapter in which Alex has grown weary of violence and contemplates the possibility of a wife and child. His child may have his own violent tendencies, Alex muses, and it is possible that he will be no more successful in controlling these urges than his own father had been. "Alex is evil, not merely misguided," Burgess wrote in the *Listener.* But he is also very human—in his love of language and music. Even his aggressiveness proves his humanity for Burgess. "Theologically, evil is not quantifiable. Yet I posit the notion that one act of evil may be greater than another, and that perhaps the ultimate act of evil is dehumanisation, the killing of the soul. . . . What my . . . parable tries to state is that it is preferable to have a world of violence undertaken in full awareness—violence chosen as an act of will—than a world conditioned to be good or harmless."

Not all reviewers agreed with those sentiments, with many decrying what they found to be gratuitous violence and titillation. The film version of the novel is still banned from public showing in England. Others saw Alex's violence as only one part of the equation; the other dominated by the violence done by the State in its attempts at rehabilitation. The overwhelming critical sentiment, however, recognized the brilliance of the language and the spirit of the intended message. Julian Mitchell, reviewing the British edition in the *Spectator,* stated, "Mixing horror with farce in his inimitable manner, Mr. Burgess develops his theme brilliantly. . . ." Stanley Edgar Hyman, an American critic and educator, noted in the *New Leader* the "savagery" and the "endless sadistic violence in the book," but also observed that Burgess, "Coming to literature by way of music . . . has a superb ear, and he shows an interest in the texture of language rare among current novelists." Hyman concluded that *A Clockwork Orange* was "an eloquent and shocking novel that is quite unique." Robert K. Morris, in his *The Consolations of Ambiguity: An Essay on the Novels of Anthony Burgess*, observed that, "Like all good satirists, Burgess lashes out with savage indignation at stupidity and blind error and lacerates our disastrous pretensions at solving human problems at the expense of human beings." Morris also drew attention to the symbolism of Alex's jump from the window—a true leap of faith in the terms of the philosopher Kierkegaard. Aggeler in *Dictionary of Literary Biography* called the book a "linguistic tour de force" and dubbed it "one of Burgess' most brilliant achievements."

Typically, however, Burgess had his own irreverent spin on the critical battle being waged over his book and the propriety of including or not including his final chapter. After Kubrick's film version of the book, Burgess's name was increasingly connected only with that one novel. But Burgess had moved on; he was far from a one-trick pony. By 1981 he had heard enough, and in an interview in *Modern Fiction Studies* declared that "I'm not particularly proud of *A Clockwork Orange*, because it has all the faults which I rail against in fiction, It's didactic. It tends to pornography. It's tricky. It's gimmicky. . . . The book is not all that interesting or important."

The Fruits of an Inquisitive Mind

The flurry of writing and publishing in the early 1960s established Burgess as an author of note, but he was not one to rest on his laurels. Increasingly, however, his wife's condition became a burden for him. Never fully recovered from the beating at the hands of GIs, she also suffered from cirrhosis of the liver brought on by alcoholism and vitamin deficiencies experienced during the couple's years together in Malaya and Borneo. In 1968, Burgess's first wife died, and a few months later he married an Italian contessa, Liliana Macellari, a philologist and translator. They moved first to Malta in 1969, then to Rome for a time, and finally settled in Monaco. As his literary repu-

tation grew, Burgess was increasingly sought as a guest lecturer at universities, especially in the United States, where he spent several semesters in the 1970s.

Burgess's fiction output never wavered, and his interests continued to grow over the years. Publication of *A Clockwork Orange* was followed by *Honey for the Bears*, and then by his Shakespeare novel, *Nothing Like the Sun: A Story of Shakespeare's Love Life*, in which the Bard's literary fecundity was explained in terms of his sexuality, a book that offended Shakespeare scholars and delighted readers. Written in an Elizabethan-style idiom, *Nothing Like the Sun* was "a clever, tightly constructed book," according to the critic D. J. Enright in *Man Is an Onion: Reviews and Essays*. Other notable novels of Burgess's middle period is *MF*, a book full of language games that reminded some reviewers of both Vladimir Nabokov and James Joyce, and *Beard's Roman Women*, in which Burgess expiates some of the guilt he felt for his first wife's condition. In *Napoleon Symphony*, Burgess created "a mock epic about the career of Napoleon Bonaparte that sometimes reads like Dickens, sometimes like Tennyson and Wordsworth, with an occasional gash of Gerard Manley Hopkins' gold-vermillion," according to R. Z. Sheppard in *Time* magazine. Beethoven's Third Symphony, the E-flat *Sinfonia Eroica*, was used to shape the narrative in four parts, making *Napoleon Symphony* the most musically determined of Burgess's novels. The Burgess scholar Robert K. Morris noted in the *Nation* that the book "is alive, lush, lyric, witty and wildly comic." Burgess also wrote for television: his screenplays included *Moses the Lawgiver* and *Jesus of Nazareth*, both of which he turned into novels. His translation and adaptation of the play *Cyrano de Bergerac* won critical attention, as well.

The book that many critics believe to be his masterpiece, *Earthly Powers*, was published in 1980, after a decade in the writing. The novel is the purported autobiography of the octogenarian playwright, Kenneth M. Toomey, an amalgam of the writers Graham Greene, Evelyn Waugh, and W. Somerset Maugham, with more than a pinch of Burgess himself thrown into the brew. In the course of the memoirs, the reader encounters Don Carlo Campanatti, destined one day to become the Pope. Toomey and Campanatti represent opposite sides of Burgess's perennial debate over inherent goodness versus inherent evil in mankind. For

If you enjoy the works of Anthony Burgess, you may also want to check out the following books:

The works of James Joyce, including *Dubliners*, 1914, and *A Portrait of the Artist as a Young Man*, 1916.

The works of George Orwell, including *Burmese Days*, 1934, *Animal Farm*, 1945, and *1984*, 1949.

Aggeler in *Dictionary of Literary Biography*, "*Earthly Powers* is mainly about the monsters that abide within the labyrinth of the human soul." Through Toomey's long and less than brilliant career, many of the horrors of the twentieth century, including the rise of Naziism, are introduced. Jeremy Treglown, writing in the *Times Literary Supplement*, felt that *Earthly Powers* was "a big, grippingly readable, extraordinarily rich and moving fiction by one of the most ambitiously creative writers working in fiction," while John Leonard noted in the *New York Times* that Burgess had written "an entertainment about God, after the laughter stops. . . . Mr. Burgess, in his best novel, subverts." And writing in the *New Yorker*, the critic George Steiner concluded that *Earthly Powers* was "a feat of imaginative breadth and of intelligence which lifts fiction high. The whole landscape is the brighter for it."

The Final Years

Burgess's output never faltered, even in the final year of his life when he knew he was dying of throat cancer. He continued to write in an amazing assortment of genres, producing both fiction and nonfiction. Sitting down to his architect's table at ten in the morning, he wrote until five in the afternoon. Among Burgess's works of criticism, Aggeler in *Dictionary of Literary Biography* draws special attention to his books on James Joyce, *Re Joyce* and *Joysprick: An Introduction to the Language of James Joyce*. Burgess also wrote on Hemingway, *Ernest Hemingway and His World*, and on another writer from the north of England, D. H. Lawrence, in his *D. H. Lawrence in Italy* and *Flame into Being: The Life and Work of D. H. Lawrence*. In the mid-1980s, Burgess also began writing his autobi-

ography, published in two parts as *Little Wilson and Big God* and *You've Had Your Time: Being the Second Part of the Confessions of Anthony Burgess*.

Burgess's fiction output also kept pace, with titles such as *The End of the World News*, *The Kingdom of the Wicked*, *The Pianoplayers*, *Any Old Iron*, and *A Dead Man in Deptford* all appearing in the last decade of his life. And toward the end, Burgess also turned his hand to adapting for the stage his most notorious novel. *A Clockwork Orange 2004*, a musical version of the book, was staged at London's Barbican Theater in 1990.

Finally, however, Burgess's second terminal diagnosis proved all too true. A life-long heavy smoker, Burgess underwent a bronchoscopy in 1992 and was told he had not long to live. A year later, on November 25, 1993, at the age of seventy-six, Anthony Burgess died in London. He left behind him thirty-four years of a writing life, years that produced a profusion of plots and characters that some have compared to Dickens's output. Writing in the *Observer* upon the death of the author, the reviewer Lorna Sage summed up Burgess's life—though not necessarily his legacy—neatly: "He lived to write, ate paper and drank ink like those Shakespeare characters infatuated with literature. He worked impossibly hard, filled every day with words, stayed in love with the language all his life—exile only made him more passionate. Now he's gone, the world of English letters has lost a generous, genial and inspirational presence, who breathed his life into the words on the page."

■ Works Cited

Aggeler, Geoffrey, "Anthony Burgess," *Dictionary of Literary Biography*, Volume 14: *British Novelists Since 1960*, Gale, 1983, pp. 159-87.

Buckley, Reid, *American Spectator*, August, 1983, pp. 38-40.

Burgess, Anthony, *A Clockwork Orange*, Norton, 1963.

Burgess, Anthony, "Clockwork Marmalade," *Listener*, February 17, 1972, pp. 197-99.

Burgess, Anthony, interview with Samuel Coale, *Modern Fiction Studies*, Autumn, 1981, p. 448.

Burgess, Anthony, *Little Wilson and Big God*, Heinemann, 1987.

Dirda, Michael, review of *On Going to Bed*, *Washington Post Book World*, June 13, 1982, p. 4.

Enright, D. J., "A Modern Disease: Anthony Burgess's Shakespeare," *Man Is an Onion: Reviews and Essays,* Open Court, 1972, pp. 34-43.

Folkart, Burt A., obituary in *Los Angeles Times,* November 26, 1993, p. A44.

Gioia, Dana, "Deathbed Confessions," *New York Times Book Review,* November 30, 1997, pp. 9-10.

Hyman, Stanley Edgar, "Anthony Burgess' Clockwork Oranges," *New Leader,* January 7, 1963, pp. 22-23.

Leonard, John, "Books in the Times," *New York Times,* November 19, 1980, p. C33.

Mitchell, Julian, "Horrorshow on Amis Avenue," *Spectator,* May 18, 1962, pp. 661-62.

Morris, Robert K., "The Bitter Fruits of Freedom," *The Consolations of Ambiguity: An Essay on the Novels of Anthony Burgess,* University of Missouri Press, 1971, pp. 55-75.

Morris, Robert K., "Anthony Burgess—'The Malayan Trilogy': The Futility of History," *Continuance and Change: The Contemporary British Novel Sequence,* Southern Illinois University Press, 1972, pp. 71-91.

Morris, Robert K., "With Flourish of Hautboys," *Nation,* August 3, 1974, pp. 87-88.

O'Hara, J. D., review of *The Clockwork Testament, or Enderby's End, New York Times Book Review,* February 2, 1975.

Sage, Lorna, and others, "Not So Poor Burgess," *Observer,* November 28, 1993, p. 2.

Sheppard, R. Z., "Grand Illusions," *Time,* May 27, 1974, pp. 92-93.

Steiner, George, "Scroll and Keep," *New Yorker,* April 13, 1981, pp. 156, 159-62.

Theroux, Paul, "Shades of Enderby," *Washington Post Book World,* March 9, 1975, pp. 1, 3.

Treglown, Jeremy, "The Knowledge of Good and Evil," *Times Literary Supplement,* October 24, 1980, p. 1189.

Vidal, Gore, *New York Review of Books,* May 7, 1987, pp. 3, 6, 8.

■ **For More Information See**

BOOKS

Adams, Robert Martin, *After Joyce: Studies in Fiction After "Ulysses,"* Oxford University Press, 1977.

Aggeler, Geoffrey, *Anthony Burgess: The Artist as Novelist,* University of Alabama Press, 1979.

Bergonzi, Bernard, *The Situation of the Novel,* University of Pittsburgh Press, 1970.

Biles, Jack I., editor, *British Novelists since 1900,* AMS Press, 1987.

Boytinck, Paul W., *Anthony Burgess: An Enumerative Bibliography,* Norwood, 1973.

Coale, Samuel, *Anthony Burgess,* Ungar, 1981.

Concise Dictionary of British Literary Biography, Volume 8: *Contemporary Writers, 1960 to the Present,* Gale, 1992.

Contemporary Literary Criticism, Gale, Volume 1, 1973, Volume 2, 1974, Volume 4, 1975, Volume 5, 1976, Volume 8, 1978, Volume 10, 1979, Volume 13, 1980, Volume 15, 1982, Volume 22, 1982, Volume 40, 1986, Volume 62, 1991, Volume 81, 1994.

DeVitis, A. A., *Anthony Burgess,* Twayne, 1972.

Dix, Carol M., *Anthony Burgess,* Longman, 1971.

Kennard, Jean E., *Number and Nightmare: Forms of Fantasy in Contemporary Fiction,* Archon Books, 1975.

Kostelanetz, Richard, editor, *On Contemporary Literature,* Avon, 1964.

Mathews, Richard, *The Clockwork Universe of Anthony Burgess,* Borgo Press, 1978.

Schoenbaum, Samuel, *Shakespeare's Lives,* Clarendon Press, 1970.

Solotaroff, Theodore, *The Red Hot Vacuum,* Atheneum, 1970.

Tilton, John W., *Cosmic Satire in the Contemporary Novel,* Bucknell University Press, 1977.

PERIODICALS

America, October 22, 1966.

Arizona Quarterly, Autumn, 1969.

Atlanta Journal and Constitution, March 1, 1987.

Atlantic Monthly, February, 1975; January, 1990; June, 1991.

Bookletter, March 31, 1975.

Books & Bookmen, December, 1965.

Carleton Miscellany, Spring, 1966.

Chicago Tribune, October 29, 1978; April 15, 1979; January 12, 1987; May 19, 1991.

Chicago Tribune Book World, November 23, 1980; March 27, 1983; September 8, 1985; October 13, 1985; May 4, 1986.

Christian Science Monitor, May 29, 1974; February 22, 1990; June 7, 1991.

Commonweal, May 28, 1971; December 6, 1974.

Contemporary Literature, Summer, 1970.

Detroit News, October 13, 1985.

Economist, October 19, 1991.

Encounter, November, 1965.

Globe and Mail (Toronto), July 7, 1984; November 16, 1985; November 23, 1985; April 5, 1986; May 24, 1986; November 29, 1986; February 28, 1987; July 11, 1987; April 29, 1989; December 14, 1991, p. C12.

Guardian, October 10, 1964; October 20, 1991.

Harper's, March, 1966.

Hudson Review, Spring, 1967; Autumn, 1967; Autumn, 1992.

Journal of Popular Culture, Summer, 1973.

Life, October 25, 1968.

Listener, February 10, 1977; June 2, 1977, p. 729; April 5, 1984, pp. 24-25.

London Magazine, February, 1964.

Los Angeles Times, November 7, 1985; March 27, 1986.

Los Angeles Times Book Review, December 14, 1980; May 30, 1982; May 1, 1983; March 16, 1986; May 10, 1987; December 31, 1989; October 21, 1990; December 8, 1991; August 15, 1993, p. 3.

Malahat Review, April, 1969.

Massachusetts Review, Summer, 1966.

National Elementary Principal, May, 1971.

National Review, May 9, 1975.

New Republic, October 15, 1966.

New Statesman and Society, April 23, 1993, p. 36.

Newsweek, February 21, 1966; June 4, 1974; October 25, 1976.

New Yorker, May 7, 1966; May 20, 1991.

New York Herald Tribune, February 8, 1965.

New York Review of Books, September 30, 1976.

New York Times, December 1, 1965; March 12, 1983; August 8, 1983; April 14, 1984; September 11, 1985; December 31, 1986; February 14, 1987; February 14, 1990.

New York Times Book Review, May 1, 1966; December 4, 1966; November 29, 1970; November 19, 1978; April 15, 1979; December 7, 1980; March 6, 1983; April 22, 1984, p. 10; September 22, 1985; March 30, 1986; June 1, 1986; November 2, 1986; February 22, 1987; February 26, 1989, p. 12; December 10, 1989; October 21, 1990; April 28, 1991; May 5, 1991; June 9, 1991; June 16, 1991; May 31, 1992.

New York Times Magazine, April 2, 1967.

Observer, November 1, 1992, p. 62.

Paris Review, Spring, 1973.

Publishers Weekly, January 31, 1972.

Punch, June 12, 1968; March 28, 1984, p. 59.

Saturday Review, July 15, 1967.

Seventeen, August, 1973.

Spectator, May 31, 1968; August 30, 1968; November 10, 1990, p. 45; October 19, 1991; January 2, 1993, p. 25; May 8, 1993, p. 28.

Time, March 21, 1983, p. 76; October 17, 1983; April 23, 1984; November 17, 1986; February 16, 1987.

Times (London), January 16, 1964; October 20, 1980; April 4, 1982; October 28, 1982; March 29, 1984; May 16, 1985; August 12, 1985; March 6, 1986; May 17, 1986; August 28, 1986; February 27, 1987; October 10, 1987; March 2, 1989; October 10, 1991.

Times Literary Supplement, November 4, 1965; October 8, 1982; November 5, 1982; December 10, 1982; December 24, 1982; March 30, 1984; May 31, 1985; October 18, 1985; November 16, 1985; April 4, 1986; August 29, 1986; February 27, 1987; April 7, 1989; October 26, 1990; October 11, 1991; April 30, 1993, p. 21.

Tribune Books (Chicago), January 12, 1987; February 15, 1987; January 29, 1989; May 19, 1991, p. 4.

Variety, May 16, 1973.

Village Voice, April 14, 1966.

Washington Post, October 30, 1978; December 26, 1980; June 13, 1982, p. 4; March 8, 1987; December 24, 1989.

Washington Post Book World, March 31, 1968; November 23, 1980; March 13, 1983; January 1, 1984; April 8, 1984; March 17, 1985; May 12, 1985; October 6, 1985; January 19, 1986; March 9, 1986; November 16, 1986; March 1, 1987; February 12, 1989; May 12, 1991, p. 1; December 22, 1991; August 15, 1993, p. 3.

Wilson Library Bulletin, May, 1965.

■ **Obituaries**

PERIODICALS

Chicago Tribune, November 26, 1993, section 3, p. 6; November 29, 1993, section 2, p. 8.

New York Times, November 26, 1993, p. B23.

Times (London), November 26, 1993, p. 23.

Washington Post, November 26, 1993, p. C6.*

—Sketch by J. Sydney Jones

Tim Cahill

■ Personal

Born c. 1944, in Nashville, TN. *Education:* University of Wisconsin, B.A. (European intellectual history); attended law school; San Francisco State, M.A. (creative writing).

■ Addresses

Home—Livingston, MT.

■ Career

Journalist and writer. Worked variously as a lifeguard, longshoreman, and warehouse worker; *Rolling Stone*, San Francisco, then New York City, associate editor and staff writer, 1971—; *Outside*, founding editor, 1976-77, and contributing editor; freelance writer.

■ Writings

Buried Dreams: Inside the Mind of a Serial Killer, Bantam (New York City), 1987.
Jaguars Ripped My Flesh: Adventure Is a Risky Business (essays), Bantam, 1987.

A Wolverine Is Eating My Leg (essays), Vintage (New York City), 1989.
Road Fever: A High-Speed Travelogue, Random House (New York City), 1991
Pecked to Death by Ducks (essays), Random House, 1993.
(Editor and contributor) *Wild Places: Twenty Journeys into the North American Outdoors*, Foghorn Press, 1996.
Pass the Butterworms: Remote Journeys Oddly Rendered (essays), Villard (New York City), 1997.

Also contributor to *The Literary Insomniac: Stories and Essays for Sleepless Nights*, edited by Elyse Cheney and Wendy Hubbert, Doubleday (New York City), 1996; author of introduction to *Everest: Mountain without Mercy*, by Broughton Coburn, National Geographic Society (Washington, DC), 1997. Contributor to periodicals, including *Discovery, Geo, Islands, National Geographic*, and *San Francisco Examiner*.

■ Sidelights

Tim Cahill may be classified as a writer of "travel" books, but critics and readers alike will agree that his are most definitely travel books with a twist. An experienced writer, editor, and journalist, Cahill has channeled his love of the outdoors and his fear of neither man nor beast into several volumes of entertaining prose. With lighthearted titles like *Jaguars Ripped My Flesh: Adventure Is a Risky Business* and *A Wolverine Is*

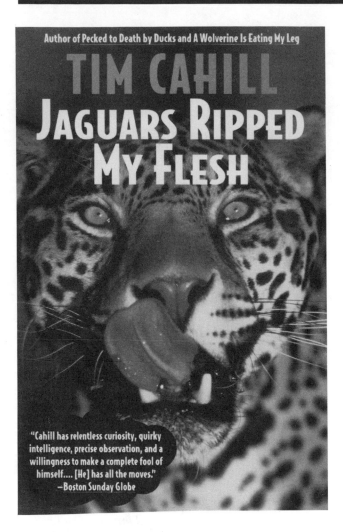

Author of Pecked to Death by Ducks and A Wolverine Is Eating My Leg

TIM CAHILL

JAGUARS RIPPED MY FLESH

"Cahill has relentless curiosity, quirky intelligence, precise observation, and a willingness to make a complete fool of himself.... [He] has all the moves."
—Boston Sunday Globe

Cahill encounters gorillas, porcupines, and Amazon ruins in this humorous journey through the wild.

Eating My Leg, his books recall the bravado of adventurers of yore . . . and swiftly undercut it with a sense of fun. Whether it be hang gliding or parachuting, mountain climbing or sea kayaking, hacking his way through jungle underbrush or traversing seemingly endless stretches of desert a la Lawrence of Arabia, Cahill knows no bounds in his pursuit of his always intriguing, always lively stories. As Pam Johnson stated in *School Library Journal,* he is a writer who "appears to have personally visited every imaginable place on Earth, . . . where he has eaten whatever has been served . . . and survived disastrous mishaps."

Born in Nashville, Tennessee, Cahill was transplanted to more northerly terrain by his parents at an early age; he would spend most of his youth in Waukesha, Wisconsin. He got bit by the writing bug even before the travel bug found him; as Cahill told interviewer David Petersen in *Bloomsbury Review:* "I secretly bought *Writer's Digest* the way some people buy pornography. I didn't want people to know I had writing aspirations—because I might *fail.*" After graduating from high school, Cahill enrolled in classes at the University of Wisconsin, where he eventually earned a B.A. in European intellectual history. He then gave law school a trial run, but he knew it wasn't for him; after a semester or so he left the world of torts and malfeasance for San Francisco State, and was awarded his M.A. in creative writing a few years later.

From Lifeguard to Journalist

While he was attending college, Cahill took odd jobs working as a lifeguard, longshoreman, warehouse worker—anything to keep the tuition paid. After graduation, and with a masters degree under his belt, he decided to get a job where he could use less brawn and more brains: he found it at the San Francisco office of *Rolling Stone* magazine, where he signed on as an associate editor and staff writer in 1971. Five years later, *Rolling Stone* packed up its West Coast office and moved east to New York City. That same year, the publishers decided to start a new magazine, *Outside.* Because of Cahill's skill as an editor and his abiding interest in the outdoors, he was the logical choice to be *Outside's* founding editor. He focused on organizing and publishing the new periodical, while also finding time to begin a column called "Out There." By 1977, however, Cahill had enough of the city. He turned over his management duties and became one of the magazine's most frequent contributors by keeping his column and serving as a contributing editor. From his new home in Livingston, Montana, he embarked on a career as freelance writer.

Cahill's first published book was *Buried Dreams: Inside the Mind of a Serial Killer.* An account of the life of John Wayne Gacy, the book was written with the help of investigative reporter Russ Ewing, who had been granted the opportunity to interview and correspond with the notorious mass murderer for several years after Gacy's arrest and imprisonment for the murder of thirty-three young men in Chicago. Gacy's killing spree lasted six years during the 1970s. He lured young men to

Cahill describes his experiences in the Himalayan Mountains, the Grand Terror of Montana, and other dangerous, bizarre, and rarely-seen places.

his suburban home before assaulting, torturing, and finally killing them, disposing of their bodies by burying them in the crawlspace under his house. All along, his gruesome deeds were masked by a placid demeanor and Gacy's reputation as an upstanding citizen. "Cahill's juggernaut of a book will go down as the definitive story," remarked a contributor in *Kirkus Reviews.* Maria Gallagher, writing in the *New York Times Book Review,* noted that the author of *Buried Dreams* "musters some surprisingly graceful prose for this fulsome subject."

In light of his later career, *Buried Dreams* is very uncharacteristic Cahill. He told Petersen that writing it was "no fun" because he was forced to go inside the mind of his subject. "I had to slip in

and out of a trance state in which I was able to think like this guy," he recalled, "which was not psychologically very healthy." Since his first book, he has shifted his focus exclusively to the adventure travel genre: "I seem to do my best work when stimulated by vaguely threatening situations," Cahill admitted to Petersen.

Travel and Adventure

After revealing the inner psyche of an extremely troubled man in *Buried Dreams,* Cahill now focused on his true calling—getting himself out of all sorts of crazy situations involving Mother Nature, and documenting them in articles and books.

In this work, Cahill writes of his many adventures in the course of a fifteen-thousand-mile journey from Tierra del Fuego to Prudhoe Bay in a record-breaking twenty-three-and-a-half days.

Jaguars Ripped My Flesh: Adventure Is a Risky Business and *A Wolverine Is Eating My Leg* feature collected essays previously published in Cahill's "Out There" column in *Outside* over a seventeen-year period. Two more books of collected essays from the author's twenty-years-worth of contributions to *Outside* would be published as *Pecked to Death by Ducks* and *Pass the Butterworms: Remote Journeys Oddly Rendered.*

The essays in *Jaguars Ripped My Flesh* are gleaned from Cahill's early contributions to *Outside*. South America and Australia are among the continents that he traverses, meeting and mingling with everyday folk in situations that Cahill imbues with humor in the retelling. Readers will learn such useful information as how to find a good auto mechanic in Latin America and how to evaluate different suggestions for dealing with shark and bear attacks (first, be sure the person giving the advice has all his limbs). While noting that "literate adventure writing" may be somewhat of an oxymoron, *Library Journal* contributor David J. Panciera praised the collection as "articulate" and "entertaining."

Scouring the Planet for Challenges

"Every once in a while, I like to flirt with some physical challenge in which the price of failure is death," Cahill writes in *A Wolverine Is Eating My Leg*. His experiences in the pages of this volume attest to achieving this desire: spelunking through tight-fitting passages deep within the earth; diving into the ocean's depths in search of poisonous snakes; and trekking across Death Valley during the dry season when the arid region more than lives up to its name. His journeys are never aimless, however, but follow what Carl Sommers calls Cahill's "fascination with death" in a *New York Times Book Review* appraisal of the volume. He ruminates on the Jonestown, Guyana, massacre instigated by Reverend Jim Jones and, in an essay titled "Love and Death in Gorilla Country," follows the trail of murdered anthropologist Dian Fossey, who once studied the mountain gorilla population of Rwanda. Even with such sobering focus, Cahill's book "balance[s] a sense of peril with playfulness," and its author makes his stories entertaining, according to Sommers. Alas, the book features no peril involving wolverines; the title is a satire on typical macho adventure-mag fare. Praising *A Wolverine Is Eating My Leg*, *Los*

The author travels from Antarctica to Kuwait and from Bali to Guatemala in his quest for the kind of adventures not found in most travel guides.

Angeles Times Book Review critic Alex Raksin called Cahill's work "An impressive collection, exploring the way the beauty and the darkness of the physical world is mirrored in the human psyche."

Cahill has even more fun with titles in *Pecked to Death by Ducks*. Here readers find the author sea kayaking in the California Gulf, bungee jumping off a bridge in Bristol, England, with the dapperly dressed members of Britain's Dangerous Sports Club, and exploring the newly discovered Lechu-gilla Cave outside Carlsbad, New Mexico. Even with all this going on, the indomitable Cahill still found the time (and energy) to fish in Guatemala, search for giant clams battling their way back from extinction in Tonga, and have a chat

If you enjoy the works of Tim Cahill, you may also want to check out the following books and films:

Sebastian Junger, *The Perfect Storm*, 1997.
John Krakauer, *Into Thin Air*, 1997.
Gary Paulsen, *The Car*, 1994.
Mountains of the Moon, written and directed by Bob Rafelson, 1990.

with diamond miners in Brazil. While *Times Literary Supplement* reviewer William Dalrymple dismissed the work as a patchwork of "self-consciously 'wacky' stunt[s]," other critics disagreed. *Los Angeles Times Book Review* critic Charles Solomon wrote that Cahill "retains a healthy sense of his own absurdity," while in *Quill & Quire* Nancy Wigston characterized the author as having "a concern for the environment and a liking for honest humanity." Praising particularly the opening essay, "Kuwait Is Burning: A Postcard from the Apocalypse," *New York Times Book Review* contributor Mark Goodman contended that Cahill magically takes readers along "on the Huck-and-Tom adventures we dreamed of as children, then sadly left behind in what passes for modern adulthood."

Pass the Butterworms: Remote Journeys Oddly Rendered is one of Cahill's most recent collections of essays. In this collection of two dozen tales, he "delivers all the goods—vibrancy, wit, intelligence—anyone could hope for from adventure travel writing," according to a *Kirkus Reviews* critic. Handy ways to avoid inhaling Congolese bees and recommendations of a steak-and-gin diet over malaria pills are among the practical information readers gain while they follow Cahill on his globe-spanning rounds. In the outer reaches of Mongolia he helps Oregon State University's Center for the Study of the First Americans by collecting samples of human hair from area residents; in Bonaire he rekindles his fascination with scuba diving; visiting the coast of British Columbia he kayaks the frigid ocean waters.

But all is not fun and games; as a reviewer in *Publishers Weekly* noted, the author "has a more reflective side, one that recognizes that the wilderness is a place to test ourselves and that progress has its contradictions." In "Among the

Karowai: A Stone Age Idyll," which serves as the concluding tale in *Pass the Butterworms*, Cahill writes: "the homogenization of humanity—seems to be the direction of history. . . . Missionaries come, followed by government in the form of soldiers and policemen and bureaucrats. And then the multinational developers arrive . . . and they promise a better life to anyone who wants to log the forest and farm the waste. . . . The result has always been the same. Everywhere. The living culture is entombed within museums."

The Ultimate Road Trip

In 1991 Cahill published a full-length, autobiographical work titled *Road Fever: A High-Speed Travelogue.* An account of the fifteen-thousand-mile, twenty-three-and-a-half-day marathon drive from Tierra del Fuego to Prudhoe Bay that got the author and driving buddy Garry Sowerby into the *Guinness Book of World Records*, Cahill's book is "agreeably cynical," according to Solomon in the *Los Angeles Times Book Review.* Noting that the volume steers away from "the in-your-face macho posturing that too often typifies" books of this nature, Solomon accepts the fact that Cahill and Sowerby made the trip for the sole purpose of notoriety and money, but wondered why the volume contained no map to put the whole South America-to-Alaska trip into perspective for geographically impaired readers.

For Cahill, even the excitement of his life up to that point had failed to provide him with some of the experiences he would encounter on this ultra-long road trip. "Well, it was the first time I'd gone into a war zone," he admitted to Petersen, explaining that "especially in South and Central America, there were lots of tense moments; . . . Sowerby and I were constantly dealing with people with guns." In Colombia alone, the pair were stopped by armed patrols over twenty times. Still, the author managed to keep his wits—and his life—and talked the whole trip into a tape recorder, which he transcribed upon returning safely to his home-base in Montana.

In addition to his own works, Cahill has served as editor and contributor to *Wild Places: Twenty Journeys into the North American Outdoors*, published by Foghorn Press. He has also contributed to works by other authors, including an essay in *The Literary Insomniac: Stories and Essays for*

Sleepness Nights and the introduction to Broughton Coburn's *Everest: Mountain without Mercy*, a publication of the National Geographic Society. His contributions to periodicals are many; magazines that contain Cahill's byline include *Discovery*, *Geo*, *Islands*, *National Geographic*, and the *San Francisco Examiner*. While he continues to avoid what he terms "issue" books, Cahill's respect and caring for the natural world underlies all his prose.

■ Works Cited

Review of *Buried Dreams: Inside the Mind of a Serial Killer*, *Kirkus Reviews*, January 1, 1986, pp. 28-29.

Cahill, Tim, *A Wolverine Is Eating My Leg*, Vintage, 1989.

Cahill, Tim, *Pass the Butterworms: Remote Journeys Oddly Rendered*, Villard, 1997.

Dalrymple, William, review of *Pecked to Death by Ducks*, *Times Literary Supplement*, August 6, 1993, p. 11.

Gallagher, Maria, review of *Buried Dreams: Inside the Mind of a Serial Killer*, *New York Times Book Review*, March 30, 1986, p. 19.

Goodman, Mark, review of *Pecked to Death by Ducks*, *New York Times Book Review*, April 11, 1993, p. 29.

Johnson, Pam, review of *Pass the Butterworms: Remote Journeys Oddly Rendered*, *School Library Journal*, September, 1997, p. 240.

Panciera, David J., review of *Jaguars Ripped My Flesh: Adventure Is a Risky Business*, *Library Journal*, October 1, 1987, p. 93.

Review of *Pass the Butterworms: Remote Journeys Oddly Rendered*, *Kirkus Reviews*, December 15, 1996.

Review of *Pass the Butterworms: Remote Journeys Oddly Rendered*, *Publishers Weekly*, December 30, 1996.

Petersen, David, "Road Fever: Tim Cahill Has It" (interview), *Bloomsbury Review*, September, 1991, p. 1.

Raksin, Alex, review of *A Wolverine Is Eating My Leg*, *Los Angeles Times Book Review*, February 19, 1989, p. 4.

Solomon, Charles, review of *Road Fever: A High-Speed Travelogue*, *Los Angeles Times Book Review*, April 5, 1992, p. 10.

Solomon, Charles, review of *Pecked to Death by Ducks*, *Los Angeles Times Book Review*, April 17, 1994, p. 8.

Sommers, Carl, review of *A Wolverine Is Eating My Leg*, *New York Times Book Review*, May 14, 1989, p. 23.

Wigston, Nancy, review of *Pecked to Death by Ducks*, *Quill & Quire*, February, 1993, p. 1.

■ For More Information See

PERIODICALS

Booklist, December 15, 1985, p. 595; October 1, 1987, p. 208; February 15, 1989, p. 972; April 15, 1993, p. 1530; February 1, 1997, p. 920.

Library Journal, January, 1993, p. 150; January, 1997, p. 128.

Los Angeles Times Book Review, June 2, 1996, p. 15.

New York Times Book Review, August 30, 1987, p. 34; May 17, 1992, p. 42; March 28, 1997, p. 17.

Observer (London), April 2, 1995, p. 22.

Publishers Weekly, January 31, 1986, p. 362; September 4, 1987; December 23, 1988, p. 78; December 14, 1992, p. 49; January 24, 1994, p. 53; December 30, 1996, p. 44.

Washington Post Book Word, April 10, 1994, p. 12; April 28, 1996, p. 12.*

—Sketch by Pamela L. Shelton

Alexander Calder

Miroglio, 1971; Calder's own ballet *Work in Progress*, produced in Rome, 1968.

Collections of Calder's work are located in Neue Nationalgalerie, Berlin, Germany; Art Moderne, Paris, France; Museum of Modern Art, Whitney Museum; Guggenheim Museum, New York City; and in Stockholm, Sweden, Philadelphia, PA, and Amsterdam, Holland.

■ Personal

Born July 22, 1898, in Philadelphia, PA; died November 11, 1976, in New York, NY; married Louisa James, 1931; children: two daughters. *Education:* Attended school in Berkeley, CA; Stevens Institute of Technology (Hoboken, NJ), M.E., 1918.

■ Career

Draftsman and engineer at logging camps, 1919-23; studied drawing and painting under Boardman Robinson at Art Students League, 1923-25, and at the Académie de la Grande Chaumiere, Paris, France, 1926-27; contributed sketches to *National Police Gazette*, New York City, 1925-26; worked on wood sculpture, and produced miniature circus, Paris, 1925-26; member of Abstraction-Creation group, Paris, 1930-31; first mobiles, 1931; lived in Roxbury, CT, after 1933, and spent much time in Sache, near Tours, France, after 1960; set designer for Martha Graham ballets, and for *Socrate* by Satie, 1935, *Provocation* by Pierre Halet, 1963, *Metaboles*, 1969, and *Eppur si muove* by Francis

■ Awards, Honors

Gold Medal of the American Academy of Arts and Letters, 1971; Grand Prix National from the French Ministry of Culture, 1974.

■ Writings

Calder's Circus, Dutton, 1964.
Calder: An Autobiography with Pictures, Pantheon, 1966.

ILLUSTRATOR

Charles Leidl, *Animal Sketching*, Sterling Publishers, 1926.
Aesop, *Fables of Aesop*, Dover Publishing, 1931.

Also illustrator of *3 Young Rats and Other Rhymes*, edited by James Johnson Sweeney, 1944; *The Rime of the Ancient Mariner*, by Samuel Taylor Coleridge,

1946; *Selected Fables*, by Jean de La Fontaine, 1948; *A Bestiary*, edited by Richard Wilbur, 1955; *Fetes*, by Jacques Prevert, 1955; *La Proue de la Table*, by Yves Elleouet, 1967; and *Santa Claus*, by D. John Grossman, 1974.

■ Sidelights

Best known as the inventor of the mobile, Alexander Calder is considered the preeminent American sculptor of the twentieth century. Calder was fascinated by motion, which led him to develop a new art form—movable sculpture. By adding movable parts to his wire and sheet metal constructions, he gave them a life of their own, allowing them to endlessly rearrange themselves in an ever-changing pattern. Later in his career, he also created looming, standing constructions of intersecting planes of steel plate which he called

Inspired by the relationships of planets and stars, Calder introduced movement into his work to develop the concept of the mobile.

stabiles. In *Artists: From Michelangelo to Maya Lin*, G. Aimée Ergas quotes a friend and critic of Calder who noted, "Public sculpture was a stuffed shirt's paradise until [he] came along." Calder felt the same way, and he once stated that "Above all, I feel art should be happy and not lugubrious."

Calder was born in 1898 to a family of artists. His mother, Nanette Lederer Calder, was an accomplished painter. His father, Alexander Milne Calder, was a prominent sculptor who carved a notable statue of George Washington on the monumental arch in Manhattan's Washington Square. Alexander Stirling Calder, his grandfather, was also a well-known sculptor; born in Aberdeen, Scotland in 1846, he created the thirty-seven-foot-high bronze effigy of William Penn that still stands on top of Philadelphia's City Hall. When he was a boy, Calder began making toys, jewelry, and gadgets from materials that he found around the house. Although he loved art, it was not Calder's first career choice.

After graduating from high school, Calder decided to become an engineer, and he attended Stevens Institute of Technology in Hoboken, New Jersey. He was an excellent and popular student, and many classmates remembered his pleasant nature and ability to make them laugh. At Stevens, Calder studied mechanical drawing, applied kinetics (the branch of science that deals with the effects of forces on the motions of bodies or with changes in a physical or chemical system), and descriptive geometry. This latter area of study would later prove useful to Calder as an artist.

After graduating from college, Calder worked at various jobs, including automotive engineer, map maker, machinery salesman, efficiency engineer, and crew member in the boiler room of a passenger ship. In 1923, he began to study at the Art Students League in New York City.

A Career in Art

Calder's first art position was as a sports illustrator for the *National Police Gazette* newspaper. Because he had a press pass, he was able to spend two weeks in the spring of 1925 sketching scenes at the Ringling Brothers Barnum & Bailey Circus. He also decorated a sporting goods store in New York City with portraits of athletes, and compiled

Calder's standing constructions of steel plate, or "stabiles," are broad, curved structures that often resemble huge spiders, animals, or dinosaurs.

a collection of drawings he had done at New York zoos in his first book, entitled *Animal Sketching*, which was published in 1926. In this year, Calder left New York for Paris.

There he enrolled in art classes and began building his first movable wood and wire sculptures in his tiny studio. The result was his famous miniature circus, whose characters are based on his New York circus drawings. Using wood, wire, rubber, cork, buttons, bottle caps, and fabric, Calder created miniature elephants, acrobats, seals, lions, and a ringmaster. Soon, Calder's circus was drawing an audience, and even important artists of the day came to watch as the "funny" American played with his "toys." The circus helped Calder to pay his bills, and it also gave him the opportunity to become known to the leaders in the Paris art community. The impact that the circus had on the intellectual and social circles in

Paris was best indicated by the fact that years later Thomas Wolfe, in his novel *You Can't Go Home Again*, would describe one of the performances, his stinging comments lashing out at the social milieu that treated art as a diversion. Calder's first show in Paris was at the Salon des Humoristes in 1927, where he exhibited circus figures, wire sculptures, and paintings of the celebrated black dancer Josephine Baker.

Next, Calder began experimenting with large-scale wire sculptures, many of which were three-dimensional. The pieces were witty and playful, made of wire and sheet metal, and full of spidery lines and curlicues. He gave them whimsical titles, such as *Blue Elephant with Red Ears, Crested Cow,* and *The Only, Only Bird. Umbrella Lamp,* which was one of his cleverest sculptures, portrayed a skinny pedestrian with a light bulb for a head holding a toy umbrella.

One of Calder's major influences was the artist Piet Mondrian, a Dutch abstractionist painter who drew austere pictures using straight black lines and white or primary-colored rectangles. "My entrance into the field of abstract art came about as a result of a visit to the studio of Piet Mondrian in Paris in 1930," Calder asserted in a 1951 essay that appeared in the *Museum of Modern Art Bulletin*. Calder visited Mondrian's studio in Paris and expressed the wish that he could see all of Mondrian's paintings set in motion. Mondrian painted primarily in black and white, using the primary colors red, blue, and yellow for accent. Calder adopted this color scheme for his own work, and he protested when he was asked to use different colors.

In 1929, Calder presented his first solo show in Paris, displaying his wood and wire sculptures. Later, the exhibition moved on to New York and Berlin. During the 1930s, Calder often traveled between New York and Paris by ship. It was on one of these trips that he met Louisa James, whom he married in 1931. As his fame grew, Calder was accepted into a number of progressive art circles. He was invited to exhibit with Abstraction-Creation in Paris, a group dedicated to the promotion of nonfigurative art through exhibitions and the publication of an almanac, and his works were displayed at an event at the Museum of Modern Art in New York. For the first issue of *Abstraction-Création, Art Non-Figuratif*, Calder prepared the following statement to accompany a reproduction of the sculpture *Little Universe*: "How does art come into being? Out of volumes, motion, spaces carved out within the surrounding space, the universe."

In *Little Universe*, Calder attempted for the first time to realize his concept of the cosmos in a three-dimensional form. The sculpture is made up of two circles of wire that intersect at right angles to form a sphere. A plastic form, which is thought to represent the universe, supports smaller solid spheres that could be asteroids or planetary bodies. Calder tried to portray his own vision of the shape and nature of the cosmos in this and other sculptures.

The Invention of the Mobile

It was during the 1930s and early 1940s that Calder developed the concept of kinetic art by introducing actual movement rather than implied motion into his work. The idea was inspired partly by the relationships of planets, stars, and other celestial bodies. Calder's first stabiles were stationary constructions developed from his wire sculptures. He suspended little balls or free-form shapes from long wires, suggesting a model of the solar system.

In 1931, Calder began creating mobiles—moving sculptures that hung from ceilings or were suspended from large bases. Calder's first exhibition of these mobiles was held at the Galerie Vignon in Paris. In an effort to convey graceful, natural movement, he experimented with weight balances. When he tried to power his mobiles with small motors, he disliked their predictable, steady motion, and found that the motion created by air or wind currents in a room was more interesting. Calder's innovation was hailed as a major advancement in modern art; art critic Waverly Root is quoted in *Modern Arts Criticism* as stating that "Calder's mobiles may well be the beginning of four-dimensional sculpture." The unique combination of his engineering expertise and his spirit of creative exploration allowed Calder to modernize the art of sculpture.

Calder's first mobiles hung from the ceiling, but Calder quickly invented several standing varieties. *Sandy's Butterfly* has been described as a mobile-stabile, but art critic and author Bernice Rose, in an introduction to *A Salute to Alexander Calder*, wrote that Calder objected to this term because he felt that "anything that moves is a mobile."

By the end of the 1930s, Calder had established a general form for his mobiles and stabiles. He often titled his works with the names of animals, including *Spider, Whale,* and *Black Beast.* His stabiles were broad, curved structures that were planted on the ground and often resembled huge spiders or dinosaurs.

Calder and his wife bought a farmhouse in Connecticut, and his studio there looked like a factory, with wires, poles, sheet metal, tools, and crates throughout. As interest in Calder's work grew, his sculptures were displayed all over the United States and Europe in the 1930s and 1940s. French author and philosopher Jean-Paul Sartre, in a catalogue for a 1946 Calder exhibition, stated, "When everything goes right a mobile is a piece of poetry that dances with the joys of life and

In the 1970s, Braniff Airlines commissioned Calder to paint his designs on this 727-200 plane.

surprises." When the Museum of Modern Art moved to its present location in New York City in 1939, Calder was commissioned to create a mobile for the stairway. In 1943, the Museum installed a large exhibition of Calder's work that included performances of *Circus* by the artist himself. The exhibition was a huge success, and commissions poured in from businesses, private citizens, and even governments all over the world. Demand was high for Calder's sculptures and for the posters, prints, rugs, and tapestries that he had designed. For the first time, Calder began to enjoy financial success, and his work was widely accepted.

Because of his newfound fame, he was commissioned to create large-scale sculptures for the Brussels World's Fair, UNESCO headquarters in Paris, and for what is now Kennedy International Airport in New York. Calder also made jewelry, designed sets and costumes for theatrical productions and ballets, illustrated books, and created toys for his children and grandchildren. He also drew and

painted with oils. In the 1970s, Braniff Airlines commissioned Calder to paint some of their jets with his designs, and he decorated a racing car for the BMW motor company.

Reputation Grows

In 1953, the Calder family, which also included two daughters, bought a house near Tours in central France. This became their primary home and Calder's main studio, although they did keep the house in Connecticut. Calder's reputation continued to grow, and by the 1960s he was one of the world's most celebrated artists. His large sculptures appeared in public places. In 1962, Calder designed one of his most famous sculptures, a gigantic black stabile called *Teodelapio*, for the city of Spoleto, Italy. The piece is more than fifty-eight feet high, and traffic drives through it. Five years later, he produced *Man* for the World's Fair in Montreal, Canada. In 1974, he created the fifty-three-foot high *Flamingo* that stands in the Fed-

If you enjoy the works of Alexander Calder, you may also want to check out the following:

The works of Bauhaus artist Paul Klee.
The paintings of fauvist Henri Matisse.
The works of surrealist Joan Miró.
The paintings of Dutch artist Piet Mondrian.

eral Center Plaza in Chicago, which complements an adjacent skyscraper by Mies van der Rohe. When Katharine Kuh of *Artist's Voice* asked Calder in a 1960 interview if he liked being commissioned to create sculptures of such considerable size, he responded, "Yes—it's more exhilarating—and then one can think he's a big shot."

Calder posters became very popular in the 1960s and 1970s, when bright colors and bold outlines fit the period perfectly. Calder contributed designs to the peace movement as well as to environmental causes and political campaigns. In 1966, Calder and his wife took a full-page ad in the *New York Times* to protest the war in Vietnam. Later, in 1972, he took out an ad to protest the Cambodian bombings.

During his lifetime, Calder received many prizes and honors, including the Gold Medal of the American Academy of Arts and Letters (1971) and the Grand Prix National from the French Ministry of Culture (1974). His last great work, a large mechanized mural for the Sears Tower in Chicago, was created two years before his death. In a 1972 essay that appeared in the book *Homage to Calder*, Gilbert Lascault wrote, "Calder's sculptures are perfect works, a mixture of delight and gravity, humor and construction. . . . These creatures who have been endowed with an independent life of their own . . . make us turn, fascinated, to their creator." When Calder died in 1976, tributes poured in from all over the world. Martin Friedman, director of the Walker Art Center in Minneapolis, Minnesota, stated in a eulogy for Calder that "He was one of the greatest form-givers America has ever produced. His art was characterized by wit, invention, and humanity. . . . His introduction of motion as a . . . component of art was an unprecedented event."

■ Works Cited

"Alexander Calder," *Modern Arts Criticism*, Volume 2, Gale, pp. 56-73.

Calder, Alexander, *Museum of Modern Art Bulletin*, Spring, 1951, pp. 8-9.

Ergas, G. Aimée, *Artists: From Michelangelo to Maya Lin*, Volume 1, UXL, 1995, pp. 34-41.

Kuh, Katharine, *The Artist's Voice: Talks with Seventeen Artists*, Harper and Row, 1962, pp. 39-51.

Lascault, Gilbert, "Calder's Contradictions and Laughter," *Homage to Calder*, Tudor Publishing Company, 1972, pp. 39-48.

Marter, Joan M., "Alexander Calder: Cosmic Imagery and the Use of Scientific Instruments," *Arts Magazine*, October, 1978, pp. 108-13.

Rose, Bernice, in an introduction to *A Salute to Alexander Calder*, Museum of Modern Art, 1969, pp. 4-24.

■ For More Information See

BOOKS

Arnason, H. H., *Calder: A Study of the Works*, Van Nostrand, 1966.

Bourdon, David, *Calder: Mobilist, Ringmaster, Innovator*, Macmillan, 1980.

Caradente, Giovanni, *Calder: Mobiles and Stabiles*, New American Library, 1968.

Guerrero, Pedro E., *Calder at Home: The Joyous Environment of Alexander Calder*, Stewart, Tabori, and Chang, 1998.

Hayes, Margaret Calder, *The Calders: A Family Memoir*, Paul S. Eriksson, 1977.

Lipman, Jean, *Calder's Universe*, Running Press, 1976.

Marchesseau, David, *The Intimate World of Alexander Calder*, translated by Eleanor Levieux and Barbara Shirey, Harry N. Adams, 1989.

Marter, Joan M., *Calder*, Cambridge University Press, 1984.

Mulas, Ugo, and Arnason, H. H., *Calder*, Viking Press, 1971.

Ragon, Michel, *Calder: Mobiles and Stabiles*, Methuen, 1967.

Venezia, Mike, *Alexander Calder*, Children's Press, 1998.

PERIODICALS

American Art Journal, July, 1979, pp. 75-85.

Art in America, Number 4, 1962, pp. 68-73; March-April, 1969, pp. 32-49; May-June, 1970, pp. 48-51.
Art News, Summer, 1973, pp. 54-58.

CATALOGS

Messer, Thomas, *Calder,* [New York], 1964.
Rose, Bernice, *A Salute to Calder,* [New York], 1969.
Sweeney, James Johnson, *Calder,* [New York], 1951.

■ Obituaries

PERIODICALS

Newsweek, November 22, 1976, p. 79.
New York Times, November 12, 1976; November 13, 1976.
Smithsonian, December, 1976, pp. 74-81.
Time, November 22, 1976, pp. 63-64.*

—Sketch by Irene Durham

Raymond Chandler

Personal

Born July 23, 1888, in Chicago, IL; died March 26, 1959, in La Jolla, CA; buried at Mount Hope Cemetery, San Diego, CA; son of Maurice Benjamin and Florence Dart (Thornton) Chandler; married Pearl Cecily (some sources say Eugenia or Eugenie) Hurlburt, 1924 (died, 1954). *Education:* Educated in England, France, and Germany.

Career

The Admiralty, London, England, worker in supplies and accounting departments, 1907; reporter for *Daily Express*, London, and *Western Gazette*, Bristol, England, both 1908-12; worked as menial laborer in St. Louis, MO, c. 1912; worked at sporting goods company in California; Los Angeles Creamery, Los Angeles, CA, accountant and bookkeeper, 1912-17; worked at bank in San Francisco, CA, 1919; *Daily Express*, Los Angeles, reporter, 1919; Dabney Oil Syndicate, Los Angeles, 1922-32, began as bookkeeper, became auditor, then vice president; writer, 1933-59. *Military service:* Served in Canadian Army, 1917-18, and in Royal Air Force, 1918-19. *Member:* Mystery Writers of America (president, 1959).

■ Awards, Honors

Nomination for Academy Award for best screenplay, Academy of Motion Picture Arts and Sciences, 1944, for *Double Indemnity*; Edgar Allan Poe Award, Mystery Writers of America, and nomination for Academy Award for best original screenplay, both 1946, both for *The Blue Dahlia*; Edgar Allan Poe Award, Mystery Writers of America, 1954, for *The Long Goodbye*.

■ Writings

NOVELS

The Big Sleep, Knopf, 1939.
Farewell, My Lovely, Knopf, 1940.
The High Window, Knopf, 1942.
The Lady in the Lake, Knopf, 1943.
The Little Sister, Houghton, 1949, published as *Marlowe*, Pocket Books, 1969.
The Long Good-Bye, Hamish Hamilton, 1953, published as *The Long Goodbye*, Houghton, 1954.
Playback, Houghton, 1958.
(With Robert B. Parker) *Poodle Springs*, Putnam, 1989.

Works also published in multi-novel volumes.

SHORT STORIES

Five Murders, Avon, 1944.

Five Sinister Characters, Avon, 1945.

Red Wind: A Collection of Short Stories, World, 1946.

Spanish Blood, World, 1946.

Finger Man, and Other Stories, Avon, 1947.

The Simple Art of Murder (includes "Trouble Is My Business" and "Pick-Up on Noon Street," and the essay "The Simple Art of Murder"), Houghton, 1950, selections published separately as *Trouble Is My Business: Four Stories from "The Simple Art of Murder,"* Pocket Books, 1951, "The Simple Art of Murder" published separately, Pocket Books, 1953.

Pick-Up on Noon Street, Pocket Books, 1952.

Pearls Are a Nuisance, Hamish Hamilton, 1953.

Killer in the Rain, edited by Philip Durham, Houghton, 1964.

The Smell of Fear, Hamish Hamilton, 1965.

Smart-Aleck Kill, Penguin, 1976.

Contributor to periodicals, including *Academy, Atlantic Monthly, Black Mask, Detection Fiction Weekly, Detective Story, Dime Detective, Spectator, Unknown,* and *Westminster Gazette.* Stories included in various anthologies.

SCREENPLAYS

(With Billy Wilder) *Double Indemnity* (adapted from James M. Cain's novel of the same title), Paramount, 1944.

(With Frank Partos) *And Now Tomorrow* (adapted from Rachel Field's novel of the same title), Paramount, 1944.

(With Hagar Wilde) *The Unseen* (adapted from Ethel Lina White's book *Her Heart in Her Throat*), Paramount, 1945.

The Blue Dahlia (produced by Paramount, 1946), edited by Matthew J. Bruccoli, Southern Illinois University Press, 1976.

(With Czenzi Ormonde) *Strangers on a Train* (adapted from Patricia Highsmith's novel of the same title), Warner Bros., 1951.

Raymond Chandler's Unknown Thriller: The Screenplay of "Playback," Mysterious Press, 1985.

OTHER

Raymond Chandler Speaking (letters, criticism, and fiction), edited by Dorothy Gardiner and Kathrine Sorley Walker, Houghton, 1962.

The Midnight Raymond Chandler (omnibus), edited by Joan Kahn, Houghton, 1971.

Chandler before Marlowe: Raymond Chandler's Early Prose and Poetry, 1908-1912, edited by Matthew J. Bruccoli, introduction by Jacques Barzun, University of South Carolina Press, 1973.

The Notebooks of Raymond Chandler, and "English Summer: A Gothic Romance," edited by Frank MacShane, Ecco Press, 1976.

(With James M. Fox) *Raymond Chandler and James M. Fox: Letters,* privately printed, 1979.

Selected Letters of Raymond Chandler, edited by Frank MacShane, Columbia University Press, 1981.

■ Adaptations

The High Window inspired the 1942 film *Time to Kill* and was filmed as *The Brasher Dubloon* with George Montgomery in 1947; *Farewell, My Lovely* was filmed as *Murder, My Sweet* with Dick Powell in 1945, and, under its original title, with Robert Mitchum in 1975; *The Big Sleep* was filmed—by director Howard Hawks from an adaptation by William Faulkner, among others—with Humphrey Bogart and Lauren Bacall in 1946, and with Robert Mitchum in 1978; *The Lady in the Lake* was filmed in 1946 by actor-director Robert Montgomery; *The Little Sister* was filmed as *Marlowe* with James Garner in 1969; *The Long Goodbye* was filmed—by director Robert Altman—with Elliott Gould in 1973.

■ Sidelights

In the late 1940s well-known British author and critic Evelyn Waugh hailed Raymond Chandler as America's "greatest living writer." Poet W. H. Auden stated that Chandler's mystery novels "should be read and judged, not as escape literature, but as works of art." Chandler himself once observed that it was not he but rather his colleague Dashiell Hammett who had taken murder "out of the Venetian case and dropped it into the alley." Perhaps, but it was Chandler who dusted it off, and, in the process of creating his Philip Marlowe character, elevated the literary genre of the hard-boiled detective story into a uniquely American art form. Writing in *Twentieth-Century Crime and Mystery Writers,* T. R. Steiner has observed that "No earlier hardboiled writer had presented such vivid evocative images of city life and of nature. Although writers like Ernest Hemingway, Ring Lardner, and Hammett had been developing a trenchant comic American written lingo, Chandler intensified and further stylized it, particularly with the comic similes and litotes that became trademarks of his style. If hardboiled fiction was, paradoxically, romance, Chandler made it even more romantic." Chandler biographer Frank MacShane viewed him as a thematic heir to Chaucer and Dickens and as such "one of the most important writers of his time, as well as one of the most delightful."

Raymond Thornton Chandler was born in Chicago on July 23, 1888, the only child of Florence and Maurice Chandler. His mother was Irish, his father an Irish-American from Philadelphia. Maurice Chandler worked for the railway and traveled a lot, which was just as well; the elder Chandler was an alcoholic who, when home, was "found drunk if he was found at all," as Tom Hiney put it in *Raymond Chandler: A Biography*.

Enjoys Proper British Upbringing

When the Chandlers divorced in 1895, Florence and her son went to England. There they moved in with Florence's mother and one of her sisters in the north London suburb of Upper Norwood. Young Raymond was raised in what one of his friends described in an essay in Miriam Gross's *The World of Raymond Chandler* as an atmosphere of "'high Victorian rectitude,' which resulted in Chandler developing a puritan streak and a fascination with the dark side of the masculine psyche."

A well-to-do Irish uncle paid Chandler's tuition at nearby Dulwich College, the same public school attended around this same time by authors P. G. Wodehouse and C. S. Forester. Chandler studied both classical and modern subjects in hopes of one day becoming a lawyer. However, money was a problem, and he quit school at sixteen. He then went to France and Germany for two years, studying languages in preparation for writing the civil service examinations. Secretly, Chandler had another ambition. "I wanted to be a writer, but I knew my Irish uncle would not stand for that," Frank MacShane quotes him as saying in his *The Life of Raymond Chandler*, "so I thought perhaps that the easy hours in the Civil service might let me do that on the side."

Chandler became a British citizen upon his return to England in 1907. He also took the civil service exams, finishing third out of eight hundred candidates overall and first in the classics test. As a result, he was offered a job at the Admiralty, which involved accounting for and distributing naval supplies. Chandler hated it, and to his family's dismay he quit after just six months. "I had too much Irish blood in me to be pushed around by suburban nobodies," Chandler told British publisher Hamish Hamilton in a 1950 letter. With help from his old classics master at Dulwich, Chandler found part-time work teaching at the college. He lasted only a term, still being intent on a literary career. Chandler got a start in that direction when he was hired as a reporter by the *Daily Express* newspaper. "Every time they sent me out on a story I would get lost," MacShane quotes him as saying; Chandler was fired as a result. But on the strength of a recommendation from a friend of his uncle, Chandler found another writing job, this one at the weekly *Westminster Gazette*, London's leading liberal newspaper. He wrote essays, book reviews, and poetry for the *Gazette* and other publications. "Chandler's early poetry, with few exceptions, is most remarkable for the fact that he managed to have it published—for payment—in a reputable magazine," Hiney noted.

In Search of Life's Purpose in U.S.

Chandler realized he was going nowhere fast. "I had the qualifications to become a pretty good second-rate poet," he recalled in a 1950 letter to Hamish Hamilton. "But that means nothing because I have the type of mind that can become a pretty good second-rate anything, and without much effort." Feeling frustrated and discouraged, in 1912 Chandler, now twenty-four, returned to the United States. On the voyage to New York, he was befriended by the Lloyds, a well-to-do family from Los Angeles. They encouraged Chandler to move west, which he did. "I arrived in California with a beautiful wardrobe, a public school accent, no practical gifts for earning a living, and a contempt for the natives which, I am sorry to say, has in some measure persisted to this day," he recalled in another 1950 letter to Hamish Hamilton. Initially, Chandler had a difficult time making a living; he worked as an apricot picker, as a tennis racket stringer, and at other menial jobs. Determined to improve his lot in life, Chandler taught himself bookkeeping. Then, with help from the Lloyds, he got an office job at the Los Angeles Creamery. He did well there and soon had saved enough money to pay his mother's way to California.

Chandler's life changed abruptly in 1917, when the United States entered World War I. Being a British citizen, he traveled to Victoria, British Columbia, where he joined the Canadian Army (Canada being part of the British Empire at that time). While fighting in the trenches in France, Chandler was knocked senseless by a German enemy artillery barrage in June 1918. After a brief recovery, he transferred into the Royal Air Force (RAF) and was sent to flying school in Lincolnshire, northeast of London. There Chandler learned to be a pilot and how to drink. "When I was . . . in the RAF I would get so plastered that I had to crawl to bed on my hands and knees and at 7:30 the next morning I would be as blithe as a sparrow and howling for my breakfast. It is not in some ways the most desirable gift," Chandler later wrote in a letter to a friend.

Return Stateside Brings Eventual Stability

The war ended in November 1918, before Chandler had the opportunity to fly in combat. Following his discharge from the military, he returned home reluctantly; Chandler was loathe to return to a workaday routine. He stopped briefly in San Francisco, working at a local newspaper and then at a bank. As had become his habit, he lasted only a few weeks in each job. Chandler went back in Los Angeles in late 1919 for two reasons: he had nowhere else to go and he had fallen in love with a woman with whom he had been corresponding. Cecilia ("Cissy") Pascal, a free-spirited former New York model, was the wife of the man in whose house Florence Chandler (now terminally ill with cancer) had been living while her son was overseas.

Chandler's mother was adamantly opposed to her son, now thirty-one, marrying Cissy, who was forty-nine and already twice married. So the couple held off in their vows until after Florence Chandler died in late January 1924. With Cissy now at his side, Chandler seemed relatively content and settled. He found work as the auditor of the Dabney Oil Syndicate, a company involved in oil exploration in the Los Angeles basin. By

In Chandler's first book, detective Philip Marlowe discovers that young Carmen Sternwood, the supposedly innocent victim of extortion, is actually a killer.

late 1923 Chandler had risen to vice president of the syndicate. Chandler and Cissy lived well; they dressed nicely, owned two new cars, and socialized with the smart set. However, as always, Chandler was a study in contradictions. He loved his job, yet he hated it; he was utterly devoted to Cissy, yet he philandered shamelessly as the age gap between them began to show. "The relationship between Chandler's marriage and his work has been a source of immense controversy among his critics," Paul Skenazy wrote in the *Concise Dictionary of Literary Biography*. And then there was the matter of Chandler's drinking. Like his father before him, he was an alcoholic who went on drinking binges and suffered from blackouts.

Drop in Fortunes Prompts First Written Efforts

Chandler's life fell apart in 1932, when he was fired from his job. After a three year lag, the Great Depression hit the oil industry hard and when Dabney ran into trouble, Chandler's drinking and erratic behavior made him expendable. Thus at age forty-four, he was again unemployed and had few prospects. Supported by an allowance of $100 per month from his old friends the Lloyds, Chandler decided to resume his writing career. Throughout his years in business, he had continued to write poetry and to dream of a literary life. "Wandering up and down the Pacific Coast in an automobile, I began to read pulp magazines, because they were cheap enough to throw away," Chandler recalled in a 1950 letter to his British publisher Hamish Hamilton. "This was in the great days of the *Black Mask* [a monthly pulp fiction crime magazine that sold for fifteen cents per copy] . . . and it struck me that some of the writing was pretty forceful and honest, even though it had its crude aspect. I decided that this might be a good way to learn to write fiction and get paid a small amount of money at the same time."

Chandler approached his new vocation methodically. He enrolled in a night course in short-story writing and began analyzing the work of successful authors such as Dashiell Hammett, Erle Stanley Gardner, and Ernest Hemingway. In a March 1957

Humphrey Bogart plays detective Philip Marlowe and Lauren Bacall plays Vivian Sternwood Rutledge in the original screen adaptation of *The Big Sleep*, released in 1946.

letter to a friend, Chandler explained his technique for learning to write. "I made a detailed synopsis of some story . . . and then tried to write [it]. Then I compared it with professional work and saw where I had failed to make an effect, or had the pace wrong, or some other mistake. Then I did it over and over again." Having mastered basic techniques, Chandler started work on a short story. He spent the next five months writing and rewriting an 18,000 word novella about a Hollywood starlet who enlists the help of a Chicago private eye named Mallory when thugs try to blackmail her. "This dark tale of extortion and racketeering contains all the hard-boiled genre's conventions: violence, corrupt officials, gangsters and gun molls, and a detective with a fast gun and a code of ethics," observed Liahna Babener in *Contemporary Authors*.

To Chandler's delight, *Black Mask* editor Joseph Shaw bought his first story, "Blackmailers Don't Shoot," and it was featured in the magazine's December 1933 issue. The fact Chandler earned just $180—a penny a word—did not trouble him; he was desperate for money and promptly went to work on a new story. "After that I never looked back, although I had a good many uneasy periods looking forward," Chandler recalled in a 1950 letter to Hamish Hamilton.

First Stories Inspired by L.A. Culture

In assessing "Blackmailers Don't Shoot" in an essay in *Down These Mean Streets a Man Must Go: Raymond Chandler's Knight*, critic Philip Durham deemed Chandler's first story "competent. The plot and theme are conventional: characterization and setting are the most interesting. From the beginning, Chandler used the technique of minute, detailed description to create character." Durham also pointed out that "Chandler began recreating the city of Los Angeles for his purposes." Having spent his youth in England, he had an outsider's perspective where U.S. culture was concerned; Chandler was at once attracted and appalled by the materialism of everyday life and by the city of Los Angeles's beauty and tawdriness. "Like Gardner and Hammett before him, Chandler drew on the irony of California's status as the Golden State," Babener wrote, "and used the setting to suggest the beguiling and corruptive power of money in American life. Ultimately, Chandler presented a more provocative Los Angeles than had

any of his predecessors." In *Nation*, contributor Thomas S. Reck would crown Chandler "the Los Angeles laureate" and claim the writer successful at capturing the true character of the city.

Two more of Chandler's short stories were published in *Black Mask* in 1934. Editor Shaw was so impressed that he began giving his new contributor star billing. Because of that, Chandler gained confidence and increased his output. He wrote eight short stories in 1935 and 1936; seven of them appeared in *Black Mask*, the other in *Detective Fiction Weekly*. "These stories, among them some of

Chandler's colorful second novel, in which an ex-con hires Marlowe to find his showgirl girlfriend, was published in 1940.

Chandler's good ones, used the city through which he had moved and the people with whom he had been associated or known about during the previous fifteen years," wrote Durham.

Chandler's total output during the 1930s amounted to twenty-one pulp fiction stories, and most critics regard the decade as his literary apprenticeship. British mystery writer Julian Symons, in an essay in *The World of Raymond Chandler,* observed: "The pulp magazines had shaped him, but once he had learned the trade they were a restriction. The novels enabled him to burst the bonds and to express the essential Raymond Chandler." In later years Chandler often questioned the quality of his early work; as Paul Skenazy pointed out, at other times, "Chandler praised [it] for the 'smell of fear which these stories managed to generate' and for their portrayal of 'a world gone wrong, a world in which . . . civilization has created the machinery for its own destruction,' a world in which 'the streets were dark with something more than night.'"

In the summer of 1938 Chandler took a break from the pulp magazines and plunged into work on his first novel, *The Big Sleep.* Recounting the book's genesis twelve years later, he told Hamish Hamilton in a letter, "I wrote *The Big Sleep* in three months, but a lot of the material in it was revamped from a couple of [my] novelettes. This gave it body, but didn't make it any easier to write. I was always a slow worker." Having done so once, Chandler began to recycle more of his early writings. His habit of "cannibalizing" his short fiction for characters, scenes, and even bits of dialogue would become the focus of critical interest when he became well known. Some observers were astounded by this practice, among them the celebrated British author and critic J. B. Priestly, one of Chandler's most influential early boosters. "As he freely confesses, Chandler was not a natural storyteller, a fertile plotter. This is proved by his habit, astonishing to me, of making use in his full-length novels of earlier short stories," Priestly observed in a 1962 essay in *New Statesman.*

The Big Sleep Receives Yawn from Critics

The Big Sleep was published in February 1939 by Alfred Knopf, who promoted the book heavily. Nonetheless, mainstream critics on both sides of the Atlantic ignored the novel, which was generally regarded as being too violent and tawdry to be taken seriously. The story's central figure is a private detective named Philip Marlowe, who is hired by an aged wheelchair-ridden tycoon named General Sternwood to investigate what initially seems to be a straightforward attempt to extort money from the General's spoiled, free-spirited young daughter Carmen. However, in the course of his investigation, Marlowe discovers the Sternwoods are not the genteel folk they seem to be, and that Carmen Sternwood is a murderer. Peter J. Rabinowitz, writing in *Texas Studies in Literature and Language,* pointed out in a 1980 article, "the novel ends not with the soothing conservative affirmation of order, but with something more politically unsettling: . . . a pervasive sense of individual despair, social chaos, and the triumph of evil."

The reaction of reviewer Will Cuppy of the *New York Herald Tribune Books* was typical of contemporary critical reaction to *The Big Sleep.* While praising the novel's "admirable hard-boiled manner," Cuppy remarked that "[Chandler] should . . . be stood in a corner and lectured upon the nature and suitable use of his talents." The book's only really favorable review, in the *Los Angeles Times* on February 19, 1939, compared Chandler to James M. Cain, the author of a 1934 bestseller called *The Postman Always Rings Twice,* a gritty, Depression-era tale about a grifter who helps an adulteress murder her husband and steal his money.

Discouraged by the critical reception for *The Big Sleep,* Chandler lamented in a letter to Knopf that reviewers "seemed more occupied with the depravity and unpleasantness of the book than with anything else." He continued, "In fact the notice from the *New York Times* . . . deflated me pretty thoroughly. I do not want to write 'depraved books.'"

Despite the lack of press attention and the hostility of those few critics who did review it, positive word-of-mouth—a "cult following," Hiney called it—resulted in ten thousand copies of *The Big Sleep* being sold in the United States and another eight thousand in Great Britain. While this was a respectable sale for a first novel of the time, Chandler only earned about $2,000 for his efforts, and he was forced to resume writing pulp fiction short stories to pay his bills.

Although initially unsuccessful, *The Big Sleep*'s appearance was noteworthy for a couple of reasons. For one, it enabled Chandler to prove to himself—and to others—that he was capable of writing novel-length fiction. In the months following the book's release, he received numerous letters of encouragement from admiring readers; two in particular stood out: those from writers John Steinbeck and S. J. Perelman. For another, *The Big Sleep* marked the debut of Chandler's signature character, detective Philip Marlowe, who some have claimed was named after Marlowe House at Dulwich College. In the words of Jerry Speir, another Chandler biographer, in his *Raymond Chandler*, "Philip Marlowe crackles to life on an cloudy October morning in the first paragraph of *The Big Sleep* . . . 'I was wearing my powder-blue suit, with dark blue shirt, tie and display handkerchief, black brogues, black wool socks with dark blue clocks on them. I was neat, clean, shaved, and sober, and I didn't care who knew it. I was everything the well-dressed private detective ought to be. I was calling on four million dollars.'"

The Birth of Philip Marlowe

In Marlowe, the book's first-person narrator, Chandler created one of the most enduring—and intriguing—characters in American fiction. Marlowe is the archetypal mid-twentieth-century American hero: a lonely, flawed, modern-day knight who stands up for the weak and the downtrodden as he tilts against the windmills of urban chaos, greed, and corruption. Critics would argue that Marlowe was everything from Chandler's literary alter ego to a middle-class existentialist, an amoral hired gun, an anti-Semite, and even a closet gay. The author's own view was less complex, but infinitely more quixotic; Marlowe was, he explained in a 1951 letter to an inquiring reader, "in revolt against a corrupt society." Those comments echoed sentiments Chandler had voiced in a 1944 *Atlantic Monthly* essay in which he described his detective hero in this way: "down [the] mean streets a man must go who is not himself mean, who is neither tarnished nor afraid. The detective in this kind of story must be such a man. He is the hero; he is everything. He must be a complete man and a common man and yet an unusual man. He must be, to use a rather weathered phrase, a man of honor—by instinct, by inevitability, without thought of it, and certainly without saying it. He must be the best man in

the world and a good enough man for any world."

The complexity of Chandler's detective hero was not the only quality that set his work apart from other pulp fiction writers. Those who read his prose were awed by its energy and superb precision. Chandler had an unequalled ear for the rhythms of everyday speech. "While Chandler's wasn't a native American voice, Philip Marlowe's invented voice is," R. W. Lid once observed in the *Kenyon Review*. Having grown up in England, Chandler studied American speech like a foreign language, and so when he used slang, colloquialisms, and wise cracks, he did it with care and great effect. Praising Chandler's ear for the vernacular, novelist Irving Wallace wrote in a 1946 *Pageant* magazine article, "His dialogue is low American—brash, unsentimental, crackling with wit. His characterizations, often in Marlowe's words, are studded with electric images: 'eyes like strange sins'; 'a smile I could feel in my hip pocket'; 'a voice that grew icicles.' On almost every page there are phrases a poet might envy: 'old men with faces like lost battles'; 'the surf curled and creamed, almost without sound, like a thought trying to form itself on the edge of consciousness.'"

Chandler was less complimentary in assessing his own writing. *The Big Sleep* was "very unequally written," he confided in a letter written to publisher Knopf a few weeks after the book's release. "There are scenes that are all right, but there are other scenes still too pulpy. Insofar as I am able, I want to develop an objective method—but slowly—to the point where I can carry an audience over into a genuine dramatic, even melodramatic novel, written in a very vivid and pungent style, but not slangy or overly vernacular."

Moves Further Afield from Pulp Fiction

Chandler's second novel, *Farewell, My Lovely*, was published in May 1940. While elements of the plot again were recycled from Chandler's earlier work, "[It] confirmed how far away from the restrictions of *Black Mask* Chandler's fiction was moving," Hiney wrote in *Raymond Chandler: A Biography*. "Though he was still using the framework of his old pulp stories, his hero, Marlowe, is even further away from being a stock pulp hero than he was in *The Big Sleep*." Even the title—which Knopf

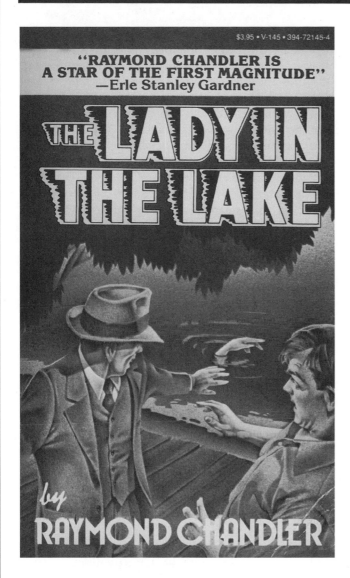

$3.95 • V-145 • 394-72145-4

"RAYMOND CHANDLER IS A STAR OF THE FIRST MAGNITUDE"
—Erle Stanley Gardner

THE LADY IN THE LAKE

by RAYMOND CHANDLER

In this fourth installment of the "Marlowe" series, the detective encounters a number of con-men and thugs as he searches for a missing woman.

had wanted changed—was considered unconventional for a detective mystery. Chandler had agonized over the book and its title for almost a year. Hiney quotes a December 19, 1939, letter in which Chandler told a writer friend, "I had to throw my second book away, so that leaves me with nothing to show for the last six months and possibly nothing to eat for the next six." Ultimately, Chandler's perfectionism paid off. Many people, Chandler included, felt *Farewell, My Lovely* was his best book.

This time out, Marlowe is hired by a hulking ex-con fresh out of prison. "Moose" Malloy—"He was big man but not more than six feet five inches tall and not wider than a beer truck"— wants the detective to find his old showgirl girlfriend Velma. What begins as a straight-forward case takes some unexpected and violent twists involving stolen jewels, crooked cops, blackmail, and murder. The neatly plotted tale ends with a bloody showdown between Moose and Velma, who has escaped her shady past and is furious at having been rediscovered. Paul Skenazy quotes a letter in which Chandler told a friend, "I shall never again achieve quite the same combination of ingredients. The bony structure was much more solid, the invention less forced and more fluent."

Unfortunately for Chandler, *Farewell, My Lovely* was ignored by critics, just as *The Big Sleep* had been. However, there were a few favorable notices, one of which particularly pleased Chandler. It appeared in the *Hollywood Citizen-News* where, Frank MacShane reports, reviewer Morton Thompson offered lavish praise for *Farewell, My Lovely*, despite his aversion to mystery novels. "I am perfectly willing to stake whatever critical reputation I possess today or may possess tomorrow on the literary future of this author. Chandler writes throughout with amazing absorption in the tasks of craftsmanship." A few months later, Isaac Anderson of the *New York Times Book Review* added his voice to a rising chorus of Chandler admirers when he observed that while *Farewell, My Lovely* was rife with violence, alcoholism, and coarse language, it was "swift moving" and "extremely well done."

Despite a vigorous advertising campaign by Knopf, sales for *Farewell, My Lovely* were disappointing. Chandler's literary reputation was growing, especially in Great Britain, but he was still largely unknown by the general public. A big reason for this was Knopf's refusal to allow cheap paperback reprints of Chandler's books, the thinking being that mass-market versions would harm his literary reputation. For now Chandler went along with this and continued struggling to survive and to write a novel that critics and the U.S. reading public would take seriously.

It took Chandler two years to finish his third Philip Marlowe novel. *The High Window* was published in August 1942. Unlike his two previous efforts, this story was entirely new and original. The plot follows Marlowe's adventures when he is hired by a woman seeking the return of a sto-

If you enjoy the works of Raymond Chandler, you may also want to check out the following books and films:

The works of Dashiell Hammett, including *The Maltese Falcon*, 1930, and *The Glass Key*, 1932.

The crime novels of John D. MacDonald, including *A Deadly Shade of Gold*, 1965, and *Cinnamon Skin*, 1982.

The mystery novels of Ross Macdonald, including *The Drowning Pool*, 1950, and *The Chill*, 1964.

Chinatown, starring Jack Nicholson, 1974.

len precious coin. The prime suspect is the estranged wife of the woman's son, but Marlowe discovers that the case is infinitely more complicated and the crooks more sinister than he ever envisioned. *The High Window* is darker, less playful, and generally less interesting than Chandler's earlier novels. This was a reflection both of his own growing frustrations and the bleakness of the international scene; the United States was now at war, and Britain's fortunes remained dim in the life-and-death struggle with Hitler.

Although there were few contemporary reviews of *The High Window*, those that did appear were generally favorable. Will Cuppy, writing in the *New York Herald Tribune Books*, applauded Chandler as "the pick of the hard-boiled scribblers"; this was a back-handed endorsement, but an endorsement nonetheless. Isaac Anderson of the *New York Times Book Review* wrote, "Raymond Chandler has given us a detective who is hard-boiled enough to be convincing without being disgustingly tough, and that is no mean achievement." Despite the positive press, sales of *The High Window* were slow. Oddly enough, as interest in his writing sagged in the United States, it continued to grow in Great Britain, where several influential critics were loud in their praise of his work.

Chandler's pessimism carried over into his next novel, *The Lady in the Lake*. This fourth installment of the Philip Marlowe series was published in 1943. It is a dark, dispirited tale in which the detective is hired to find a missing woman named Crystal Kingsley. Once again, Marlowe becomes entangled in what Hiney describes as "the usual pulp trail of crooked cops, corpses, and blackjacks." By the end of the story, Marlowe has been beaten up and unsuccessfully framed for murder and the missing woman is dead, as are several other characters. Chandler would later say that *The Lady in the Lake* was the only one of his books that he could not bear to reread. The irony was that as he himself was becoming discouraged, more reviewers were warming to his writing. Elizabeth Bullock of *Book Week* lauded *The Lady in the Lake* as "a story as finely balanced as a precision instrument and as exciting to watch at work." A reviewer writing in the *New Yorker* described the book as "Tough, beautifully organized and with a great deal more meat on its bones than the usual story of this type." And Desmond McCarthy of the London *Sunday Times* hailed *The Lady in the Lake* as "a brilliant whodunit."

The burgeoning popularity of Chandler's writing came about in part at least because of the runaway success of a twenty-five cent Avon paperback edition of *The Big Sleep*. Knopf had finally agreed to allow the publication after reluctantly concluding that Chandler was never going to be a success, and three hundred thousand copies of the Avon edition of Chandler's first novel were sold in the United States and another fifteen thousand in a special GI version. A cheap edition of *Farewell, My Lovely* was even more successful, ringing up sales of more than one million copies. Mass market versions of Chandler's books—the very thing Knopf felt would ruin the author's literary career—proved to be his salvation.

Success in Novels Sparks Screenplay Offers

Chandler's sudden fame led to him being hired as a movie screenwriter in 1943 by Paramount Studios. He started at $1,700 per week—more than he had earned in his best days in the oil industry. Originally, Chandler was recruited to work with director Billy Wilder on a screen adaptation of James M. Cain's novel *Double Indemnity*. Chandler never worked well with others, and he did not get along with Wilder. Despite their creative and personal differences, the two men produced a memorable screenplay that earned an Oscar nomination in 1944. Chandler remained on the payroll of the Hollywood studios off-and-on over the next seven years. During this period, he worked on scripts for a handful of films, most notably *The Blue Dahlia*, which in 1946 won him a second Oscar nomination, and *Strangers on a Train,* for which he teamed-up with legendary British director Alfred Hitchcock, whom Chandler also disliked.

In addition to Chandler's own screenwriting efforts, his work reached the world in the form of movies based on his books. Chandler's novels were suddenly hot properties in Hollywood, despite problems with the film censors who objected to their violence, strong language, and sexual content. Sometimes the titles of Chandler's stories were changed, as was the case with *Farewell, My Lovely,* which was filmed as *Murder, My Sweet* in 1945 with Dick Powell as Philip Marlowe. Other times, Chandler's titles remained unchanged, as was the case when Humphrey Bogart and Lauren Bacall starred in a classic 1946 screen version of *The Big Sleep.*

Burdened by his own growing cynicism about his writing and by his habitual problems with alcohol, Chandler was unable to finish another book in the years between 1943 and 1949. As Skenazy reported, in 1948 Chandler quipped, "Five years of fighting Hollywood has not left me with many reserves of energy." Having grown frustrated and embittered about his life in Hollywood, Chandler and his wife (who was now in failing health) moved to La Jolla, a suburb of San Diego. Away from Los Angeles, where he and Cissy had resided for almost forty years, Chandler became increasingly moody. He fired his business manager and his secretary and sought relief from the inner demons that tortured him by drinking and by writing long letters to anyone who cared to write to him. "He acquired a long list of correspondents; as he wrote in one of his more self-dramatizing moments: 'all of my best friends I have never met,'" noted Skenazy.

Chandler poured the frustrations and anger of his Hollywood years into his next novel, *The Little Sister,* which was published in October 1949 (by Houghton Mifflin, Chandler having cut his ties with Knopf). In this story, Marlowe goes looking for a missing boy named Orrin Quest. As the story progresses, Chandler pokes sarcastic fun at the movie industry. "Hollywood's bitchiness seems . . . to have embraced Chandler," Frank MacShane observed. Readers who were familiar with Chandler's work also noticed that Philip Marlowe, like his literary creator, was beginning to show his age. Hiney points out that American critics at the time were ambivalent towards *The Little Sister*; for example, a *Time* reviewer commented that Chandler was "in danger of becoming a talented hack." At the same time, the British reception for *The Little Sister* was much more positive. Novelist Elizabeth Bowen commented in *Tatler* that "no consideration of modern American literature ought, I think, to exclude him."

Despite the mixed reviews, *The Little Sister* was one of Chandler's most successful books. It sold well in the United States and Britain and in foreign language editions, especially in France. A further indication of Chandler's growing audience

Chandler garnered the Edgar Allan Poe Award for this 1953 mystery that many critics believed to be his best and most ambitious work.

was the fact he now received offers for the rights to create both television and radio series based on his Philip Marlowe character. As well, mainstream publishers were suddenly interested in his early fiction. A dozen of the better short stories—Chandler excluded any that he had cannibalized for his novels—were reprinted in 1950 in an anthology called *The Simple Art of Murder*. Paul Skenazy notes that the appearance of *The Little Sister* and *The Simple Art of Murder* marked a shift in the way Chandler himself approached his writing; in a letter to a friend he reportedly said that from then on he intended to "write what I want as I want to write it."

The result was the 1953 novel *The Long Goodbye*. Many critics regard this book as Chandler's most personal and most ambitious. According to Jerry Speir, it was his "last great effort to push the mystery novel out of its stereotyped niche. Unlike any of its predecessors, it takes on the whole modern society as its subject." The plot explores Marlowe's relationship with Terry Lennox, a "gentleman drunk," who becomes a suspect in the murder of his wife. When Lennox's body turns up in a Mexican town, Marlowe sets out to investigate the background and circumstances of his friend's death. Predictably, the answers that he uncovers are as surprising as they are violent and nasty.

Critical Acclaim and Personal Tragedy

Unlike Chandler's early novels, *The Long Goodbye* was widely reviewed, and many of those reviews were stunningly positive. Frank MacShane took a broad view when he wrote, "From the beginning of the book it is obvious that Chandler intended *The Long Goodbye* to be his major effort as a novelist. It has an expansiveness that his other books lack." William F. Nolan, writing in *The Black Mask Boys,* praised the work as Chandler's "finest, most mature writing achievement."

On December 12, 1954, Chandler's wife of thirty-one years died after a long battle with fibrosis of the lungs. She was eighty-four. Increasingly in recent years, Chandler's life had revolved around Cissy, and he took her death hard. So hard, in fact, that his literary career was effectively over, for he would never again work in a sustained manner. Chandler went on a prolonged drinking binge in late 1954. Ten weeks later, a failed sui-

cide attempt led to his being institutionalized briefly. Afterward, he left La Jolla and moved to London, where he took up residence in a hotel and basked in the celebrity that he enjoyed in the British capital. Chandler drank, lived a desultory lifestyle, and lavished money on friends and a succession of women, at least two of whom he talked about marrying. He continued trying to write, but produced just one more work of note, a 1958 Marlowe novel called *Playback* that was based on a failed screenplay that Chandler had written in 1947. He simply inserted Philip Marlowe into the action and rewrote the plot to account for his new protagonist. Two elements of the story set *Playback* apart from Chandler's earlier tales: the setting is not Los Angeles, but rather the suburbs of San Diego, and the book ends with Marlowe accepting a marriage proposal.

Critical assessment of *Playback* was—and still is—divided. "It is a disappointing and relatively uninspired work," wrote Liahna Babener. Jerry Speir disagreed, noting that while the novel lacks much of the energy and character development of Chandler's best work, "it still displays the characteristic Chandlerian wit and provides certain insights into the author and his attitude toward his work in his later years."

Playback proved to be the last thing that Raymond Chandler wrote. He was in the Scripps Clinic in La Jolla, suffering from pneumonia, when he died on March 26, 1959, at the age of seventy. In the years since his death Chandler has not been forgotten. His novels are still in print, and his literary reputation remains strong due to the ongoing interest in his writing by literary scholars. As well, numerous anthologies of Chandler's short stories and essays have been published. Philip Marlowe has been introduced to new generations of fans by fresh movie adaptations of Chandler's novels, and in a 1989 novel called *Poodle Springs*, a fragment of a book that Chandler was working on at the time of his death and which was finished by Robert B. Parker.

■ Works Cited

Anderson, Isaac, "New Mystery Stories," *New York Times Book Review,* November 17, 1940, p. 29.

Anderson, Isaac, review of *The High Window, New York Times Book Review,* August 16, 1942, p. 17.

Babener, Liahna, essay on Raymond Chandler, *Contemporary Authors,* Volume 129, Gale, 1990.

Bullock, Elizabeth, review of *The Lady in the Lake,* *Book Week,* November 11, 1943, p. 11.

Chandler, Raymond, "The Simple Art of Murder," *Atlantic Monthly,* December 1944, pp. 53-59.

Cuppy, Will, "Mystery and Adventure: 'The Big Sleep'," *New York Herald Tribune Books,* February 5, 1939, p. 12.

Cuppy, Will, review of *The High Window, New York Herald Tribune Books,* August 23, 1942, p. 17.

Durham, Philip, "The Tale-Teller," *Down These Mean Streets a Man Must Go: Raymond Chandler's Knight,* University of North Carolina Press, 1963, pp. 22-30.

Hiney, Tim, *Raymond Chandler: A Biography,* Chatto & Windus, 1997.

Review of *The Lady in the Lake, New Yorker,* November 6, 1943, p. 108.

Lid, R. W., "Philip Marlowe Speaking," *Kenyon Review,* spring, 1969, pp. 153-78.

MacShane, Frank, *The Life of Raymond Chandler,* Dutton, 1976.

MacShane, Frank, *Selected Letters of Raymond Chandler,* Columbia University Press, 1981.

McCarthy, Desmond, review of *The Lady in the Lake, Sunday Times* (London), October 29, 1944.

"Murder at the Old Stand," *Time,* October 3, 1949, pp. 82-83.

Nolan, William F., *The Black Mask Boys,* Morrow, 1985.

Priestly, J. B., "Close-up of Chandler," *New Statesman,* March 16, 1962, pp. 379-80.

Rabinowitz, Peter J., *Texas Studies in Literature and Language,* summer, 1980.

Reck, Thomas S., "Raymond Chandler's Los Angeles," *Nation,* December 20, 1975, pp. 661-63.

Skenazy, Paul, "Raymond Chandler," *Concise Dictionary of American Literary Biography,* Volume 5: *The Age of Maturity, 1929-1941,* Gale, 1989.

Speir, Jerry, *Raymond Chandler,* Ungar, 1981.

Steiner, T. R., *Twentieth-Century Crime and Mystery Writers,* St. James Press, 1996, pp. 186-88.

Symons, Julian, "An Aesthete Discovers the Pulps," *The World of Raymond Chandler,* edited by Mirian Gross, A & W Publishers, 1977.

Wallace, Irving, "He Makes Murder Pay," *Pageant,* July, 1946, pp. 126-29.

■ For More Information See

BOOKS

Benstock, Bernard, editor, *Art in Crime Writing: Essays on Detective Fiction,* St. Martin's Press, 1983.

Bruccoli, Matthew J., *Kenneth Millar/Ross Macdonald: A Checklist,* Gale, 1971.

Bruccoli, Matthew J., *Raymond Chandler: A Descriptive Bibliography,* University of Pittsburgh Press, 1979.

Cawelti, John G., *Adventure, Mystery, and Romance: Formula Stories as Art and Popular Culture,* University of Chicago Press, 1976.

Chandler, Raymond, *The Simple Art of Murder,* Houghton, 1950.

Dictionary of Literary Biography Documentary Series, Volume 6: *Hardboiled Mystery Writers,* Gale, 1989.

Durham, Philip, *Down These Mean Streets a Man Must Go: Raymond Chandler's Knight,* University of North Carolina Press, 1963.

Eames, Hugh, *Sleuths, Inc.,* Lippincott, 1977.

Fine, David, editor, *Los Angeles in Fiction,* University of New Mexico Press, 1984.

Goulart, Ron, editor, *The Hardboiled Dicks: An Anthology and Study of Pulp Detective Fiction,* Pocket Books, 1967.

Hamilton, Cynthia S., *Western and Hard-Boiled Detective Fiction in America: From High Noon to Midnight,* University of Iowa Press, 1987.

Knight, Stephen, *Form and Ideology in Crime Fiction,* Macmillan, 1980.

Lambert, Gavin, *The Dangerous Edge,* Grossman, 1976.

Luhr, William, *Raymond Chandler and Film,* Ungar, 1982.

Madden, David, *Tough Guy Writers of the Thirties,* Southern Illinois University Press, 1968.

Marling, William H., *Raymond Chandler,* Twayne, 1986.

Maugham, W. Somerset, *The Vagrant Mood,* Doubleday, 1953.

Most, Glenn W., and William W. Stowe, editors, *The Poetics of Murder: Detective Fiction and Literary Theory,* Harcourt, 1983.

Newlin, Keith, *Hardboiled Burlesque: Raymond Chandler's Comic Style,* Brownstone, 1984.

Pendo, Stephen, *Raymond Chandler on Screen: His Novels into Film,* Scarecrow, 1976.

Porter, Dennis, *The Pursuit of Crime: Art and Ideology in Detective Fiction,* Yale University Press, 1981.

Powell, Lawrence Clark, *California Classics: The Creative Literature of the Golden State,* Ward Ritchie, 1971.

Ruehlmann, William, *Saint with a Gun: The Unlawful American Private Eye,* New York University Press, 1974.

Thorpe, Edward, *Chandlertown: The Los Angeles of Philip Marlowe,* Vermilion, 1983.

Twentieth-Century Literary Criticism, Gale, Volume 1, 1978, Volume 7, 1982.

Wells, Walter, *Tycoons and Locusts: A Regional Look at Hollywood Fiction of the Thirties,* Southern Illinois University Press, 1973.

Wolfe, Peter, *Something More than Night: The Case of Raymond Chandler,* Bowling Green State University Press, 1985.

PERIODICALS

Antaeus, spring-summer, 1977.
Atlantic Monthly, November, 1945.
Black Mask, April, 1933.
Chicago Tribune, October 12, 1989.
Clues: A Journal of Detection, fall-winter, 1980.
Commentary, February, 1963.
Kenyon Review, spring, 1979.
London Magazine, December, 1959.
Los Angeles Times Book Review, June 27, 1976.

Massachusetts Review, winter, 1973.
Nation, April 23, 1960; September 4, 1960.
New Republic, May 7, 1962.
New Statesman, April 9, 1949.
Newsweek, May 14, 1945; October 31, 1949.
New Yorker, March 11, 1962.
New York Times, May 9, 1946.
New York Times Book Review, September 27, 1949.
New York Times Magazine, December 23, 1973.
Partisan Review, May-June, 1947.
Southern Review, summer, 1970.
Time, October 3, 1949.

■ Obituaries

PERIODICALS

New York Times, March 27, 1959.
Times (London), March 28, 1959.*

—Sketch by Ken Cuthbertson

Wes Craven

■ Personal

Full name Wesley Earl Craven; born August 2, 1939, in Cleveland, OH; son of Paul (a factory worker) and Caroline (a secretary; maiden name, Miller) Craven; married Bonnie Susan Broecker (divorced, 1970); married Millicent Eleanor Meyer (a flight attendant), July 25, 1982 (divorced, 1985); children: (first marriage) Jonathan, Jessica. *Education:* Wheaton College, B.A., 1963; Johns Hopkins University, M.A., 1964. *Politics:* Egalitarian. *Hobbies and other interests:* Flying, playing classical guitar, art, cinema, jazz and classical music, carpentry, gardening, traveling.

■ Addresses

Office—Wes Craven Films, Metro-Goldwyn-Mayer Television, 10000 West Washington Blvd., Suite 3016 Culver City, CA 90232. *Agent*—Lin Radner, International Creative Management, 8899 Beverly Blvd., Los Angeles, CA 90048.

■ Career

Screenwriter, director, and producer of films and television programs. Westminster College, New Wilmington, PA, professor, 1964-65; Clarkson University, Potsdam, NY, professor of humanities, 1965-67; worked as a high school teacher in Madrid, Spain, and Waddington, NY, 1967-68. Worked variously as a messenger, post-production assistant, and synch-up assistant to filmmaker Sean Cunningham. Co-director of "Tales to Tear Your Heart Out," and *Stranger in Our House* (television movie), NBC-TV, 1978; director of television shows, including *The Twilight Zone* (episodes include "A Little Peace and Quiet," "Word Play," "Shatterday," "Chameleon," "The Road Not Taken," "Her Pilgrim Soul," and "Dealer's Choice"), CBS-TV, 1985; *Casebusters* (made-for-TV movie), 1986; and *Nightmare Cafe*, 1992.

Director of films, including *Deadly Friend*, Warner Bros., 1986; *The Serpent and the Rainbow*, Universal, 1988; *Vampire in Brooklyn*, 1995; *Scream*, Miramax, 1996; and *Scream 2*, Miramax, 1997. Assistant producer of *Together* (also known as *Sensual Paradise*), New Line Cinema, 1971. Executive producer of films and television shows, including *The People Next Door* (series), CBS-TV, 1989; *Mindripper*, WarnerVision, 1995; *Wishmaster*, 1997; and *Carnival of Souls*, 1998. Actor in *Shocker*, 1989; *Fear in the Dark* (documentary), Arts & Entertainment, 1991; *Body Bags*, 1993; *Wes Craven's New Nightmare*, 1994; *The Fear*, 1995; an episode of *The Shadow Zone* (television series), 1996; and *Scream*, 1996. Advisor for *Bloodfist II*, Concorde, 1990. *Member:* Writer's Guild of America, Director's Guild of America, Screen Actors Guild.

■ Awards, Honors

Best picture award, London Film Festival, and honors, Sitges Film Festival (Spain), both 1978, both for *The Hills Have Eyes*; most popular film designation, Madrid Film Festival, 1980, for *Deadly Blessing*; Critic's Choice award, French Science-Fiction and Horror Film Festival, and best horror film nomination, Academy for Science Fiction, Fantasy, and Horror, both 1984, and best horror film award, Avoriaz International Festival of Fantasy and Science-Fiction Films, 1985, all for *A Nightmare on Elm Street*; best director, Madrid Film Festival, 1988; grand prize, Avoriaz International Festival of Fantasy and Science-Fiction Films, 1992, for *The People under the Stairs*.

■ Writings

SCREENPLAYS

(And director and editor) *Last House on the Left*, American International, 1972.

(And director and editor) *The Hills Have Eyes*, Castle Hill, 1977.

(With Glenn M. Benest and Mathew Barr, and director) *Deadly Blessing*, United Artists, 1981.

(And director) *Swamp Thing*, AVCO-Embassy, 1981.

(With Richard Rothstein, and director) *Invitation to Hell* (television movie), ABC-TV, 1984.

(And director) *A Nightmare on Elm Street*, New Line Cinema, 1984.

(And director) *The Hills Have Eyes: Part II*, VTC, 1985.

(With J. D. Feigelson, and director) *Chiller* (television movie), CBS-TV, 1985.

The Twilight Zone (television series pilot), CBS-TV, 1985.

(With Bruce Wagner, and executive producer) *A Nightmare on Elm Street Part III: Dream Warriors*, New Line Cinema, 1987.

Flowers in the Attic, New World, 1987.

(And director and executive producer) *Shocker*, Universal, 1989.

(And director and executive producer) *Night Visions* (movie), NBC-TV, 1990.

(And director and executive producer) *The People under the Stairs*, Universal, 1991.

(And executive producer), *Nightmare Cafe* (television series), NBC-TV, 1992.

(And director) *Wes Craven's New Nightmare*, New Line Cinema, 1994.

Also author of film treatments and script rewrites. Writer for cabaret comedy.

Editor of films, including *It Happened in Hollywood*, Screw Film, 1972; *You've Got to Walk It like You Talk It or You'll Lose That Beat*, JER Pictures, 1972; and *The Carhops*, 1980.

■ Adaptations

A series of books based on characters created by Craven were adapted by Bob Italia and published by Abdo & Daughters in 1992. The screenplay of *Scream* was adapted by Kevin Williamson as *Scream: A Screenplay*, Hyperion, 1997.

■ Work in Progress

Three films for Miramax, including *Fiddlefest*, about a violin teacher.

■ Overview

When *Last House on the Left*, a film written and directed by a former English professor from Cleveland, appeared in U.S. theaters in the early 1970s, audiences rioted and attacked projectionists. Two decades later, that film would be hailed as an underground classic of the horror genre, and its co-writer and co-director, Wes Craven, was credited with revitalizing an industry and exciting audiences. Craven's films were not only shockingly gruesome, they featured more complex characters, carried subtle messages about America and violence, and terrified viewers at a deep, psychological level. Mobs of young people gathered at theaters not to riot, but to be among the first to watch films like *A Nightmare on Elm Street*. Craven's work was in demand in the television and film industries, and he even began to take minor acting roles in several films. Despite the influence which Craven had on the horror genre and the remarkable commercial success of his horror films, by the 1990s Craven was ready to demonstrate he had more to offer as a filmmaker than nightmare stories. Nevertheless, his horror films, including *Wes Craven's New Nightmare* (which he wrote and directed), and *Scream* and *Scream 2* (which he directed), were his most successful works in the later 1990s.

Craven was born in Cleveland, Ohio, to parents involved in a troubled marriage. Paul Craven left the family when Wes, his youngest child, was just four years old, and he died a year later. Still, Craven remembers being scared of his father. As he told Jayne Margetts in *Celluloid: The Film Files*,

The monstrous Freddy Krueger brought Craven fame and a number of awards in 1984, and went on to inspire six sequels and a television series.

"I think I've based a lot of my films around fear-some men, which I think comes from my perception of my father." The loss of his father, and his mother's resulting work schedule, made Craven's childhood difficult. While his mother worked, he spent lunch times, afternoons, and evenings after school in the home of a friend. "I remember the psychic tension of being without parents, mostly because my mother was working and my father wasn't there, and the sense of having to go into something that was very scary by myself," he told Dieter Miller in an interview for *Authors and Artists for Young Adults* (*AAYA*). "That was when I started to have nightmares."

Craven's family suffered financial difficulties. Until he was in high school, the family had no television and no car. The Cravens were forced to live in rough neighborhoods, and they had to move frequently. "I was always getting to know new kids at school. . . . I think that's part of the reason why I became my own storyteller and learned how to think in extreme cases," Craven explained.

Ponders Questions of Heaven and Hell

Craven's family, after the loss of Wes's father, was a close one. Caroline Craven raised the children in a strict Baptist faith. No drinking, smoking, dancing, card-playing, or watching movies were allowed. So Craven explored the world through books. He worked as a public library page when he was fifteen years old, and, as he told Marc Mancini in *Film Comment*, "started reading everything I could get my hands on." After high school Craven went to Wheaton College, which he described for *AAYA* as a "Liberal Arts fundamentalist school." There he studied literature and psychology, became fascinated by the work of Ovid, and pondered the descent-into-hell theme in literature. Craven polished his skills as a writer and editor of the college literary magazine, but, as he recalled to *AAYA*, was denounced for printing stories that took up subjects the church did not consider proper, and the magazine was cancelled for one year.

Eventually, the refusal of the people who shared his religion to indulge intellectual freedom prompted Craven to abandon the Baptist faith. While attending graduate school at Johns Hopkins, he wrote and edited for literary magazines, explored the works of Baber and Tillich, and "read my way through other great minds to make the transition from Christianity into a larger humanistic philosophy." Craven replaced the "very rigid views" of his childhood with "a broader view of consciousness and the holiness of life itself."

After graduating from Johns Hopkins in 1964, Craven married and found a job as a professor of humanities at Westminster College. While he enjoyed the rich intellectual environment, as well as the time an academic career allowed him to spend with his family, he did not enjoy the more "formal and political" aspects of teaching. He was in his late twenties when he began to seriously pursue his interest in filmmaking, and he eventually decided to leave academia to become a filmmaker. "I can't explain quite where" the fascination with filmmaking came from, Craven told *AAYA*. "Maybe it was due to my being disallowed films as a youngster, or the fact that my friend's father with whom I spent so much time while my mother worked was an avid [amateur] filmmaker."

Dream of Film Work Requires Sacrifice

The decision to go into filmmaking turned Craven's life upside down. For two summers he looked for work, and when he quit his job teaching college he worked as a high school teacher and then as a messenger in a film post-production house. "That was embarrassing and very, very scary because I didn't know whether I would ever get to make a film at all," he revealed to *AAYA*. Craven and his family suffered financial difficulties during this period, and his wife was upset by the disruption his career decision had caused. She and Craven divorced in 1970.

Craven, intent on achieving his goal, continued to work as a messenger. He met Sean Cunningham, who would later originate the "Friday the 13th" series of movies. Cunningham hired Craven to work for him, and ten months later they had become friends. As Craven explained to *AAYA*, "When Sean got the offer to make a scary feature film, he said 'Why don't we do it together?' and offered me the job of writing, directing, and cutting it." Craven, who still did not know much about filmmaking, took the opportunity and "really just learned by doing."

Despite his inexperience, Craven's work as a writer, director, and editor met with success. The outcome of his collaboration with Cunningham, *Last House on the Left*, which has been described by some critics as violent and disturbing, has earned a reputation as a cult favorite. The story of the film, based on Ingmar Bergman's *The Virgin Spring*, begins as two teenaged girls on their way to a concert featuring a rock group known for its violent performances stop to try to buy marijuana from a young man they meet. They are kidnapped, raped, and gruesomely murdered by the man and his friends. The four criminals—three men and one woman—hide the bodies and then stop at a randomly selected house. Although the killers do not realize it, the house belongs to the parents of one of the girls they have slain. When the parents realize that their guests are criminals, and that they have killed their daughter, they viciously avenge themselves by murdering each member of the group one by one.

While the violence of the film disturbed some members of its audiences, *Last House on the Left*, made for just $90,000, had reaped box-office rewards of millions of dollars by the mid-1990s, and could still be seen occasionally in theaters—except where it was banned. Some critics, including Robin Wood of *Film Comment*, have interpreted the film seriously. According to Wood, *Last House on the Left* "analyzes the nature and conditions of violence and sees them as inherent in the American situation. . . . No act of violence in the film is condoned, yet we are led to understand *every* act as the realization of potentials that exist within us all, that are intrinsic to our social and personal relationships."

Craven's next film, which he created with Cunningham, won critical acclaim. *The Hills Have Eyes* follows the story of a family on vacation. Driving towards California in a motor home, the group experiences car trouble in an isolated desert area. Another family, savage and living alone in the desert, finds and attacks them. The vacationing family struggles to survive at all costs. *The Hills Have Eyes* was recognized by Wood of *Film Comment* as being more than just another horror film; he believed it was a commentary on the American family. Receiving prizes at film festivals in London and Spain, it is considered among Craven's best works.

Craven's next few films did not meet with the success of his early efforts. *Deadly Blessing*, which he wrote and directed, is the story of a woman whose husband is mysteriously killed after he abandons his religious group. When her friends come to visit her, the religious group tries to drive the women away. *Swamp Thing* is a spoof of 1950s horror movies, and features a scientist who has been accidentally transformed into a monster.

A Nightmare on Elm Street Fulfills Craven's Dreams

Craven worked for five years to finish the fifth film he wrote and directed. Fascinated by dreaming (he began to record his own dreams in college), and inspired by actual newspaper articles about teenagers who fought off sleep only to die screaming in their beds, Craven created *A Nightmare on Elm Street.* This film, which *New Statesman* critic Frances Wheen called "a most elegant shocker," made Craven's name a household word. As Damian Cannon of *Movie Reviews UK* noted in 1997, *A Nightmare on Elm Street* also marked "a significant change in fortune for the moribund horror industry."

The main character in *A Nightmare on Elm Street* is its monster: Freddy Krueger, a scarred man with a striped sweater and knives on his fingers. (Craven named the monster after a neighborhood bully who used to try to beat him up, and after one of his earliest villains, Krug). Krueger, once human, was burned by townspeople who accused him of killing children. Existing now only in the dream world, he hopes to avenge himself by murdering the children of those who killed him as they sleep and dream. According to Craven, the film is about more than suspense and gore. He told *AAYA*, "An intellectual person can see *Nightmare on Elm Street* as a study of consciousness and another can see it as a hell of a ride. They are both right."

While executives at New Line, which released *A Nightmare on Elm Street*, began the production of sequels to the film, Craven went on to other projects. He directed television movies and series, including episodes for *The Twilight Zone*. He also created a sequel to *The Hills Have Eyes*. In *The Hills Have Eyes: Part II*, which Craven wrote and directed in 1985, the survivors from the first movie return to the desert with a group of teenagers, and the fighting begins anew with the remaining members of the savage family. Released before Craven felt it was complete, this film did not please him, and it did not receive the critical

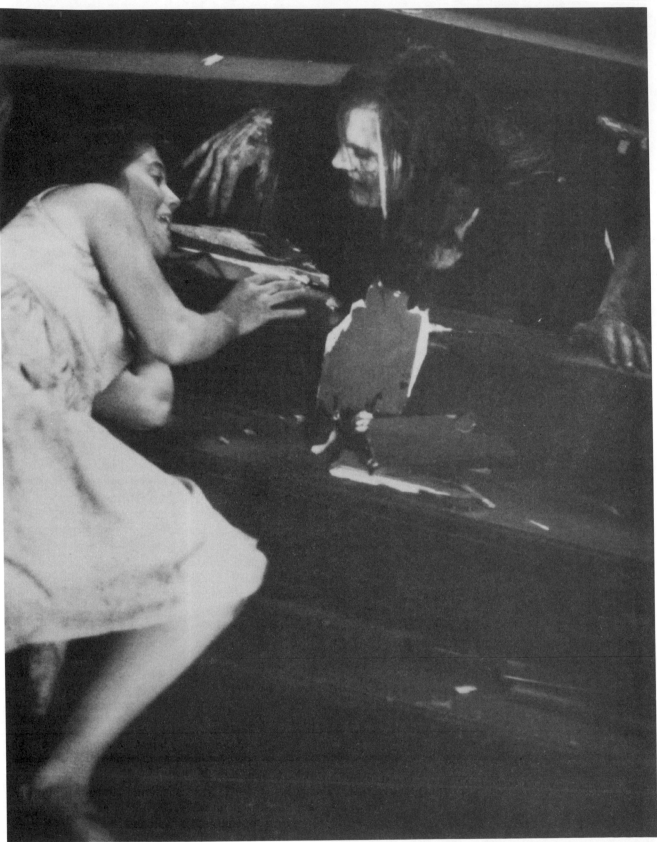

An elderly landlord couple kill all the adults in the building, and hide any children who find out about it, in the 1991 film *The People Under the Stairs*.

attention of its predecessor. Craven also directed a film about a teenaged scientist who builds a robot that has the ability to hate. In *Deadly Friend*, the robot kills people in his creator's neighborhood, including the scientist's girlfriend. The scientist dismantles the robot, but places its computer chip in the brain of his dead girlfriend. Like the robot, she becomes a killer. *Deadly Friend* is not considered among Craven's better works.

Craven, who did not participate in the creation of the first *Nightmare on Elm Street* sequel, cowrote *A Nightmare on Elm Street Part III: Dream Warriors* and was the film's associate producer. Set in a small town, the film begins as teenagers are committing suicide. Others, and those attempting suicide, explain that they are having nightmares about Freddy Krueger. The dream sequences in this film are noted for their original and graphic qualities; in one scene, Freddy almost swallows a victim whole. This third chapter of the "phenomenally successful horror series," as *TV Guide Online* called it, was produced with a budget of more than $4 million dollars, and made almost $9 million dollars on its first weekend (and more than $40 million dollars overall).

Craven's next work as a director, *The Serpent and the Rainbow*, was set in Haiti and took a great deal of effort to produce. In this film, a young scientist attempts to learn about the drugs that turn people into zombies. As he explores a local culture that practices voodoo, he jeopardizes his own life. Ironically, the lives of the writers and directors of this film were also in danger as they filmed in Haiti. One screenwriter became seriously ill after experimenting with voodoo, and due to political unrest, the filmmakers had to be evacuated from their shooting location on Haiti.

Shocker, which Craven wrote, directed, and produced, appeared in 1989. It features a TV repairman and mass murderer who is convicted of murder and electrocuted. Horace Pinker, the killer, sends his spirit into the electric lines and takes refuge in the video world. By inhabiting bodies and machines, Pinker forces unsuspecting people to seek out and attempt to murder his son. Throughout the film, dream sequences and references to other horror films appear, as do clips from actual, disturbing news events. Craven has explained in *Film Comment* that *Shocker* reflects the thinking he has done about television. According to Craven, television "anesthetizes us into a hypnotic state." We "welcome" television, like a Trojan horse, "into our house, not thinking about the threats it holds." *Shocker,* ambitious, and to some, overwhelming, was not as well received as *A Nightmare on Elm Street.*

■ Update

By 1990 Craven was known as the "Guru of Gore," the "Sultan of Slash," and the "Maven of Mayhem." He insisted in an *AAYA* interview that such terms do not represent him well, and that there is more to him than what he reveals in his horror films. Craven did attempt to move toward other genres during the decade. Nevertheless, he continued to make horror films, and these provided his greatest successes. The seventh sequel to *A Nightmare on Elm Street* surprised critics and audiences alike with its originality, and *Scream,* and *Scream 2,* which Craven directed, won immense popularity among teen viewers.

Inspired by a news story he heard, Craven wrote and directed *The People under the Stairs*, released in 1991. This work features an elderly couple, acting as landlords, who kill any adult who comes near their home. However, the couple, referred to as Man and Woman, are more interested in children. They have a neglected, tormented daughter, Alice, and they want a perfect male child. They steal a number of boy babies, but their desire for a perfect boy is complicated by their own paranoia: whenever the stolen children hear or see evidence of the couple's murderous activities, Man and Woman maim their sensory organs, and put the imperfect children in the basement. Trouble for Man and Woman begins when Fool, a young man living in the ghetto, attempts to rob the landlords. He finds the people under the stairs and, although he barely escapes with his life, returns to save the day.

Critics picked up on the social messages in *The People under the Stairs*. According to a *TV Guide Online* reviewer, Craven's film "doesn't stop at making viewers squirm on a personal level; it has a socio-political agenda as well—economic exploitation is equated with mythic monstrosity." Other critics noted that this film was not as frightening as some of Craven's other films. Richard Harrington of the *Washington Post*, for one, wrote that *The People under the Stairs* "hardly figure and they hardly scare."

Craven, who had nothing to do with four of the "Nightmare on Elm Street" sequels, wrote and directed the seventh film in the series. This may have seemed a difficult task, because in the sixth Freddy feature, the villain is finally killed. The premise of the seventh film, however, is that the original *Nightmare* films made Freddy Krueger a real force with power in the actual world. *Wes Craven's New Nightmare*, which Craven wrote and directed, was released in 1994.

In Craven's *New Nightmare*, the original actress from the first *Nightmare* movie plays herself. She begins to have nightmares about Krueger (whom she believes to be a film character). She also begins to receive telephone calls from someone behaving like Freddy. Meanwhile, her young son also has nightmares about Freddy, and it is not long before her husband is killed—presumably, by Freddy. The actress agrees to be in a new movie

Wes Craven (playing himself) is preparing as a means of stopping the maniacal Freddy from inhabiting the real world. Much of the action in the movie takes place as the actress fights valiantly to save her son from the evil celluloid menace.

Critics lauded Craven's *New Nightmare*. Desson Howe of the *Washington Post* called it "a great movie, easily the most brilliant of the . . . series." Roger Ebert, writing in the Chicago *Sun-Times*, concluded, "I haven't been exactly a fan of the 'Nightmare' series, but I found this movie, with its unsettling questions about the effect of horror on those who create it, strangely intriguing." According to Richard Harrington, also writing in the *Washington Post*, the work "recaptures the dark soul of the original through a clever conceit: Everyone plays both their real selves and their Elm Street roles, and the blurring of boundaries is confusingly entertaining."

Neve Campbell (left) and Rose McGowan portray teenagers stalked by a killer in Craven's innovative and popular 1996 horror film, *Scream*.

In 1995, in a departure from his earlier work, Craven directed a film conceived by Eddie Murphy titled *Vampire in Brooklyn*. The film, at once an attempt at comedy, mystery, and horror, features Murphy as a Caribbean vampire named Maximillian who has come to Brooklyn to find a mate. The film generally received poor reviews, though Murphy, who starred as Maximillian, received much of the blame.

Scream Awakens Horror Fans

Craven's 1996 blockbuster horror film *Scream* begins as a teenaged girl (portrayed by Drew Barrymore) is home alone, making popcorn. The telephone rings and, answering the phone, she begins to flirt with the man on the line, then hangs up on him. He continues to call, finally threatening her, revealing that he is just outside her home, and telling her he will kill her if she cannot successfully answer his question (regarding the killer in the film, *Friday the 13th*). The man, dressed in a black robe with a distorted black-and-white mask, viciously murders the girl's boyfriend, who has arrived for a visit, and then her; the girl's parents eventually return home to find her body hanging from a tree. The double murder shocks the small town.

While some students at Woodsboro High School make light of the murders, a young woman named Sidney—played by Neve Campbell—is especially bothered by them; a year earlier, her own mother had been raped and murdered. The evening after the first murders, Sidney receives a call from the killer, and she is subsequently attacked by the masked man. Cleverly, Sidney uses her computer to request police help. Before the police arrive, however, her boyfriend shows up to "save" her. When Sidney sees that he has a cellular phone, she tells police she suspects he is the attacker.

From that point on, Sidney is pursued by the killer, and other murders occur; the audience is presented with a series of characters who each seem to be likely suspects. Throughout the movie, Gale Weathers, a reporter working on a book about the murder of Sidney's mother and the murder trial of suspect Cotton Weary, investigates the new murders. She tries to get as close as she can to the teens involved by befriending a police deputy.

If you enjoy the works of Wes Craven, you may also want to check out the following books and films:

The works of Stephen King, including *Carrie*, 1974, and *The Tommyknockers*, 1987.

The horror novels of R. L. Stine, including *Broken Hearts*, 1993, *The Dare*, 1994, and *Superstitions*, 1995.

I Know What You Did Last Summer, starring Jennifer Love Hewitt, 1997.

Scream was perceived by critics as innovative because its characters make references to other horror films, and even to the genre of horror films itself. (For example, in *Scream*, as a group of teens at a party watches one famous horror film, one young man lists the rules for survival). *Scream*, according to Robert B. DeSalvo in *Movieline*, is a "clever, punchy and even frightening thriller." Other critics maintained that the film incorporates elements of every major horror flick since Alfred Hitchcock's horror masterpiece *Psycho*. While Ebert, reviewing the film for the Chicago *Sun-Times*, found *Scream* to contain "an incredible level of gore," he thought the violence was "defused by the ironic way the film uses it and comments on it." However, Ebert added, for "some viewers, it will not be, and they will be horrified." Describing *Scream* as "icky," *San Francisco Chronicle* critic Peter Stack noted that themes in the film included "the unabashed linkage of sex and violence," and "the rendering into powerlessness of the police or other adult protectors." Owen Gleiberman of *Entertainment Weekly* online called the work "deft, funny, shrewdly unsettling," and noted that the teens in the show "have such intricate knowledge of the formulas of grade-Z horror that when those formulas start to come alive, it confirms their worst fears."

Craven's Web site carries the information that *Scream*, which was created with an initial budget of $15 million, brought in $103 million. The film was such a success that its creators released a sequel by the following Christmas. As Ray Pride related on *NewCityNet*, the writer and director, beginning work before they had a completed script, did not even let the cast in on the ending until partway through the filming.

In *Scream 2*, the survivors of *Scream* return. This time, though, they are students at Windsor College. The annoying reporter, Gale Weathers, has written a book about the events that occurred in the first movie; her book, in turn, has been adapted as a film titled *Stab*. Critics appreciated the satire in *Scream 2*, which goes beyond that of the first movie to overtly and subtly discuss the genre of the horror film, and its meaning and effects in and on American culture. "It's . . . well, it's about as good as the original," wrote Ebert in the *Chicago Sun-Times*. He asked, "Will a movie like this, by educating its audience to the conventions and silly cliches of horror films, defuse the violence and make them less likely to be influenced?" Susan Wloszczyna of *USA Today* wrote that "the satire is more sophisticated" in *Scream 2*, while Carol Buckland of *CNNinteractive* exclaimed that "Wes Craven and screenwriter Kevin Williamson have done something special with 'Scream 2.'" The work, according to Buckland, "actually manages to transcend a few of the silver screen traditions it sends up." "'Scream 2' isn't particularly scary," wrote Mick LaSalle of the *San Francisco Chronicle*. "But the picture works mainly as a nasty comedy." Developed with an initial budget of $23 million, as noted on Craven's Web site, *Scream 2* earned $33 million in its first weekend, prompting the filmmakers to consider making still another sequel.

In a 1980 article in *Film Comment*, Robin Wood described Craven as "gentle, troubled, and quiet-spoken." Craven, who lives in Los Angeles with his pets, considers himself to be well organized and hardworking, and says he still reads a great deal. Although making horror films has brought Craven wealth and fame, he has continually dealt with the disdain of many adults for his work, as well as the impact of his movies on his own public image. In an interview with *DGA* magazine published on Craven's Web site, the filmmaker explained that horror films are "guilty pleasures to a lot of people. They're really sustained only by a young audience that doesn't give a damn about all those proprieties because they're kind of involved in that visceral life because they are in the middle of their passage from childhood to adulthood." Craven also believes, as he explained on his Web site, that people "arrive at wherever they're going to be very early." In any case, Craven does not suffer from nightmares anymore. His films allow him "to process those nightmares into films and thereby get control of them. It's like putting the genie back in the bottle," he explained online on *SimulChat*. The films he makes may do the same for others, he noted in his discussion with Jane Margetts: "Kids today have fears and they need a way to process their terror in a positive and fun manner."

■ Works Cited

Buckland, Carol, "'Scream 2': Horror's Hippest Hoot," *CNNinteractive*, http://www.cnn.com/SHOWBIZ.

Cannon, Damian, review of *A Nightmare on Elm Street*, *Movie Reviews UK*, http://www.film.unet.com/movies/reviews.

Craven, Wes, Web site at http://www.wescraven.com.

Craven, Wes, interview with Dieter Miller for *Authors and Artist for Young Adults*, Volume 6, Gale, 1990.

Craven, Wes, interview in *SimulChat*, at http://magenta.com/~philion/SimulChat, October 31, 1995.

Craven, Wes, interview with Jayne Margetts, in *Celluloid: The Film Files*, at http://www.thei.aust.com/isite/craven, March, 1997.

DeSalvo, Robert B., "Top of the Pop," *Movieline*, July, 1997.

Ebert, Roger, review of *Wes Craven's New Nightmare*, *Sun-Times* (Chicago), October 14, 1994.

Ebert, Roger, online review of *Scream*, *Sun-Times* (Chicago) at http://www.suntimes.com/ebert/ebert_reviews/1996/12/122006.html.1

Ebert, Roger, online review of *Scream 2*, *Sun-Times* (Chicago) at http://www.suntimes.com/ebert/ebert_reviews/1997/12/121203.html.

Gleiberman, Owen, "Hack to Basics," *Entertainment Weekly*, January 10, 1998.

Harrington, Richard, review of *The People under the Stairs*, *Washington Post*, November 6, 1991.

Harrington, Richard, review of *Wes Craven's New Nightmare*, *Washington Post*, October 14, 1994.

Howe, Desson, review of *Wes Craven's New Nightmare*, *Washington Post*, October 14, 1994.

LaSalle, Mick, "Terror Gets Fresh Voice in 'Scream 2,'" *San Francisco Chronicle*, December 12, 1997.

Mancini, Marc, "Professor Gore," *Film Comment*, September-October, 1989.

Review of *A Nightmare on Elm Street Part III: Dream Warriors*, *TV Guide Online*, http://www.tvguide.com/movies/mopic/pictures.

Review of *The People under the Stairs*, *TV Guide Online*, http://www.tvguide.com/movies/mopic/pictures.

Pride, Ray, online review of *Scream 2, NewCityNet*, http://www.weeklywire.com/filmvault/chicago.

Stack, Peter, "Satirical 'Scream' Is out for Blood—and Lots of It," *San Francisco Chronicle*, December 20, 1996.

Wheen, Frances, review of *A Nightmare on Elm Street, New Statesmen*, September 6, 1985.

Wloszczyna, Susan, review of *Scream 2, USA Today*, December 11, 1997.

Wood, Robin, "Neglected Nightmares," *Film Comment*, March-April, 1980, pp. 24-48.

■ For More Information See

BOOKS

International Directory of Films & Filmmakers, second edition, Volume 2, edited by Nicholas Thomas, St. James Press, 1991.

Newman, Kim, *Nightmare Movies: A Critical History of the Horror Film from 1968*, [London], 1988.

Newsmakers, Issue 3, Gale, 1997.

PERIODICALS

Fangoria, October, 1984; February, 1986.
Film Comment, July-August, 1978, p. 49.
Hollywood Reporter, February 5, 1988.
Journal of Popular Film, fall, 1990.
Literature/Film Quarterly, number 3, 1985.
Los Angeles Times, February 27, 1987; October 18, 1989; October 27, 1989; November 18, 1989.
New York Times, February 27, 1987; October 28, 1989, p. A16.
People Weekly, November 13, 1989, pp. 159-60; January 12, 1998.
Rolling Stone, October 6, 1988.
Starbust, April, 1992.
Sun-Times (Chicago), February 14, 1988.
Time, September 5, 1988.
Time Out, June 1, 1988.

WEB SITE

http://www.wescraven.com.*

—*Sketch by R. Garcia-Johnson*

Helen Cresswell

■ Personal

Born July 11, 1934, in Nottinghamshire, England; daughter of J. E. and Annie Edna Clarke Cresswell (a homemaker); married Brian Rowe, April 14, 1962; children: Candida, Caroline. *Education:* King's College, University of London, B.A. (honors), 1955. *Religion:* Church of England. *Hobbies and other interests:* Collecting antiques, walking, visiting the seashore, "ticking"—exploring new places, philosophy, gardening, and "collecting coincidences."

■ Addresses

Home—Old Church Farm, Eakring, Newark, Nottinghamshire NG22 0DA, England. *Agent*—A. M. Heath, 79 St. Martin's Lane, London WC2N 4AA, England.

■ Career

Writer. Worked as a literary assistant to a foreign author, fashion buyer, and teacher, and did tele-vision work for British Broadcasting Corporation. *Member:* International PEN, Society of Authors.

■ Awards, Honors

Nottingham Poetry Society Award for best poem submitted in annual competition, 1950; Carnegie Medal runner-up, British Library Association, 1967, for *The Piemakers,* 1969, for *The Night-Watchmen,* 1971, for *Up the Pier,* and 1973, for *The Bongleweed; Guardian* Award for children's fiction runner-up, 1967, for *The Piemakers,* and 1968, for *The Signposters;* runner-up for best children's original television drama, Television Writers Guild of Great Britain, 1972, for "Lizzie Dripping"; *Absolute Zero: Being the Second Part of the Bagthorpe Saga* was named a *School Library Journal* Best Book, 1978; *Absolute Zero* and *Bagthorpes Unlimited: Being the Third Part of the Bagthorpe Saga* were selected as "Children's Choice" by the International Reading Association, both 1979; Whitbread Literary Award runner-up for best children's novel, Booksellers Association of Great Britain and Ireland, 1982, for *The Secret World of Polly Flint;* Phoenix Award, Children's Literature Association, 1988, for *The Night-Watchmen; Up the Pier, The Winter of the Birds, Ordinary Jack: Being the First Part of the Bagthorpe Saga, Absolute Zero,* and *Bagthorpes Unlimited* were all named Notable Books by the American Library Association; *Up the Pier, The Winter of the Birds,* and *Ordinary Jack* were named to the *Horn Book* honor list; *Classic Fairy Tales* was selected as an Artists and Writers Guild book.

■ Writings

JUVENILE

Sonya-by-the-Shore, illustrated by Robbin Jane Wells, Dent, 1960.

The White Sea Horse (also see below), illustrated by Robin Jacques, Oliver & Boyd, 1964, Lippincott, 1965.

Pietro and the Mule, illustrated by Maureen Eckersley, Oliver & Boyd, 1965, Bobbs-Merrill, 1970.

Where the Wind Blows, illustrated by Peggy Fortnum, Faber, 1966, Funk & Wagnalls, 1968.

The Piemakers, illustrated by V. H. Drummond, Faber, 1967, Lippincott, 1968, new edition illustrated by Judith G. Brown, Macmillan, 1980.

A Day on Big O, illustrated by Shirley Hughes, Benn, 1967, Follett, 1968.

A Tide for the Captain, illustrated by Robin Jacques, Oliver & Boyd, 1967.

The Signposters, illustrated by Gareth Floyd, Faber, 1968.

The Sea Piper, illustrated by Robin Jacques, Oliver & Boyd, 1968.

Rug Is a Bear, illustrated by Susanna Gretz, Benn, 1968.

Rug Plays Tricks, illustrated by Susanna Gretz, Benn, 1968.

The Barge Children, illustrated by Lynette Hemmant, Brockhampton Press, 1968.

The Night-Watchmen, illustrated by Gareth Floyd, Macmillan, 1969.

A Game of Catch, illustrated by Gareth Floyd, Oliver & Boyd, 1969, illustrated by Ati Forberg, Macmillan, 1977.

A Gift from Winklesea, illustrated by Janina Ede, Brockhampton Press, 1969.

A House for Jones, illustrated by Margaret Gordon, Benn, 1969.

Rug Plays Ball, illustrated by Susanna Gretz, Benn, 1969.

Rug and a Picnic, illustrated by Susanna Gretz, Benn, 1969.

The Outlanders, illustrated by Doreen Roberts, Faber, 1970.

Rainbow Pavement, illustrated by Shirley Hughes, Benn, 1970.

The Wilkses, illustrated by Gareth Floyd, BBC Publications, 1970.

John's First Fish, illustrated by Prudence Seward, Macmillan, 1970.

At the Stroke of Midnight: Traditional Fairy Tales Retold, illustrated by Carolyn Dinan, Collins, 1971.

The Bird Fancier, illustrated by Renate Meyer, Benn, 1971.

Up the Pier, illustrated by Gareth Floyd, Faber, 1971, Macmillan, 1972.

The Weather Cat, illustrated by Margery Gill, Benn, 1971.

The Beachcombers, illustrated by Errol Le Cain, Macmillan, 1972.

The White Sea Horse and Other Stories from the Sea (contains *The White Sea Horse*, *The Sea Piper*, and *A Tide for the Captain*), Chatto & Windus, 1972.

Bluebirds over Pit Row, illustrated by Richard Kennedy, Benn, 1972.

Jane's Policeman, illustrated by Margery Gill, Benn, 1972.

The Long Day, illustrated by Margery Gill, Benn, 1972.

Roof Fall!, illustrated by Richard Kennedy, Benn, 1972.

Short Back and Sides, illustrated by Richard Kennedy, Benn, 1972.

The Beetle Hunt, illustrated by Anne Knight, Longman, 1973.

The Bongleweed, illustrated by Ann Strugnell, Macmillan, 1973.

The Bower Bird, illustrated by Margery Gill, Benn, 1973.

The Key, illustrated by Richard Kennedy, Benn, 1973.

Cheap Day Return, illustrated by Richard Kennedy, Benn, 1974.

The Trap, illustrated by Richard Kennedy, Benn, 1974.

Shady Deal, illustrated by Richard Kennedy, Benn, 1974.

Two Hoots, illustrated by Martine Blanc, Benn, 1974, Crown, 1978.

Two Hoots Go to Sea, illustrated by Martine Blanc, Benn, 1974, Crown, 1978.

Butterfly Chase, illustrated by Margery Gill, Kestrel, 1975.

The Winter of the Birds, Faber, 1975, Macmillan, 1976.

Awful Jack, illustrated by Joanna Stubbs, Hodder & Stoughton, 1977.

Donkey Days, illustrated by Shirley Hughes, Benn, 1977.

The Flyaway Kite, illustrated by Bridget Clarke, Kestrel, 1979.

My Aunt Polly by the Sea, illustrated by Margaret Gordon, Wheaton, 1980.

Nearly Goodbye, illustrated by Tony Morris, Macmillan, 1980.

Penny for the Guy, illustrated by Nicole Goodwin, Macmillan, 1980.

Dear Shrink, Macmillan, 1982.

The Secret World of Polly Flint, illustrated by Shirley Felts, Faber, 1982, Macmillan, 1984.

Ellie and the Hagwitch, illustrated by J. Heap, P. Hardy, 1984.

Petticoat Smuggler, illustrated by Shirley Bellwood, Macmillan, 1985.

Whodunnit, illustrated by Caroline Browne, J. Cape, 1986.

Greedy Alice, illustrated by Martin Honeysett, Deutsch, 1986.

Moondial, Faber, 1987.

Trouble, Gollancz, 1987.

Dragon Ride, illustrated by Liz Roberts, Kestrel, 1987.

Time Out, Lutterworth, 1987.

The Story of Grace Darling, Viking, 1988.

Rosie and the Boredom Eater, Heinemann, 1989.

Whatever Happened in Winklesea?, Lutterworth, 1989.

Almost Goodbye Guzzler, Black, 1990.

Hokey Pokey Did It, Ladybird, 1990.

(Editor) *The Puffin Book of Funny Stories*, illustrated by A. Macleod, Viking, 1992.

The Return of the Psammead, illustrated by John Holder, BBC Books, 1993.

Classic Fairy Tales, illustrated by Carol Lawson, HarperCollins, 1993.

The Watchers: A Mystery at Alton Towers, Viking Penguin, 1993, Macmillan, 1994.

Giant!, Cambridge University Press, 1994.

Polly Thumb, Simon & Schuster, 1994.

Mystery at Winklesea, Hodder & Stoughton, 1995.

Stonestruck, Viking Penguin, 1995.

Birdspell, illustrated by Aafke Brouwer, Heinemann, 1995.

Mystery Stories, illustrated by Adrian Reynold, Kingfisher, 1996.

The Little Sea Horse, illustrated by Jason Cockroft, Hodder & Stoughton, 1996.

Mister Maggs, illustrated by Jamie Smith, Piccadilly, 1996.

Bag of Bones, Hodder & Stoughton, 1997.

"JUMBO SPENCER" SERIES

Jumbo Spencer, illustrated by Clixby Watson, Brockhampton Press, 1963, Lippincott, 1966.

Jumbo Back to Nature, illustrated by Leslie Wood, Brockhampton Press, 1965.

Jumbo Afloat, illustrated by Leslie Wood, Brockhampton Press, 1966.

Jumbo and the Big Dig, illustrated by Leslie Wood, Brockhampton Press, 1968.

"LIZZIE DRIPPING" SERIES

Lizzie Dripping, illustrated by Jenny Thorne, BBC Publications, 1972.

Lizzie Dripping by the Sea, illustrated by Faith Jacques, BBC Publications, 1974.

Lizzie Dripping and the Little Angel, illustrated by Faith Jacques, BBC Publishing, 1974.

Lizzie Dripping Again, illustrated by Faith Jacques, BBC Publications, 1974.

More Lizzie Dripping, illustrated by Faith Jacques, BBC Publications, 1974.

Lizzie Dripping and the Witch (also see below), BBC Books, 1991.

"TWO HOOTS" SERIES

Two Hoots in the Snow, illustrated by Martine Blanc, Benn, 1975, Crown, 1978.

Two Hoots and the Big Bad Bird, illustrated by Martine Blanc, Benn, 1975, Crown, 1978.

Two Hoots and the King, illustrated by Martine Blanc, Benn, 1977, Crown, 1978.

Two Hoots Play Hide and Seek, illustrated by Martine Blanc, Benn, 1977, Crown, 1978.

"BAGTHORPE" SERIES

Ordinary Jack: Being the First Part of the Bagthorpe Saga, illustrated by Jill Bennett, Macmillan, 1977.

Absolute Zero: Being the Second Part of the Bagthorpe Saga, illustrated by Jill Bennett, Macmillan, 1978.

Bagthorpes Unlimited: Being the Third Part of the Bagthorpe Saga, illustrated by Jill Bennett, Macmillan, 1978.

Bagthorpes Versus the World: Being the Fourth Part of the Bagthorpe Saga, illustrated by Jill Bennett, Macmillan, 1979.

Bagthorpes Abroad: Being the Fifth Part of the Bagthorpe Saga, illustrated by Jill Bennett, Macmillan, 1984.

Bagthorpes Haunted: Being the Sixth Part of the Bagthorpe Saga, illustrated by Jill Bennett, Macmillan, 1985.

Bagthorpes Liberated: Being the Seventh Part of the Bagthorpe Saga, illustrated by Jill Bennett, Faber/Macmillan, 1989.

The Bagthorpe Triangle, illustrated by Jill Bennett, Faber, 1992.

Bagthorpes Besieged, illustrated by Jill Bennett, Hodder & Stoughton, 1995.

Meet Posy Bates, Bodley Head, 1990, Macmillan, 1992.

Posy Bates, Again!, Bodley Head, 1991, Macmillan, 1994.

Posy Bates and the Bag Lady, illustrated by Kate Aldous, Bodley Head, 1993, Macmillan, 1993.

TELEVISION PLAYS

Dick Whittington (based on original fairy tale), British Broadcasting Corporation (BBC), 1974.

For Bethlehem Read Little Thraves (adult), BBC-TV, 1976.

Lizzie Dripping and the Witch, BBC-TV, 1977.

The Day Posy Bates Made History, BBC-TV, 1977.

The Secret World of Polly Flint (series), Central TV, 1985.

The Haunted School (eight-part miniseries), BBC/ Revcom (France)/Australian Broadcasting Co., 1986.

Moondial (six-part series), BBC-TV, 1988.

(Adaptor) Edith Nesbit, *Five Children and It,* BBC-TV, 1991.

The Return of the. Psammead (series) BBC-TV, 1993.

Also author of screenplays for *The Watchers* (television series), 1995.

OTHER

Contributor of stories to *Winter's Tales for Children 4,* Macmillan (London), 1968; *Winter's Tales,* Macmillan, 1969; *The World of Ballet,* Collins, 1970; *Bad Boys,* Puffin, 1972; *Author's Choice Two,* Hamish Hamilton, 1973, Crowell, 1974; *Bakers Dozen,* Ward, Lock, 1973, Lothrop, 1974; *My England,* Heinemann, 1973; *Christmas Holiday Book,* Dent, 1973; *Summer Holiday Book,* Dent, 1973; *Cricket's Choice,* Open Court Publishing, 1974; *Birthday Book,* Dent, 1975; *The Cat-Flap and the Apple Pie and Other Funny Stories,* W. H. Allen, 1979; *They Wait,* Pepper Press, 1983; *Over the Rainbow,* St. Michael, 1983; *The Methuen Book of Animal Tales,* Methuen, 1983; *Shades of Dark,* Patrick Hardy Books, 1984; *Shivers in the Dark,* Magnet Books, 1984; *I Like This Story,* Puffin, 1986; and *Hidden Turnings,* Greenwillow, 1989. Contributor of essays to *A Sense of Story: Essays on Contemporary Writers for Children,* edited by John Rowe Townsend, Lippincott, 1971, and *The Thorny Paradise: Writers on Writing for Children,* edited by Edward Blishen, Penguin, 1975.

Also contributor of short stories and poetry to *Cornhill Magazine.*

■ **Adaptations**

Lizzie Dripping and the Witch was adapted and produced as a stage play at Unicorn Theater, London, 1979. Television plays made from Cresswell's books include *The Piemakers,* BBC-TV, 1967; *The Signposters,* BBC-TV, 1968; *The Night-Watchmen,* BBC-TV, 1969; *The Outlanders,* BBC-TV, 1970; *Lizzie Dripping* (series), BBC-TV, 1973, 1975; *Jumbo Spencer* (series), BBC-TV, 1976; and *The Bagthorpe Saga,* BBC-TV, 1981.

■ **Sidelights**

Helen Cresswell has written dozens of books running the gamut from fantasy to humor; even her most realistic works have something of the absurd or fantastical about them. A prolific writer, Cresswell has managed to maintain a high standard of quality throughout her career, winning many awards and pleasing children and young adults throughout the world. Perhaps some of her success is due to the respect she has for her audience. "I have a very strong sense of childhood," Cresswell admitted in *Children's Books and Their Creators,* "and like to be talking to human beings before they have become capable of pose or hypocrisy or prejudice."

Born in England in 1934, Cresswell had a childhood that was studded with pleasant times, but also haunted by the abuse she received at the hands of her father. One of her earliest memories is of her father going into a rage on Christmas day, hitting her and throwing a cup of hot tea at her mother. Mr. Cresswell was often drunk and in a bad mood; the house was frequently messy and cluttered. However, there were also good memories. She wrote in an essay in *Something about the Author Autobiography Series (SAAS)* that "at that same table [where my father flew into a rage] my mother serves glorious fruit dumplings for Sunday dinners, and Irish stews, and homemade fish cakes. And at that same table I sit and write some of my early poems while the kettle spits and simmers."

The Cresswell family home also contained a bookcase with a veritable library of books on it which became a magical place for her. "The bottom shelf is the *Encyclopaedia Britannica*, the one above a complete edition of Shakespeare in twenty-one volumes with full-colour plates and engravings. I know and love them all and weave my own sad stories about the floating Ophelia and transmogrified Bottom."

Cresswell did very well in school, despite her chaotic family life. In addition, her brother Peter was her mother's favorite, so Cresswell felt that she needed to do something to prove herself unique. "I manage to win her approval by being top of the class, writing poetry, winning scholarships," she would later recall. Her poetry writing also became a way for her to escape the realities of her life. "It is lying in [my] bed that I start to make up poems inside my head, and sitting on it that I write poems and stories. I have a passion for words, I play with them as other children play with bricks, I go into another world," Cresswell wrote in *SAAS*.

As a comfort to her while she was a child, Cresswell collected things she found to be pretty and hid them in a little cache under her bed. "I collect beautiful things—pieces of coloured glass like jewels, veined stones, a saucer painted with violets," she admitted to *SAAS*. "One day at a friend's house we explore her mother's dressing table and find a powder compact of mother of pearl. I am enchanted. It joins my other treasures under the mattress, and I visit it from time to time to gaze and gloat. This is my undoing. The compact is missed, the treasure trove is discovered and dismantled, I am disgraced." Soon after this, she found a more secure home for a newly created collection, near the fence in her backyard. This collection became a glimpse at her life to come, where her treasure trove of hidden thoughts, feelings, and experiences would be used to form her later stories.

Cresswell won a scholarship to the private Nottingham Girls' High School when she was ten. She excelled there, too, learning poetry, producing the school play, and playing sports with the other girls. However, at twelve, she began to experience terrible back pains. Her parents were Christian Scientists, a religion that encourages its members not to seek medical help but to maintain a positive mental attitude when one is ill. Young Cresswell followed these Christian Science dictates yet got increasingly sicker, until the school

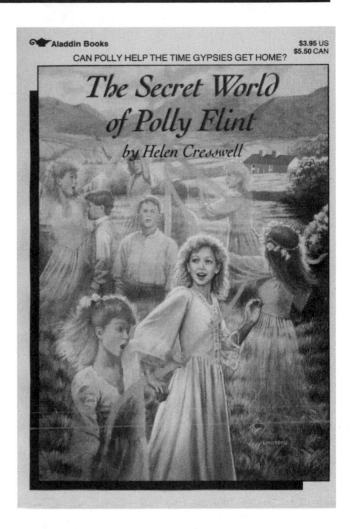

In this 1982 work, a girl is befriended by a band of Time Gypsies.

sent home a note to her mother regarding her pallor. Cresswell's mother purchased rouge for her daughter's cheeks and sent her back to school. Soon, however, the pain became too much to bear, and Cresswell was sent to the hospital where she was put into a body cast. Her hospitalization caused her to be put back into the earlier grade when she returned to school.

Creating Her Inner Cache

The many stresses in her life caused Cresswell to cope by turning inward. She commented in *SAAS* that "For the latter part of my childhood I am two people. I am the popular class clown, one of the top clique. But my real, secret self is the one who sits up into the early hours to finish poems."

Partially, this is because of a revelation she had before she was a teenager. She recounted to *SAAS* an experience that changed her life view and became a basis for much of her later work. She was "walking, on a very hot day, down Davis Road. . . . The world about me is suddenly foreign. I think 'This is not real,' I think it, and I know it. Then 'I don't belong here—what am I doing here?' I think it, and I know it, and am transfixed by the knowledge. . . . At that moment the boundaries of reality are irrevocably shifted. I have a new secret treasure and it is hidden, not under a mattress or in a hole in the wall, but within my own self."

Cresswell went on to leave her unhappy home life, get married, have a family, and become a successful writer for children. But she confessed in *SAAS* that much of the inspiration for her later writing would be drawn from these early years. "The most interesting part of any writer's life is her childhood. They are the only years that count in the sense that they hold the key to what she writes, and why. . . . This, after all, is what writers really do—try to make sense of the world."

Cresswell has written several series for young adults, one featuring a character who first appeared in the 1963 work *Jumbo Spencer*. Jumbo is a young man who decides to become a local reformer through both grandiose and trivial plans that include painting an unusual crosswalk so a neighbor can make a trip to the post office with ease. Cresswell continued writing about her irrepressible character in three other books and even adapted the stories for television. Cresswell's "Lizzie Dripping" series began as scripts for a television series and were transformed by her into books published between 1972 and 1991. Lovable Lizzie Dripping is a fantasy-seeking teenager whose dreaminess gets her into more trouble in her village. The "Posy Bates" series, published from 1990 to 1993, which also made its way into book form, is similar to the "Lizzie" books in its episodic nature, comedic touches, and strong writing.

Cresswell's "Bagthorpe" series involves some of her most well-developed comical characters. The stories are veritable cult favorites in Britain. Catherine L. Elick wrote in *Dictionary of Literary Biography* that "here is comedy of the highest order, deriving not just from fast-paced preposterous plots but from character taken to the brink

This 1989 work marks the seventh appearance of the eccentric, humorous Bagthorpe family.

of caricature and from a style wisely restrained in the face of so much inanity." The Bagthorpe family includes Grandma Bag, a fiercely competitive woman who cheats at games and almost busts up the bingo parlor when she is about to lose; Tess, a thirteen year old who not only reads Voltaire for fun but has a black belt in judo and plays the oboe; and Father Bagthorpe, a self-professed literary genius and scriptwriter for television, keen for family argument but allergic to any kind of housework. Elick claimed that "although the books are much less well known to American than to British children, Bagthorpe humor does translate; however, mainly the older and more gifted readers on both sides of the Atlantic best appreciate the sometimes sophisticated wit. Some critics claim to have grown weary of this irrepressible clan . . . most readers and critics, however, greet each new volume in the continuing saga with shouts of joy."

Enchanted Fantasies

Cresswell is also very well known for her fantasy books, including her early effort, *The White Sea Horse* (1964). Elick claimed that "even though *The White Sea Horse* must be viewed as apprentice work, it does broach themes important to much of Cresswell's writing: the right of all creatures to live free, untrammeled lives and the threat posed to their existence by human greed and ignorance."

In *The Piemakers* (1967), Cresswell combines strong character development and humor with a well-tooled fantasy plot. The Roller family belongs to a long line of piemakers who live in Danby Dale. One day, they are commissioned to bake a pie to serve two hundred people, including the king. Naively, they ask brother Crispin to help them make the huge pie, but he sabotages it instead by adding pepper to it. Arthy Roller decides to torch his pie house rather than suffer his reputation by not having the pie done. Later, the town blacksmith forges a huge pie dish that is floated down the river to a secret barn where an oven has been set up. The Rollers finish a pie large enough to serve two thousand, and enter it in a local contest where the king samples it and declares it delicious.

Cresswell received critical praise, honors, and awards for *The Piemaker;* among these were being named runner-up for the Carnegie Medal and receiving the Guardian Award for children's fiction. Margery Fisher, critiquing the work in *Growing Point*, heaped lavish praise upon the novel: "The book is clean and crisp as a pie-crust and it has the power . . . to embrace within comic fantasy an evanescent, elusive beauty of mood and scene. There can be few children who will not be captivated by the adventures of the Piemakers." A *Junior Bookshelf* reviewer was also captivated by the tale, indicating that "Here is treasure. Helen Cresswell's story of the piemakers of Danby Dale is extremely funny—a rare enough quality in a book for children—and equally serious. . . . This is one of those rare books which makes an immediate impression and confirms it with each re-reading."

In her 1969 work, *The Night-Watchmen,* Cresswell "takes a commanding stride forward," according to a critic in the *Times Literary Supplement*. Two tramps, Josh and Caleb, appear in a small English village, posing as night watchmen at a small excavation. They also befriend Henry, a young boy from the village, who remains curious about their purpose. Barbara Wersba, writing in the *New York Times Book Review,* observed that the tramps' "dialogue is complicated and romantic; a dark past is hinted at, escapes, enemies, journeys." In *Children's Literature in Education,* Anne Merrick stated that *The Night-Watchmen* "is a subtle weave of humour, mystery, reality and fantasy, leaving one enriched by its vision, with words and phrases caught in the memory. It is not fairytale fantasy completely divorced from life but the revelation of imaginative possibilities which exist in the ordinary and not quite ordinary things that lie around us."

Uncontrollable Weed

Cresswell's 1973 book, *The Bongleweed,* is a fantasy story set in a contemporary time. The book focuses on Becky and her parents, Else and Finch, who watch as a huge weed overtakes the sedate Pew Gardens virtually overnight. The townspeople grow fearful as the Bongleweed chokes that garden and many others in the village. However, Becky and her parents find themselves in awe of the mysterious and powerful weed. As head gardener at Pew, Finch refuses to destroy the weed. Just before he is forced to by the villagers, a killing frost destroys the weed. Elick claimed that the Bongleweed "symbolizes those infinite possibilities usually left to slumber dormant just below the surface of things but which can be called miraculously to life by the power of the creative imagination." This book earned Cresswell her fourth Carnegie Medal nomination.

Growing Point reviewer Margery Fisher opined that in *The Bongleweed,* "as it dances its way along with chatter and musing and laughter and plain domestic veracity, there is what amounts to a hymn in praise of the odd, the unheralded, the wayward, the unnecessary but essential elements of life. Like all Helen Cresswell's books, this one gives the impression that its form has been dictated and shaped by an idea that could not possibly take any other form than that of a fantasy for the young." Michele Landsberg, in her *Reading for the Love of It: Best Books for Young Readers,* claimed the story uses images from Adam and Eve: "Not one youngster in a thousand may explicitly recognize the images of puberty, the echoes of the Garden of Eden, in this lovely and funny story, but many will respond to its energy without knowing why."

Introduces Science-Fiction Theme

The Secret World of Polly Flint (1982) and *Moondial* (1987) are two popular fantasy stories with similar plots. In both stories, the main characters have to leave their homes because a parent is convalescing after a grave accident. Both heroines learn how to use time travel as a way to help others. Polly Flint encounters Time Gypsies while having a maypole dance in her home village of Wellow, England. She helps them find their way back to their mythic village in another time dimension. In *Moondial* Minty Kane encounters three hapless children from the Dickensian era who are misfits in their own time. She works to find them a happy home, but is only able to keep them in the moontime, a timeless place where they will be left alone. Penelope Lively complimented *The Secret World of Polly Flint*, writing in the *Times Educational Supplement*: "A whiff of sentiment here and there, maybe, but dialogue and pace that are models of how it can be done in the right hands." Denise M. Wilms, in *Booklist*, claimed that *Moondial* is "another first-rate piece of storytelling from this amazingly versatile writer."

Cresswell's 1993 work, *The Watchers: A Mystery at Alton Towers*, casts Katy and Josh, two inhabitants of a children's home, into a world where time travel is also possible. The children run away and hide in Alton Towers, an amusement park in their town, where they meet a cast of characters who appear after hours. A parallel Alton Towers turns out to be a shelter for homeless children who are taken care of by a magician. Katy and Josh, however, must also confront an evil boy who calls himself the King and who wants to gain control of the magical world. Maeve Visser Knoth wrote in *Horn Book* that "readers will become immediately involved in the fantasy."

1995's *Stonestruck* follows Jessica as her home is destroyed in London as a result of Hitler's repeated bombing of the city during World War II. Her family sends her to a Welsh castle to live while the war rages on. She feels that the castle

If you enjoy the works of Helen Cresswell, you may also want to check out the following books and films:

Betsy Byars, *The Not-Just-Anybody Family*, 1986.
Polly Horvath, *The Happy Yellow Car*, 1994.
Marc Talbert, *Toby*, 1987.
Back to the Future, starring Michael J. Fox, 1985.

is inhabited by ghosts, including those of a chain of children endlessly caught in a game of tag. With the help of poor London evacuees, Jessica is able to stop the evil haunting. Mandy Cheethem, writing in *Magpies*, called *Stonestruck* "an excellent ghost story with scenes that will chill the bones."

Cresswell admits that her career sprang from a childhood that was less than fulfilled. "I see now that most of the stories I have written have their roots deep in my childhood. My early fantasies, in particular, have at their core the sense of two worlds coexisting, the ordinary life of every day and another, more significant dimension," she related in *SAAS*. She has woven this childhood inspiration into a wealth of stories, many, significantly, about children caught between two worlds. In *SAAS* she sums up the effect of her childhood on her career: "whatever I am now is contained in those years, and whatever I have written. And that is that. You can't give up on your childhood."

■ Works Cited

Cheethem, Mandy, review of *Stonestruck*, *Magpies*, September, 1995, p. 33.

Cresswell, Helen, essay in *Something about the Author Autobiography Series*, Volume 20, Gale, 1995, pp. 101-21.

"Danger—Men at Work," review of *The Night-Watchmen*, *Times Literary Supplement*, June 26, 1969, p. 687.

Elick, Catherine L., "Helen Cresswell," *Dictionary of Literary Biography*, Volume 162: *British Children's Writers since 1960, First Series*, Gale, 1996, pp. 83-92.

Fisher, Margery, review of *The Piemakers*, *Growing Point*, April, 1967, pp. 882-83.

Fisher, Margery, review of *The Bongleweed*, *Growing Point*, January, 1974, p. 2318.

Knoth, Maeve Visser, review of *The Watchers: A Mystery at Alton Towers*, *Horn Book*, March/April, 1995, pp. 192-93.

Landsberg, Michele, "Fantasy," *Reading for the Love of It: Best Books for Young Readers*, Prentice Hall, 1987, pp. 157-82.

Lively, Penelope, review of *The Secret World of Polly Flint*, *Times Educational Supplement*, November 19, 1982, p. 34.

Merrick, Anne, "'The Night-Watchmen' and 'Charlie and the Chocolate Factory' as Books to Be Read to Children," *Children's Literature in Education*, Spring, 1975, pp. 21-30.

Review of *The Piemakers*, *Junior Bookshelf*, April, 1967, p. 111.

Silvey, Anita, editor, *Children's Books and Their Creators*, Houghton, 1995, p. 179.

Wersba, Barbara, review of *The Night-Watchmen*, *New York Times Book Review*, November 8, 1970.

Wilms, Denise M., review of *Moondial*, *Booklist*, October 1, 1987, pp. 317-18.

■ **For More Information See**

BOOKS

Baskin, Barbara H., and Karen H. Harris, *Books for the Gifted Child*, Bowker, 1980.

Children's Literature Review, Volume 18, Gale, 1989.

In Defence of Fantasy: A Study of the Genre in English and American Literature since 1945, Routledge, 1984.

Twentieth-Century Children's Writers, fourth edition, St. James Press, 1995.

PERIODICALS

Booklist, December 15, 1994, pp. 752-53.

Books and Bookmen, February, 1973; November, 1975; June, 1980.

Books for Keeps, January, 1987, pp. 12-13; January, 1998, p. 19.

Bulletin of the Center for Children's Books, November, 1989, p. 53.

Children's Literature in Education, March, 1971; July, 1971, pp. 51-59; spring, 1975, pp. 21-30.

Five Owls, January/February, 1990, p. 40.

Growing Point, December, 1975, pp. 2272-73.

Horn Book, February, 1973, p. 52; November/December, 1989, pp. 769-70.

Junior Bookshelf, June, 1970, pp. 135-39; December, 1992, p. 253; February, 1993, pp. 19, 28; October, 1995, pp. 182-83.

Listener, November 10, 1977.

Magpies, July, 1993, p. 33.

New York Times Book Review, November 8, 1970.

School Librarian, November, 1992, p. 145; November, 1997, p. 190.

Spectator, December 5, 1992, p. 49.

Times Literary Supplement, June 6, 1968, p. 584; April 4, 1969; July 2, 1970, p. 714; December 3, 1971, p. 1516; November 23, 1973, p. 1428; December 5, 1975, p. 1457; July 23, 1982, p. 794.

Tribune Books (Chicago), October 10, 1982.

Voice of Youth Advocates, April, 1995, p. 20.*

—Sketch by Nancy Rampson

Tom Feelings

worked as freelance illustrator for Ghana television programs and for newspapers and other businesses in Ghana. *Military service:* U.S. Air Force, illustrator in Graphics Division in London, England, 1953-57, became airman first-class.

■ Personal

Born May 19, 1933, in Brooklyn, NY; son of Samuel (a taxicab driver) and Anna (Nash) Feelings; married Muriel Grey (a school teacher), February 18, 1968 (divorced, 1974), married Dr. Dianne Johnson (a professor of English), 1992; children: (first marriage) Zamani, Kamali. *Education:* Attended School of Visual Arts, 1951-53, 1957-60.

■ Addresses

c/o Anna Morris, 21 St. James Pl., Brooklyn, NY 11205.

■ Career

Ghana Publishing Company, Ghana, West Africa, illustrator for African Review, 1964-66; Government of Guyana, Guyana, South America, teacher of illustrators for Ministry of Education, 1971-74; artist and illustrator. University of South Carolina, Columbia, associate professor of art, 1989-96. Has

■ Awards, Honors

Certificate of Merit for exhibition, Society of Illustrators, 1961, 1962, 1967, and 1968; Nancy Bloch Memorial Award, Downtown Community School, 1968, and Lewis Carroll Shelf Award, 1970, both for *To Be a Slave; To Be a Slave* also received a Newbery Honor Book citation from the American Library Association, 1969; Caldecott Honor Book citations, American Library Association, 1972, for *Moja Means One*, and 1975, for *Jambo Means Hello*; Art Books for Children citations, Brooklyn Museum and Brooklyn Public Library, 1973, 1974, and 1975, for *Moja Means One; Boston Globe-Horn Book* Award, 1974, Art Books for Children citation, 1976, and American Book Award nomination, 1981, for *Jambo Means Hello*; Woodward School annual book award, and Brooklyn Museum citation, both 1973, American Library Association notable book citation and placement on *Horn Book* honor list, all for *Black Pilgrimage*; School of Visual Art outstanding alumni achievement award, 1974; Children's Book Showcase award, Children's Book Council, 1977, for *From Slave to Abolitionist*; Coretta Scott King Book Award, American Library Association, 1979, for *Something on My Mind*, 1994, for *Soul*

Looks Back in Wonder, and 1996, for *The Middle Passage: White Ships/Black Cargo;* National Endowment for the Arts visual arts grant, 1982; Award of Excellence in children's book art and first place for literary children's book, both Multicultural Publishers Exchange, 1991, for *Tommy Traveler in the World of Black History;* Top Ten Best Books for Young Adults, American Library Association, 1996, for *The Middle Passage: White Ships/Black Cargo.*

■ Writings

SELF-ILLUSTRATED

Black Pilgrimage (autobiography), Lothrop, 1972.

Tommy Traveler in the World of Black History (adapted from his comic strip "Tommy Traveler in the World of Negro History" [also see below]), Writers & Readers, 1991.

The Middle Passage: White Ships/Black Cargo, Dial, 1995.

Author of introduction and illustrator for *Now Sheba Sings the Song* (also see below), Dial, 1987. Also author and illustrator of the comic strip "Tommy Traveler in the World of Negro History," published in the *New York Age* (now defunct), c. 1958-59; and of a comic book on black Revolutionary War hero Crispus Attucks. Contributor of articles to *Black World* and *Horn Book.*

ILLUSTRATOR

Rolland Snellings, *Samory Toure,* Nommo Associates, 1963.

Letta Schatz, *Bola and the Oba's Drummers,* McGraw, 1967.

Eleanor Heady, compiler, *When the Stones Were Soft: East African Folktales,* Funk, 1968.

Robin McKown, *The Congo: River of Mystery,* McGraw, 1968.

Osmond Molarsky, *Song of the Empty Bottles,* Walck, 1968.

Julius Lester, editor, *To Be a Slave,* Dial, 1968.

Nancy Garfield, *The Tuesday Elephant,* Crowell, 1968

Julius Lester, compiler, *Black Folktales,* Baron, 1969.

Ruskin Bond, *Panther's Moon,* Random House, 1969.

Rose Blue, *A Quiet Place,* F. Watts, 1969.

Kathleen Arnot, *Tales of Temba: Traditional African Stories,* Walck, 1969.

(With Marylyn Katzman) Jane Kerina, *African Crafts,* Lion Press, 1970.

Muriel Feelings, *Zamani Goes to Market,* Seabury, 1970.

Muriel Feelings, *Moja Means One: Swahili Counting Book,* Dial, 1971.

Muriel Feelings, *Jambo Means Hello: Swahili Alphabet Book,* Dial, 1974.

Lucille Schulberg Warner, adapter, *From Slave to Abolitionist: The Life of William Wells Brown,* Dial, 1976.

Nikki Grimes, *Something on My Mind,* Dial, 1978.

Joyce Carol Thomas, *Black Child,* Zamani Productions, 1981.

Eloise Greenfield, *Daydreamers,* Dial, 1981.

Maya Angelou, *Now Sheba Sings the Song,* Dial, 1987.

Talking with Artists, Bradbury, 1992.

Maya Angelou, Askia Toure, and Langston Hughes, *Soul Looks Back in Wonder,* Doubleday, 1994.

Also illustrator for *We Are One,* 1972, and *Brotherman: The Odyssey of Black Men in America,* edited by Herb Boyd and Robert Allen, 1995; works included in *On-the-Spot Drawings,* Watson-Guptill, 1976, *Flights of Color,* Ginn, 1982, and *Dreams and Decisions,* McMillan, 1983; contributor to periodicals, including *Cricket, Freedomways, Harper's, Liberator, Look,* and *Pageant.*

■ Sidelights

Renowned artist and professor of art Tom Feelings is known for his ability to expose the reality of life for African Americans, combining the beauty and warmth of the culture with suffering and pain. For more than thirty years, he has illustrated award-winning books for children and young adults.

Born and raised in Brooklyn, New York, Feelings knew at a young age that he would be an artist. "The first time I remember getting any recognition of my talent was in kindergarten from a schoolteacher who took me by the hand and showed a drawing I had done to teachers in other classes," he wrote in an essay for the *Something about the Author Autobiography Series* (SAAS). That year, he lived with his mother Anna and sister Flo in the Brownsville section of Brooklyn. His mother and father had split up when he was two, but Feelings remembered that his father never lived far away. When he was little, Feelings' mother collected welfare, but when World War II broke out his mother and many other women were able to get jobs, and the family moved to the Bedford-Stuyvesant section of Brooklyn. "Our new block, Putnam Avenue . . . looked clean and it even had four trees, something rare in Brownsville," Feelings said.

However, looks were deceiving. There were gangs in Bedford-Stuyvesant, and sometimes even gang killings. "As you got older, ten on up, fear as a young boy in Bed-Sty was tied mostly to gang wars and the chance of getting killed, even if you didn't belong to a gang. For if you were neutral (or smooth) you were liable to get whipped by both groups. Strangely, most of the kids in my block didn't belong to any fighting gangs," Feelings said. He attributes this lack of gang activity on Putnam Avenue to the influence of the Edwardses, a family of immigrants from the West Indies with eight children (six boys and two girls) born in the United States. The Edwardses became an extended family for many young people on Putnam Avenue, and many spent as much time at the Edwardses as they did at home. "The Edwards parents did not seem to feel that it was useless to try to compete in the 'white world' outside of our community." Feelings said. "They gave off the confidence that you could succeed in anything if you worked hard enough and acquired sufficient education. I was to learn much later in life that this confidence came partly from having been born and raised in countries which were completely or mainly black."

Despite his lack of gang activity, Feelings still remembers the fear he felt growing up. "We lived between two gangs, the Bishops and the Robins, and couldn't for the longest time go five blocks in either direction because we stood to get whipped in either direction," he told SAAS. "So we did a lot of running. We didn't think it was any different for black people any other place. All we knew was Bed-Sty."

A Whole New World

To avoid the fighting, Feelings began to spend more and more time at home and in school drawing and painting comic book characters, and inventing characters and plots for each story. Then Feelings heard about an art teacher who was teaching a class at the Police Athletic League (PAL) at Wynn Center. It was right in the middle of "Robin" turf, ten blocks from his home on Putnam Avenue, but Feelings decided that it was worth the risk to meet a real artist. It was at the PAL that he met Mr. Thipadeaux, a man of Creole descent from New Orleans. "So I went and met Mr. Thipadeaux, who was not only a live artist, but a black artist," Feelings recalled in SAAS. Thipadeaux discouraged Feelings from copying from comic books and encouraged him to draw and paint his own impressions of the world around him. Soon, despite his fear and occasional run-ins with the gang members, Feelings was rushing to the center every day after school.

Feelings' days were beginning to revolve around drawing. At home, his mother would fold blank paper, stitch it together on her sewing machine, and tell him to "draw a book." He also began to use the library at this time. Once, while preparing for an assignment for Negro History Week, he discovered another room to the library. In SAAS Feelings recalled an incident that would change his life. "When I asked the librarian where I could find books on George Washington Carver and Booker T. Washington, she pointed to a room where some inventive librarian had put all of the books dealing with black people. Here, for the first time, I could read about people who looked like me. It was a whole new world. . . . My head was filled with so many unanswered questions. Why had all the black people I read about gone through so much? Why were they made into slaves? Why were they treated so badly in America?"

Feelings spent more and more time drawing and painting, especially during the winter months. He took Mr. Thipadeaux's advice and began to do more watercolors from real life. Soon he began to win medals in city-wide PAL competitions. One of Feelings' paintings, which showed his grandmother's red brick house in Cape May, [NJ], won a top medal and was shown on a television show known as *Teen Canteen*. "I used to sit on the screened porch [of his grandmother's house] for long hours on warm, lazy summer afternoons, watching my grandmother rocking in her favorite chair and doing what she called 'rubbernecking'— looking at all the people go by and making personal comments on each one," Feelings explained in SAAS.

By then, it was time for high school, and Feelings hoped to attend a school that focused on art, like Industrial Arts High School or Music and Arts High School. But when he went to Industrial Arts High School, Feelings was told the school was too far out of his district and that his academic grades were not high enough to be accepted there. His counselor suggested he attend George Westinghouse Vocational High, which had a full art curriculum. "My mother was as disappointed as I was," Feelings told *SAAS*. "It would have been wonderful to go to a school whose whole emphasis was on art. But I tried to forget my disappointment, and on graduation, both my mother and I were pleased and excited when I was called up on stage to win the medal for the best artist of the graduating class of the spring of 1947."

Because he had a gift for art that was recognized at an early age, Feelings felt pressure to "make it" and to work his way out of poverty, especially as he entered his teen years. "Most people don't know what they want to be until they are well into their teens. But it was already clear to me and everyone around me that if I could survive the pitfalls out on the streets, I was going to be an artist," Feelings explained in *SAAS*.

Avoiding Pitfalls

There were many pitfalls on the streets of Bed-Sty, and

Feelings's illustrations accompanied Maya Angelou's 1987 work, *Now Sheba Sings the Song.*

things were getting worse. Kids quit school because they were tired of being poor. They took dead-end jobs that they hated, and they drank, smoked pot, and got involved in all types of hustling. Pimping and prostitution, always common in Bed-Sty, were becoming more prevalent and apartments that were once safe were now being robbed. Heavy drugs were also becoming more common. "Around the corner from me . . . you could see young people who were only a couple of classes ahead of me before finishing or dropping out of school, standing on the corner all day, their eyes always red in a blank, bottomless stare . . . their bodies bending over in a horrible, slow-motion, long nod. It was all out there for me to see, and it could happen to me," Feelings wrote.

Soon after he started high school, Feelings applied for his first real job as a messenger for a garment manufacturer in the garment center in Manhattan. It was his first chance to move around the city's office buildings by himself. "The first day went fine," he recalled. But by the end of the second day, the white man who was his boss handed him a broom. Said Feelings, "I refused to take it. I had not expected this. I argued that I was hired as a delivery boy, not a janitor. To me, even at fourteen, the broom meant something else. The broom meant something I did not want to become." He was fired on the spot. When he returned home, his sister said that he was spoiled and lazy and that he should have taken the broom. But his mother's response was different. She was silent for a while, then said, "Don't worry. You'll get another job. The kind you want."

Feelings did get another job: delivering Western Union telegrams. He took the telegrams to people in expensive apartments and marveled at the contrast between his own life in Bed-Sty and the 'rich white lives' in the area around Grand Central Station. Although he enjoyed delivering telegrams to expensive apartments and houses, he was more excited about the deliveries he made to art studios and publishing houses. He enjoyed viewing the artwork in the lobbies and watching art directors talking to artists about the work. "But in all that time, never once did I see a black person in any of the offices unless he was a janitor. There didn't seem to be much hope for my dreams," Feelings said in *SAAS*.

Feelings described his high school as a "blackboard jungle." He had two art teachers: Mr. Singer, an excellent watercolorist who taught drawing, painting and poster making, and Mr. Schulman, who taught lettering and silk-screen printing. The classes were designed to help students learn to make a living from their artwork. But many boys were not interested in art, and many were bored as they waited until their sixteenth birthday for the opportunity to drop out of school. Fights broke out often.

Feelings was still going to the PAL after school, but Mr. Thipadeaux informed him that he was leaving. He was replaced by a younger artist, Mr. Bilah, who had just converted to the Orthodox Islamic faith. Mr. Bilah's drawings had a spiritual quality, and Feelings considers them an influence on his own work.

Graduation time was coming, and Feelings believed that he would not be able to get a job in art. The Korean War was in full swing, and he also faced the possibility of being drafted. Mr. Schulman told him of a scholarship to the Cartoonists and Illustrators School. At first, Feelings did not want to apply because he did not feel that he could win the scholarship. Later, he found out that Mr. Schulman had gone down to the school, filled out an application for Feelings, and had even talked to the director of the school on his behalf. Feelings agreed to go for an interview.

A Turning Point

The interview did not go well; Feelings became frustrated because of the questions that were asked. The director wanted to know if his parents were married, or how long they had been separated. Feelings had found out years before that his parents had never married. "Though it didn't conform to the 'legitimate' images of families in those books I read or stories I heard on the radio, my reality was that I did have a father and mother. . . . They didn't live together, but my father was near enough for me to see him whenever I wanted to. He was *real*," Feelings told *SAAS*.

Although he bristled at the director's questions, Feelings hid his anger. "It was obvious that this could be a turning point in my life," Feelings added. "I could be given the chance to acquire the tools of a trade for which I could express myself, if not verbally, on paper. I wanted that

Feelings's wordless 1995 book, *The Middle Passage: White Ships/Black Cargo,* is comprised of sixty-four illustrations depicting the African slave trade.

scholarship badly, for I knew it would mean a chance for a different life, a chance to avoid the frustration of my dreams. But I did not want to be humiliated. I resented all white people at that moment because they controlled my life."

Feelings won a three-year scholarship to the Cartoonists and Illustrators School. His mother was as pleased as he was; he found out later that she had arranged to borrow the money if he hadn't won the scholarship. That summer, Feelings worked in a hospital so he could pay for his art supplies. He began to study life drawing, art theory, color, and perspective, and moved from writing and laying out comic book pages to other forms of storytelling. One teacher at the school told Feelings that "Comic strips are for entertaining—not for sending messages or getting one's personal feelings involved." Over the years, Feelings' functional forms have moved from comic books to magazine illustration to book illustration, depending on how much content and personal feeling he is trying to project.

In 1957, after a four-year stint in the U.S. Air Force, Feelings enrolled in the School of Visual Arts to study illustration and painting. The period was one of non-objective painting, abstract expressionism, and the beginning of pop art, where the lack of emotion in one's work was deliberate and thought to be profound. Feelings felt that the work of this time came from the head, not the heart. "But the heart is linked to emotion, and that emotional quality is what breathes life into the work, pulling it together and giving it a powerful heartbeat. That's exactly what I wanted in my work," he told *SAAS.*

"In 1958, when the civil rights movement was at its peak," Feelings wrote, "I did my own assignments"—depicting the protest marches against discrimination, the first battles for school integration, and other subjects that drew from life in the black community. He took his drawing pad everywhere and started sketching black children. "When I asked to draw them—and they never questioned that activity—and when they felt that I liked them and saw their own beauty in my eyes, they gave it right back, and the drawings flowed." But Feelings also noticed some troubling signs. The children "would say, 'Wait, I want to fix my hair. Will you draw my nose smaller? Don't make my lips too large.' And I could feel the strains and the pain of the present that were rooted in the aching past. Slowly this feeling moved into all my painting—a dark, somber, intense mood echoing black rage, negative self images, frustration, and a vivid awareness of the direct and indirect struggle between the races," Feelings noted in *SAAS*.

In the late 1950s, Feelings published his first printed work, the comic strip entitled "Tommy Traveler in the World of Negro History" in the now-defunct *New York Age*. The strip centered around a young man who looked through a doctor's book collection to find information about famous blacks that he could not find in public libraries. "Tommy read and, each time, fell asleep dreaming himself in the story he'd just read. Tommy was really me," Feelings said.

As a black American, Feelings knew why many black adults were in pain. He also noted a difference between black children in the North and the South. In the early 1960s, he was sent on assignment to New Orleans for *Look* magazine; he was struck by the uninhibited warmth, dignity, and joy of black children there compared to the negative feelings from which black children in the North seemed to suffer. When he saw the happiness of the children in the South, Feelings wanted to understand the source of their joy. It was then that he decided to go to Africa.

In 1964, he arrived in Ghana, where he stayed for two years. Working as an illustrator for the government of Ghana, Feelings also drew the things and people around him. "Living in Africa reaffirmed much that was positive that I had deep inside me about black people. Africa helped make my drawings more fluid and flowing; rhythmic lines started to appear in my work, and a dance consciousness surfaced," Feelings told *SAAS*. Through his illustrations in Africa, he tried to show what he saw in the faces of the people there. In *Children's Books and Their Creators*, Feelings was quoted as saying he saw "a glow that came from within, from a knowledge of self, a trust in life, or maybe from a feeling of being part of a majority in your own world." The book *Black Pilgrimage* deals with his life experiences, the biases he has faced as a black artist in America, and the reasons that he moved his family to Ghana. In this book, he combines artwork with informal autobiographical sketches and statements concerning his beliefs about black art and consciousness and the importance of a strong Africa for black Americans.

Feelings also began using color in his paintings, and even his black-and-white paintings became brighter. "In America my colors were muted, monochromatic, and somber. In Africa they became more vivid and alive," he told *SAAS*. Feelings wanted to bring this light back to America for young black children to see and feel. In 1966, he returned home with a strong sense of purpose and a portfolio of images.

The timing was right; publishers in America were finally viewing books for black children as viable commercial projects. But Feelings' books did not look like the others that were being published at the time. In the late 1960s, most children's books in America were bright and colorful. "I chose to limit my colors," Feelings said in *SAAS*. "It is my way of speaking and pulling my audience in quietly," he added.

Throughout his career, Feelings has concentrated on illustrating books with African and African American themes. In an interview in *Pauses*, he told Lee Bennett Hopkins that he decided to illustrate books for children "because I was concerned about the lack of positive imagery among African American children, a lack that I felt had existed since my own childhood years." When he returned to the United States, he began to collaborate on books written by black authors. He provided illustration for Julius Lester's book *To Be a Slave*, and worked with Muriel Feelings, his wife at that time, to produce *Moja Means One* and *Jambo Means Hello*. These two books, which have won numerous awards, were designed to introduce children to the Swahili alphabet and counting system. Through his illustrations in these books, Feelings was able to accurately depict everyday life in Africa. In *Horn Book*, reviewer Anita Silvey wrote that *Jambo Means Hello* "has been engendered by an intense, personal vision of Africa—one that is warm, all-enveloping, quietly strong, and filled with love."

In *To Be a Slave*, Feelings attempted to show the joy and sadness that characterized the experiences of African Americans. In an article he wrote for *Horn Book*, Feelings described how he and other black artists strive to capture the black experience in their work: "We celebrate life; we can take the pain; we have endured it. We don't want our experience just stated or told to us in a flat way. . . . Whatever it is, it must always sing for us."

In the early 1970s, Feelings was recruited by the government of Guyana in South America, a small independent Third World country. His assignment was to head the children's book project and train young illustrators in that country. With relatively small printing presses, most work was limited to two-color projects, so Feelings began experimenting with printing on tone or mottled paper to get the feeling of full color. "I rediscovered the lesson of my ancestors—improvising within a restrictive form," Feelings told *SAAS*. "In Guyana, we learned to do more—with less. I brought this information back with me when I returned to America."

Soul Looks Back in Wonder (1993) is a collection of poems from a number of well-known contemporary African American poets, including Maya Angelou, set to pictures that Feelings drew when he was in Ghana, Senegal, Guyana, and the United States. In *Booklist*, reviewer Hazel Rochman observed that "In powerful pictures, Feelings celebrates 'African creativity'." A critic in *Publishers Weekly* described the poems as "uniformly uplifting, with affirming messages about the heritage, strength, and dreams of African Americans." In the *Wilson Library Bulletin*, Donnarae MacCann and Olga Richard wrote that "In Feelings' book, African and African American experiences are thoroughly blended."

History Is More Than Facts

The Middle Passage: White Ships/Black Cargo is considered one of Feelings' most important books. In an article in the *University of South Carolina Times*, Feelings relates that "An African friend asked me what happened to our African ancestors when they were taken away on the ships. I wanted to answer him, but couldn't."

When Feelings returned to the United States, the question haunted him. He describes *The Middle Passage* as his answer to his African friend. The book, which took him twenty years to complete, is a collection of sixty-four black-and-white illustrations suffused with blue and warm, brown overtones that depict life on the ships that brought

---

If you enjoy the works of Tom Feelings, you may also want to check out the following:

The classic works of such artists as Francisco Goya, Paul Gauguin, and Vincent van Gogh.
The works of African American artists such as Elizabeth Catlett, Romare Bearden, Charles White, and Jacob Lawrence.

---

slaves from Africa to America. In this book, Feelings alternates between abstract and realistic images to depict the suffering and desperation felt by Africans, who were beaten, force-fed, and chained in small, cramped spaces on the ships.

In an introduction to *The Middle Passage*, Feelings discussed his reasons for creating the work: "I began to see how important the telling of this particular story could be for Africans all over this world, many who consciously or unconsciously share this *race memory*, this painful experience of the Middle Passage." He added, "But if this part of our history could be told in such a way that those chains of the past, those shackles that physically bound us together against our wills could, in the telling, become spiritual links that willingly bind us together now and into the future—then that painful Middle Passage could become, ironically, a positive connecting line to all of us whether living inside or outside of the continent of Africa."

The book has no text. It begins with a double-page spread showing the dignity and happiness of a proud people living in their homeland. This is followed by scenes of village raids and use of force to get the captives on the ships to come to America. White enforcers are depicted more as wisps than as defined people, while black people are drawn with sharp definition. The pictures on the last pages of the book shows the survivors (about one-third of those who were captured) arriving at the slave markets, still filled with pride and strength with their heads held high. In *Booklist*, reviewer Donna Seaman described *The Middle Passage* as "testimony not only to our capacity for evil, but also to the triumph of the spirit and of beauty." In a review of the book in *Bookbird*, *The Middle Passage* was commended "for showing young people that history is more than facts. . . ." Barbara Hawkins, reviewing the work in *School Library Journal*, called *The Middle Passage* "A powerful rendered reality that all teens deserve the opportunity to experience." In *Horn Book*, Hanna B. Zeiger pointed out that "Tom Feelings' drawings engage eye, mind, and heart as they speak eloquently of the infamy and suffering of the Middle Passage." Speaking of *Middle Passage* to Karin Schill in the *Augusta Chronicle*, Feelings said "I clearly did this book for black people so it would be something that inspires them. But because it's in the form of a book, anyone can look at it and be affected by it. This book is also for whites who claim they can't recognize what racism feels like."

In an interview in *Horn Book*, Feelings said, "When I am asked what kind of work I do, I answer, 'I am an illustrator, a storyteller in picture form, who tries to reflect and interpret life as I see it.' When I am asked who I am, I say, 'I am an African who was born in America.' Both answers connect me specifically to my past and present. For I believe I bring to my work a quality which is rooted in the culture of Africa and expanded by the experience of being Black in America." In 1989, Feelings became an associate professor of art at the University of South Carolina at Columbia. He is now retired and lives in Columbia, South Carolina, with his wife, Dianne.

■ Works Cited

Bishop, Rudine Sims, "Tom Feelings and *The Middle Passage*," *Horn Book*, July/August, 1996, pp. 436-42.

Feelings, Tom, "The Artist at Work: Technique and the Artist's Vision," *Horn Book*, November/December, 1985, pp. 685-95.

Feelings, Tom, *Something about the Author Autobiography Series*, Volume 19, Gale, 1995.

Feelings, Tom, *The Middle Passage: White Ships/Black Cargo*, Dial, 1995.

Hawkins, Barbara, review of *The Middle Passage: White Ships/Black Cargo*, *School Library Journal*, February, 1996, p. 132.

Hopkins, Lee Bennett, *Pauses: Autobiographical Reflection of 101 Creators of Children's Books*, HarperCollins, 1995.

MacCann, Donnarae, and Olga Richard, review of *Soul Looks Back in Wonder*, *Wilson Library Bulletin*, June, 1994.

Review of *The Middle Passage: White Ships/Black Cargo*, *Bookbird*, Winter, 1996.

"Retired art professor completes magnum opus," *University of South Carolina Times*, November 2, 1995.

Rochman, Hazel, review of *Soul Looks Back in Wonder*, *Booklist*, November 1, 1993.

Schill, Karin, "Passage of Darkness," *Augusta Chronicle*, August 24, 1996.

Seaman, Donna, review of *The Middle Passage: White Ships/Black Cargo*, *Booklist*, October 15, 1995, p. 376.

Silvey, Anita, review of *Jambo Means Hello*, *Horn Book*, August, 1974, p. 367.

Silvey, Anita, "Tom Feelings," *Children's Books and Their Creators*, Houghton Mifflin, 1995.

Review of *Soul Looks Back in Wonder*, *Publishers Weekly*, November 8, 1993.

Zeiger, Hanna B., review of *The Middle Passage: White Ships/Black Cargo*, *Horn Book*, March/April, 1996, pp. 223-24.

■ For More Information See

BOOKS

Innocence and Experience: Essay and Conversations on Children's Literature, Lothrop, 1987.

Children's Literature Review, Volume 5, Gale, pp. 104-8.

Something about the Author, Volume 69, Gale, 1992, pp. 54-58.

PERIODICALS

Booklist, June 15, 1972; February 15, 1994, p. 1080; March 15, 1994, pp. 1336, 1356, 1360; January 1, 1996, p. 738; March 15, 1996, pp. 1274, 1289.

Bulletin of the Center for Children's Books, September, 1972; January, 1994, p. 152; December, 1995, p. 125.

Horn Book, March, 1985; May, 1985.

New York Times Book Review, May 7, 1972; April 7, 1996, p. 21.

Publishers Weekly, February 20, 1987; November 6, 1995, p. 80.

School Library Journal, December, 1996, p. 33.

Tribune Books (Chicago), February 13, 1994, p. 6; February 11, 1996, p. 6.

Wilson Library Bulletin, April, 1994, pp. 124-25.

OTHER

Head and Heart (biographical film), New Images, 1976.

Website biography of Tom Feelings at http://www.penguin.com.*

—Sketch by Irene Durham

Mel Glenn

■ Personal

Born May 10, 1943, in Zurich, Switzerland (U.S. citizen born abroad); son of Jacob B. (a physician) and Elizabeth (Hampel) Glenn; married Elyse Friedman (a teacher), September 20, 1970; children: Jonathan, Andrew. *Education:* New York University, A.B., 1964; Yeshiva University, M.S., 1967. *Religion:* Jewish.

■ Addresses

Home—4288 Bedford Ave., New York, NY 11229. *Office*—Abraham Lincoln High School, Brooklyn, NY 11235.

■ Career

U.S. Peace Corps, Washington, DC, volunteer English teacher in Sierra Leone, West Africa, 1964-66; English teacher at a public junior high school, New York City, 1967-70; Abraham Lincoln High School, New York City, English teacher, 1970—.

Member: Society of Children's Book Writers and Illustrators, Authors Guild.

■ Awards, Honors

Best Books for Young Adults, American Library Association (ALA), 1982, and Golden Kite Honor Book plaque, Society of Children's Book Writers and Illustrators, both for *Class Dismissed!: High School Poems;* Best Books, *School Library Journal,* 1986, and Christopher Award, 1987, both for *Class Dismissed II: More High School Poems;* Best Books for Young Adults, ALA, 1992, for *My Friend's Got This Problem, Mr. Candler;* Top Ten Best Books for Young Adults, ALA, 1997, Edgar Allan Poe Award nomination, for *Who Killed Mr. Chippendale? A Mystery in Poems.*

■ Writings

POETRY

Class Dismissed! High School Poems, illustrated with photographs by Michael J. Bernstein, Clarion, 1982.

Class Dismissed II: More High School Poems, illustrated with photographs by Michael J. Bernstein, Clarion, 1986.

Back to Class, illustrated with photographs by Michael J. Bernstein, Clarion, 1989.

My Friend's Got This Problem, Mr. Candler: High School Poems, illustrated with photographs by Michael J. Bernstein, Clarion, 1991.

Who Killed Mr. Chippendale? A Mystery in Poems, Lodestar, 1996.

The Taking of Room 114: A Hostage Drama in Poems, Lodestar, 1997.

Jump Ball: A Basketball Season in Poems, Lodestar, 1997.

FICTION

One Order to Go, Clarion, 1984.
Play-by-Play, Clarion, 1986.
Squeeze Play: A Baseball Story, Clarion, 1989.

Sidelights

Mel Glenn is a teacher and writer whose special knack lies with his keen ability to portray the everyday concerns and challenges of teenagers. As Glenn stated to Jeffrey Copeland in *Speaking of Poets*, "I'm a writer because I am a teacher. If I weren't a teacher, I couldn't get near the stories I write about." Glenn's poems, written in free verse and simple language, "reach out to adolescents, even those who are not ordinarily readers of poetry," Teri S. Lesesne remarked in *Twentieth-Century Young Adult Writers*. Lesesne added that Glenn's work "highlights the trials and tribulations, the angst and anxiety, and the joys and wonders of adolescence."

Born in Switzerland, Glenn and his family moved to the United States in 1945, his father already a U.S. citizen. His father, a doctor, also wrote a medical column for a Yiddish paper in New York. Glenn's first real writing experience was helping his father with the text of the articles. Glenn recalled to Copeland, "I really think there is a little gene on my chromosome that says 'write, write, write!' My influences were environmental and also hereditary."

Growing up in Brooklyn, Glenn once recalled, "I adored the Brooklyn Dodgers and afternoons spent in the local park shooting baskets till it was far too late to see the hoop." Later, Glenn attended New York University and worked four years for the school newspaper. He began as a sports reporter but later developed a feature column. As he admitted to Copeland in *Speaking of Poets*, "I thought that when I finished college I would somehow go into journalism."

Peace Corps Beckons

However, Glenn was temporarily sidetracked. A Peace Corps representative, who he had interviewed, gave him an application. The corps came calling after his college graduation in 1964. At that time, the nation was still reeling from the tragic death of President John F. Kennedy, and Glenn remembers feeling a slight sense of nobility in joining the Peace Corps. Glenn became an English teacher in the small republic of Sierra Leone, West Africa. Glenn once stated, "I found out, between bouts of dysentery and rains that lasted for days, that I really loved teaching. I loved it all—the class discussions, marking reports in fractured English. But most of all, I loved the students."

Naturally, when Glenn returned to the United States in 1967, he took a teaching position with a junior high school in Brooklyn. In 1970, he joined the teaching staff of which he still belongs, at Lincoln High School, the very high school he had graduated from in 1960. It is at Lincoln High School where Glenn's literary career began. Glenn told Copeland, "I can give an exact date for my beginning as a writer for young people: January 1, 1980. It was a New Year's resolution of mine. Another teacher in school had shown me a manuscript, and I thought it was horrible. . . . So January 1, 1980, I wrote my first poem." It would be the first of a slew of poems, based on his "natural outgrowth from teaching." His teaching and counseling duties have given Glenn a wealth of information for his poems, and have also let Glenn reflect on his own adolescence, as he stated in the *Seventh Book of Junior Authors and Illustrators*: "I write because I remember how it felt not to make the basketball team, how it felt to worry about tests, how if felt finding my way through the teenage social labyrinth." These experiences, which can be shared by all, pour out of Glenn's work.

Glenn's first work, *Class Dismissed! High School Poems*, was based on Edgar Lee Master's *Spoon River Anthology*. *Class Dismissed!* is a collection of seventy poems, each titled after a fictional student with real problems, such as a teenage girl who discovers she's pregnant, or a thief and his victim. Glenn commented, "One of the things in

If you enjoy the works of Mel Glenn, you may also want to check out the following books:

Anthologies by Lee Bennett Hopkins, including *Voyages: Poems by Walt Whitman*, 1988.
Collections by Paul Janeczko, including *Preposterous: Poems of Youth*, 1991.
Ron Koertge, *Diary Cows*, 1981.

teaching that's important to me is that every kid is a gift and every kid has a story. It's these stories I focus on in my writing." Candy Bertelson, in the *School Library Journal*, stated that the characters are "very 'real' kids, who are easy to identify," and went on to say that the poems will "reach many young people who don't ordinarily read poetry." A critic in *Bulletin of the Center for Children's Books* described each poem as "direct and concise, candid in tone, and varied in subject and attitude." Glenn does such a convincing job portraying the emotions of the students that James Campbell, writing in *Voice of Youth Advocates*, remarked, "at first, I thought these verses were by high school students."

Addressing Teen Concerns

Glenn published a sequel titled *Class Dismissed II: More High School Poems*, "a second collection of poems about high school students written by an affectionate and insightful high school teacher," wrote a critic in the *New York Times Book Review*. The collection is devoted to teenage concerns, from prom to parents to such grave matters as nuclear arms. As Luvada Kuhn commented in *Voice of Youth Advocates*, "all characters are fictional, but their struggle to bring the world into focus is real, totally honest, and realistically appealing." A critic in the Chicago *Tribune Books* concurred, stating, "young adults will appreciate this honesty and the realism with which they are portrayed in this collection." Although Roger Sutton in *Bulletin of the Center for Children's Books* argued that adolescents are "capable of greater sophistication than this collection offers," *Booklist* reviewer Stephanie Zvirin concluded that Glenn's "angst-ridden adolescence . . . will likely find a comfortable home right next to its predecessor."

Taking a similar angle to the teen years as both *Class Dismissed!* and *Class Dismissed II*, the 1989 work *Back to Class* "offers the same clear, fresh insight into the adolescent world," stated Kathleen Whalin in the *School Library Journal*. "The poems tell about, rather than show, the pleasure and pain Glenn so carefully observes," Tony Manna added in *Voice of Youth Advocates*. The book is a collection, as Glenn offers in his introductory note, of "fictional composites of the many students and teachers I have worked with through the years." A critic in *Kirkus Reviews* said that "the simple language and clearly stated themes makes this accessible to the most unpracticed poetry reader."

Glenn continues with "further slice-of-life vignettes about high school," as Nancy Vasilakas wrote in *Horn Book*, with *My Friend's Got This Problem, Mr. Candler: High School Poems*, only the view is now from students and their families as they talk to their high school guidance counselor. The book focuses on the perspectives, experiences, and feelings of high school students which "have a stark intensity that will strike a chord of recognition and compassion in teenagers," explained Diane Tuccillo in *Voice of Youth Advocates*. She praised Glenn further, writing, "this is the most cohesive and best of the Glenn/Bernstein books to date."

In *Who Killed Mr. Chippendale?: A Mystery in Poems* Glenn takes a different approach to his poetry while still incorporating his expertise of the high school arena. The book revolves around the reactions of students, companions, teachers, and even the community over the random shooting of Mr. Chippendale, an English teacher at Tower High. "Glenn delivers a starkly realistic view of modern high school life," Sharon Korbeck remarked in *School Library Journal*, "A clever idea, executed in a thoughtful, compelling and thoroughly accessible manner." More than a whodunit, a *Kirkus Reviews* critic stated, the work allows readers to decide the identity of the killer, "as they appreciate the multiple ironies here, search for clues, and look for echoes of their own peers and teachers in these vignettes."

Tower High is again the backdrop for Glenn's book, *The Taking of Room 114: A Hostage Drama in Poems*, in which the author "has demonstrated his dramatic mastery in fashioning a gripping story, told completely in poems," stated M. Jerry Weiss in *Teaching and Learning Literature*. The story takes place on a June school day when a veteran history teacher snaps and holds his first period class hostage at gunpoint. The teacher slips notes under the door, piecing together his reasons for the takeover. The poems reflect the thoughts and reactions of the students during the crisis. Mike Angelotti in the *ALAN Review* commended Glenn for his "great delicacy and truth the psyches of people and institutions that compose the greater school community."

Life Becomes Fiction

Glenn draws from his own experiences when he writes. He once said, "I write about what I know." In *Play-by-Play*, Glenn tells the story of a young boy named Jeremy, who hasn't found his niche in the athletic world, unlike his best friend Lloyd. Then Jeremy is introduced to soccer. Glenn continued, "The material was all around me. My son Jonathon, was actively involved in a local soccer league . . . as a writer, I tried to pay close attention to the language, characteristics, and social mores of nine-year-olds."

Another work in which Glenn drew on his experiences, *One Order to Go,* is set in a Brooklyn candy store—"the old kind," Glenn once recalled, "where you can get a real malted and egg cream. The story concerns a young boy who is not sure about his future. I am sure that a large part of it is autobiographical. . . . You bring to your characters a sense of your own personal values and memories." Richie Linder is a slacker who would rather be chasing his dream of becoming a news correspondent than attending school. His short-tempered father does not help matters, making Richie work behind the lunch counter during his free time. Things come to a head when Richie confronts his father about his future plans. Deborah Locke, writing in *School Library Journal,* found the book lacked the "perception, sensitivity and poignancy" of Glenn's other award-winning writing. Stephanie Zvirin noted in *Booklist* that "the pace is rather slow . . . but principle characters are distinctive and credible."

A more recent publication, *Jump Ball: A Basketball Season in Poems,* takes the reader back to Tower High, this time during their basketball championship season. The story is told through the eyes of the players, fans, teachers, parents, and bystanders. A *Kirkus Reviews* contributor stated that "the author expertly creates dramatic tension with early hints of the tragedy to come." The tragedy came when the team bus goes out of control on an icy road, which, the critic added, "gives the story a bitter, discouraging cast."

Glenn is still teaching and writing, with many projects on the horizon. His ability to write about the hardships of adolescence is testimony to his compassion and expertise in the classroom. "I write to remember," he once stated. "I write to open up the lines of communication, to explain my past to myself and others. On a certain level we are all emotionally fourteen. Good writing can put us in touch with who we were and who we are. When you grow up you realize the adult world is just composed of everyone you went to high school with." Glenn continued, "If, as it has happened, a kid says to me after reading one of my poems, 'I've felt just like that,' I know that I have succeeded as both a poet and a teacher. There are few joys that come close."

■ Works Cited

Angelotti, Mike, review of *The Taking of Room 114: A Hostage Drama in Poems, ALAN Review,* fall, 1997.

Review of *Back to Class, Kirkus Reviews,* October 15, 1988.

Bertelson, Candy, review of *Class Dismissed! High School Poems, School Library Journal,* October, 1982, p. 160.

Campbell, James, review of *Class Dismissed! High School Poems, Voice of Youth Advocates,* August, 1982, p. 44.

Review of *Class Dismissed! High School Poems, Bulletin of the Center for Children's Books,* September, 1982, p. 9.

Review of *Class Dismissed II: More High School Poems, New York Times Book Review,* March 1, 1987, p. 31.

Review of *Class Dismissed II: More High School Poems, Tribune Books* (Chicago), May, 1987, p. 5.

Copeland, Jeffrey S., interview with Mel Glenn, *Speaking of Poets,* National Council of Teachers of English, pp. 17-26.

Glenn, Mel, *Back to Class,* Clarion, 1989.

Glenn, Mel, essay in *Seventh Book of Junior Authors and Illustrators,* H. W. Wilson, 1996, pp. 110-11.

Review of *Jump Ball: A Basketball Season in Poems, Kirkus Reviews,* August, 1997, p. 1305.

Korbeck, Sharon, review of *Who Killed Mr. Chippendale?: A Mystery in Poems, School Library Journal,* July, 1996.

Kuhn, Luvada, review of *Class Dismissed II: More High School Poems, Voice of Youth Advocates,* February, 1987, p. 297.

Lesesne, Teri S., "Mel Glenn," *Twentieth-Century Young Adult Writers,* 1st edition, St. James Press, 1994, pp. 248-49.

Locke, Deborah, review of *One Order to Go, School Library Journal,* December, 1984, p. 89.

Manna, Tony, review of *Back to Class, Voice of Youth Advocates,* February, 1989, pp. 300-1.

Sutton, Roger, review of *Class Dismissed II: More High School Poems, Bulletin of the Center for Children's Books,* February, 1987, p. 107.

Tuccillo, Diane P., review of *My Friend's Got This Problem, Mr. Candler: High School Poems, Voice of Youth Advocates,* February, 1992, p. 394.

Vasilakas, Nancy, review of *My Friend's Got This Problem, Mr. Candler: High School Poems, Horn Book,* November/December, 1991, p. 757.

Weiss, M. Jerry, review of *The Taking of Room 114: A Hostage Drama in Poems, Teaching and Learning Literature,* November/December, 1997, pp. 82-83.

Whalin, Kathleen, review of *Back to Class, School Library Journal,* January, 1989, p. 98.

Review of *Who Killed Mr. Chippendale?, Kirkus Reviews,* June, 1996.

Zvirin, Stephanie, review of *One Order to Go, Booklist,* October, 1984, p. 211.

Zvirin, Stephanie, review of *Class Dismissed II: More High School Poems, Booklist,* December 1, 1986, p. 567.

■ **For More Information See**

PERIODICALS

ALAN Review, winter, 1997; winter, 1998.

Booklist, September 15, 1991, p. 134; June 1, 1996, p. 1688; March 1, 1997.

Bulletin of the Center for Children's Books, March, 1997, pp. 247-48.

Kirkus Reviews, May 1, 1996; February 1, 1997.

Publishers Weekly, July 8, 1996, p. 85.

School Library Journal, April, 1997.

Voice of Youth Advocates, December, 1996; February, 1998, p. 400.*

—*Sketch by Kelly Druckenbroad*

Lorraine Hansberry

Member: Dramatists Guild, Ira Aldrich Society, Institute for Advanced Study in the Theater Arts.

■ Personal

Born May 19, 1930, in Chicago, IL; died of cancer, January 12, 1965, in New York, NY; buried in Beth-El Cemetery, Croton-on-Hudson, NY; daughter of Carl Augustus (a realtor and banker) and Nannie (Perry) Hansberry; married Robert B. Nemiroff (a music publisher and songwriter), June 20, 1953 (divorced, March, 1964). *Education:* Attended University of Wisconsin, Art Institute of Chicago, Roosevelt College, and New School for Social Research, and studied in Guadalajara, Mexico, 1948-50. *Hobbies and other interests:* Ping-pong, skiing, walking in the woods, reading biographies, conversation.

■ Career

Playwright. Worked variously as a clerk in a department store, a tag girl in a fur shop, an aide to a theatrical producer, and as a waitress, hostess, and cashier in a restaurant in Greenwich Village run by the family of Robert Nemiroff; associate editor, *Freedom* (monthly magazine), 1952-53.

■ Awards, Honors

New York Drama Critics Circle Award for Best American Play, 1959, for *A Raisin in the Sun;* named "most promising playwright" of the season, *Variety,* 1959; Cannes Film Festival special award and Screen Writers Guild nomination, both 1961, both for screenplay *A Raisin in the Sun.*

■ Writings

PLAYS

A Raisin in the Sun (three-act; produced on Broadway, 1959; also see below), Random House, 1959, with introduction by Robert Nemiroff, Vintage, 1994.

The Sign in Sidney Brustein's Window (three-act; produced on Broadway, 1964), Random House, 1965.

Les Blancs (two-act; produced on Broadway, 1970), Hart Stenographic Bureau, 1966, published as *Lorraine Hansberry's "Les Blancs",* adapted by Robert Nemiroff, S. French (New York City), 1972.

To Be Young, Gifted, and Black: A Portrait of Lorraine Hansberry in Her Own Words (produced Off-

Broadway, 1969), illustrated by Hansberry, edited by Robert Nemiroff, introduction by James Baldwin, Prentice-Hall, 1969, adapted by Nemiroff, S. French, 1971.

Les Blancs: The Collected Last Plays of Lorraine Hansberry (includes *The Drinking Gourd* and *What Use Are Flowers?*), edited by Robert Nemiroff, Random House, 1972, published as *Lorraine Hansberry: The Collected Last Plays*, New American Library, 1983.

A Raisin in the Sun (expanded twenty-fifth anniversary edition) [and] *The Sign in Sidney Brustein's Window*, New American Library, 1987.

OTHER

A Raisin in the Sun (screenplay), Columbia, 1960.

(Author of text) *The Movement: Documentary of a Struggle for Equality* (collection of photographs), Simon & Schuster, 1964, published as *A Matter of Colour: Documentary of the Struggle for Racial Equality in the U.S.A.*, Penguin (London), 1965.

Lorraine Hansberry Speaks Out: Art and the Black Revolution (recording), Caedmon, 1972.

Contributor to anthologies, including *American Playwrights on Drama*, 1965; *Three Negro Plays*, Penguin, 1969; and *Black Titan: W. E. B. Du Bois*. Also contributor to periodicals, including *Negro Digest*, *Freedomways*, *Village Voice*, and *Theatre Arts*.

■ Adaptations

A musical version of *The Sign in Sidney Brustein's Window* was produced on Broadway in 1972; *Raisin*, a musical version of *A Raisin in the Sun*, was produced on Broadway in 1973. *A Raisin in the Sun* was recorded on audiocassette, Caedmon, 1972.

■ Sidelights

Lorraine Hansberry is an African American writer who achieved a number of important firsts during her short life; she was the first black woman to write a play that was produced on Broadway as well as the first black and youngest woman to win the New York Drama Critics Circle Award. This play, titled *A Raisin in the Sun*, was also the first Broadway play to be directed by an African American—Lloyd Richards—in over fifty years.

During her short life, Hansberry completed two plays and left three others uncompleted; a sixth piece would be assembled after her death from excerpts from her writings. Although she only lived until the age of thirty-four, her achievements helped to pave the way for other African Americans who wanted their plays to be produced.

Hansberry was born into a middle class family on the South side of Chicago in 1930. Her father was a successful real estate broker, and when Hansberry was eight he deliberately violated the city's covenant laws by moving into a segregated white neighborhood. With the help of the National Association for the Advancement of Colored Persons (NAACP), Hansberry's father took his case to the Illinois Supreme Court. The court ruled that the laws, which sanctioned housing discrimination, were unconstitutional. During the trial, white neighbors harassed the Hansberry family. On one occasion, a brick that was thrown through their home's living room window barely missed Hansberry's head. Because her parents were so dedicated to the struggle for civil rights, Hansberry learned about sacrifice and injustice at an early age. Even though he won a victory in court, Hans-berry's father was disappointed that his legal victory brought about little change. He had plans to move his family to Mexico, but he died in 1945. Although her father supposedly died of a cerebral hemorrhage, Hansberry would later remark that "American racism helped kill him."

Hansberry first became interested in theater when she was in high school. In 1948 she began attending the University of Wisconsin, where she spent two years. It was there that she took a course in stage design and saw the plays of Henrik Ibsen and Sean O'Casey for the first time. Later, she studied painting at the Art Institute of Chicago (then Roosevelt College) and in Guadalajara, Mexico. She moved to New York in 1950 and worked at a number of jobs while she wrote short stories and plays. She worked as an associate editor and reporter for Paul Robeson's monthly *Freedom* magazine, and she also became politically active. She was on a picket line protesting discrimination at New York University when she met Robert Nemiroff, a white man who became a songwriter and producer after the couple married in 1953. Nemiroff encouraged Hansberry in her writing and even went so far as to salvage discarded pages from the wastebasket near her typewriter.

A First in Theater

Although she had been working on three uncompleted plays and an unfinished semi-autobiographical novel before she began working on *A Raisin in the Sun*, the play was to be Hansberry's first completed work. In an interview with the *New York Times*, quoted in an essay by Michael Adams in the *Dictionary of Literary Biography*, Hansberry talked about what inspired her to write this play. "One night, after seeing a play I won't mention," she said, "I suddenly became disgusted with a whole body of material about Negroes. Cardboard characters. Cute dialect bits. Or hip-swinging musicals from exotic scores." She channeled her anger into her writing. One night in 1957, while Hansberry and Nemiroff were entertaining their friends Burt D'Lugoff and Philip Rose, they read the play aloud. To their surprise, Rose announced the next morning that he would like to produce the play on Broadway.

A Raisin in the Sun is the story of a black family living in a run-down apartment in Chicago. The characters include Walter Lee, a chauffeur, his wife Ruth, who works occasionally as a maid, their ten-year-old son Travis, Walter's mother Lena, and his sister Beneatha, a college student. All members of the family are unhappy with their lives, but they look forward to some improvements because of a ten-thousand-dollar life insurance payment they will be receiving on the death of Walter's father. The family members discuss how to spend the money: Walter wants to use the money to buy a liquor store, Beneatha wants to use the money for her medical school tuition, and Lena wants to buy a nice house in an all-white neighborhood. Lena makes a $3,500 down-payment on the house and puts $3,500 in the bank for Walter and $3,500 for Beneatha. But Walter gives the money to his business partner, who runs away with it and shatters the family's dreams. To make matters worse, Walter agrees to accept money from a representative of the white neighborhood in exchange for not moving there. He later realizes that he would be sacrificing his manhood if he accepted the money, and he rejects the offer. At the end of the novel, the family realizes that they will still have to struggle, but that they love each other despite their weaknesses.

The title of *A Raisin in the Sun* comes from a question posed by Langston Hughes in his 1951 poem "Harlem:"

What happens to a dream deferred?

Does it dry up
like a raisin in the sun?
Or fester like a sore—
And then run?
Does it stink like rotten meat?
Or crust and sugar over—
like a syrupy sweet?

Maybe it just sags
like a heavy load.

Or does it explode?

A Raisin in the Sun was a solid success in tryouts all over the country, and it made its Broadway debut on March 11, 1959, at the Ethel Barrymore Theatre. In June of that year, Hansberry was named the "most promising playwright" of the season. *A Raisin in the Sun* would become the longest-running black play in Broadway's history.

A Raisin in the Sun enjoyed immense popularity because it explored a universal theme—the search for freedom and a better life. Writing in *Commentary*, Gerald Weales pointed out that "Walter Lee's difficulty . . . is that he has accepted the American myth of success at its face value, that he is trapped, as Willy Loman [in Arthur Miller's *Death of a Salesman*] was trapped by a false dream. In planting so indigenous an image at the center of her play, Miss Hansberry has come as close as possible to what she intended—a play about Negroes which is not simply a Negro play."

Other critics agreed with Weales' assessment. Writing in *Saturday Review*, Henry Hewes declared that in Hansberry's *A Raisin in the Sun* "we have at last a play that deals with real people." Critic Harold Clurman, in the *Nation*, noted that "*A Raisin in the Sun* is authentic: it is a portrait of the aspirations, anxieties, ambitions, and contradictory pressures affecting humble Negro fold in an American big city." *New York Times* critic Brooks Atkinson concurred, stating that "*A Raisin in the Sun* has vigor as well as veracity."

The play's original run on Broadway lasted for nineteen months and a total of 530 performances. Hansberry sold the movie rights of *A Raisin in the Sun* to Columbia Pictures in 1959, and in 1960 she wrote two screenplays. In the new screenplays, Hansberry added some provocative new scenes that pointed out problems that African Americans were facing at the time. However, Columbia allowed none of these new scenes or any new material to appear in the film version, which was basically a shortened version of the play. In 1961 the film version of the drama was released, starring Sidney Poitier as Walter Lee and Claudia McNeil as Mama. For the film, Hansberry won a special award at the Cannes Film Festival, and her screenplay was nominated for a Screen Writers Guild Award.

Entering the Limelight

The success of *A Raisin in the Sun* made Hansberry an instant celebrity, and she found herself enjoying it. She appeared on countless radio and television talk shows and attempted to answer letters from almost everyone who wrote to her. She was fun-loving and would often reply whimsically to questions, but she never shied away from a serious question and could cause discomfort for even hardened interviewers such as Mike Wallace.

In 1960 Hansberry faced censorship again when producer-director Dore Schary asked her to write a play on slavery for television. The play was to be the first in a series of five dramas to be written by leading playwrights to commemorate the centennial of the Civil War. When Schary told the management of NBC that he had asked a black playwright to create a drama about slavery, they asked what her attitude was toward it. When he learned that this question was not a joke, Schary realized that the project would not survive. It was later cancelled, but Hansberry used the material she had developed in a play she called *The Drinking Gourd*. This work was published posthumously in 1972, and scenes from it were included in another play, *To Be Young, Gifted, and Black*.

It is believed that *The Drinking Gourd* was inspired in part by stories told to Hansberry by her mother and grandmother. Hansberry's grandfather, who was a slave, escaped from his master and hid in the Kentucky hills while his mother brought food to him. The play was also influenced by the enormous amount of reading that Hansberry did on the topic of slavery before and after she was asked to write the play. The result is a disturbing but strongly unified drama about sympathetic characters at three social levels—slave owners, poor whites, and slaves—each caught in a dehumanizing chain of events that threatens to destroy them all.

Hiram Sweet is the slave master, and Hannibal, his mother Rissa, and his sweetheart Sarah are slaves. Sweet keeps the slaves in a state of ignorance and forces them to perform hard, unrewarding labor. Hannibal responds by malingering and doing only half of the work that his master wants him to complete in the cotton fields. He also talks the master's younger son, Tommy, into teaching him to read. Meanwhile, Rissa, who has worked with Sweet since he started the plantation, tries to use her position as cook and quasi-confidante to pressure Sweet to take her son out of the fields so that he will not continue to be defiant. Although work in the fields is strenuous, Rissa and Sarah know that the life of a house slave is also hard. Finally, their situation becomes so difficult that the three decide they can no longer tolerate it and must flee no matter what the risk.

The situation of Zeb Dudley, a poor white man, is not much better. Because he has only a small farm and no slaves, he is not able to compete with the big plantations. He must decide whether to leave the South and try to make a home in the West or take a job as an overseer so that his children can eat. He decides to become an overseer and is forced to commit brutal acts, such as putting out the eyes of Hannibal because he learned to read.

Even Sweet finds that slavery forces him to do things that are damaging spiritually and physically. He once thought of himself as a humane master because his slaves only worked nine-and-a-half-hour days. Now, declining market prices and diminishing yields force him to make the slaves work longer and harder, which, in some cases, will probably lead to death. Sweet also sees that the continued competition between the North and the South will eventually lead to a war that the South cannot win. He becomes so worried that his health worsens and he is forced to turn control of the plantation over to his ruthless son Everett.

Everett sets out to undermine everything that Sweet has done. He is the one who makes the decision to blind Hannibal, but it is Sweet who pays the price for it—Rissa blames Sweet for the attack and will not come to his rescue when he

In 1959 the playwright received the New York Drama Critics Circle Award for *A Raisin in the Sun*, with its Broadway debut starring Claudia McNeil and Sidney Poitier.

collapses from tension. At the end of the play, the Civil War is beginning and the narrator reveals that he has decided to fight for the North because "it is possible that slavery might destroy itself . . . it is more possible that it would destroy these United States first."

In 1961 Hansberry and her husband moved from Greenwich Village to a house in Croton-on-Hudson, a tranquil wooded area of New York State within commuting distance of New York City. From this peaceful place, Hansberry was able to balance her public and private commitments. She continued to be politically active: in 1962 she mobilized support for the Student Non-Violent Coordination Committee (SNCC) in its struggle against segregation in the South; she spoke against the House Un-American Activities Committee and

the Cuban missile crisis; and she wrote *What Use Are Flowers?*, a play about life after an atomic war.

At Work until the End

In 1963 Hansberry was diagnosed with cancer. Undaunted, she continued to write and to work for various causes. A scene from *Les Blancs*, a play that was in progress, was staged at the Actors Studio Writers Workshop. In May she and others met with Attorney General Robert Kennedy to discuss the racial crisis. At this time, Kennedy was unable to understand or comprehend the urgency of blacks, and the meeting was emotionally charged. In June Hansberry chaired a meeting in Croton-on-Hudson to raise money for the SNCC. Five days later, she underwent an unsuccessful cancer operation.

If you enjoy the works of Lorraine Hansberry, you may also want to check out the following books and films:

Christopher Paul Curtis, *The Watson Go to Birmingham—1963*, 1995.
Rosa Guy, *The Music of Summer*, 1992.
Rita Williams-Garcia, *Blue Tights*, 1988.
Hoops Dreams, an acclaimed documentary, 1994.

In 1964 the SNCC prepared a book titled *The Movement: Documentary of a Struggle for Equality*. The book contained photos of horrifying and distressing aspects of the black experience in America, including lynchings, savagely beaten demonstrators, and substandard housing. The photographs were coupled with a sharply worded text written by Hansberry.

Hansberry's marriage to Nemiroff ended in 1964, but she continued to work with him, and the two saw each other daily until her death. Even as she underwent radiation and chemotherapy treatments, Hansberry worked on a number of projects, including *The Sign in Sidney Brustein's Window*, which was being produced by Nemiroff and Burton D'Lugoff. Hansberry attended the opening of the play at the Longacre Theater.

Aside from *A Raisin in the Sun*, *The Sign in Sidney Brustein's Window* is Hansberry's only other completed play. It was a commercial and critical failure, but it attracted a group of passionate supporters. The lead character, Sidney Brustein, is a liberal but apolitical man who is drawn into action when he agrees to work for a reform candidate in a city election. Sidney soon discovers that people can have good ideals but may be personally corrupt or weak in ways that invalidate their theoretical commitment. Some of the characters include a black friend of Sidney's who is prejudiced and a homosexual friend who is sexually manipulative. Writing in *Contemporary American Dramatists*, Gerald M. Berkowitz remarked that *The Sign in Sidney Brustein's Window* "is excessively talky, and secondary characters are either underwritten . . . or overwritten. . . . Still, it is a failure of accomplishment rather than of conception and one can see the core of a play that might

have been stronger had Hansberry (who was terminally ill at the time of production) been able to work on it more."

For the most part, the initial reviews of *The Sign in Sidney Brustein's Window* were not positive. Walter Kerr, for example, writing in the *New York Herald Tribune*, stated that the problems Brustein encounters "are much too small, finicky and familiar to serve as a carryall." Generally, mixed reviews mean instant death for a Broadway play, but a large number of Hansberry's supporters contributed time, money, and publicity to keep the play running for 101 performances. *The Sign in Sidney Brustein's Window* ran until the playwright's death on January 12, 1965.

Many critics were disappointed because *The Sign in Sidney Brustein's Window*, which is set in the Greenwich Village flat of a white man, was so different from *A Raisin in the Sun*. However, Hansberry refused to be limited in her writing, and at the time of her death she was working on a wide range of projects, including an opera about the Haitian revolutionary Toussaint L'Ouverture; a musical based on the *Laughing Boy*, a novel about the Navajos by Oliver LaFarge; and a drama about the ancient Egyptian ruler Akhnaton.

During the last year and a half of her life, Hansberry also spent considerable time working on *Les Blancs*, a play about Africa. She also worked on a play about the eighteenth-century feminist Mary Wollstonecraft. On May 1, 1964, she was released from the hospital to deliver a speech to the winners of the United Negro College Fund writing contest, for which she first coined the phrase "To be young, gifted, and Black." She did not finish *Les Blancs*, but left extensive notes and held long discussions with Nemiroff so that he could finish the play after she died. Nemiroff did finish the play, and it opened at the Longacre Theater on November 15, 1970. It received mixed reviews and closed after forty-seven performances.

Les Blancs is the story of the radicalizing of a white reporter, Charles Morris, and a black intellectual, Tshembe Matoseh. Morris travels to the mythical African country of Zalembe to meet the leader of the country, Reverend Torvald Neilsen. He learns that Neilsen acts as a Great White Father caring for his irresponsible black children. Morris then comes to the conclusion that only a violent revolution will help to liberate the country. The revolution does occur, and Matoseh is forced to kill his own brother.

When Hansberry died, six hundred people attended her funeral, and Paul Robeson delivered the eulogy. Nemiroff remained dedicated to Hansberry and her work. He was appointed her literary executor, and he collected her writings and words and presented them in the autobiographical montage *To Be Young, Gifted, and Black.* He also edited and published her three unfinished plays—*Les Blanc, The Drinking Gourd,* and *What Use Are Flowers?* "It's true that there's a great deal of pain for me in this," Nemiroff told Arlynn Nellhause of the *Denver Post,* "but there's also a great deal of satisfaction." *To Be Young, Gifted, and Black* was made into a play that ran Off-Broadway in 1969.

C. W. E. Bigsby, writing in *Confrontation and Commitment: A Study of Contemporary American Drama, 1959-66,* stated that "Hansberry's death at the age of thirty-four has robbed the theatre of the one Negro dramatist who has demonstrated her ability to transcend parochialism and social bitterness." Clive Barnes, in the *New York Times,* described Hansberry as "a master of the dramatic confrontation." According to Jeanne Noble, writing in *Beautiful, Also, Are the Souls of My Black Sisters,* among Hansberry's last words were, "I think when I get my health back I will go into the South to find out what kind of revolutionary I am." Although she never got the chance, Hansberry contributed to the civil rights movement in the United States by inspiring readers and theatergoers in both her own generation and those that have followed.

■ Works Cited

Adams, Michael, "Lorraine Hansberry," *Dictionary of Literary Biography,* Volume 7: *Twentieth-Century American Dramatists,* Gale, 1981, pp. 247-54.

Atkinson, Brooks, "The Theater: 'A Raisin in the Sun'," *New York Times,* March 12, 1959.

Barnes, Clive, "The Sign in Sidney Brustein's Window," *New York Times,* January 27, 1972.

Berkowitz, Gerald M., "Lorraine Hansberry," *Contemporary American Dramatists,* St. James Press, 1994, pp. 247-48.

Bigsby, C. W. E., "Lorraine Hansberry," *Confrontation and Commitment: A Study of Contemporary American Drama, 1959-66,* University of Missouri Press, 1968, pp. 156-73.

Clurman, Harold, review of *A Raisin in the Sun, Nation,* April 4, 1959, pp. 301-2.

Hewes, Henry, "A Plant Grows in Chicago," *Saturday Review,* April 4, 1959, p. 28.

Kerr, Walter, "Sign in Sidney Brustein's Window," *New York Herald Tribune,* October 16, 1964.

Nellhause, Arlynn, *Denver Post,* March 14, 1976.

Noble, Jeanne L., *Beautiful, Also, Are the Souls of My Black Sisters: A History of the Black Women in America,* Prentice-Hall, 1978.

Weales, Gerald, "Thoughts on 'A Raisin in the Sun'," *Commentary,* June, 1959, pp. 527-30.

■ For More Information See

BOOKS

Authors in the News, Volume 2, Gale, 1976.

Black Literature Criticism, Gale, 1992.

Carter, Steven R., *Hansberry's Drama: Commitment amid Complexity,* University of Illinois Press, 1991.

Cherry, Gwendolyn, and others, *Portraits in Color,* Pageant Press, 1962.

Concise Dictionary of Literary Biography, Volume 1: *The New Consciousness: 1941-1968,* Gale, 1988, pp. 244-58.

Contemporary Literary Criticism, Gale, Volume 17, 1981, Volume 62, 1991.

Cruse, Harold, *The Crisis of the Negro Intellectual,* Morrow, 1967.

Dictionary of Literary Biography, Volume 38: *Afro-American Writers after 1955: Dramatists and Prose Writers,* Gale, 1985.

Drama Criticism, Volume 2, Gale, 1992.

Keppel, Ben, *The Work of Democracy: Ralph Bunche, Kenneth B. Clarke, Lorraine Hansberry, and the Cultural Politics of Race,* Harvard University Press, 1995.

McKissack, Patricia C., and Fredrick L. McKissack, *Young, Black, and Determined: A Biography of Lorraine Hansberry,* Holiday House, 1997.

Nemiroff, Robert, *The 101 Final Performances of "Sidney Brustein": Portrait of a Play and Its Author,* published with *A Raisin in the Sun* and *The Sign in Sidney Brustein's Window,* New American Library, 1966.

Scheader, Catherine, *They Found a Way: Lorraine Hansberry,* Children's Press, 1978.

PERIODICALS

Commonweal, September 5, 1969, pp. 542-43; January 22, 1971.

Denver Post, March 14, 1976.

Esquire, November, 1969.

Freedomways, winter, 1963; summer, 1965; fourth quarter, 1978.

Life, January 14, 1972.

New Republic, June 9, 1959.

New Yorker, May 9, 1959.

New York Post, March 22, 1959.

New York Times, March 8, 1959; March 12, 1959; April 9, 1959; November 9, 1983; August 15, 1986.

Theatre Journal, December 1986, p. 441-52.

Washington Post, November 16, 1986; December 2, 1986; November 16, 1989, pp. F1-F3.

Women's Wear Daily, November 16, 1970.

■ **Obituaries**

PERIODICALS

Antiquarian Bookman, January 25, 1965.

Books Abroad, spring, 1966.

Newsweek, January 25, 1965.

New York Times, January 13, 1965.

Publishers Weekly, February 8, 1965.

Time, January 22, 1965.*

—Sketch by Irene Durham

Oscar Hijuelos

1977-84; writer, 1984—; Hofstra University, Hempstead, NY, professor of English, 1989—. *Member:* International PEN.

■ Awards, Honors

Received "outstanding writer" citation from Pushcart Press, 1978, for the story "Columbus Discovering America"; Oscar Cintas fiction writing grant, 1978-79; Bread Loaf Writers Conference scholarship, 1980; fiction writing grant from Creative Artists Programs Service, 1982, and from Ingram Merrill Foundation, 1983; Fellowship for Creative Writers award from National Endowment for the Arts, and American Academy in Rome Fellowship in Literature from American Academy and Institute of Arts and Letters, both 1985, both for *Our House in the Last World;* National Book Award nomination, National Book Critics Circle Prize nomination and Pulitzer Prize for fiction, all 1990, all for *The Mambo Kings Play Songs of Love.*

■ Personal

Surname is pronounced "E-way-los"; born August 24, 1951, in New York, NY; son of Pascual (a hotel worker) and Magdalena (a homemaker; maiden name, Torrens) Hijuelos; divorced; two children. *Education:* City College of the City University of New York, B.A., 1975, M.A., 1976. *Religion:* Catholic. *Hobbies and other interests:* Pen-and-ink drawing, old maps, turn of the century books and graphics, playing musical instruments, jazz ("I absolutely despise modern rock and roll"), archeology.

■ Addresses

Home—211 West 106th St., New York, NY 10025. *Office*—Hofstra University, English Department, 1000 Fulton Ave., Hempstead, NY 11550. *Agent*—Harriet Wasserman Literary Agency, 137 East 36th St., New York, NY 10016.

■ Career

Transportation Display, Inc., Winston Network, New York City, advertising media traffic manager,

■ Writings

NOVELS

Our House in the Last World, Persea Books (New York City), 1983.

The Mambo Kings Play Songs of Love, Farrar, Straus (New York City), 1989.

The Fourteen Sisters of Emilio Montez O'Brien, Farrar, Straus, 1993.

Mr. Ives' Christmas, HarperCollins (New York City), 1995.

Work represented in anthology *Best of Pushcart Press III,* Pushcart, 1978.

■ Adaptations

The Mambo Kings Play Songs of Love was adapted as the film *The Mambo Kings* in 1992.

■ Sidelights

The son of Cuban immigrants who settled in New York City, Oscar Hijuelos is a Pulitzer Prize-winning author who is best known for his novel *The Mambo Kings Play Songs of Love.* Although he

In the 1940s, two Cuban brothers find fame playing the mambo in New York in this nostalgic Pulitzer Prize winner.

writes entirely in English, Hijuelos was the first Latino novelist to receive the Pulitzer Prize in English, and he was one of the first of a growing group of Hispanic writers to be read by a broad American audience. He provides a look at the bittersweet experiences of immigrant life in compelling and accessible prose.

Hijuelos was born on August 24, 1951, in New York City. He grew up on 118th Street in the section of New York known as Spanish Harlem, just a few blocks from where he lives today. During his teenage years, Hijuelos told Michael Coffey in *Publishers Weekly,* "I was always in a band, mostly with Puerto Rican guys; we played Top-40 stuff and some Latin things." Hijuelos attended both Catholic and public schools, and graduated from the City University of New York with a master's degree in creative writing. After graduation, he worked in an advertising agency and then traveled throughout Europe. "As a kid I used to play a lot of music," he said in an interview with Margo Jefferson in the *New York Times Book Review.* "Then I had to grow up."

Hijuelos' parents came to New York in the 1940s from the Oriente province of Cuba, which he described to Coffey as " . . . home to Desi Arnaz, Fidel Castro, Batista, Jose Lima, Alejo Carpentier." His first novel, published in 1983 and entitled *Our House in the Last World,* is the story of the Santinio family, another family who emigrated to the United States from Cuba in the 1940s. The novel begins in Cuba in the 1930s and describes the courtship and early years of marriage for Alejo Santinio, a "small town dandy," and Mercedes Sorrea, his shy wife. The couple arrive in Spanish Harlem in 1943 and look forward to living the American dream, but reality soon sets in when Alejo is forced to take a low-paying job as a hotel cook and their sons Horacio and Hector pass their days in squalor. What makes things worse for the Santinios is that many of their friends and relatives thrive in America. Alejo begins drinking heavily and Mercedes becomes bitter and high-strung. Resentful of her husband, she eventually withdraws into a fantasy world filled with Cuban ghosts. Horacio, the oldest son, turns into a rebellious boy who makes his name on the mean streets of New York. His frail younger brother Hector, whose character is central to the novel, becomes isolated from his Cuban roots. When Alejo dies suddenly in 1969, the family is on the verge of collapsing.

Antonio Banderas and Armand Assante star in the 1992 movie, *The Mambo Kings.*

An Immigrant Story

In *Our House in the Last World*, Hijuelos provides readers with a glimpse of the diversity of experiences for immigrants. Cleveland *Plain Dealer* critic Bob Halliday noted that Hijuelos is "especially eloquent in describing the emotional storms" that transform the Santinios as they "try to assimilate the rough realities of Spanish Harlem in terms of the values and personal identities they have inherited from their homeland." Throughout the novel, Hector is concerned about his manhood and worries that he is a freak because he is not as "Cuban" as his father or his older brother. His feelings of inadequacy are worsened by Alejo's excesses; despite the constant complaints of his wife, Alejo continues to spend his free time away from home drinking and womanizing. Hector must struggle to establish his own identity as a Cuban American without becoming like his father.

Many critics praised the work for its lyrical prose. In *Library Journal*, Mary Ellen Quinn wrote that "this first novel is recommended for its vivid images. . . ." In the *New York Times Book Review*, critic Edith Milton points out that "There is more than a touch of satire in Mr. Hijuelos's writing, but he never loses the syntax of magic, which transforms even the unspeakable into a sort of beauty."

Hijuelos won the Rome Fellowship in Literature from the American Academy and Institute of Arts and Letters in 1985 for *Our House in the Last World*. While he was in Italy, Hijuelos developed a love for archeology and began digging for treasures at archeological digs. "Nothing like Indiana Jones," he joked to Jefferson, "just lug labor, lots of mud and wheelbarrows."

Recreating the Past

According to Hijuelos, Latin people characteristically are absorbed by thoughts of the past. Memory plays an important role in *The Mambo Kings Play Songs of Love*, the winner of the Pulitzer Prize for Literature. *The Mambo Kings Play Songs of Love* is the story of two Cuban brothers, Cesar and Nestor Castillo, who immigrate to New York in the late 1940s. They form an orchestra known as the Mambo Kings and achieve one night of fame when they appear as Ricky Ricardo's cousins on an episode of *I Love Lucy*.

The Mambo Kings are as different from one another as were Horacio and Hector in *Our House in the Last World*. Nestor is a moody, melancholy man who writes the brothers' greatest hit, "Bellisima Maria de mi Alma" ("Beautiful Maria of My Soul"), a ballad about a girl who broke his heart in Cuba. Nestor works constantly on the tune, and his constant rewriting yields twenty-two versions of the song. He continues to rewrite the ballad until he dies in a car accident.

Cesar, on the other hand, is a consummate ladies' man with slicked-back hair and a considerable libido. He resembles his idol, Desi Arnaz; both men were born in Santiago de Cuba, have a strong Cuban accent and pretty-boy looks, and play the congo drum. Both men spend a large amount of time chasing women and come to regret it. Cesar dies broke and alone in a seedy New York tenement, playing a stack of old Mambo King records.

Although Nestor and Cesar are the main characters in the book, the first character that is introduced in the novel is Eugenio, Cesar's nephew, who serves as the vehicle for the story. In the book's prologue, Eugenio gives his account of seeing the *I Love Lucy* rerun. In the epilogue of *The Mambo Kings Play Songs of Love*, Eugenio is visiting Arnaz's ranch in California after his uncle's death. The men sip Dos Equis beer and reminisce about the Mambo Kings. Eugenio is the source of the novel's point of view, its attitudes, and its values. The rest of the book is written as a series of flashbacks through the eyes of Cesar. Writing in the *Dictionary of Literary Biography*, Gustavo Perez Firmat noted that "Like Hijuelo's first novel, *The Mambo Kings* is written 'from' Cuba but 'toward' the United States." He added that "the novel is able to occupy an eccentric place somewhere between Havana and Harlem. . . ."

For the most part, critics raved about *The Mambo Kings Play Songs of Love*. "Hijuelo's American dream is as strong and rich and sweet as Cuban coffee . . . ," wrote Bob Shacochis of the *Washington Post Book World*. Lewis Beale of the *Detroit Free Press* described the book as "an elegy to a glittering, long past, a memory book in the best sense of the term." "*The Mambo Kings* is not a quick read, but it is a deeply rewarding book," observed Michael Dorris in the *Detroit News*. A critic in *Publishers Weekly* stated that "Hijuelos' pure storytelling skills commission every incident with a life and breath of its own." Writing in the

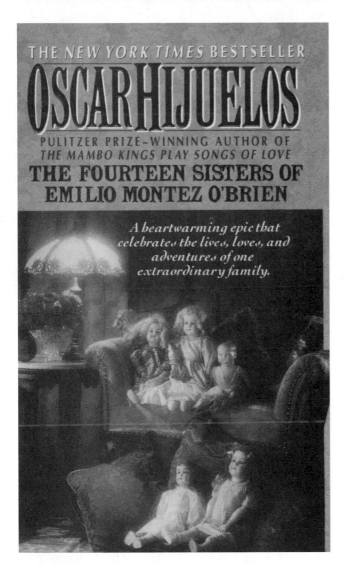

THE *NEW YORK TIMES* BESTSELLER

OSCAR HIJUELOS

PULITZER PRIZE-WINNING AUTHOR OF
THE MAMBO KINGS PLAY SONGS OF LOVE

THE FOURTEEN SISTERS OF EMILIO MONTEZ O'BRIEN

A heartwarming epic that celebrates the lives, loves, and adventures of one extraordinary family.

Spanning an entire century, this work traces the extraordinary lives of fifteen siblings, the children of an Irish father and a Cuban mother.

Chicago *Tribune Books*, Joseph Coates declared, "The novel leaves one with the . . . sense of voracity at the heart of the American dream that chews up talented people and spits out what's left, that magnifies personal faults, along with regrets, and turns them into self-destruction. . . ."

A Feminine Perspective

In Hijuelos' next novel, *The Fourteen Sisters of Emilio Montez O'Brien*, he moves from the male perspective to tell his story through the eyes of fourteen women. *Fourteen Sisters* is the story of the family of Nelson O'Brien, an Irish immigrant who traveled to Cuba during the Spanish-American War. While he is there, he meets, falls in love with, and marries Mariela Montez, a beautiful Cuban girl. After the war, the O'Briens move to a small town in Pennsylvania and Nelson works as a photographer and runs the local movie theater. At the same time, Mariela is busy bearing and raising the couple's fourteen daughters and their last child, a boy named Emilio. In an interview with Susannah Hunnewell of the *New York Times Book Review*, Hijuelos remarked that he came up with the idea for *Fourteen Sisters* when he was staying with a friend in rural Pennsylvania. Hijuelos told Hunnewell that he had a dream about "a house full of women. . . . I wanted to portray a world in which women were very powerful," he noted.

The book is big and ambitious and spans an entire century. The reader is able to look into the lives of different members of the Montez O'Brien clan. Although the sisters are the title characters of the book, a large part of the book deals with the exploits of Emilio as he fights in World War II, beds his way through Greenwich Village after the war, plays Tarzan and Sam Spade-style detectives in B movies in Hollywood, and eventually achieves fame as a celebrity photographer. The lives of the sisters of Emilio are less developed, critics believed, because there are so many of them, and because they are defined primarily by their relationships with men. Writing in *Times Literary Supplement*, Nick Hornby stated, "*The Fourteen Sisters of Emilio Montez O'Brien* is at all times readable and diverting. . . . Most of the time, however, it succeeds only in providing a basic lesson in how to write a fashionable blockbuster novel. . . ." Janice C. Simpson offered a different view in *Time*: "Reading *The Fourteen Sisters of Emilio Montez O'Brien* is like leafing through the pages of a treasured family album."

A Christmas Carol for the Nineties

Mr. Ives' Christmas, Hijuelos' fourth novel, is the story of Edward Ives, who was born in the 1920s and spent his early years in an orphanage. He was later adopted by a kind man who had also been adopted, so he has no background of his own. Ives seizes on his adopted father's Catholicism with a passion and considers religion such an emotional experience that he sometimes bursts

If you enjoy the works of Oscar Hijuelos, you may also want to check out the following books and films:

Lori M. Carlson, *Where Angels Glide at Dawn: New Stories from Latin America,* 1990.

Nicholosa Mohr, *El Bronx Remembered: A Novella and Stories,* 1975.

Gary Soto, *Jesse,* 1994.

Like Water for Chocolate, based on the novel by Laura Esquival, 1993.

---

into tears during Mass. When he is first introduced in the novel, it is the 1950s, and Ives has taken a year off from his job as a commercial artist at a New York advertising agency to walk around New York and look at churches. For different reasons, one of which is that he looks "like a Spaniard," Ives is also drawn to New York's Hispanic community, which is dominated by Puerto Ricans and Cubans.

Hijuelos presents Ives by looking at different Christmases in his life. Christmas is the time of year when Ives meets Annie, his wife-to-be; when he and Annie are married; and when his son Robert, who wants to be a priest, is killed in a random shooting. This pivotal event puts Mr. Ives' sense of himself to the test. Because the boy who killed his son is Puerto Rican, Ives finds himself resenting a community for which he once felt a special affinity. The killing also puts a strain on his marriage, which never regains its passion. By the end of the novel, Ives is no longer a cheerful man, but he is still a good one.

Writing in the *Los Angeles Times Book Review,* critic Benjamin Cheever remarked that Hijuelos "tells a story that is nearly 2,000 years old and yet in doing so presents us with a book that is truly startling in its novelty." Marie Arana-Ward, in the *Washington Post Book World,* noted that "The message of Ives's Christmases—of any Christmas, as anyone who has read Dickens or Miles or Hijuelos knows—is that though life may bring a man to the darkest nadir, faith can lead him out again." Jack Miles, in the *New York Times Book Review,* wrote that "The shortest of Oscar Hijuelos's recent novels, *Mr. Ives' Christmas* is in my judgment

both the deepest and the best." Other critics were less enthusiastic about the work. "Although much of *Mr. Ives' Christmas* shows an awareness of nuance and detail, the clear-cut contrast at its heart, between the goodness of Mr. Ives and the evil of what has befallen him, is too polarized to engage the reader fully," declared David Horspool in the *Times Literary Supplement.* Critic Roseanne Daryl Thomas, in the Chicago *Tribune Books,* stated, "Centered around a lifetime of Christmases, the tale of Mr. Ives is meant, I suppose, to be a Christmas story. . . . I only wish that Hijuelos had taken the blanket off the church bells."

In his interview with Coffey in *Publishers Weekly,* Hijuelos summed up his views as a novelist in the following way: "People want to go out and have fun—they want to find magic and romance and they want to find poetry and fall in love and be loved to death. People live this dream and then they hit real life again. And there are arbiters of that dream—that's what entertainers are all about. . . . And I think novelists and poets, or the worlds inside their works, are too. What I want to do is entertain and give readers something that can help them live more happily, just like characters in a song of love."

■ Works Cited

Arana-Ward, Marie, "Spirits of the Season," *Washington Post Book World,* December 10, 1995.

Beale, Lewis, review of *The Mambo Kings Play Songs of Love, Detroit Free Press,* August 20, 1989.

Cheever, Benjamin, "Believing by Rote," *Los Angeles Times Book Review,* December 17, 1995, pp. 3, 12.

Coates, Joseph, "When Cuban Musicians Dream the American Dream," *Tribune Books* (Chicago), August 13, 1989, p. 6.

Coffey, Michael, *PW Interviews: Oscar Hijuelos, Publishers Weekly,* July 21, 1989, pp. 42, 44.

Dorris, Michael, review of *The Mambo Kings Play Songs of Love, Detroit News,* September 3, 1989.

Firmat, Gustavo Perez, "Oscar Hijuelos," *Dictionary of Literary Biography,* Volume 145: *Modern Latin-American Fiction Writers, Second Series,* Gale, 1994.

Halliday, Bob, review of *Our House in the Last World,* Cleveland *Plain Dealer,* July 17, 1983.

Hornby, Nick, "In Ripe Old Age," *Times Literary Supplement,* August 6, 1993, p. 19.

Horspool, David, "A Christian Message," *Times Literary Supplement,* December 8, 1995, p. 20.

Hunnewell, Susannah, "A House Filled with Women," *New York Times Book Review*, March 7, 1993, p. 6.

Jefferson, Margo, "Dancing into the Dream," *New York Times Book Review*, August 27, 1989.

Review of *The Mambo Kings Play Songs of Love*, *Publishers Weekly*, June 2, 1989, p. 68.

Miles, Jack, "The Ghost of a Christmas Past," *New York Times Book Review*, December 3, 1995.

Milton, Edith, "Newcomers in New York," *New York Times Book Review*, May 15, 1983, pp. 12-13.

Quinn, Mary Ellen, review of *Our House in the Last World*, *Library Journal*, June 1, 1983, p. 1157.

Shacochis, Bob, review of *The Mambo Kings Play Songs of Love*, *Washington Post Book World*, August 20, 1989.

Simpson, Janice C., "Sister Act," *Time*, March 29, 1993, pp. 63-65.

Thomas, Roseanne Daryl, "A Winter's Nap," *Tribune Books* (Chicago), December 24, 1995, p. 2.

■ For More Information See

BOOKS

Contemporary Literary Criticism, Volume 65, Gale, 1990.

PERIODICALS

Americas Review, Volume 22, numbers 1-2, pp. 274-76.

Bloomsbury Review, May, 1990, p. 5.

Boston Globe, November 18, 1990, p. 21.

Chicago Tribune, August 9, 1990, p. 1; May 30, 1993, Section 6, p. 5.

Chicago Tribune Book World, July 17, 1983.

Christian Century, May 22, 1996, p. 581.

Cosmopolitan, March, 1993, p. 16.

Entertainment Weekly, March 19, 1993, p. 57.

Horn Book, May-June, 1995, p. 316.

Insight on the News, October 23, 1989, p. 56.

London Review of Books, September 23, 1993, p. 23.

Los Angeles Times, April 16, 1990, p. 1.

Los Angeles Times Book Review, September 3, 1989, p. 1; March 14, 1993, pp. 3, 8.

Los Angeles Times Magazine, April 18, 1993, pp. 22-28, 54.

New Republic, March 22, 1993, pp. 38-41.

New Statesman, December 15, 1995, p. 64.

Newsweek, August 21, 1989, p. 60.

New York, March 1, 1993, p. 46.

New Yorker, March 29, 1993, p. 107; August 21, 1995, pp. 126-27.

New York Times, September 11, 1989, p. C17; April 1, 1993, p. C17.

Observer (London), July 25, 1993, p. 53.

People, April 5, 1993, p. 26.

Philadelphia Inquirer, July 17, 1983.

Publishers Weekly, April 15, 1983, p. 42; February 1, 1991, pp. 17-21.

Time, August 14, 1989, p. 68; March 29, 1993, pp. 63, 65.

Tribune Books (Chicago), January 3, 1993, p. 6.

U. S. Catholic, May, 1996, p. 46.

Village Voice, May 1, 1990, p. 85.

Washington Post Book World, March 14, 1993, pp. 1, 10.

World Literature Today, winter, 1994, p. 127.*

—Sketch by Irene Durham

Jack Kerouac

around the United States and Mexico; was a fire lookout for the U.S. Agriculture Service in northwest Washington, 1956. *Military service:* U.S. Merchant Marine, 1942-43; U.S. Navy, 1943. *Member:* Authors Guild, Authors League of America.

■ Personal

Born Jean-Louis Lebris de Kerouac, on March 12, 1922, in Lowell, MA; died October 21, 1969, of a stomach hemorrhage in St. Petersburg, FL; buried in Lowell, MA; son of Leo Alcide (a printer) and Gabrielle-Ange (a shoe-factory worker; maiden name, Levesque) Kerouac; married Frankie Edith Parker, August 22, 1944 (marriage annulled, 1945); married Joan Haverty, November 17, 1950 (divorced); married Stella Sampas, November 18, 1966; children: (second marriage) Jan Michele Hackett. *Education:* Attended Horace Mann School for Boys, New York, NY; attended Columbia College, 1940-42; attended New School for Social Research, 1948-49. *Religion:* Roman Catholic. *Hobbies and other interests:* Reading, walking, late TV movies, tape-recording FM musical programs.

■ Career

Writer. Worked at odd jobs in garages and as a sports reporter for the Lowell (MA) *Sun*, 1942; was a railroad brakeman with the Southern Pacific Railroad, San Francisco, CA, 1952-53; traveled

■ Awards, Honors

American Academy of Arts and Sciences grant, 1955; Allen Ginsberg and other poets created the Jack Kerouac School of Disembodied Poetics at the Naropa Institute in Boulder, CO.; *Moody Street Irregulars: A Jack Kerouac Newsletter*, edited by Joy Walsh and Michael Basinski, was established in 1978.

■ Writings

(Under name John Kerouac) *The Town and the City,* Harcourt (New York City), 1950, reprinted under name Jack Kerouac, Grosset (New York City), 1960, reprinted, Harcourt, 1978.

(Under name John Kerouac) *Visions of Gerard* (also see below), Farrar, Straus (New York City), 1963, reprinted under name Jack Kerouac, McGraw (New York City), 1976.

Contributor to *Columbia Review* (under pseudonym Jean-Louis Incogniteau) and to *New World Writing* (under pseudonym Jean-Louis).

NOVELS; UNDER NAME JACK KEROUAC

On the Road, Viking (New York City), 1957, reprinted, Penguin (New York City), 1987, critical edition with notes by Scott Donaldson published as *On the Road: Text and Criticism*, Penguin, 1979.

The Dharma Bums, Viking, 1958, reprinted, Buccaneer Books (Cutchogue, NY), 1976.

The Subterraneans (also see below), Grove (New York City), 1958, 2nd edition, 1981.

Doctor Sax: Faust Part Three, Grove, 1959, reprinted, 1988.

Maggie Cassidy: A Love Story, Avon (New York City), 1959, reprinted, McGraw, 1978.

Excerpts from Visions of Cody, New Directions (New York City), 1959, enlarged edition published as *Visions of Cody*, McGraw, 1972 (published with *The Visions of the Great Rememberer*, by Allen Ginsberg, Penguin, 1993).

Tristessa, Avon, 1960 (published in England with *Visions of Gerard*, Deutsch, 1964), reprinted, McGraw, 1978.

Big Sur, Farrar, Straus, 1962, reprinted, McGraw, 1981, new edition with foreword by Aram Saroyan, Penguin, 1992.

Desolation Angels, Coward (New York City), 1965.

Satori in Paris (also see below), Grove, 1966, reprinted, 1988.

Vanity of Duluoz: An Adventurous Education, 1935-46, Coward, 1968.

Pic, Grove, 1971 (published in England with *The Subterraneans* as *Two Novels*, Deutsch [London], 1973; published with *Satori in Paris*, Grove, 1986).

Also author, with William S. Burroughs, of unpublished novel "And the Hippos Were Boiled in Their Tanks," and of unpublished novels "The Sea Is My Brother," "Buddha Tells Us," and "Secret Mullings about Bill."

POETRY; UNDER NAME JACK KEROUAC

Mexico City Blues: Two Hundred Forty-Two Choruses, Grove, 1959, reprinted, 1987.

Hugo Weber, Portents, 1967.

Someday You'll Be Lying, privately printed, 1968.

A Lost Haiku, privately printed, 1969.

Scattered Poems, City Lights (San Francisco, CA), 1971.

(With Albert Saijo and Lew Welch) *Trip Trap: Haiku along the Road from San Francisco to New York, 1959*, Grey Fox (San Francisco, CA), 1973.

Heaven and Other Poems, Grey Fox, 1977.

San Francisco Blues, Beat Books, 1983.

Hymn: God Pray for Me, Caliban (Dover, NH), 1985.

American Haikus, Caliban, 1986.

Pomes All Sizes, with introduction by Allen Ginsberg, City Lights, 1992.

Old Angel Midnight, Grey Fox, 1993, new edition edited by Donald Allen, with prefaces by Ann Charters and Michael McClure, Grey Fox, 1993.

Book of Blues, with introduction by Robert Creeley, Penguin, 1995.

SOUND RECORDINGS; UNDER NAME JACK KEROUAC

Jack Kerouac Steve Allen Poetry for the Beat Generation, Hanover, 1959.

Jack Kerouac Blues and Haikus, Hanover, 1959.

Readings by Jack Kerouac on the Beat Generation, Verve, 1959.

The Jack Kerouac Collection, Rhino (Santa Monica, CA), 1990.

OTHER; UNDER NAME JACK KEROUAC

(Contributor) *January 1st 1959: Fidel Castro*, Totem, 1959.

Rimbaud, City Lights, 1959.

The Scripture of the Golden Eternity (philosophy and religion), Corinth Books (Chevy Chase, MD), 1960, new edition, 1970, new edition with introduction by Eric Mottram, City Lights, 1994.

(Author of introduction) *The Americans*, photographs by Robert Frank, Grove, 1960, revised and enlarged edition, 1978.

Lonesome Traveler (autobiography), McGraw, 1960, reprinted, Grove, 1989.

(Ad lib narrator) *Pull My Daisy* (screenplay), Grove, 1961.

Book of Dreams, City Lights, 1961.

A Pun for Al Gelpi (broadside), [Cambridge], 1966.

A Memoir in Which Is Revealed Secret Lives and West Coast Whispers, Giligia (Aurora, OR), 1970.

Two Early Stories, Aloe Editions, 1973.

Home at Christmas, Oliphant, 1973.

(With Allen Ginsberg) *Take Care of My Ghost, Ghost* (letters), limited edition, Ghost Press, 1977.

Une veille de Noel, Knight, 1980.

(With Carolyn Cassady) *Dear Carolyn: Letters to Carolyn Cassady*, Unspeakable Visions (California, PA), 1983.

Good Blonde & Others, edited by Donald Allen, Grey Fox, 1993.

Jack Kerouac: Selected Letters, 1940-1956, edited with introduction and commentary by Ann Charters, Viking, 1995.

The Portable Jack Kerouac (omnibus volume), edited by Ann Charters, Viking, 1995.

A Jack Kerouac ROMnibus (CD-ROM), Largely Literary Designs (Morrisville, NC), 1995.

Also author of *Before the Road: Young Cody and the Birth of Hippie,* and of *Not Long Ago Joy Abounded at Christmas,* 1972. Author of pamphlet, *Nosferatu* (Dracula), New York Film Society, 1960. Contributor to periodicals, including *Ark-Moby, Paris Review, Evergreen Review, Big Table, Black Mountain Review,* and *Chicago Review.* Contributor of regular column, "The Last Word," to *Escapade,* 1959-61.

One of Kerouac's notebooks is housed at the University of Texas, Austin; five notebooks and a typescript are housed in the Berg Collection of the New York Public Library; some of the author's correspondence with Allen Ginsberg is housed at the Butler Library of Columbia University; other letters are housed in the Gary Snyder Archives at the library of the University of California, Davis.

■ Adaptations

The Subterraneans was adapted as a film of the same title by Metro-Goldwyn-Mayer in 1960, starring George Peppard and Leslie Caron; a play based on Kerouac's life and works was produced in New York in 1976; a film based on *On the Road* is scheduled for release in 1998.

■ Sidelights

Jack Kerouac died, as he had spent much of his adult life, writing. The morning of October 20, 1969, he was sitting in front of his television at his home in St. Petersburg, Florida, jotting down notes when a vein in his stomach ruptured. A hard-drinking man, Kerouac had been a walking time bomb for years. His youthful athletic frame had long ago given way under the pressure of an erratic life-style and too much hard liquor: Twenty hours later, after numerous transfusions, he was dead. Kerouac was only forty-seven when he died; an old forty-seven with decades of writing behind him, and thousands of miles traveled

in a ceaseless seeking after the "It" he had first talked about in the novel *On the Road*—the vision, the reality underlying the seemingly random and meaningless events of life in the twentieth century.

Only two months earlier the nation had watched its youth cavort at Woodstock, the first of the mega-rock concerts. His friend and fellow Beat writer William Burroughs said of Kerouac that his writings and influence "opened a million coffee bars and sold a trillion Levis to both sexes. . . . Woodstock rises from his pages." But at his death, Kerouac was largely forgotten except for his one commercial success, *On the Road.* He lived out his last years writing and drinking. A barroom beating the previous spring had sent him into self-imposed seclusion in his St. Petersburg home with his wife and his mother, whom he had vowed to take care of years before. The beating also sent him into a bout of heavy drinking, mindless television viewing, and ceaseless listening to Handel's *Messiah* on the record player. He was increasingly cut off from his former friends, especially the poet Allen Ginsberg who had crossed the bridge from Beat lyricist to hippie guru. Saddened by the Vietnam war, but even more by what seemed to him the unpatriotic stance of youth vis-a-vis the war, Kerouac was, in his personal life, out of synch with the times. All that remained for him at the end was the work, and that no longer came with the old fire.

There were the usual eulogies at Kerouac's death, but most accented his identity with the Beat Generation, a term he had coined in 1948. *Time* magazine dubbed him a "shaman of the Beat Generation" in its obituary, but barely mentioned that he was a writer. For years thereafter Kerouac's literary reputation floundered. Aside from *On the Road, The Subterraneans,* and *The Dharma Bums,* his books did not sell well during his lifetime; they fared not much better when he was dead. Critics generally regarded him as an aberration of the 1950s, a "kind of cultural dinosaur," according to Matt Theado in *Dictionary of Literary Biography Yearbook 1995,* "an emissary of a post-World War II fad of deviant behavior—social impudence, jazz, coffeehouses, dope."

Slowly however, that situation changed. His "masterpiece," according to Theado, *Visions of Cody,* was published in 1972 to tepid reviews, but it set the stage for a renewed critical assessment. Then came a Kerouac conference in Colorado in 1982 and new critical studies. Kerouac's reputation has continued to grow over the years, so that by the 1990s most of his books are back in print, biographies have been written, his collected letters published, and *The Portable Jack Kerouac* brought out by Viking, a sure sign that he has resurfaced on the literary map of the nation. His novels have begun to make it into the canon, as well, to be taught at universities as more than a historical curiosity: works to be placed on the shelf next to Ernest Hemingway, William Faulkner, John Dos Passos, and Thomas Wolfe. In a 1995 review of *The Portable Jack Kerouac*, Ann Douglas noted in the *New York Times Book Review* that "Kerouac's work represents the most extensive experiment in language and literary form undertaken by an American writer of his generation."

Slowly also, the real Kerouac has surfaced, not the Beat caricature. He is now recognized as a man of deep contradictions and complexity: the athlete-aesthete, the devoutly Catholic and conservative breaker of mores, a ceaseless man of the road who was in fact fearful of driving and of being driven, the creator of "spontaneous writing" who was at the same time a technically elegant stylist. Kerouac was, at bottom, a reluctant rebel. He was brought up to value the life of home and family, both of which cultural shibboleths he ultimately rejected, driven on by his need to create, to explore, to grow. Fueled by the destructive effects of benzedrine and booze, Kerouac's was a short journey in time.

A French-Catholic Upbringing

Central to Kerouac's life was his Catholic upbringing. Born on March 12, 1922, to French-Canadian parents in working-class Lowell, Massachusetts, Kerouac was firmly shaped by the precepts of Roman Catholicism. Another shaping influence was the fact that Kerouac spoke a local dialect of French, *joual*, before he spoke English, a language he only began learning at age six. Born Jean-Louis Lebris de Kerouac, Ti Jean—as he was called by his family—was the youngest of three children. Kerouac's early life was relatively comfortable and secure. His father Leo was a former insurance salesman from the French-speaking portion of Quebec who opened a print shop in Lowell and made a good living. Yet the first of what George Dardess in *Dictionary of Literary Biography* calls

"decisive and painful ruptures" in Kerouac's life came just after his fourth birthday when his older brother Gerard died of rheumatic fever. During his brother's illness, Kerouac had grown very close to Gerard, and his death brought about something like a spiritual crisis in the young Kerouac. Catholicism was teaching him of the power of God, yet His absence and seeming indifference was glaring at the time of Gerard's death. Years later, his brother still informed Kerouac's thoughts, inspiring him to write *Visions of Gerard*, part of his ongoing cycle of works recording his own life.

"In no time at all we were back on the main highway and that night I saw the entire state of Nebraska unroll before my eyes. A hundred and ten miles an hour straight through, an arrow road, sleeping towns, no traffic, and the Union Pacific streamliner falling behind us in the moonlight. I wasn't frightened at all that night; it was perfectly legitimate to go 110 and talk and have all the Nebraska towns—Ogallala, Gothenburg, Kearney, Grand Island, Columbus—unreel with dreamlike rapidity as we roared ahead and talked."

Jack Kerouac, *On the Road*

Kerouac, soon called Jack by his youthful playmates, was a strong child, athletic and physically outgoing, though very shy. He received first communion in 1929 and served as an altar boy at the same church, Jean Baptiste Cathedral, where later his own funeral service would be held. A devout child, still Kerouac was drawn to the physical life of sensation. As Dardess noted, "the apparent split between the spirit and the flesh was one that troubled Kerouac throughout his life," a schism that affected his literary themes and style. Kerouac attended a Catholic grammar school and then a public junior high where he began to make more English-speaking friends and to feel at home in his second language. He formed an early love for reading and writing, and in the eighth grade was strongly influenced by an English teacher who encouraged his attempts at storytelling. It was about then he began a life-long habit of carrying small notebooks with him to record scenes, dialogue, and inspirations. Radio programs such as "The Shadow" and films also proved a strong influence. As a high school student he paid more attention to his own tastes in reading—from the Harvard classics and contemporaries such as Hemingway and William Saroyan—than to his class assignments. He remained a voracious reader all his life, schooling himself in literature from around the world.

During this developmental period, his secure family life was coming asunder, the second of Dardess's ruptures. In 1936, the Merrimac River flooded Lowell, causing considerable damage to Leo Kerouac's print shop. This damage, on top of the hard economic times brought on by the Great Depression, spelled ruin for the business. Kerouac's father sold out and was forced to take odd jobs that took him away from the family for long stretches of time. His family also moved from their home into cheaper lodgings in Lowell, and Kerouac, the only remaining son, soon began feeling the tug of family responsibility. His prowess on the football field partly made up for these other setbacks, and as a star halfback, he won scholarships to both Boston College and Columbia University. Opting for Columbia, it seemed that he was well on his way to making up for the hard times brought on by the sale of his father's business. During his senior year in high school, he also made two friendships that would inform his later life and work: he found a soul mate in Sebastian Sampas, whose sister he would later marry, and a love interest in Mary Carney, whom he later wrote of in *Maggie Cassidy: A Love Story*.

Into the Big World of New York

Kerouac did not immediately enter Columbia, but required a year at the Horace Mann School to bring him up to the standards of the Ivy League. His year at Horace Mann was well spent, as he earned good grades and led his football team to a championship. His extensive reading and experiments in writing continued also, and he made pocket money writing term papers for his preppie fellow students. He was also learning about life in the city and began a life-long love of jazz, feeling a special affinity for the improvisation and free-association found in this musical form. Entering Columbia in 1940, his football career was put on hold with a broken leg. His studies fared not much better, for he followed his own passions in reading, spending time with the works of Thomas Wolfe instead of chemistry, which he failed.

Meanwhile his family life was continuing to disintegrate as his parents moved to New Haven, Connecticut, where his father found new employment. The next year, the fall of 1941, saw the gathering clouds of war, and football was the furthest thing from Kerouac's mind. Bad blood between him and the coach did not help matters, and Kerouac finally walked away from university life. For a time, he rejoined his family, working variously as a grease monkey and a sports reporter, then moved to Washington, D. C., where he worked for a short period on the construction of the Pentagon. Finally, in March 1942 he joined the U.S. Merchant Marine and sailed on the S. S. *Dorchester* on an ammunition run to Greenland. The following fall he was back at Columbia for another abortive try at the football team but soon returned to his family, waiting to be drafted. Eventually, he decided to join up instead of waiting, enlisting in the U.S. Navy in February 1943.

But the regimented military life was not one he could abide. He was soon cashiered out of the Navy, after putting down his rifle on the drill field and heading for the base library. Termed an "indifferent character," Kerouac earned an honorable discharge after a short stay in the psychiatric ward of Bethesda Naval Hospital. By this time, Kerouac's family had settled in Ozone Park, Queens, the father working in a printing shop and Kerouac's mother employed at a shoe factory. Leo Kerouac looked on his son as a failure; the secure nest was gone for Kerouac. He took up for a time with old Columbia friends in Manhattan, especially Edie Parker, an art student from a wealthy Michigan family. By June 1943 he had shipped out again in the Merchant Marine, on an ammunition run to Liverpool. On board he began writing a novel he called "The Sea is My Brother," and gained insight to his mission as a writer from reading John Galsworthy's family tale, *The Forsyte Saga*. Kerouac determined that he too would write a series of connected stories about his life and adventures.

Back in New York, he fell in with friends of Edie Parker: Lucien Carr, Allen Ginsberg, and William Burroughs. Though Carr and he were closest initially, it was Ginsberg and Burroughs who would have most influence on him over the years. The influence flowed both ways, for Kerouac convinced both men to write, giving Ginsberg the title of his first great poem, "Howl," and supplying Burroughs with the title for his equally famous *Naked Lunch*, even typing the manuscript for him. Burroughs, the oldest of the three, had worked as an adman, exterminator, and detective, and in turn introduced Kerouac to the works of Spengler, Nietzsche, and Celine. Burroughs also introduced Kerouac to the use of amphetamines.

Kerouac's friendship with Carr floundered after Carr killed a man, and Kerouac was involved as a material witness to the crime. Leo Kerouac, disgusted with his son and his friends, refused to bail him out. Kerouac turned to Edie Parker, proposing marriage so that she could borrow family money for the bail. But the marriage was more or less in name only, and by late 1944, Kerouac was again sailing with the Merchant Marine, only to jump ship and set up in New York. For the next months, Kerouac, Burroughs, and Ginsberg were inseparable friends, analyzing literature, philosophizing about the state of the world, and taking drugs together. In December 1945, partly as a result of his heavy use of benzedrine, Kerouac contracted thrombophlebitis and was confined to a hospital bed. That same month, his father Leo was diagnosed with stomach cancer and forced to quit his job. The following May, Kerouac's father died, extracting a deathbed promise from his son to take care of his mother.

In the event, the mother took care of her son, for when Kerouac joined her at the Ozone Park home, he sat down to write his first published novel, *The Town and the City*. Two years in the writing, that novel was ultimately brought out in 1950, and is his most conventional work, much influenced by the style of his early literary model, Thomas Wolfe. Kerouac took as his theme the split between the two worlds of the hometown, with its traditional values, and the big city, with all its physical and psychic stimulations and dangers. The story deals with the disintegration of a family as each of its members goes his or her own way in the world, a novel with large touches of autobiography.

Writing of the book was slowed somewhat by the entrance of a new and quite powerful friend into Kerouac's life, Neal Cassady, who became a source of literary inspiration. Cassady, born in Denver,

Colorado, was not an intellectual like Ginsberg or Burroughs. Instead he was a spirited hell-raiser: He stole his first car when he was fourteen; by the time he was twenty-one, he'd stolen five hundred cars and been arrested ten times, convicted six times, and spent fifteen months in jail. But Cassady didn't steal cars for mere profit; he took them for the thrill of driving them, for the freedom of the open road. He was like a shot of adrenaline, an invitation to anarchy. Kerouac accepted. In 1947 Kerouac made the first of his numerous transcontinental trips, hitchhiking to Colorado to visit Cassady, and then continuing on to San Francisco, eventually to return to New York by bus.

The Beat Generation and *On the Road*

By September 1948, Kerouac had finished his first novel, but it would take another year to sell it. It was that very fall, in a conversation with another friend, John Clellon Holmes, that Kerouac first coined the term "Beat Generation" to denote a whole generation of young men and women who felt cut off from a society controlled by industrialism and militarism. On one level, the term connotes "beat" as in beaten down by technology and the loss of the human scale; on another level it denotes "beatitude" as Dardess noted in *Dictionary of Literary Biography*—"the happy release of emotions no longer entrapped by observance of the forms."

Kerouac was doing his best to get beyond observance of literary forms as well as lifestyle ones. He increasingly stood on the side of racial, political, and economic outcasts of society, and in his fiction he was consciously moving away from traditional literary forms such as he employed in his first novel, *The Town and the City*. Cassady helped in this venture, providing not only a protagonist for Kerouac's fiction but inspiring the style in his letters. Kerouac later typified these letters from Cassady in a *Paris Review* interview with Ted Berrigan as "all first person, fast, mad, confessional, completely serious, all detailed." In one such letter—a small novella in length—Cassady described a seduction and love affair with a woman he had met on a bus. To Kerouac, for whom the improvisations of jazz were such a delight, this free-form style of writing offered exactly what he had been seeking: a new form with which to get beneath the layer of civility that separated him from his material. As Dardess observed in *Dictionary of Literary Biography*, this new style, or "spontaneous prose" as Kerouac called it, "was the way by which the inner mind, trapped as Kerouac finally felt it to be by social, psychological, and grammatical restrictions, could free itself from its muteness and take verbal shape in the outside world. The result of this liberation would not be chaotic, however, since the inner mind was innately shapely and would cause the words with which it expressed itself to be shapely." As the biographer Dennis McNally noted in his *Desolate Angel: Jack Kerouac, the Beat Generation, and America*, Kerouac's prose innovation had parallels in music and the visual arts: "At roughly the same time and place and in response to the same stimuli—a world at once accelerating and constricting—the painter Jackson Pollock and the musician Charlie Parker had accomplished similar revolutions in their own art forms."

Kerouac employed his "spontaneous prose" in a twenty-day burst of writing, typing onto a continuous roll of teletype paper the 175,000 words of the first draft of *On the Road*, a novel that featured Cassady in the guise of Dean Moriarty and himself as Sal Paradise. This was not Kerouac's first attempt at telling the story of his friendship with Cassady: Two earlier versions came to nothing, though they had paved the way for Kerouac's burst of creativity in April 1951. Critics are quick to point out, however, that as the novel was not published for another six years and saw many revisions from this initial teletype version, that *On the Road* is not a pure representation of Kerouac's spontaneous prose style. The books that followed, though, largely were such creations.

On the Road is divided into five parts, chronicling the incessant travels of Sal and Dean back and forth across America in search of what Dean calls "IT," or as Dardess explained, "the moment of spontaneous ecstasy when all things are known in their greatest purity." The quest for "IT" takes them to Denver, San Francisco, New York, New Orleans, and Mexico, and along the frenetic way women and male friends are met and lost, drugs taken, cars stolen, sex played at. Kerouac's old friends, Burroughs and Ginsberg, make appearances in the novel: Burroughs as Old Bull Lee, a heroin addict, and Ginsberg as the poet Carlo Marx. Episodic rather than plot-driven, *On the Road* is a picaresque novel in the tradition of what has come to be known as "road literature," narratives in which travel itself becomes a quest. As such, it has been compared to other quintessentially American works such as Mark Twain's *The Adventures of Huckleberry Finn.*

Acting as narrator, Sal sometimes travels with Dean, sometimes on his own, or sometimes with other Beat friends. His adventures and quests take him to derelict apartments, bordellos, and the jungles of Mexico. But it is Dean, "madman angel and bum" as he is described in the book, who is the motive force for the voyage toward self. "Yes he's mad," Sal says of Dean, but he is attracted to Dean because of this madness. His old friends and college buddies "were in the negative, nightmare position of putting down society and giving their tired bookish or political or psychoanalytical reasons. . . . Dean just raced in society, eager for bread and love; he didn't care one way or the other." Sal eagerly tags along with the Denver madman on adventures in the American grain. "With the coming of Dean Moriarty began the part of my life you could call my life on the road," Sal says. "Dean is the perfect guy for the road because he actually was born on the road, when his parents were passing through Salt Lake City in 1926, in a jalopy, on their way to Los Angeles."

Set between the winter of 1947 and the late fall of 1950, the book initially details Sal's adventures along Route 6, "one long red line. . .that led from the tip of Cape Cod clear to Ely, Nevada, then dipped down to Los Angeles." But Sal has misread the map lines, and ends up on his first trip stranded in the Catskills, from where he takes a bus to Chicago. He continues his journey ever West by hitchhiking and hopping trains, encountering along the way both social outcasts and Beat intelligentsia. Hoboes, waitresses, field workers, truck drivers, and women on the run from their husbands are all included in Kerouac's gallery of characters, all of whom exhibit Dean's chronic restlessness. At one point, Sal sets up a temporary domestic relationship with a young Mexican girl, Terry, and her small boy, only to send her back to her own home when times get tough. "I could feel the pull of my own life calling me," Sal writes. "I shot my aunt a penny postcard across the land and asked for another fifty."

But as the travels continue, the talk more and more turns to God and religion; to "IT," an experience that will give the ceaseless wandering reason and purpose. Christian religion as well as Buddhist symbolism converge, with the road becoming the Tao, the way. And in Mexico, the two finally go their separate ways, with Dean ever-driven to travel on. Sal, meanwhile returns to New York and gives up the road for a woman he has found to pin his dreams on. In a sense, the novel is not so much a paean to the mad freedom of Dean Moriarty as it is a novel of Sal's growth from childlike worship of his friend to the slow realization of how trapped Dean is in his quest. Sal has a vision of Dean, noted Carole Gottlieb Vopat in the *Midwest Quarterly*, "not as sweet, holy goof but as the Angel of Death, burning and laying waste whatever he touches."

On the Road did not find a publisher for six years, and upon publication in 1957 it earned a great deal of critical attention, most of which was negative. One bright light in the reviews came from Gilbert Millstein in the *New York Times*. Millstein observed that there "are sections of *On the Road* in which the writing is of a beauty almost breathtaking." Noting that the novel was a testament for the Beat Generation just as Hemingway's "*The Sun Also Rises* came to be regarded as the testament of the 'Lost Generation,'" Millstein concluded that *On the Road* "is a major novel." But other reviewers strongly disagreed. The critic and Hemingway biographer, Carlos Baker, writing in *Saturday Review,* complained of the hollowness of the lives portrayed in the novel, and concluded that Kerouac "can write when he chooses. . . . This dizzy travelogue gives him little chance but to gobble a few verbal goofballs and thumb a ride to the next town."

More reviews in the same vein followed. David Dempsey observed in the *New York Times Book Review* that "*On the Road* is a stunning achievement. But it is a road, as far as the characters are concerned, that leads nowhere. . . ." While Thomas F. Curley noted in *Commonweal* Kerouac's "bravura style," he also observed that the characters in the novel displayed "a frenzied need for love and order without the strength or the faith to make the love that would create that order." Gene Baro, in the *New York Herald Tribune Book Review,* observed that Kerouac's characters are "sexually promiscuous, drink-and-drug ridden, thieving, lying, betraying. . . . They spend themselves gladly and savagely; their joys are hysterical and obsessive, their sorrows sentimental or incoherent." Indeed, much of the early negative criticism of Kerouac was not so much about his qualities as a writer, but as a chronicler of a life seen by many in 1950s America as disruptive and challenging to the order of things. Such criticism, as Dardess pointed out in *Dictionary of Literary Criticism,* said "much. . .about the depths of these critics' fears of their emotions and of their pride in the narrow limits of their intellects. But it did not say much of anything about *On the Road.*"

"The Legend of Duluoz"

Such reviews, however, were still in the future for Kerouac. No publisher would touch the book initially. Kerouac's personal life continued to be as chaotic as that of his fictional personas. Not long before the writing of *On the Road,* Kerouac's marriage to Edie Parker had been annulled, and in November 1950, he married Joan Haverty, though that marriage was not destined to last long, either. The same month Harcourt, Brace—Kerouac's publishers for *The Town and the City*—rejected *On the Road,* Haverty tossed him out of their apartment and started divorce proceedings, informing him in the process that she was pregnant with his child. But for years Kerouac denied paternity, "partly out of fear of having to support the child," according to Dardess, "partly out of fear, evidently unfounded, that the child was not his. Kerouac's insufficiency as a husband . . . was second only to his insufficiency as a father."

Kerouac kept on writing. Setting up home again with his mother, he also set about creating a Proustian testament to his life and adventures which he came to call "The Legend of Duluoz," the name he used for himself in several later novels. As Ann Charters noted in *Dictionary of Literary Biography,* this fictionalized autobiography was "one of the most ambitious projects conceived by any modern American writer in its scope, depth, and variety. Kerouac intended in his old age to gather his books together in a uniform binding and insert the real names of his contemporaries into the narratives so that his larger designs might be more apparent." The novel sequence, though not published in chronological order, would eventually include *Visions of Gerard,* a picture of Kerouac's childhood and the death of his beloved brother; *Doctor Sax: Faust Part Three,* another look at his youth but through a surrealist lens; *Maggie Cassidy,* a recounting of Kerouac's first love with Mary Carney; *Vanity of Duluoz: An Adventurous*

If you enjoy the works of Jack Kerouac, you may also want to check out the following:

William Burroughs, *Naked Lunch*, 1959.
Lawrence Ferlinghetti, *A Coney Island of the Mind*, 1958.
Allen Ginsberg, the seminal poem "Howl," 1956.

Education 1935-46, a chronicle of his football years at Horace Mann and Columbia; *On the Road*, which was his report of the late 1940s; *Visions of Cody*, a much more "spontaneous prose" version of the Moriarty material; *The Subterraneans*, a retelling of Kerouac's love affair in 1953 with an African American woman; *The Dharma Bums*, relating his West Coast adventures in Buddhism and his friendship with the poet, Gary Snyder; *Tristessa*, a novel describing a love affair in Mexico City in the mid-1950s; *Desolation Angels*, a chronicle of the year before publication of *On the Road*; *Big Sur*, a novel that shows Kerouac's bitterness and despair in the early 1960s as he slipped into alcoholism; and *Satori in Paris*, the story of a trip Kerouac made to that city in 1965 to trace his family tree. But as Charters noted in *Dictionary of Literary Biography*, "The larger design of Kerouac's 'Legend of Duluoz' has been overshadowed by the popularity of three novels, *On the Road* (1957), *The Dharma Bums* (1958), and *The Subterraneans* (1958)."

Throughout the early 1950s Kerouac continued to write in obscurity, living sometimes with his mother, at other times with friends in Mexico City, Tangier, and San Francisco, supporting himself at times as a brakeman on the Southern Pacific Railroad and as a fire lookout in Washington state. All the while he continued to flesh out the precepts of his "spontaneous prose" style. By 1955 Beat poets were beginning to come into their own, and Ginsberg's *Howl* was the subject of a high-profile obscenity trial the following year. The public was becoming more and more interested in these writers, and finally Malcolm Cowley at Viking championed the manuscript of *On the Road* for publication. Though critics may have quibbled about the merits of *On the Road*, the public eagerly bought it, and Kerouac's book became a bestseller; overnight Kerouac himself became the spokesperson for the Beat Generation.

Though he had a desk full of unpublished manuscripts, he responded to his publishers' call for more material with a ten-day burst of writing about his experiences in 1955 studying Buddhism with Gary Snyder. That book, *Dharma Bums*, became another of Kerouac's most popular titles, with Snyder being given the fictional name of Japhy Ryder and Kerouac assuming the persona of Ray Smith. Such name changes were insisted upon by Kerouac's publishers in order to avoid possible lawsuits. Ray and Japhy are modern religious wanderers seeking dharma, or truth. In the course of the book, published in 1958, Snyder/Ryder has a vision of "a great rucksack revolution . . . refusing to submit to the general demand that they consume . . . all that crap they didn't really want anyway such as refrigerators, TV sets . . . certain hair oils and deodorants and general junk you finally see a week later in the garbage anyway." It was an accurate prophecy of the hippies of the next decade.

The Subterraneans was also published in 1958, though written several years before in three benzedrine-enhanced nights of typing. The story of Kerouac's love affair with a black woman in 1953, it "was closest in its narrative and its sexual detail to a Henry Miller novel," according to Charters. She goes on to say that "There is no search for an alternative life-style in this novel. Here Kerouac confronted himself directly, and in his honesty describing his failure to love the black girl 'Mardou' he created one of his most dramatic illustrations of the basic theme of his work, his belief that 'All life is suffering'." As Charters went on to point out in *Dictionary of Literary Biography*, the publication of these three books sealed Kerouac's critical fate. The hedonistic joyriding of *On the Road*, the "rucksack revolution" proposed in *The Dharma Bums*, and the explicit interracial sexuality of *The Subterraneans* "angered many reviewers in the repressive McCarthy era." Kerouac's message was the culprit here, not his medium. The critics gathered to shoot the messenger.

The Beaten and the Beatified

Though Kerouac's accumulated manuscripts continued to be published throughout the late 1950s and early 1960s, he was unable to finish another manuscript for four years after writing *The Dharma Bums*. Retreating from the press, the fans, and the bright lights of publicity, Kerouac lived for a time in a remote cabin in California's Big Sur, where he suffered an alcoholic breakdown. This was recounted in his *Big Sur*, published in 1962, a book that deals with the negative effects of fame, and was better received than much of his other work, perhaps because it showed the demise of the Beat myth, the end of the joyride. For years critics had complained of Kerouac's "spontaneous prose," claiming as the author Truman Capote once did, that it was typing, not writing.

Increasingly through the 1960s Kerouac wrote less and less, and drank more and more. In his 1968 *Paris Review* interview with Ted Berrigan, Kerouac noted how all the old joy had gone out of writing: "I had a ritual once of lighting a candle and writing by its light and blowing it out when I was done for the night . . . also kneeling and praying before starting . . . but now I simply hate to write." In 1966, Kerouac married Stella Sampas, the sister of his childhood friend from Lowell. In the final years she helped take care of Kerouac's mother, who had suffered a stroke and lived with them in New England and in Florida. By the end, Kerouac's "spontaneous prose" had become too hard to sustain. His storytelling was confined largely to the barrooms of Lowell or St. Petersburg, Florida. In 1968 his great friend, Neal Cassady, died in Mexico, burnt out on drugs and alcohol. Kerouac followed him to the grave the next year, an all but forgotten figure of the Beat Generation.

Yet with changing times and mores, and with the death of Kerouac's wife and the subsequent passing of the estate to her brother who is more proactive in initiating release of hitherto unpublished Kerouac material, Kerouac is enjoying a posthumous renaissance. At the time of his death, Kerouac's estate was worth $91; by the mid-1990s the estate was estimated to be worth $10 million, and legal battles were being fought between Jan Kerouac, the author's daughter, and John Sampas, Stella Sampas's brother. With renewed sales has come a resurrection of critical attention, and the Kerouac achievement is finally receiving a more balanced assessment. Reviewing *The Portable Jack Kerouac* in the *New Yorker*, the writer Joyce Carol Oates contended that "the evidence of Jack Kerouac's oeuvre is that, for all its flaws, it, and he, deserved to be treated better by the censorious 'literary' critics of his time. . . . *The Portable Jack Kerouac* may well be seminal in a reevaluation of Kerouac's position in the literature of mid-twentieth-century America—a richly varied affluence of 'high' and 'low' art that permanently changed the course of our fiction."

In reviewing that same book as well as Kerouac's *Selected Letters*, a critic in the *Chicago Tribune* observed that the letters greatly helped to fill in the background to the writing of *On the Road*, "one of the most important American novels of this century." Fittingly, that novel, as Dardess pointed out in *Dictionary of Literary Biography*, ends with a question mark about the dream of finding the illusive "IT." Sal Paradise's discovery in *On the Road* that "the true nature of 'IT'—the knowledge of 'IT' is for mortals inextricably bound up with joy and creativity but also with loss and death," Dardess concluded. He went on to add that this realization is reminiscent of Nick Carroway's final attitude toward Gatsby's dream in the novel, *The Great Gatsby*; "wonder at its purity and grandeur, dismay at its cost." The same might be said for the life and quest of Jack Kerouac.

■ Works Cited

Baker, Carlos, "Itching Feet," *Saturday Review*, September 7, 1959, pp. 19, 32-33.

Baro, Gene, "Restless Rebels in Search of—What?," *New York Herald Tribune Book Review*, September 15, 1957, p. 4.

Berrigan, Ted, "The Art of Fiction XLI," *Paris Review*, Summer, 1968, pp. 60-105.

Charters, Ann, *Dictionary of Literary Biography*, Volume 2: *American Writers Since World War II*, Gale, 1978, pp. 255-61.

Curley, Thomas F., "Everything Moves, but Nothing Is Alive," *Commonweal*, September 13, 1957.

Dardess, George, "Jack Kerouac," *Dictionary of Literary Biography*, Volume 16: *The Beats: Literary Bohemians in Postwar America*, Gale, 1983.

Dempsey, David, "In Pursuit of 'Kicks'," *New York Times Book Review*, September 8, 1957, p. 4.

Douglas, Ann, review of *The Portable Jack Kerouac*, *New York Times Book Review*, April 9, 1995.

Kerouac, Jack, *On the Road*, Viking, 1957.

Kerouac, Jack, *The Dharma Bums*, Viking, 1958.

McNally, Dennis, *Desolate Angel: Jack Kerouac, the Beat Generation, and America*, McGraw, 1979.

Millstein, Gilbert, review of *On the Road*, *New York Times*, September 5, 1957, p. 27.

Oates, Joyce Carol, "Down the Road," *New Yorker*, March 27, 1995, pp. 96-100.

Review of *The Portable Jack Kerouac* and *Selected Letters*, "A Second Act for Kerouac," *Chicago Tribune*, March 26, 1995, section 14, pp. 1, 9.

Theado, Matt, "The Jack Kerouac Revival," *Dictionary of Literary Biography Yearbook 1995*, Gale, 1996, pp. 272-80.

Time, October 31, 1969.

Vopat, Carole Gottlieb, "Jack Kerouac's 'On the Road'," *Midwestern Quarterly*, Summer, 1973, pp. 386-407.

■ For More Information See

BOOKS

Anstee, Rod, editor, *Jack Kerouac: The Bootleg Era: A Bibliography of Pirated Editions*, Water Row Press, 1994.

Authors in the News, Volume 1, Gale (Detroit, MI), 1976.

Balakian, Nona, and Charles Simmons, *The Creative Present: Notes on Contemporary American Fiction*, Doubleday (New York City), 1963.

Bartlett, Lee, *The Beats: Essays of Criticism*, McFarland (Jefferson, NC), 1981, pp. 115-26.

Cassady, Carolyn, *Heart Beat: My Life with Jack and Neal*, Creative Arts Book Co. (Berkley, CA), 1977.

Cassady, Carolyn, *Off the Road: My Years with Cassady, Kerouac, and Ginsberg*, Morrow (New York City), 1990.

Challis, Chris, *Quest for Kerouac*, Faber (Winchester, MA), 1984.

Charters, Ann, *Kerouac: A Biography*, Straight Arrow (San Francisco), 1973, reprinted, St. Martin's (New York City), 1994.

Charters, Ann, *A Bibliography of Works by Jack Kerouac, 1939-1975*, Phoenix Book Shop (New York City), 1975.

Clark, Tom, *Jack Kerouac*, Harcourt (San Diego, CA), 1984, reprinted, Paragon House (New York City), 1990.

Concise Dictionary of American Literary Biography: The New Consciousness, 1941-1968, Gale, 1987.

Contemporary Literary Criticism, Gale, Volume 1, 1973, Volume 2, 1974, Volume 3, 1975, Volume 5, 1976, Volume 14, 1980, Volume 29, 1984, Volume 61, 1990.

Cook, Bruce, *The Beat Generation*, Scribner (New York City), 1971.

Dictionary of Literary Biography Documentary Series, Volume 3, Gale, 1983.

Donaldson, Scott, editor, *On the Road: Text and Criticism*, Viking, 1979.

Feied, Frederick, *No Pie in the Sky: The Hobo as American Culture Hero in the Works of Jack London, John Dos Passos, and Jack Kerouac*, Citadel (Secaucus, NJ), 1964.

Fiedler, Leslie, *Waiting for the End*, Stein & Day (Briarcliff Manor, NY), 1964.

French, Warren, editor, *The Fifties: Fiction, Poetry, Drama*, Everett/Edwards (DeLand, FL), 1970.

French, Warren, *Jack Kerouac*, Twayne (Boston, MA), 1986.

Fuller, Edmund, *Man in Modern Fiction: Some Minority Opinions on Contemporary American Writings*, Random House (New York City), 1958.

Gaffie, Luc, *Jack Kerouac: The New Picaroon*, Postillion Press (Southfield, MI), 1977.

Gifford, Barry, *Kerouac's Town*, Capra (Santa Barbara, CA), 1973, revised edition, Creative Arts Book Co., 1977.

Gifford, Barry, and Lawrence Lee, *Jack's Book: An Oral Biography of Jack Kerouac*, St. Martin's (New York City), 1978, reprinted, 1994.

Ginsberg, Allen, *Allen Verbatim: Lectures on Poetry, Politics, Consciousness*, McGraw, 1974.

Hipkiss, Robert A., *Jack Kerouac: Prophet of the New Romanticism*, University of Kansas Press (Lawrence, KS), 1977.

Holmes, John Clellon, *Nothing More to Declare*, Dutton (New York City), 1967.

Huebel, Harry Russell, *Jack Kerouac*, Boise State University (Boise, ID), 1979.

Hunt, Tim, *Kerouac's Crooked Road: Development of a Fiction*, Archon Books (Hamden, CT), 1981.

Jarvis, Charles E., *Visions of Kerouac*, Ithaca Press (Lowell, MA), 1973, third edition, 1994.

Johnson, Joyce, *Minor Characters: A Young Woman's Coming-of-Age in the Beat Orbit of Jack Kerouac*, Anchor Books (New York City), 1994.

Jones, Granville H., *Lectures on Modern Novelists*, Carnegie Institute (Pittsburgh, PA), 1963.

Jones, James T., *A Map of Mexico City Blues: Jack Kerouac as Poet*, Southern Illinois University Press (Carbondale, IL), 1992.

Kerouac, Jack, *Lonesome Traveler*, McGraw, 1960.

Kerouac, Jack, and Allen Ginsberg, *Take Care of My Ghost, Ghost*, limited edition, Ghost Press, 1977.

Kerouac, Jack, and Carolyn Cassady, *Dear Carolyn: Letters to Carolyn Cassady*, Unspeakable Visions, 1983.

Lindberg, Gary, *The Confidence Man in American Literature*, Oxford University Press (Oxford, England), 1982.

McClure, Michael, *Scratching the Beat Surface: Essays on New Vision from Blake to Kerouac*, Penguin, 1994.

McDarragh, Fred W., *Kerouac and His Friends: A Beat Generation Album*, William Morrow (New York City), 1985.

McDarragh, Fred W., and Gloria S. McDarragh, *Beat Generation: Glory Days in Greenwich Village*, Schirmer (New York City), 1996.

Milewski, Robert J., *Jack Kerouac: An Annotated Bibliography of Secondary Sources, 1944-1979*, Scarecrow (Metuchen, NJ), 1981.

Montgomery, John, *The Kerouac We Knew: Unposed Portraits: Action Shots*, Fels & Firn (Kentfield, CA), 1982.

Moore, Harry T., editor, *Contemporary American Novelists*, Southern Illinois University Press (Carbondale, IL), 1964.

Motier, Donald, *Gerard: The Influence of Jack Kerouac's Brother on His Life and Writing*, Beaulier Press (Harrisburg, PA), 1991.

Nicosia, Gerald, *Memory Babe: A Critical Biography of Jack Kerouac*, Grove, 1983, reprinted, University of California Press (Berkeley, CA), 1994.

Nisonger, T. E., *Jack Kerouac: A Bibliography of Biographical and Critical Material, 1950-1979*, Bull Bibliography, 1980.

Parker, Brad, *Jack Kerouac: An Introduction*, Lowell Corporation for the Humanities (Lowell, MA), 1989.

Parkinson, Thomas, editor, *A Casebook on the Beat*, Crowell (New York City), 1961.

Podhoretz, Norman, *Doings and Undoings*, Farrar, Straus, 1964.

Tanner, Tony, *City of Words*, Harper (New York City), 1971.

Tytell, John, *Naked Angels: The Lives and Literature of the Beat Generation*, McGraw, 1976.

Waldmeir, Joseph J., editor, *Recent American Fiction*, Houghton (Boston, MA), 1963.

Weinreich, Regina, *The Spontaneous Poetics of Jack Kerouac: A Study of Fiction*, Southern Illinois University Press, 1987.

PERIODICALS

American Literature, May, 1974.
Atlantic, July, 1965.
Best Sellers, February 15, 1968.
Books, December, 1966.
Books Abroad, Summer, 1967.
Books and Bookmen, May, 1969.
Chicago Review, Winter-Spring, 1959.

Chicago Tribune, August 22, 1986; March 16, 1994, p. 8.
Commonweal, February 2, 1959.
Contemporary Literature, Summer, 1974.
Critique: Studies in Modern Fiction, Volume 14, number 3, 1973.
Detroit Free Press, November 13, 1986.
Detroit News, November 23, 1995, p. 3F.
Esquire, June, 1983, pp. 158-60, 162-64, 166-67.
Evergreen Review, Summer, 1958; Spring, 1959.
Harper's, October, 1959.
Hudson Review, winter, 1959-60; spring, 1967.
Illinois Quarterly, April 1973, pp. 52-61.
Listener, June 27, 1968.
Los Angeles Times, September 19, 1986; September 20, 1986; June 4, 1992, p. 1E.
National Observer, February 5, 1968; December 9, 1968.
New Republic, April 24, 1995, p. 43.
New Statesman, November 23, 1973.
Newsweek, December 19, 1960.
New York Post, March 10, 1959.
New York Review of Books, May 20, 1965; April 11, 1968.
New York Times, May 4, 1965; June 8, 1965; January 9, 1973; April 16, 1986; June 11, 1995, p. 8.
New York Times Book Review, May 2, 1965; February 26, 1967; February 18, 1968; January 28, 1973; April 9, 1995, p. 2.
Observer (London), November 19, 1967.
Observer Review, November 19, 1967.
Partisan Review, Volume 40, number 2, 1973.
Playboy, June, 1959.
Prairie Schooner, Spring, 1974.
Reporter, April 3, 1958.
Review of Contemporary Fiction, Volume 3, number 2, 1983; Spring, 1995, pp. 161-62.
Saturday Review, January 11, 1958; May 2, 1959; June 12, 1965; December 2, 1972.
Small Press Review, March, 1983.
South Atlantic Quarterly, Autumn, 1974.
Spectator, November 24, 1967; March 28, 1969; August 10, 1974; August 24, 1974.
Stand, Volume 16, number 2, 1975.
Tamarack Review, Spring, 1959.
Time, February 23, 1968.
Times Literary Supplement, May 26, 1966; February 1, 1968; March 27, 1969; April 6, 1973; November 2, 1973; September 13, 1974; April 22, 1977; September 1, 1995, p. 22.
Village Voice, September 18, 1957; November 12, 1958.
Virginia Quarterly Review, Spring, 1973.
Washington Post, October 22, 1969; August 2, 1982.

Washington Post Book World, April 8, 1973; March 12, 1995, pp. 1, 14.

OTHER

A Jack Kerouac ROMnibus (CD-ROM), Largely Literary Designs, 1995.
What Happened to Kerouac? (documentary film), produced by Richard Lerner, 1986.

■ **Obituaries**

PERIODICALS

Detroit Free Press, October 22, 1969.
L'Express, October 27-November 2, 1969.
Newsweek, November 3, 1969.
New York Times, October 22, 1969.
Publishers Weekly, November 3, 1969.
Rolling Stone, November 29, 1969.
Variety, October 29, 1969.
Village Voice, October 30, 1969; November 28, 1969.
Washington Post, October 22, 1969.*

—Sketch by J. Sydney Jones

Ken Kesey

■ Personal

Full name, Ken Elton Kesey; born September 17, 1935, in La Junta, CO; son of Fred A. and Geneva (maiden name, Smith) Kesey; married Faye Haxby, May 20, 1956; children: Shannon, Zane, Jed (deceased), Sunshine. *Education:* University of Oregon, B.A., 1957; Stanford University, graduate study, 1958-61, 1963.

■ Addresses

Home—85829 Ridgeway Rd., Pleasant Hill, OR 97401. *Agent*—Sterling Lord Literistic, Inc., 660 Madison Ave., New York, NY 10021.

■ Career

Multi-media artist and farmer. Night attendant in psychiatric Veterans Administration Hospital, Menlo Park, CA, 1961; president, Intrepid Trips, Inc. (motion picture company), 1964.

■ Awards, Honors

Woodrow Wilson fellowship; Saxton Fund fellowship, 1959; Distinguished Service award, State of Oregon, 1978; Robert Kirsch Award, *Los Angeles Times*, 1991.

■ Writings

One Flew Over the Cuckoo's Nest (novel), Viking, 1962, new edition with criticism, edited by John C. Pratt, 1973.

Sometimes a Great Notion (novel), Viking, 1964.

(Contributor) *The Last Whole Earth Catalog: Access to Tools*, Portola Institute, 1971.

(Editor with Paul Krassner and contributor) *The Last Supplement to the Whole Earth Catalog*, Portola Institute, 1971.

(Compiler and contributor) *Kesey's Garage Sale* (interviews and articles, including "Tools from My Chest," "An Impolite Interview with Ken Kesey," and the screenplay "Over the Border"), introduction by Arthur Miller, Viking, 1973.

(Author of introduction) Paul Krassner, editor, *Best of "The Realist": The Sixties' Most Outrageously Irreverent Magazine*, Running Press, 1984.

Demon Box (essays, poetry, and stories, including "The Day Superman Died," "Good Friday," "Finding Doctor Fung," "Run into the Great Wall," and "The Search for the Secret Pyramid"), Viking, 1986.

Little Trickler the Squirrel Meets Big Double the Bear (juvenile), Penguin, 1988.

(Under joint pseudonym O. U. Levon [an anagram for "University of Oregon novel"] with Robert Bluckner, Ben Bochner, James Finley, Jeff Forester, Bennett Huffman, Lynn Jeffress, Neil Lindstrom, H. Highwater Powers, Jane Sather, Charles Varani, Meredith Wadley, Lidia Yukman, and Ken Zimmerman, and author of introduction) *Caverns* (mystery novel), Penguin, 1989.

The Further Inquiry (autobiographical screenplay), Viking, 1990.

The Sea Lion (juvenile), Viking, 1991.

Sailor Song, Viking Penguin, 1992.

(With Ken Babbs) *Last Go Round: A Dime Western*, Viking Penguin, 1994.

Also author of two unpublished novels, "End of Autumn" and "Zoo," and "Seven Prayers by Grandma Whittier," an unfinished novel serialized between 1974 and 1981 in *Spit in the Ocean*, a magazine Kesey published sporadically during the 1970s and 1980s. His play, *Twister*, was first performed in 1994. Work included in anthologies, including *Stanford Short Stories 1962*, edited by Wallace Stegner and Richard Scowcroft, Stanford University Press, 1962. A collection of Kesey's manuscripts is housed at the University of Oregon.

■ Adaptations

One Flew Over the Cuckoo's Nest was adapted for the stage by Dale Wasserman and produced on Broadway at the Cort Theatre on November 13, 1963, revived in 1971, and adapted for film by United Artists in 1975; *Sometimes a Great Notion* was adapted for film by Universal in 1972.

■ Sidelights

Writer Ken Kesey has often said that he would rather live a novel than write one—be a lightning rod rather than a seismograph. A lightning rod is exactly what Kesey has been, attracting not only the admiration of the literary establishment with his early novel, *One Flew Over the Cuckoo's Nest*, but also the crackle and spark of a younger generation with his experiments with LSD and antics with the Merry Pranksters. "Kesey is a pivotal figure between the Beats and the Hippies," noted Ann Charters in *Dictionary of Literary Biography*, "the leader and chief chronicler of the activities of his associates, the Merry Pranksters." Along with Neal Cassady, of Jack Kerouac fame, Kesey helped to pioneer the psychedelic drug culture with its mixed-media "happenings," and in the doing became as much a folk hero for the hippie generation as Cassady had become for the Beats.

A down-home Oregon boy, voted most likely to succeed by his high school class in Springfield, Oregon, Kesey formed a new persona once at Stanford's school of creative writing in the late 1950s, assuming the avant garde aesthetics of the day—growing a beard, playing folk music, finding a new interest in Eastern religions, and using marijuana and psychedelics. In his critical study, *Ken Kesey*, Stephen L. Tanner noted the two-fold tugs of Kesey's life: "Ken Kesey's career as a writer can best be understood in relation to two geographical locations: western Oregon and the San Francisco Bay area. These are the centers for the important shaping influences of his life." Tanner goes on to describe the tension in Kesey's fiction as the push and pull between these two poles, "between country and city . . . between family roots and individual discovery; between traditional Christian values and those of a new counterculture; between respectability and outlawry; between old ways and rural life and dayglo paint and amplified rock music; and between the straight and drug cultures."

These tensions are clearly present in Kesey's two major works, and are in place also in recent fiction, including *Sailor Song*, his first novel after a nearly three-decade hiatus. Central to Kesey's work is the individual who stands up to the forces of a mechanized, soulless, authoritarian world, whether it be Randle Patrick McMurphy in *One Flew Over the Cuckoo's Nest* battling the metaphorical powers of the "Combine" as personified in Nurse Ratched, or Hank Stamper fighting a losing battle against the union which wants to organize all independent loggers in *Sometimes a Great Notion*. Kesey's rugged individualism harkens back to western themes, but his message goes beyond such easy labeling, and he also employs large doses of transcendental wisdom and consciousness expansion in both incident and theme.

A Hard Shell Baptist, Born and Raised

Kesey was born on September 17, 1935, in La Junta, Colorado, the first child of Fred and Geneva

Kesey, both of whom were products of a long line of farmers and ranchers. His forebears were, as he described the Stampers in *Sometimes a Great Notion,* "a stringy-muscled brood of restless and stubborn west-walkers." A second son, Joe, called Chuck by family and friends, was born three years later. Kesey spent most of his first ten years in Colorado. His initial visit west to Oregon came about when his father, grown restless with waiting to be called up for the navy in late 1941, took his family for a visit to his parents in Eugene, Oregon. For the next year the family stayed in the Eugene area, father Fred working in a local creamery. Once Fred was called up for service in World War II, the mother and her two sons returned to Colorado, where they remained until war's end. In 1946 the family returned permanently to the Eugene area, where Fred took up the dairy business.

Fred Kesey became a successful and well-liked leader in the business, founding a cooperative for dairy farmers and retailing under the name Darigold. Kesey was close to his father, a person he identified, as Tanner noted, "with the John Wayne image." Both father and son were stubborn and hard-headed, and Kesey early on learned a love for the outdoors from his father. He and his brother went duck and deer hunting and trout and salmon fishing with their dad. Raised in the Willamette Valley at a time before large population incursions, Kesey led a life close to nature and family. Weekly visits to Grandfather Kesey's farm involved big dinners and arm-wrestling contests with cousins and uncles. The Kesey clan was fiercely competitive, and Kesey was no exception to that rule. Additionally, storytelling was still a strong tradition of the post-frontier farming community, and the vernacular was rich from both the farming and logging trades. Kesey learned a love of language and of story from his rough-hewn relatives.

If Kesey learned the ways of the natural world from his father, he heard the word of God from his Baptist maternal grandmother, Grandma Smith. As Kesey told Linda Gaboriau in a *Crawdaddy* interview, he is "a hard shell Baptist, born and bred." A churchgoer and avid reader of the Bible, Kesey's grandmother instilled at least a modicum of her beliefs in her grandson. Decades later, in his compilation, *Kesey's Garage Sale,* Kesey reported that the Bible still topped the list of things he considered his personal tools, valid equipment for

any sort for living. The occurrence of a small epiphany when Kesey was an adolescent might also have contributed to his future literary endeavors. A stream that once ran through the Kesey backyard had been covered over with rocks and concrete, forming a sort of tunnel after the stream had dried up. One day, Kesey and his brother followed this tunnel into the darkness only to discover an accordion. Squeezed, the instrument emitted no sound. Taking it apart, Kesey discovered a note in the valve of one of the bellows, as he told Gordon Lish in *Genesis West.* The note read: "What the hell you looking in here for, Daisy Mae?" Kesey achieved something like enlightenment at that moment, he later related. That someone long ago had put this message in the accordion betting that someone else at some future time would read it was like a revelation to him. "A mystery for people to wonder about," Kesey told Lish. "Well, that's what I want for my books."

Kesey followed his father in another example—a love of reading. Fred Kesey was addicted to the works of Zane Grey, and young Kesey became so, as well. His love for that Western writer never really left Kesey, and he named his second son Zane after the author. Edgar Rice Burroughs also got considerable attention from the adolescent Kesey, as did comic books of the day. Kesey's love of the comic book form can be seen in his later works as well, a fact noted by more than one critic and reviewer. Kesey met his future wife, Faye Haxby, when they were both seventh-graders, working on class decorations. The two went together throughout high school in Springfield, where Kesey excelled in athletics, especially wrestling. His competitive spirit paid off in this endeavor, as it did in class work in general. Other youthful interests that have never left Kesey are a love of acting and magic. Sending away for Batman decals as a kid, Kesey was awarded with a supplement—a book of simple magic tricks. From that day on, Kesey learned the trade of a magician, loving to perform for friends and family. Soon he was on to ventriloquism and hypnotism. It was this interest in heightened consciousness that ultimately led him to experimenting with drugs. As he related to Gaboriau, he went "from hypnotism into dope. But it's always been the same trip, the same kind of research."

Kesey's interest in acting and stage illusions took precedence over writing in his high school and most of his college years. A love for acting led him to major in speech and communications at the nearby University of Oregon, while Faye attended Oregon State University in Corvallis. During summers, Kesey migrated to Hollywood in hopes of finding acting work, but the closest he came was working on various movie and television sets. Kesey's college career was a successful one by all standards. Recipient of the Fred Lowe Scholarship as the outstanding Northwest college wrestler, he placed second in the AAU tournament his senior year after dislocating his shoulder. He also participated in plays and won thespian awards for his efforts and maintained a high grade point average despite all his other commitments.

Kesey's college major also led him into writing for television and radio, his first formal training in the medium. From the outset, his writing was influenced by the visual techniques of television and film—the flashback, dissolve, quick cut, fade-in, and simultaneous action in different locations—techniques that would inform his later fiction. This taste of writing was enough to set Kesey penning short stories, some with the "flavor of Faulkner and Flannery O'Connor," according to Tanner. More and more, Kesey came to see himself as a writer rather than an actor, but in fact his entire life would eventually become theater: nonstop performance art.

The year before graduation, Faye and Kesey married, and upon graduation, Kesey definitely determined to become a writer. He worked for a year at the family creamery, writing his first novel, "End of Autumn," an unpublished work about college athletics. Finally recommended for and winning a Woodrow Wilson Fellowship, he attended Stanford's creative writing program, a decision that changed his life entirely.

Perry Lane

Stanford was a day's drive from Eugene, but a world away culturally, especially that segment of it into which Kesey fell. Classes in creative writing were taught by Wallace Stegner, Richard Scowcroft, Malcolm Cowley (who later became Kesey's editor at Viking), and Frank O'Connor. Equally influential were Kesey's fellow students who went on to make writing careers of their own: Larry McMurtry of *Lonesome Dove* fame,

nature writer and novelist Wendell Berry, and novelist Robert Stone.

Perhaps most influential of all, however, was Perry Lane, the block-long enclave where Kesey and Faye took up residence. A corner of bohemia on the Stanford campus, Perry Lane housed an eccentric collection of people who helped pioneer the use of LSD and many of the hallmarks of what became known as hippie culture. A microcosm of the Beat life of San Francisco's North Beach, Perry Lane secured Kesey's liberation from the Baptist, rural, sports-oriented world of his youth. In a tape-recorded discussion of his early years quoted by Tanner, Kesey admitted that Perry Lane was the most important world for him: "all that came before led to it; all that comes after will be the results of it." Under the influence of Jack Kerouac's recently published *On the Road*, Kesey began his own Beat novel, "Zoo," a story of North Beach which won him the $2,000 Saxton prize from Stanford, but which was rejected by several publishers and remains unpublished today.

It was a fellow inhabitant of Perry Lane, Vic Lovell, who first turned Kesey on to drug experiments being conducted at the Veterans Administration Hospital at Menlo Park. Participants were paid $20 a session for experimenting with drugs such as LSD, peyote-derived mescaline, and psilocybin. At the same time, to supplement his income, Kesey took a job as night attendant at the psychiatric ward of the Veterans Hospital. The coincidence of these two events marked another turning point in Kesey's life and career.

One Flew Over the Cuckoo's Nest

As Charters noted in *Dictionary of Literary Biography*, "Kesey became absorbed in the drug experiments at the hospital and in the life of the psychiatric ward at his night job. Sometimes he would go to work high on hallucinogens and feel able to see into the faces of the patients, and one night a vision came to him under the influence of peyote: the hallucinated face of an American Indian." It was this vision that inspired Kesey to begin a new novel, one set in a psychiatric ward and narrated by his visionary Native American. The resulting work was *One Flew Over the Cuckoo's Nest*, a "brilliant first novel," according to a critic in *Time*, and a novel that has found its way into the canon, to be taught both at high schools and

The 1975 film *One Flew Over the Cuckoo's Nest*, starring Jack Nicholson, received Academy Awards for best actor, best actress, best director, best adapted screenplay, and best picture.

colleges, produced on Broadway, and filmed in an award-winning movie. Over the years, the novel has sold millions of copies worldwide and remains an anthem, a soul-cry for the nonconformist individual battling the powers of conformity.

Kesey began writing the novel during his stints at the Veterans Hospital, some of it composed under the effect of drugs. By this time he was no longer an official student of the Stanford creative writing program, but was allowed to sit in on a class taught by Malcolm Cowley in the fall of 1960. Cowley himself had a long and distinguished career both as a writer and an editor. He had written of the Lost Generation of Hemingway and company in Paris of the 1920s, and had most recently edited the Beat writer Jack Kerouac at Viking. In Kesey, he saw something new and original and encouraged the young man to go forward with his novel, making suggestions especially as to narrative problems—the incorporation of his peyote-induced visions into a coherent dramatic fabric. Kesey was a quick take, and reworked his novel as it continued to grow. When it was finished, he sent it off to Cowley, now back at Viking, and the novel was immediately taken by that prestigious publishing house.

Set in a mental hospital somewhere in the Northwest, *One Flew Over the Cuckoo's Nest* is "tightly organized," according to Tanner, writing in *Dictionary of Literary Biography*, "consisting of four symmetrical parts linked by consistent patterns of imagery associated with the opposition of nature and the machine." The book is narrated by Chief Bromden, an enormous schizophrenic patient at the hospital, a mixture of white and American Indian cultures. The Chief has managed to stay out of the hands of the dreaded "Combine," the leveling powers of authority, by playing deaf and mute. Many of Kesey's drug-induced visions of society are, in fact, introduced through the Chief, who is something of an innocent witness to the microcosm of cruelty within the confines of the ward, where supposedly normative behavior is forced on patients. The Chief sees the desire of the staff to control the lives of the patients as deriving from electronic circuitry behind the hospital's walls.

Into this controlled environment prances Randle Patrick McMurphy, a gambling, swaggering "hundred-percent American con man," as he describes himself in the novel. McMurphy has, in fact, conned his way into the mental ward to avoid hard labor at a state work farm. McMurphy breathes new life into the sterile life of the ward, bucking up the spirits of the hen-pecked, intellectual Harding, and of Billy Bibbit who is dominated by his mother. But McMurphy's antics soon bring him face to face with the ultimate authority figure, Nurse Ratched, or Big Nurse, whose trick is to divide and conquer in the ward. If the red-haired, fast-talking McMurphy is something of an arrogantly masculine hero to the men, he is a continual threat to Ratched and her authority and power.

McMurphy soon has the men out on a fishing expedition and later throws a wild party at the hospital during which Bibbit loses his virginity to a prostitute. McMurphy thereafter attempts unsuccessfully to escape, and Bibbit, after Nurse Ratched threatens to tell his mother about his immorality, kills himself. Thus, McMurphy is finally driven to attacking Nurse Ratched. Restrained, he is ultimately lobotomized to level him out, to make him "normal." But Chief Bromden denies Ratched her victory: He smothers McMurphy and subsequently escapes to Canada, healthy and sane.

Upon publication, Kesey's book won favorable reviews in popular magazines and newspapers. Kesey's blending of cinematic techniques with a colloquial, hallucinated prose style was a new phenomenon, and won him praise and a wide readership. With the advent of the 1970s, Kesey's anti-authoritarian message and the structural complexity of his novel began to gain scholarly attention, as well, and the work has now become standard academic reading despite some criticism for alleged immorality. Reviewers and critics have viewed the book variously as an updated Western with the white man and Indian duo firmly in place, as a biblical allegory with McMurphy performing a Christ-like sacrifice with his lobotomy, and as a straight ahead adventure-drama about the individual's struggle for freedom from institutionalized repression of any sort. Other critics have debated alleged sexism and racism in the novel, as the main symbol of oppression is the female Nurse Ratched, along with her assistants, primarily black.

Writing in *Books*, Rose Feld noted soon after publication of *One Flew Over the Cuckoo's Nest* that "Undoubtedly there will be controversy over some of the material in Ken Kesey's novel, but there can be none about his talent. His is a powerful book . . . written with sustained vitality and force which hold the reader until the final word." Feld concluded that "this is a first novel of special worth." William Peden, writing in *Saturday Review*, largely concurred with this assessment, dubbing the book "extremely impressive," and noting that beneath the "suspense-charged action" and beyond the "violence and horseplay and the exaggeration and the comedy," Kesey presented "a continuous life-and-death struggle between good and evil, tyranny and freedom, love and hate." Peden found that Kesey created "a world that is convincing, alive, and glowing. . . . His is a large, robust talent, and he has written a large, robust book." Reviewing the novel in *Critique: Studies in Modern Fiction*, Irving Malin called the book "Gothic," noting that in Kesey's world, the categories of sane and insane are turned around. "The insane do *see*," Malin wrote, "they are less innocent than the slaves of the Combine. . . . In the upside down world, the 'cuckoo's nest,' 'insane' and 'sane' are meaningless words." Malin concluded that *One Flew Over the Cuckoo's Nest* was "an honest, claustrophobic, stylistically brilliant first novel which makes us shiver as we laugh—paradoxically, it keeps us 'in balance' by revealing our madness."

Writing in the *Explicator*, William S. Doxey went on to attempt an explanation of Kesey's title. Initially, Doxey pointed out, it is clear that it comes from the children's folk rhyme of which two lines are cited in the novel's epigraph: " . . . one flew east, one flew west / One flew over the cuckoo's nest." An obvious reading of "cuckoo's nest" would derive from the colloquial term for being insane, "an easily understood metaphor for the setting," according to Doxey. However, Doxey also noted that the actual cuckoo bird has no nest, that it lays its eggs in the nests of other birds who are tricked into raising cuckoo offspring as their own. In this reading, McMurphy might have planted the seed of rebellion in the minds of the other men in the ward, enabling them to "fly" over or out of the cuckoo's nest.

Other reviewers have focussed on the various messages the book may or may not communicate. Richard Blessing observed the Western frontier message in a review in *Journal of Popular Culture*: "Essentially, the McMurphy who enters the ward is a frontier hero, an anachronistic paragon of rugged individualism, relentless energy, capitalistic shrewdness, virile coarseness, and productive strength. He is Huck Finn with muscles, Natty Bumppo with pubic hair. He is the descendant of the pioneer who continually fled civilization and its feminizing and gentling influences." Thomas H. Fick enlarged on this frontier theme in *Rocky Mountain Review of Language and Literature*, noting that "McMurphy pays the steep but unavoidable price of monolithic heroism on the modern frontier: he chooses to share himself in the end and must pay with his life. *Cuckoo's Nest* is a powerful novel which effectively translates into contemporary terms the enduring American concern with a freedom found only in—or between—irreconcilable oppositions."

Several reviewers have noted McMurphy's Christlike similarities, both in the shock-therapy sessions in which he is laid out as if on the cross, and in his final sacrifice for his fellow inmates—his lo-

botomy and death. Ronald Wallace, writing in *The Last Laugh: Form and Affirmation in the Contemporary American Comic Novel*, while pointing out the comic and comic-book origins of Kesey's novel, also draws attention to "allusions to the Christian story" in three main episodes: "the fishing trip, the shock therapy, and the orgy." Wallace also noted that "at the end, Bromden participates in a comic communion, partaking of McMurphy's body by killing it."

If McMurphy was a quintessential Western hero for some, he was sexism and racism on two legs for other critics. One of the opening salvoes in this debate was fired by Marcia L. Falk in a letter to the editor in the *New York Times*, December 5, 1971. Falk asked why the villain of the piece, Nurse Ratched, had to be a woman, and answered her own question: "because Kesey hates and fears women." Falk also leveled the charge of white

In the 1960s Kesey traveled in this bus with the Merry Pranksters, a group who shared his interest in hallucinogenic drugs.

racism at the play adaptation of the novel. Other critics and feminist reviewers have added to the charges. Robert Forrey, for example, in *Modern Fiction Studies*, claimed that "the premise of the novel is that women ensnare, emasculate, and, in some cases, crucify men." Such criticisms have been met on many fronts. One reviewer noted that as the book was narrated through the distorted vision of Chief Bromden, any sexism or racism was due to that narrator and not McMurphy's actions. Others point out that nurses at mental institutions tended to be women when Kesey was writing; workers in the wards often were black. Wallace, in *The Last Laugh*, noted that there was no misogyny intended in Kesey's portrayal. And Janet R. Sutherland, writing in *English Journal*, concluded that "*One Flew Over the Cuckoo's Nest* is not obscene, racist, or immoral, although it does contain language and scenes which by common taste would be so considered. Like all great literature, the book attempts to give an accurate picture of some part of the human condition, which is less than perfect." Tanner, in his critical study, *Ken Kesey*, also observed that the alleged obscenity in the novel should be looked at as a means rather than an end. "McMurphy is a coarse and vulgar personality, but the victory wrought by him is not merely a triumph of coarseness and vulgarity." Tanner advised that McMurphy's example "should not be taken on face value; it is symbolic on an unconventional, almost cartoon level of values that are conventional in the most positive and universal sense: self-reliance, compassion for the weak, hope, perseverance, self-sacrifice, and harmony with nature."

Sometimes a Great Notion

Kesey was too busy writing to listen to the critics. Immediately after publication of *One Flew Over the Cuckoo's Nest*, Kesey and his wife returned to Oregon for the summer to gather material for his next novel. Hanging out with loggers in bars and on their way to and from work, he collected stories and language that would make his new book breathe life. In the fall, he returned to Stanford and worked on the new novel, but the quiet literary life was not for Kesey. A whirlwind of energy spun off from the Beat generation blew into his life. Neal Cassady, sidekick of Kerouac on their cross-country adventures, drove up in a Jeep one night, and the two men became fast friends. Cassady was something of a McMurphy come to life, a fast-talking con man in his own right, having served two years in San Quentin for possession of marijuana. As Charters noted in *Dictionary of Literary Biography*, "Cassady fueled his energy with amphetamines, but he also shared Kesey's interest in hallucinogenic drugs." Cassady fit in perfectly with the group on Perry Lane, who had progressed beyond the LSD-laced bowl of Kool-Aid to form a band of self-dubbed Merry Pranksters, out to turn the straight world on . . . or at least on its head. Kesey soon bought a house in nearby, but far more secluded, La Honda. He also purchased an old International Harvester bus which the band painted day-glo colors. Cassady was elected their driver on trips.

Meanwhile, Kesey's Oregon novel kept growing. *Sometimes a Great Notion* tells the story of a logging family who defy a labor union as well as the entire local community by going it alone during a strike. Set in and near the fictional logging town called Wakonda, the story revolves around the competition of two half-brothers, Hank Stamper, the rugged individual fighting the union, and Lee, the intellectual aesthete—two sides to Kesey's own character. Summoned by Hank to help out during the strike, Lee returns to Oregon in search of more than roots. He is also set on revenge for the seduction of his biological mother by Hank. He gets his chance with Hank's wife, Viv, who eventually leaves the brothers to battle without her, and they do come to understand each other better by novel's end.

Sometimes a Great Notion is "a large and ambitious novel," according to Tanner, writing in *Dictionary of Literary Biography*, told in both first and third person. It is a stylistic romp for Kesey, as well, employing such devices as parenthetical remarks, capital letters to reflect absurdities, and time shifts that allow for expressionistic character development. Comparing Kesey to William Faulkner and Thomas Wolfe, Granville Hicks in the *Saturday Review* commented that Kesey "is, indeed, an extravagant writer . . . but most of the time he has himself under control." In general, critical response to *Sometimes a Great Notion* was nowhere near as favorable as it was for *One Flew Over the Cuckoo's Nest*. Irving Malin provided cautionary advice for the author in *Books Abroad*. "Kesey wants to eat the whole world. But he does not realize that such Captain Marvel-like desire can be destructive, especially to his real talent. . . . In flexing his muscles, he wounds himself. His great notion,

If you enjoy the works of Ken Kesey, you may also want to check out the following books and films:

Aidan Chambers, *The Toll Bridge*, 1995.
Chris Crutcher, *Ironman*, 1995.
Jan Slepian, *The Night of the Bozos*, 1983.
The King of Hearts, starring Alan Bates, 1966.

which does not do justice to his Gothic muse, is admirable but suicidal."

Once again, however, Kesey was too busy with other concerns to listen to the critics. To commemorate publication of this second book, Kesey and his Merry Pranksters initiated their legendary trip to the East—legendary in that it was later recorded by the pop-journalist Tom Wolfe in his *The Electric Kool-Aid Acid Test.* In the course of his travels, Kesey met Timothy Leary, the guru of hallucinogens, and Jack Kerouac, of Beat fame. The poet Allen Ginsberg also became a friend back in California, and for the next few years, Kesey lived a chaotic life of happenings and Merry Prankster be-ins and acid tests. This high-life came screeching to a halt, however, when Kesey was arrested for marijuana possession in 1965, and then fled to Mexico, a "tarnished Galahad" as the presiding judge called him, to escape serving jail time. But after six months on the run, and a near-death experience for his son, Jed, Kesey came back to California and served a half-year sentence in the San Mateo Sheriff's Honor Camp. Thereafter, Kesey and his family resettled in Oregon, near his brother's and father's farms, in Pleasant Hill, close to Eugene.

Sounds of Silence

Kesey left the fast life behind, and he also left writing behind for the time. Hippie pilgrims came to call, but Kesey was no longer the psychedelic guru; he had become a farmer and family man. After the death of Neal Cassady in 1968, he was moved to write "The Day after Superman Died," a story later included in his 1986 collection *Demon Box*, but otherwise his creative efforts for the next decades were spent other than in piling words together to create novels. He was a con-

tributor to *The Whole Earth Catalogue* and for several years put out his own journal, *Spit in the Ocean*, which carried his and other contributors' works. He also ran the family farm.

He put his revolt against the excesses of the 1960s into print with his 1973 *Kesey's Garage Sale*, a loose, comic-book compilation of Prankster archives and assorted writings which included the screenplay of his flight to Mexico, "Over the Border." In that screenplay, Kesey seemingly turns his back on the former life of drugs and pranks. Devin Deboree, the Kesey double in the screenplay, is described at the end as someone who had "amped out on too much something; I don't know whether it was psychedelics, electronics or heroics." In the end, Deboree/Kesey was looking for a way to get off his own bus.

Oregon provided a refuge for Kesey, and over the years his silence became his trademark. Unlike the silence of J. D. Salinger, however, Kesey's was taken by critics to mean he had no more creative juices left. His *Demon Box* did little to convince these critics that he was back on track again. Daniel Pyne observed in the *Los Angeles Times Book Review* that Kesey's new book offered "illumination," but for others it was fire without light. Henry Allen, writing in *Washington Post Book World*, noted that Kesey "comes off the way he always has, as a big, strong, charming, failed, talented, childish, self-indulgent and now middle-aged man trying to fight back despair with main force. . . . But maybe the power will switch back on and he'll finally give us the legendary novel he's supposed to be writing about Alaska."

For Kesey, such criticism stung, but he took it as a given that the Eastern literary establishment would never understand what he was trying to do. His activities over the years included media events and theater; he lived life rather than wrote it. He helped to raise a family and lost his son in a tragic traffic accident. He also taught creative writing at his alma mater, and wrote, in concert with his students, a mystery, *Caverns*, which the class subsequently published. Meanwhile, Kesey also kept on writing that novel about Alaska.

Kesey Rebounds

Kesey published a couple of juvenile novels in the late 1980s and early 1990s, as well as an autobiographical play about the Prankster days, *The Further Inquiry*. In 1992 he finally published the big Alaska book, *Sailor Song*, set in the early twenty-first century, and featuring Ike Sallas who lives in the fishing village of Kuniak. The village is invaded by a production company come to film the Eskimo legend *The Sea Lion* (the title of one of Kesey's juvenile books). A reviewer in *Publishers Weekly* commented that Kesey's "baroque humor" was "in top form" as he "skewers religious cults, organized lodges and land developers," and the reviewer concluded that *Sailor Song* was "a gargantuan novel of epic dimensions that feeds on the need for love and heroes at a time when 'the hero business ain't so hot.'" The novel garnered an impressive array of praise and substantial sales. Kesey's 1994 *Last Go Round: A Dime Western*, about Oregon's Pendleton round-up, coauthored with his longtime friend, Ken Babbs, "portrays rodeo as a show mounted at the cost of both human and animal life," according to a *Publishers Weekly* critic.

Kesey, who suffered a mild stroke in the fall of 1997, continues to live and work in Oregon. His achievement has largely been pegged to his first novel, *One Flew Over the Cuckoo's Nest*, but as Charters wrote in *Dictionary of Literary Biography*, Kesey "is one of America's most significant contemporary authors. . . . His prophecy is not the nihilistic message of coming doom but the optimistic belief in available grace, and his books are a vital testimony to the endurance of hope and humor in this country's literature." Once dubbed the "Paul Bunyan of the Beat movement" by the poet Lawrence Ferlinghetti, Kesey personifies, as Charters concluded, "the spontaneity, humor and hope that is at the heart of Beat literature."

■ Works Cited

Allen, Henry, "Ken Kesey on the Road Again," *Washington Post Book World*, August 19, 1986, p. 9.

Blessing, Richard, *Journal of Popular Culture*, Winter, 1981.

Charters, Ann, "Ken Kesey," *Dictionary of Literary Biography*, Volume 16: *The Beats: Literary Bohemians in Postwar America*, Gale, 1983, pp. 306-15.

Doxey, William S., *Explicator*, December, 1973, p. 16.

Falk, Marcia L., letter to the editor, reprinted in *One Flew Over the Cuckoo's Nest: Text and Criticism*, Viking, 1973, pp. 450-53.

Feld, Rose, "War inside the Walls," *Books*, February 25, 1962, p. 4.

Fick, Thomas H., "The Hipster, the Hero, and the Psychic Frontier in 'One Flew Over the Cuckoo's Nest'," *Rocky Mountain Review of Language and Literature*, Numbers 1-2, 1989, pp. 19-32.

Forrey, Robert, *Modern Fiction Studies*, Volume 21, 1975.

Gaboriau, Linda, "Ken Kesey: Summing up the '60's; Sizing up the '70's," *Crawdaddy*, December, 1972, p. 38.

Hicks, Granville, "Beatnik in Lumberjack Country," *Saturday Review*, July 25, 1964, pp. 21-22.

Kesey, Ken, *One Flew Over the Cuckoo's Nest*, Viking, 1962.

Kesey, Ken, *Sometimes a Great Notion*, Viking, 1964.

Kesey, Ken, *Kesey's Garage Sale*, Viking, 1973.

Review of *Last Go Round: A Dime Western*, *Publishers Weekly*, April 25, 1994, pp. 53-54.

Lish, Gordon, "What the Hell You Looking in Here for, Daisy Mae?," *Genesis West*, Number 2, 1963, p. 27.

Malin, Irving, "Ken Kesey: 'One Flew Over the Cuckoo's Nest'," *Critique: Studies in Modern Fiction*, Fall, 1962, pp. 81-84.

Malin, Irving, *Books Abroad*, Spring, 1965, p. 218.

Review of *One Flew Over the Cuckoo's Nest*, *Time*, February 16, 1962, p. 90.

Peden, William, "Gray Regions of the Mind," *Saturday Review*, April 14, 1962, pp. 49-50.

Pyne, Daniel, review of *Demon Box*, *Los Angeles Times Book Review*, August 31, 1986, pp. 1, 6.

Review of *Sailor Song*, *Publishers Weekly*, June 22, 1992, p. 45.

Sutherland, Janet R., "A Defense of Ken Kesey's 'One Flew Over the Cuckoo's Nest'," *English Journal*, January, 1972, pp. 28-31.

Tanner, Stephen L., *Dictionary of Literary Biography*, Volume 2: *American Novelists since World War II*, Gale, 1978, pp. 261-66.

Tanner, Stephen L., *Ken Kesey*, Twayne, 1983.

Wallace, Ronald, "What Laughter Can Do: Ken Kesey's 'One Flew Over the Cuckoo's Nest'," *The Last Laugh: Form and Affirmation in the Contemporary American Comic Novel*, University of Missouri Press, 1979, pp. 90-114.

■ For More Information See

BOOKS

Acton, Jay, Alan Le Mond, and Parker Hodges, *Mug Shots: Who's Who in the New Earth*, World Publishing, 1972.

Allen, Mary, *The Necessary Blankness: Women in Major American Fiction of the Sixties*, University of Illinois Press, 1976.

Billingsley, Ronald G., *The Artistry of Ken Kesey*, University of Oregon, 1971.

Concise Dictionary of American Literary Biography, 1968-1988, Gale, 1989.

Contemporary Literary Criticism, Gale, Volume 1, 1973, Volume 3, 1975, Volume 6, 1976, Volume 11, 1979, Volume 46, 1987, Volume 64, 1990.

Cook, Bruce, *The Beat Generation*, Scribner, 1971.

Harris, Charles B., *Contemporary American Novelists of the Absurd*, College & University Press, 1971.

Krassner, Paul, *How a Satirical Editor Became a Yippie Conspirator in Ten Easy Years*, Putnam, 1971.

Labin, Suzanne, *Hippies, Drugs, and Promiscuity*, Arlington House, 1972.

Leeds, Barry H., *Ken Kesey*, Ungar, 1981.

Perry, Paul, *On the Bus: The Complete Guide to the Legendary Trip of Ken Kesey and the Merry Pranksters and the Birth of the Counterculture*, Thunder's Mouth Press, 1990.

Porter, M. Gilbert, *The Art of Grit: Ken Kesey's Fiction*, University of Missouri Press, 1982.

Wolfe, Tom, *The Electric Kool-Aid Acid Test*, Farrar, Straus, 1968.

PERIODICALS

Annals of the American Academy of Political and Social Science, Volume 376, 1968.

CEA Critic, Volume 37, 1975.

Cithara, Volume 12, 1972.

Critique: Studies in Modern Fiction, Volume 13, 1971.

Esquire, September, 1992, pp. 158-210.

Free You, Volume 2, 1968.

Journal of American Studies, Volume 5, 1971.

Journal of Narrative Technique, Volume 9, 1979.

Lex et Scientia, Volume 13, issues 1-2, 1977.

Modern Fiction Studies, Volume 19, 1973.

Nation, February 23, 1974.

New Statesman, October 10, 1986.

New Yorker, April 21, 1962; December 1, 1975.

New York Herald Tribune, February 25, 1962; July 27, 1964; August 2, 1964.

New York Review of Books, September 10, 1964.

New York Times, July 27, 1964; January 18, 1966; March 12, 1966; October 21, 1966; August 4, 1986, September 17, 1992, July 7, 1994.

New York Times Book Review, February 4, 1962; August 2, 1964; August 18, 1968; October 7, 1973; August 4, 1986; September 14, 1986; December 31, 1989; January 21, 1990; December 9, 1990, July 10, 1994.

Northwest Review, Spring, 1963; Spring, 1977.

People, March 22, 1976.

Rolling Stone, March 7, 1970; September 27, 1973; July 18, 1974; October 5, 1989.

Time, July 24, 1964; February 12, 1965; September 8, 1986, April 29, 1996, p. 73.

Times Literary Supplement, February 24, 1966; February 25, 1972.

Voice Literary Supplement, February 2, 1990.

Washington Post, June 9, 1974.

Western American Literature, Volume 9, 1974; Volume 10, 1975; Volume 22, 1987.

Wisconsin Studies in Contemporary Literature, Volume 5, 1964; Volume 7, 1966.*

—Sketch by J. Sydney Jones

Barry Levinson

■ Personal

Born April 6, 1942, in Baltimore, MD; son of Irv (in appliance business) and Vi (Krichinsky) Levinson; married Valerie Curtin (a screenwriter and actor; divorced, 1982); married Diana Mona (an artist); children: Jack, Sam, Patrick Mona, Michelle Mona. *Education:* Attended Community College of Baltimore and American University. *Politics:* Democrat.

■ Addresses

Office—Baltimore Pictures, 5555 Melrose Ave., Los Angeles, CA 90038. *Agent*—Creative Artists Agency, 9830 Wilshire Blvd., Beverly Hills, CA 90212.

■ Career

Actor, producer, director, and writer. Member of stand-up comedy and writing team with actor Craig T. Nelson, c. 1969-72; actor in television shows, including *The Lohman and Barkley Show,* 1969, *The Tim Conway Comedy Hour,* 1970, and *The Carol Burnett Show,* 1974-75. Actor in motion pictures, including *Silent Movie,* 1976, *High Anxiety,* 1978, and *History of the World, Part I,* 1981. Director of motion pictures, including *Diner,* 1982, *The Natural,* 1984, *Young Sherlock Holmes,* 1985, *Good Morning, Vietnam,* 1987, *Tin Men,* 1987, *Rain Man,* 1988, *Avalon,* 1990, *Bugsy,* 1991, *Toys,* 1992, *Jimmy Hollywood,* 1994, *Disclosure,* 1994, *Sleepers,* 1996, *Wag the Dog,* 1998, and *Sphere,* 1998. Producer or co-producer of motion pictures, including *Bugsy,* 1991, *Toys,* 1992, *Jimmy Hollywood,* 1994, *Disclosure,* 1994, *Sleepers,* 1996, *Donnie Brasco,* 1997, *Home Fries,* 1997, *Wag the Dog,* 1998, and *Sphere,* 1998. Director and producer of television productions, including *Homicide: Life on the Street,* NBC, 1993—. Executive producer of television productions, including *The Second Civil War,* HBO, 1997, and *Oz,* HBO, 1997. Cofounder and president of production company Baltimore Pictures, Hollywood, CA, 1989—. *Member:* Directors Guild, Writers Guild, Screen Actors Guild.

■ Awards, Honors

Emmy Awards, Academy of Television Arts and Sciences, best writing in a variety or music program, 1974 and 1975, and outstanding achievement in a comedy, variety, or music series, 1976, all for *The Carol Burnett Show;* Academy Award nominations, best original screenplay, 1979, for *. . . And Justice for All,* and 1982, for *Diner;* Academy Award, best director, and award from Directors Guild for outstanding achievement, both 1988, both for *Rain Man;* Writers Guild Award for best screenplay, and Academy Award nomination, best original screenplay, 1990, both for *Avalon;* Academy Award nominations, best director and best picture, both 1991, Golden Globe Award for best picture, and Associated Foreign Press Award for best picture, all for *Bugsy;* outstanding directorial achievement for dramatic series nomination, Directors Guild, 1993, Emmy Award for best director, Academy of Television Arts and Sciences, 1993, Peabody Award, 1993 and 1995, Writers Guild Award, 1994 and 1995, and Nancy Susan Reynolds Award, 1996, all for *Homicide: Life on the Street.*

■ Writings

SCREENPLAYS; AND DIRECTOR

Diner, Metro-Goldwyn-Mayer/United Artists, 1982.
Tin Men, Buena Vista, 1987.
Avalon, TriStar, 1990.
(With Valerie Curtin; and producer) *Toys,* Twentieth Century-Fox, 1992.
(And producer) *Jimmy Hollywood,* Paramount, 1994.
(And producer) *Sleepers* (based on a book by Lorenzo Carcaterra), Warner Bros., 1996.

OTHER SCREENPLAYS

(With Mel Brooks, Ron Clark, and Rudy DeLuca) *Silent Movie,* Twentieth Century-Fox, 1976.
(With Mel Brooks, Ron Clark, and Rudy DeLuca) *High Anxiety,* Twentieth Century-Fox, 1978.
(With Valerie Curtin) *. . . And Justice for All,* Columbia, 1979.
(With Valerie Curtin) *Inside Moves,* Associated Film Distributors, 1980.
(With Valerie Curtin) *Best Friends,* Warner Bros., 1982.
(With Valerie Curtin and Robert Klane) *Unfaithfully Yours* (adapted from Preston Sturges's film of the same title), Twentieth Century-Fox, 1984.

TELEVISION SERIES

(With Craig T. Nelson and others) *The Lohman and Barkley Show,* NBC-TV, 1969. (With Craig T. Nelson and others) *The Tim Conway Comedy Hour,* CBS-TV, 1970.

(With Craig T. Nelson and others) *The Marty Feldman Comedy Machine,* ABC-TV, 1972.
(With Craig T. Nelson and others) *The John Byner Comedy Hour,* CBS-TV, 1972.
(With others) *The Carol Burnett Show,* CBS-TV, 1974-75.

BOOKS

Avalon, Tin Men, and Diner: Three Screenplays, Atlantic Monthly Press, 1990.
David Thompson, editor, *Levinson on Levinson,* Faber and Faber, 1992.

■ Sidelights

Academy award-winning director, screenwriter, and producer Barry Levinson began his show business career in the late 1960s as a comedian and found success in every Hollywood path he took, but most notably as a director of movies, including *Wag the Dog, Diner, The Natural,* and *Good Morning, Vietnam.* Critics such as Peter Stack of the *San Francisco Chronicle* have hailed Levinson as a golden talent. Stack proclaimed that in his movie *Sleepers,* Levinson showed "a genius for depicting male bonding in shades of humor mixed with sorrow."

The Baltimore native reached a milestone in his career in 1988 when he won the best director Oscar for *Rain Main.* Then, in 1991, *Bugsy,* which he directed and produced, was nominated for ten Academy Awards including best picture and best director. As a screenwriter, Levinson has received three Academy Award nominations for *. . . And Justice for All, Diner* and *Avalon.* Levinson went on to launch his own production company, Baltimore Pictures, which produced the critically acclaimed movies *Quiz Show* and *Donnie Brasco.* Then he was drawn to television where he wowed audiences with *Homicide: Life on the Streets,* a police drama that takes on a documentary look by using hand-held cameras, giving viewers the sense that they are actually following real-life homicide detectives.

The son of an electronics businessman, Levinson was born in Baltimore and delights in taking his audiences back to his hometown. *Homicide: Life on the Streets* and a trilogy of his films—*Diner, Tin Men,* and *Avalon*—were all set in Maryland's larg-

Levinson wrote the screenplay for *Diner*, his directorial debut, in which future stars Kevin Bacon, Mickey Rourke, Daniel Stern, and Timothy Daly are part of a group of friends in Baltimore making the difficult transition into manhood.

est city. Before his entertainment career, Levinson sold encyclopedias and used cars while attending junior college in Baltimore. He landed a part-time job at a television station after he transferred to American University in Washington, D.C., where he majored in broadcast journalism. Levinson has never forgotten how to tell his audiences a story.

Westward Bound

After seven years in and out of school (without getting a degree), Levinson drove to Los Angeles, where he began taking acting lessons. While Levinson isn't known for his acting, his resume does include small parts in *Jimmy Hollywood, Quiz Show, Diamonds on the Silver Screen, Rain Man, History of the World: Part I, High Anxiety*, and *Silent Movie*. Early in his career Levinson worked as a stand-up comedian, and his partner at one

point was Craig T. Nelson, who went on to star in the popular television sitcom *Coach*. Meanwhile, Levinson began dating Valerie Curtin, an actress, whom he married in 1975. Levinson landed jobs as a writer for television's *The Lohman and Barkley Show, The Tim Conway Comedy Hour, The Marty Feldman Comedy Machine*, and *The Carol Burnett Show*, which later won an Emmy Award as television's best comedy. While he worked on *The Carol Burnett Show*, Levinson also launched his screenwriting career when he collaborated on a script for Mel Brooks's 1976 comedy *Silent Movie*, a farce about a band of bungling filmmakers. He also contributed to the screenplay for Brooks's *High Anxiety*, which is a spoof of film director Alfred Hitchcock's thrillers, *Vertigo, The Birds*, and *Psycho*.

In 1979, Levinson and Curtin wrote . . . *And Justice for All*, a black comedy about the American legal system. Although it was nominated for a best original screenplay Oscar by the Academy of Motion Pictures, it was not received favorably by critics. Undeterred, Levinson and Curtin teamed up again. Their next project was *Inside Moves*, a film about the patrons of a blue-collar bar. The characters included a suicide attempt survivor, an aspiring basketball player, and a prostitute. A *TV Guide* reviewer gave *Inside Moves* a lukewarm assessment. "Despite a predictable plot and an abundance of stereotypes—the product of a surprisingly clunky script by Barry Levinson . . . and Valerie Curtin—this is a well-meaning film with strong performances all around," the reviewer said.

Levinson rebounded in 1982 when he made his directorial debut with *Diner*, which he also wrote. The film is a "thoughtful, charming sleeper," according to a *TV Guide* reviewer; Levinson "takes us back to the late-1950s Baltimore of his youth,

Robin Williams starred as a comic radio broadcaster during the Vietnam War in *Good Morning, Vietnam*.

brilliantly evoking that era through carefully drawn characters." The film is about five friends who meet regularly at their favorite diner. Each has his own problems. One, a football fanatic, is considering marriage but is obsessed with the idea that his fiancee has to be a fan, too; he wants her to pass a Baltimore Colts football quiz before he will marry her. Another friend is disenchanted by marriage because he thinks his wife doesn't understand him. A third has a pregnant girlfriend, but he can't convince her to get married. Another buddy is rich, bright, and usually drunk, and the fifth friend is a hairdresser who studies law and chases women. The movie was nominated for an Academy Award for best original screenplay. "There's a lot more growing to be done, and that growing—or failure to grow—is what *Diner* is made of," Gene Siskel wrote in the *Chicago Tribune*.

One year after Levinson's success with *Diner*, he again collaborated with Curtin to write *Best Friends*, which fared poorly. Meanwhile, his marriage to Curtin also went sour; the couple divorced in 1982. While filming *Diner*, Levinson had met Diana Mona, who lived in Baltimore with her two children. She and Levinson married, and they had two more children of their own. Although they were no longer married, Curtin and Levinson in 1984 teamed up again to write *Unfaithfully Yours*, an update of director Preston Sturges's 1948 classic comedy about an orchestra conductor who mistakenly suspects his wife of infidelity.

Director's Chair Beckoned Again

Levinson also returned to directing in 1984 with the baseball film *The Natural*, which starred Robert Redford as Roy Hobbs, a once-promising ballplayer who is making a comeback as a hitter. Hobbs becomes the major league's oldest rookie sixteen years after his career appeared over when he was wounded by a deranged woman. Actress Glenn Close received a best supporting actress for her role in the film, which was a huge box office hit. In the wake of the success of *The Natural*, Levinson began directing *Young Sherlock Holmes*, about the legendary British sleuth during his schoolboy years. Holmes is determined to expose an evil band inhabiting a temple beneath London. After this movie, Levinson returned to his native Baltimore for *Tin Men*, his second film as both writer and director. This story, set in 1963, is

In 1984 Levinson directed Robert Redford in *The Natural*, the story of a wounded baseball player who makes a comeback sixteen years later.

about a conflict between two aluminum siding con-artists. Levinson did another 1960s film in 1987 when he directed *Good Morning, Vietnam,* a highly popular comedy-drama about the wartime exploits of Adrian Cronauer, a real-life comic radio broadcaster who was expelled from Saigon after broadcasts were too critical of America's wartime practices during the Vietnam War. Lawrence O'Toole, a reviewer for *Maclean's,* said Levinson "deftly meshes the comic and dramatic tones."

Levinson's next project was directing *Rain Man,* a story about two brothers as they travel from Cincinnati to Los Angeles. Raymond, played by Dustin Hoffman, is an autistic savant who is incapable of emotionally bonding with others, but has an uncanny, computer-like ability with math. His brother, Charlie, portrayed by Tom Cruise, is an opportunist who learns to develop a sincere

love for his older brother. *Newsweek* contributor David Ansen enthusiastically applauded the movie and called it a "fascinating, touching and unsettling character study." The film won Academy Awards for best picture, best director, best screenplay, and best actor (for Hoffman). It also won the Golden Bear at the Berlin film festival. Shortly after the overwhelming success he realized with *Rain Man,* Levinson formed Baltimore Productions with his longtime friend Mark Johnson, a producer; however, after several successes, they parted amicably. In another effort to maintain this link with his childhood hometown, Levinson also took part in buying the Baltimore Orioles baseball team with a group of investors.

The city of his youth became the setting for Levinson's next movie, *Avalon,* the story of an immigrant family in Baltimore from 1914 to the mid-1960s. As writer and director, Levinson, at forty-nine, recalled memories told by his grandfather. Reviewers found the film heartwarming and inspirational. "Perhaps the transforming element is his ability to tap into his love for the material," said reviewer Hal Hinson of the *Washington Post*. "But, Levinson never allows himself to be washed overboard with emotion. . . . [He] lays out these scenes with a rapturous attention to detail. And what's evoked is not so much the mood of the time as the spirit of his characters' memories of it." *Avalon* failed to attract audiences, even when it received an Academy Award nomination for best original screenplay.

Levinson's next project was directing the film *Bugsy*, which starred Warren Beatty as Bugsy Siegel, a flamboyant gangster who became popular in Hollywood and Las Vegas before he was murdered in the late 1940s. Levinson captured an Academy Award best director nomination for his

work on this film. Riding high on a tide of winners, his next work was *Toys*, a 1992 film that flopped and was booed by the critics. The story, directed by Levinson and cowritten by Levinson and Curtin, is about a Hollywood toy lover's determination to takeover a family-owned toy factory from a cynical, opportunistic relative. In an interview with Jesse Kornbluth in *Premiere*, Levinson made no apologies for the movie: "I look at *Toys* and think, I did what I was trying to do," he said. "When you make a film like that, you know you're dealing with no pre-sell, no reference points—it's dangerous."

Small Screen Success

Stepping away from the big screen, Levinson returned to the place he began his career. This time he wore both the director and producer hats in

Levinson received the Academy Award for best director for *Rain Man*, a 1988 film about an autistic savant (Dustin Hoffman, right) and his opportunistic brother (Tom Cruise).

Homicide: Life on the Street, a critically-acclaimed television show that in 1993 won him an Emmy Award for best director. In addition, *Homicide* has won or been nominated for several other major awards. The show follows a group of Baltimore homicide detectives in their day-to-day struggle to clear cases from the division's unsolved murder file. Levinson gave *Homicide* a gritty, documentary look by using hand-held cameras on location in Baltimore. Levinson told Kornbluth that he used spontaneity in filming the show. "For *Homicide*, I thought, Let's not take so much time in the production process—let's shoot faster and use the crudity as an element."

Never idle for long, in 1993 Levin teamed with editor David Thompson to write the book *Levinson on Levinson*, and the following year he went back to the big screen directing and scripting *Jimmy Hollywood*, a story about a Hollywood low-life and aspiring actor turned vigilante. In 1994, Levinson worked as director and producer of *Disclosure*, the film adaptation of Michael Crichton's best-selling novel about the high-tech world of a major computer software corporation. In 1996, Levinson wrote and directed *Sleepers* from the memoirs of Lorenzo Carcaterra. The story centers around four friends who are members of a New York City youth gang. Their exploits land them in reform school where they are humiliated and sexually abused by guards. Most of the action takes place after the boys are grown. Two of the gang track down the guards and murder them. On trial for the act, a third member of the gang, now an assistant district attorney, is assigned to the case.

In 1997 Levinson enjoyed great success producing *The Second Civil War*, *Donnie Brasco*, and *Home Fries*. Later he worked as director and co-producer of *Sphere* and *Wag the Dog*. *Donnie Brasco*, written by Paul Attanasio and produced by Levinson and three partners, is the true story of Joe Pistone, an FBI agent who infiltrates the Mafia by ingratiating himself with a low-level member named Lefty. "There's a fresh fascination and poetry to Donnie Brasco's exquisitely detailed, you-are-there portrait of how the Mob actually works," wrote Owen Gleiberman, a reviewer for *Entertainment Weekly*.

Meanwhile, *Wag the Dog* was a popular movie about accusations of sexual dalliances against the American president eleven days before the election. His advisers tell him to get the United States involved in a war to divert the public's attention.

If you enjoy the works of Barry Levinson, you may also want to check out the following films:

Network, an Academy Award-winning film, 1976.
Stand By Me, starring River Phoenix, 1986.
Goodfellas, directed by Martin Scorsese, 1990.

In an uncanny parallel to real life, the movie closely depicted actual events in early 1998, when President Bill Clinton, accused of having sexual affairs, talked of launching a war with Iraq. Leah Rozen, writing in *People*, called *Wag the Dog* a "profoundly cynical but also profoundly funny political satire. . . ."

Two months later, the movie *Sphere*, based on Michael Crichton's novel, was released. The story delves into the science fiction world with Dustin Hoffman playing a psychologist who is sent to what he thinks is a plane crash site. It turns out to be a crash site of a spaceship from the year 1709. Critics gave the film mixed reviews. Mick LaSalle of the *San Francisco Chronicle* stated that "Experience tells us to expect *Sphere* to succumb to formula and blow it. It never does. It remains, from start to finish, an adult, thinking-person's movie." He went on to say, however, that the "emotionally satisfying" ending "collapses under scrutiny. . . ."

Levinson has long grown confident with his work and his instincts. He told Kornbluth that he does no revisions, because "I have an idea. The pieces just evolve." Before being honored with a 1997 retrospective of his work at Mill Valley Festival in California, in an interview with Marilyn Beck and Stacy Jenel Smith, Levinson said: "I think it's easier to do the work than to look back on the work you've done." In fact, he said, he avoids watching a film after it's released—probably, because this prolific artist is already too busy working on his next project.

■ Works Cited

Ansen, David, review of *Rain Man*, *Newsweek*, December 19, 1988, p. 57.

Beck, Marilyn, and Smith, Jenel, *Detroit Free Press*, October 8, 1997.

Review of *Diner* at http://www.tvguide.com/movies.

Gleiberman, Owen, review of *Donnie Brasco*, *Entertainment Weekly*, March 7, 1997.

Hinson, Hal, review of *Avalon*, *Washington Post*, October 5, 1990.

Review of *Inside Moves* at http://www.tvguide.com/movies.

Kornbluth, Jesse, interview with Barry Levinson, *Premiere*, April, 1994, pp. 101-3, 148.

LaSalle, Mick, review of *Sphere*, *San Francisco Chronicle*, February 13, 1998.

O'Toole, Lawrence, review of *Good Morning, Vietnam*, *Maclean's*, January 4, 1988, p. 61.

Rozen, Leah, review of *Wag the Dog*, *People*, January 12, 1998.

Siskel, Gene, review of *Diner*, *Chicago Tribune*, July 2, 1982.

Stack, Peter, review of *Sleepers*, *San Francisco Chronicle*, April 4, 1997.

■ For More Information See

PERIODICALS

Chicago Tribune, October 19, 1979; July 2, 1982; February 10, 1984; March 15, 1987.

Entertainment Weekly, May 5, 1995, p. 54.

Los Angeles Times, May 7, 1982; December 16, 1982; February 10, 1984; March 6, 1987.

Newsweek, March 2, 1987, p. 78; January 4, 1988, pp. 50-51; January 16, 1989, pp. 52-56; April 11, 1994, p. 74.

New Yorker, January 11, 1988; April 4, 1994, pp. 97-98.

New York Times, December 19, 1980; April 2, 1982; December 17, 1982; February 10, 1984; March 6, 1987; March 15, 1987; September 15, 1989.

Rolling Stone, May 13, 1982; January 12, 1989; April 21, 1994, p. 95.

Time, February 20, 1984; May 14, 1987.

Washington Post, May 14, 1982; February 15, 1984; March 13, 1987.*

—Sketch by Diane Andreassi

Herman Melville

■ Personal

Born August 1, 1819, in New York, NY; died September 28, 1891, in New York, NY; buried in Woodlawn Cemetery, Bronx, NY; son of Allan (an importer) and Maria (Gansevoort) Melvill; married Elizabeth Knapp Shaw, August 4, 1847; children: Malcolm, Stanwix, Elizabeth, Frances. *Education:* Attended New York Male High School, and Albany Classical School. *Religion:* Dutch Reformed Church.

■ Career

Writer, 1844-91; Customhouse, New York, NY, inspector of customs, 1866-85. Worked in various occupations and professions, including bank clerk, assistant clerk in a fur store, farmer, teacher, cabin boy, and seaman. Lecture tour, 1857-60.

■ Writings

FICTION

Typee: A Peep at Polynesian Life, two volumes, Wiley & Putnam, 1846, revised edition published as *Typee; or, A Narrative of a Four Months Residence among the Natives of a Valley of the Marquesas Islands*, two volumes, John Murray [London], 1846, published as *Typee: A Romance of the South Seas*, Harcourt, 1920, new edition published as *Typee: Four Months Residence in the Marquesas*, Pacific Basin Books, 1985.

Omoo: A Narrative of Adventure in the South Seas, Harper & Brothers, 1847, Dutton, 1907, new edition, Pacific Basin Books, 1985.

Mardi: And a Voyage Thither, two volumes, Harper & Brothers, 1849, St. Boltolph Society, 1923, New American Library, 1964, new edition published as *Mardi*, Hendricks House, 1987.

Redburn: His First Voyage, Harper & Brothers, 1849, Doubleday, 1957, Holt, 1971.

White Jacket; or, The World in a Man-of-War, Harper & Brothers, 1850, United States Book Co., 1892, Northwestern University Press, 1970.

Moby-Dick; or, The Whale, Harper & Brothers, 1851, Dutton, 1907, Dodd, 1979, (published in England as *The Whale*, three volumes, Richard Bentley, 1851), published as *Moby-Dick*, illustrated by Seymour Fleishman, Scott, Foresman, 1948, adapted for young readers by Felix Sutton and illustrated by H. B. Vestal, Grosset, 1956, adapted by Patricia Daniels, Raintree, 1981, adapted by Joanne Fink (juvenile edition) illustrated by Hieronimus Fromm, Silver, 1984.

Pierre; or, The Ambiguities, Harper & Brothers, 1852, Dutton, 1929, new edition edited by Henry A. Murtay, Farrar, Straus, 1949.

Israel Potter: His Fifty Years of Exile, Putnam, 1855, Doubleday, 1965, published as *The Refugee*, T. B.

Peterson & Brothers, 1865, published as *His Fifty Years of Exile (Israel Potter)*, Sagamore Press, 1957.

The Piazza Tales (includes "Benito Cereno" and "Bartleby the Scrivener"), Dix & Edwards, 1856, Russell, 1963.

The Confidence Man: His Masquerade, Dix & Edwards, 1857, Holt, 1964, new edition published as *Confidence-Man*, Archon Books, 1987.

Billy Budd and Other Prose Pieces, edited by Raymond W. Weaver, Constable, 1924, published as *Billy Budd and Other Tales*, New American Library, 1961, published as *Billy Budd, Sailor*, edited by Harrison Hayford and Merton M. Sealts, Jr., University of Chicago Press, 1962, also published as *Billy Budd, Foretopman*, illustrated by Robert Quackenbush, F. Watts, 1968, published as *Billy Budd: An Inside Narrative*, Bobbs-Merrill, 1975.

Benito Cereno, illustrated by E. McKnight Kauffer, Nonesuch Press, 1926, another edition illustrated with wood engravings by Garrick Palmer, Imprint Society, 1972.

POETRY

Battle-Pieces and Aspects of the War, Harper & Brothers, 1866, School Facsimiles, 1979.

Clarel: A Poem and Pilgrimage in the Holy Land, Putnam, 1876, new edition edited by Walter E. Bezanson, Hendricks House, 1973.

John Marr and Other Sailors with Some Sea Pieces, DeVinn Press, 1888, Folcroft, 1975, published as *John Marr and Other Poems*, Princeton University Press, 1922, published as *John Marr*, Menhaden Press, 1980.

Timoleon Etc., Caxton, 1891, published as *Timoleon*, Folcroft, 1976.

OTHER

The Apple-Tree Table and Other Sketches, Princeton University Press, 1922, Greenwood, 1969.

Family Correspondence of Herman Melville, 1830-1904, edited by Victor H. Paltsits, New York Public Library, 1929, Haskell, 1976.

Journal Up the Straights: October 11, 1856-May 5, 1857, edited by Raymond W. Weaver, Cooper Square, 1935.

Journal of a Visit to London and the Continent 1849-1850, edited by Eleanor Melville Metcalf, Harvard University Press, 1948.

Journal of a Visit to Europe and the Levant, October 11, 1856-May 6, 1857, edited by Howard C.

Horsford, Princeton University Press, 1955, Greenwood, 1976.

The Letters of Herman Melville, edited by Merrell R. Davis and William H. Gilman, Yale University Press, 1960.

Herman Melville: Authentic Anecdotes of Old Zack, edited and with an introduction by Kenneth Starosciak, privately printed, 1973.

The Essential Melville, edited by Robert Penn Warren, Ecco Press, 1987.

Catskill Eagle (children's fiction), illustrated by Thomas Locker, Putnam, 1991.

COLLECTIONS

John Marr and Other Poems, introduction by Henry Chapin, Princeton University Press, 1922.

The Works of Herman Melville, sixteen volumes, Constable, 1922-24.

Poems, Containing Battle-Pieces, John Marr and Other Sailors, Timoleon, and Miscellaneous Poems, Constable, 1924, Russell, 1963.

Shorter Novels of Herman Melville, Liveright, 1928, new edition, 1978.

Romances of Herman Melville: Typee, Omoo, Mardi, Moby Dick, White Jacket, Israel Potter, Redburn, Pickwick Publishers, 1928.

Billy Budd, "Benito Cereno," [and] The Enchanted Isles, Press of the Readers Club, 1942.

Selected Poems of Herman Melville, edited by William Plomer, Hogarth Press, 1943.

Selected Poems, edited by F. O. Matthiessen, New Directions, 1944.

Collected Poems of Herman Melville, edited by Howard P. Vincent, Packard & Co., 1947.

Complete Works of Herman Melville, seven volumes, Hendricks House, 1947-69.

The Complete Stories of Herman Melville, edited by Jay Leyda, Random House, 1949.

Billy Budd and Other Stories, Lehmann, 1951.

The Complete Stories, edited by Jay Leyda, Eyre and Spottiswoode, 1951.

Selected Writings of Herman Melville: Complete Short Stories, Typee, [and] Billy Budd, Foretopman, Modern Library, 1952.

The Portable Melville, edited by Jay Leyda, Viking, 1952, Penguin, 1978.

Billy Budd [and] The Piazza Tales, Anchor Books, 1956.

Typee [and] Billy Budd, edited by Milton R. Stem, Dutton, 1958.

Four Short Novels, Bantam, 1959.

Selected Tales and Poems, edited by Richard Chase, Rinehart, 1960.

Three Shorter Novels of Herman Melville, Harper, 1962.

Billy Budd [and] Typee, Washington Square Press, 1962.

Herman Melville: Stories, Poems, and Letters, edited by R. W. B. Lewis, Dell, 1962.

Melville: The Best of Moby Dick and Typee; also Billy Budd Complete, Platt & Munk, 1964.

Selected Poems, edited by Hennig Cohen, Doubleday, 1964.

Billy Budd [and] "Benito Cereno," illustrated with paintings by Robert Shore, Heritage Press, 1965.

Billy Budd, [and] The Encantadas, Airmont, 1966.

Great Short Works, Harper, 1966.

Three Stories, illustrated with wood engravings by Gartick Palmer, Folio Society, 1967.

Five Tales, Dodd, 1967.

Billy Budd, Sailor and Other Stories, edited by Harold Beaver, Penguin, 1967.

The Writings of Herman Melville, six volumes, edited by Harrison Hayford, Hershel Parker and G. Thomas Tanselle, Northwestern University Press, 1968-71.

Billy Budd and Other Stories, Houghton, 1970.

Great Short Works of Herman Melville, edited by Warner Berthoff, Harper, 1970.

Herman Melville: Voyages, Hallmark Editions, 1970.

Selected Poems of Herman Melville, edited by Robert Penn Warren, Random House, 1970.

On the Slain Collegians, edited and illustrated with woodcuts by Antonio Frasconi, Farrar, Straus, 1971.

Selected Poems, edited by F. O. Matthiessen, Folcroft, 1972.

Poems of Herman Melville, edited by Douglas Robillard, College & University Press, 1976.

Billy Budd, Sailor; The Piazza Tales, illustrated by J. William Myers, Franklin Library, 1978.

Collected Poems, edited by Howard P. Vincent, Hendricks House, 1981.

Typee, Omoo, Mardi, edited by G. Thomas Tanselle, Library of America, 1982.

Typee: A Peep at Polynesian Life; Omoo: A Narrative of Adventures in the South Seas; Mardi: And a Voyage Thither, Cambridge Press, 1982.

Redburn, His First Voyage; White Jacket, or, The World in a Man- of-War; Moby-Dick, or, The Whale, Cambridge Press, 1983.

Moby Dick; The Confidence Man; The Piazza Tales; Billy Budd, Octopus, 1984.

Pierre, Israel Potter, The Piazza Tales, The Confidence Man, Billy Budd, Uncollected Tales, edited by Harrison Hayford, Library of America, 1985.

The Piazza Tales and Other Prose Pieces: 1839-1860, edited by Harrison Hayford and Hershel Parker, Northwestern University Press, 1986.

Journals, edited by Howard Horsford and Lynn Horth, Northwestern University Press, 1989.

Correspondence, edited by Lynn Horth, Northwestern University Press, 1993.

Herman Melville: Selected Poems, Arion Press, 1995.

Three Short Novels: Bartleby, Benito Cereno, Billy Budd, North Books, 1996.

Complete Short Fiction, Knopf, 1997.

Billy Budd, Sailor and Selected Tales, Oxford University Press, 1997.

Contributor to *Literary World, Yankee Doodle, Putnam's Monthly*, and *Harpers Monthly*.

The Houghton Library at Harvard University has letters, travel journals, and manuscripts for *Billy Budd*, short stories—including notes and a partial rough draft for "The Confidence Man"—poems, and other shorter writings. The Duyckinck Collection and the Berg Collection at the New York Public Library include letters from Melville and his family. The University of Virginia Library also has letters and manuscripts.

■ Adaptations

MOTION PICTURES

The Sea Beast (based on *Moby-Dick, or, The Whale*; silent film), starring John Barrymore, 1926; *Moby Dick; or, The White Whale*, starring John Barrymore and Joan Bennett, Warner Bros., 1930; *Omoo-Omoo, the Shark God*, starring Ron Randell, Devera Burton, and Trevor Bardette, Elsa Pictures, 1949; *Herman Melville's Moby Dick*, Contemporary Films, 1954; *Moby Dick*, starring Gregory Peck and Richard Basehart, Warner Bros., 1956; *Enchanted Island* (based on *Typee*), Warner Bros., 1958; *Bartleby* (based on a tale by Melville), Audio-Visual Services, 1962; *Billy Budd* (based on the play by Louis O. Coxe and Robert H. Chapman from the novel *Billy Budd, Foretopman*), starring Robert Ryan, Peter Ustinov, Melvyn Douglas, and Terence Stamp, Allied Artists, 1962; *The Trial of Billy Budd, Sailor*, Teaching Film Custodians, 1965; *A Discussion of Herman Melville's Bartleby*, Encyclopaedia Britannica Educational Corp, 1969; *Books Alive: Moby Dick*, Bailey Films, 1969; *The Great American Novel: Moby Dick*, Bailey Films, 1969, BFA Educational Media, 1971; *Bartleby by Herman Melville*, Encyclopaedia

Britannica Educational Corp., 1969; *Moby Dick*, USA Network, 1998.

PLAYS

Henry Reed, *Moby Dick, a Play for Radio*, J. Cape, 1947; Louis O. Coxe and Robert Chapman, *Billy Budd, a Play in Three Acts*, Princeton University Press, 1951; *Moby Dick*, adapted by Orson Welles, produced at Duke of York's Theatre, London, June 16, 1955, produced in New York at Ethel Barrymore Theatre, starring Rod Steiger, November 28, 1962; *Moby Dick-Rehearsed: A Drama in Two Acts*, Samuel French, 1965; Robert Lowell, *The Old Glory* (theater trilogy based on stories by N. Hawthorne and a novella by Melville), Noonday Press, 1966, revised edition, Farrar, Straus, 1968; James M. Salem, *Herman Melville's The Court Martial of Billy Budd: A Play in One Act*, Dramatic Publishing, 1969; *Pequod* (based on *Moby Dick; or, The Whale*), produced at Mercury Theatre, New York, NY, June 29, 1969; Guy Williams, adaptor, *Billy Budd; and, Moby Dick: Adapted for the Stage*, Macmillan (London), 1969; Tony Napoli, adaptor, *Moby Dick*, Lake Education, 1996.

RECORDINGS

Moby Dick, Decca, 1960, Spoken Arts, 1963, (cassette), Caedmon, Analog Audion Cassette, 1995; *Billy Budd*, Stereo Drama, General Electric, 1963; *Moby Dick: Selections*, Folkways Records, 1965; *Moby Dick by Herman Melville*, adapted by Brainerd Duffield, Listening Library, 1971; *Moby Dick* (excerpts), Caedmon, 1975; *Billy Budd* (record; cassette), Caedmon; *The Confidence Man: A Comic Fable: Opera in Two Parts*, T. Presser Co., 1982.

■ Sidelights

"Call me Ishmael. Some years ago—never mind how long precisely—having little or no money in my purse, and nothing particular to interest me on shore, I thought I would sail about a little and see the watery part of the world." So begins what Hennig Cohen in *Dictionary of Literary Biography* called "One of the few American books recognized as a world classic," the allegorical tale of seagoing adventure and whale-hunting, *Moby Dick; or, The Whale*. Penning these opening lines, Herman Melville could just as easily have been describing himself instead of his narrator. As a young man of twenty-one without prospects on land, Melville too shipped out to discover the world, and in so

doing discovered in himself the urge to be a writer. At sea for almost four years, Melville accumulated enough material for many novels. Also like the narrator of *Moby Dick*, Melville can be compared to the Biblical Ishmael, whose name has come to be synonymous with exile or outcast. In a way, Melville served an internal exile in his literary life, his serious works such as *Moby Dick* and *The Confidence Man: His Masquerade* undervalued in his lifetime. Except for his first two fictional narratives of his adventures in the South Seas, *Typee: A Peep at Polynesian Life* and *Omoo: A Narrative of Adventure in the South Seas*, his novels did not sell well and were little understood. It took over half a century for his leviathanic epic, *Moby Dick*, to begin to gain recognition as a great American novel.

At the time of his death in 1891, Melville was long forgotten by the literary community as well as the general reading public, having spent the last decades of his life writing poetry instead of the seagoing adventures by which he had made his name. Yet among his papers, he left behind the manuscript of a novella, *Billy Budd, Sailor*, that would be considered "one last triumph" for Melville, according to A. Robert Lee in a *Dictionary of Literary Biography* essay on the author's short fiction. Published three decades after his death, *Billy Budd* was eagerly received at a time when Melville's literary achievements were being rediscovered and he was assuming his place as an American original, to be compared with Nathaniel Hawthorne and Mark Twain. As Melville's reassessment progressed in the first half of the twentieth century, his total output was put under the lens for examination, and critics began to look beyond *Moby Dick*. "Melville's place in the history of American literature is no longer in doubt," noted Lee. "Nor, central though it is, can *Moby Dick* be called the sole reason for assigning him that place. For just as his other novels, his poetry, his logs and correspondence contribute to that achievement, so, too, do his short stories." Prominent among those stories are "Bartleby, the Scrivener," and "Benito Cereno," both published in magazines of the day and later collected in *The Piazza Tales*.

Rugged Early Years

Melville once wrote to his friend and fellow author, Nathaniel Hawthorne, that "Until I was twenty-five, I had no development at all. From my twenty-fifth year I date my life." Melville's metaphorical rebirth occurred when he returned home after four years at sea and discovered that he had the stuff of an author in him. His actual birth, however, took place on August 1, 1819, in New York City. Born the third of eight children to Allan and Maria Gansevoort Melvill (the final "e" was added to the name in 1832), Melville's early years were comfortable and secure. On both parental sides, he was descended from Revolutionary War kin. His grandfather, Major Thomas Melvill, took a leading part in the Boston Tea Party, and General Peter Gansevoort, who earned his commission under George Washington, was a hero of the Saratoga campaign. Melville's relations on his mother's side, the Gansevoorts, were a prominent Dutch-American family from the Hudson River region, and his father hailed from a respected Boston family. Allan Melvill would turn to his father Thomas when he was in financial need, but at the time of Melville's birth things were looking up for the family with the father's import business doing well. Melville and his siblings were baptized in the Dutch Reformed Church, and by all accounts the mother raised her children in accordance with strict Calvinist ethics.

Melville was sent to the New York Male School in 1825, "somewhat backward in speech and somewhat slow in comprehension," according to his father, as quoted in Jay Leyda's *The Melville Log: A Documentary Life of Herman Melville, 1819-1891*. The father went on to tell his son's future schoolmasters, however, that "you will find him as far as he understands men and thinks both solid and profound, and of a docile and amiable disposition." Hardly high praise, but Melville did well at the school, displaying the potential for being a scholar except for the fact that he was more interested in worldly affairs than in studying.

This easy childhood came to an abrupt end, however, when Allan Melvill's business had to be closed. The father had overextended himself and in order to recoup his losses, moved his family from New York City to Albany and became involved in the fur trade. In the event, that business also ended in failure, and in 1832 Melville's father died, deeply in debt. The family was thus reliant upon the generosity of well-to-do relatives and Melville was forced, at age twelve, to leave school and find employment.

Melville first worked for an uncle at his farm in Pittsfield, Massachusetts, then in 1834 he began clerking at his brother Gansevoort's store in Albany. Back in that city, he also re-entered the Albany Classical School to continue with his education. But when Gansevoort's business too collapsed, in 1837, Melville took a teaching position at a Pittsfield country school, dealing with thirty children of all ages. It was at about this time that Melville experimented with writing, publishing newspaper articles under a pseudonym. In 1839, he first put to sea, working as a cabin boy on the merchant ship *St. Lawrence* hauling cotton to Liverpool.

There was little in the way of personal experience that Melville did not later rework in his novels. Just as he included aspects of his father's death and the family's straitened financial circumstances in the 1852 work *Pierre; or, The Ambiguities*, so too did he employ the events of his summer's service aboard the *St. Lawrence* in the novel, *Redburn: His First Voyage*. The trip was both romantic and traumatic, instilling in Melville a love for the sea, but also confronting him with the hard life of a sailor. "Miserable dog's life is this of the sea!" he wrote in *Redburn*. "Commanded like a slave, and set to work like an ass! Vulgar and brutal men lording it over me, as if I were an African in Alabama. Yes, yes, blow on ye breezes, and make a speedy end to this abominable voyage!" It was in this narrative that Melville would first refer to himself, via his protagonist, as "a sort of Ishmael," both fatherless and a drifter.

Returning home to find his mother's financial situation even worse than before, he set to teaching school once again, only to have the school fold before the end of the term and neglect to pay his wages. He had tried the sea to find his fortune; now he set out to the West like many other young men of his generation. Visiting his uncle Thomas in Illinois and discovering that there was little that relative could do to help him secure his future, Melville turned back, but not before he saw the open prairies, visited the headwaters of the Mississippi, and took a steamboat part of the way on his return journey—experiences he would later incorporate in his deeply symbolic novel, *The Confidence Man*. But literary fodder would not help feed his family. Back in New York, he once again opted for the sea. In December 1840, he signed on the whaling ship *Acushnet* as a twenty-one-year-old, just under five feet ten inches, who had few prospects on dry land.

The Watery Part of the World

The *Acushnet* set sail from Fairhaven, Massachusetts, on January 3, 1841, bound for the South Seas. Such voyages generally lasted three to four years, and though Melville did not long remain with his original ship, his personal voyage would fit that norm. The outward journey took him south to Rio de Janeiro, round Cape Horn, up the coast of South America through the Galapagos Islands, and on to the Marquesas Islands. If, as a younger crew member on board the *St. Lawrence* he had found life difficult, life on board the whaler *Acushnet* was even more severe. "The usage on board her was tyrannical," he later wrote in his first novel, *Typee*. "The sick had been inhumanely neglected; the provisions had been doled out in scanty allowance; and her cruizes were unreasonably protracted. The captain was the author of these abuses; it was in vain to think that he would either remedy them, or alter his conduct, which was arbitrary and violent in the extreme." With no means of redress, having left civil law behind on land, and with a crew of "dastardly and mean-spirited wretches," Melville and his friend, Richard Tobias Greene, jumped ship at Nukuhiva, Marquesas, on July 9, 1842, making their way to an inland valley populated by the fierce Taipis or Typee tribe, supposedly cannibalistic. Part guest, part prisoner, Melville remained with the tribe for a month, until he was able to escape, rescued by an Australian whaler, *Lucy Ann*. This first part of his adventures would later form the core of his novel, *Typee*.

Melville stayed with the *Lucy Ann* as far as Tahiti, where he and ten other men were put ashore, imprisoned for mutiny. But once again he managed to escape, to the island of Eimo where he worked for a time on a potato farm. In November 1842 he signed with a whaler out of Nantucket, the *Charles and Henry*, island-hopping as far as Hawaii, or the Sandwich Islands as they were then known, and finally disembarked at Honolulu in May 1843. These further adventures would later be incorporated in his sequel to *Typee*, entitled *Omoo*. Then in August of the same year, Melville signed on as an enlisted seaman aboard the frigate *United States*, bound for Boston, with stopovers at the Marquesas, Tahiti, Valparaiso,

Callao, and Rio, reproducing his outward-bound journey. On board the naval vessel, he was subject to another sort of tyranny, the authoritarian military hierarchy at sea enforced by the lash. Experiences on board this vessel would later serve as inspiration for his novel, *White Jacket; or, The World in a Man-of-War*.

On October 14, 1844, Melville was discharged from the U.S. Navy in Boston. By this time Melville's brother Gansevoort had become a lawyer and a powerful figure in the Democratic party. Melville headed to Lansingburgh, the village near Albany where his family was now living. Finding his family an appreciative audience for his yarns and seagoing tall tales, he was soon encouraged to put these stories down on paper.

Early Successes

Melville wrote his first novel during the winter of 1844 and 1845, and by the summer he had in hand a work—part fact, part fiction—detailing a young man's desertion from a whaling ship and his escape into a tropical valley in the Marquesas Islands. As Lee noted in *Dictionary of Literary Biography*, the "adventure-filled story blends suspense with romance, a daring mix of sailors' high jinks, amateur anthropology, and reportings of cannibalism and other hidden tribal rituals and rites." Additionally, Melville calls into question in *Typee* the whole idea of what is civilized and what is primitive, pitting the natives' cannibalism against the equally reprehensible practices of colonialism and missionary zeal. In this, Melville adapted a cultural relativism and a penchant for paradox and moral ambiguities which would characterize much of his later work.

Melville's first attempts at publishing his work in the United States came to nothing, as publishers believed that it was pure fiction rather than a recounting of a young seaman's adventures. Not only was the writing too sophisticated for such a person, but the tales were thought too fantastical to have actually occurred. Finally, Melville's brother, bound for England as Secretary of the American Legation, took the manuscript with him and was able to place the novelization with the publisher John Murray. British publication helped him find a U.S. publisher, Wiley & Putnam. Thus the book came out in early 1846 and was a distinct success, both critically and financially.

Nathaniel Hawthorne, already a noted author of short stories by this time, declared in the *Salem Adviser* that *Typee* was "a very remarkable book . . . lightly but vigorously written. . . . The narrative is skillfully managed, and in a literary point of view, the execution of the work is worthy of the novelty and interest of its subject." The only negative criticism that came the book's way was from the religious press, which took exception to Melville's unflattering portrayal of missionaries in the South Seas, and from reviewers who thought the book a fabrication. These latter criticisms were laid to rest when Melville's friend from his *Typee* adventures, Toby Greene, came forward to say that the story was in fact true.

Melville was encouraged by this initial success to go ahead with another autobiographical novel,

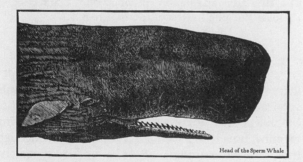

MOBY-DICK

or, The Whale

BY HERMAN MELVILLE

Head of the Sperm Whale

The Arion Press edition as designed by Andrew Hoyem

with illustrations by Barry Moser

and a Note on the California Edition by James D. Hart

This classic allegorical tale uses a variety of styles and literary forms to grapple with themes including good and evil and man versus nature.

Omoo, for which he received a $400 advance from the publisher Harper & Brothers. Recounting Melville's island-hopping adventures after escaping from the Taipis, this second novel was also a success, selling out its first edition of 3,000 copies in the first week. Horace Greeley noted in the *Weekly Tribune* of New York that the new novel "proves the author a born genius, with few superiors either as a narrator, a describer, or a humorist." The poet Walt Whitman, writing in the *Daily Eagle*, recommended *Omoo* "as thorough entertainment—not so light as to be tossed aside for its flippancy, nor so profound as to be tiresome."

Publication of this second novel also brought Melville freelance work for a new journal, *Literary World*, and for *Yankee Doodle*. Encouraged by these successes, Melville felt secure enough to embark on a marriage to Elizabeth Shaw, daughter of the Chief Justice of Massachusetts. After a honeymoon in Canada, the couple set up house in New York where Melville began work on a new book. At this time, he also discovered the works of Shakespeare. Much influenced by these, he struggled to find an individual voice for his third novel, *Mardi: And a Voyage Thither*. As Lee noted in *Dictionary of Literary Biography*, "The book is an endeavor to create nothing less than a world allegory, but its too evident symbolism and literariness fail to come off." A critical and financial failure, *Mardi* sent Melville back to his early successful formula of autobiographical writing. With the birth of his first son the same month as publication of *Mardi*, it was important that he find firm financial ground once again.

Melville therefore quickly published two narratives of which he was personally dismissive, but which Lee, among others, found to be worthy successors to his earlier fiction. "Both are lively, dramatic, shipboard stories," Lee observed. *Redburn* recounts Melville's first seagoing adventures on the *St. Lawrence*, and *White Jacket* details life aboard a navy ship and draws on his own experience on the *United States*. The second novel is notable especially for Melville's ability to create and maintain a sustained symbol, the white jacket which sets the narrator apart from the rest of the crew— a sort of cloak of innocence. *White Jacket* was also in part influential in securing the abolition of flogging in the United States Navy.

With American proofs of *White Jacket* in hand, Melville personally set sail for England to try and find a friendly publisher there, as the abysmal sales of *Mardi* had set his reputation back. While publishers were looking at the proofs, Melville took an excursion to the Continent, visiting Paris, Brussels, Cologne, and the Rhineland, and returned to London to find that the publisher Bentley was offering 200 pounds for the British rights to *White Jacket*. This helped somewhat to dispel Melville's financial worries, but such concerns were never far from his mind. His father's example was always at work on him, and finances were to plague him all his life.

Back in the United States, Melville bought—with the help of his father-in-law—a farm in Pittsfield, Massachusetts, and moved his family to the country. In 1850 he began writing his fifth novel, one that would secure him, long after his death, literary immortality.

The Whiteness of the Whale—*Moby Dick*

For all his novels Melville conducted large amounts of research in histories, personal narratives, and even scientific tracts, combining such knowledge with his own personal experience. So too with his new book about whaling, Melville harkened back to his experiences aboard the whaler *Acushnet*, but also read far and wide. In 1839, J. N. Reynold recounted the true tale of a notorious whale in "Mocha Dick," published in the *Knickerbocker Magazine*. This story obviously stuck with Melville in his own whaling yarn, which soon bore the working title *Moby Dick*. Initially he planned a straightforward account of life on a whaler, for at the time the American whaling fleet was preeminent in the world and interest among the public was high. But slowly, in his researches and readings, Melville began to invest the story with more symbolic content.

That first summer of writing, he also reviewed Hawthorne's *Mosses from an Old Manse*, met the older author, and was profoundly influenced by Hawthorne's truth in his fiction, comparing him to Shakespeare in his subsequent magazine article. Publication of Hawthorne's *The Scarlet Letter* only increased Melville's respect, giving him a new direction for his own book as well as for his literary career. According to Cohen in *Dictionary of Literary Biography*, "Hawthorne was the catalytic force that confirmed [Melville] in the direction his 'strange sort of book' was moving and in his will-

The 1956 film adaptation of *Moby Dick* stars Gregory Peck as the peg-legged Captain Ahab.

ingness thereby to court failure." Instead of a safe, semi-autobiographical account of whaling life, Melville opted for allegory, creating a sprawling, teeming novel of psychological and symbolic richness. In the summer of 1850 he promised his London publisher the new manuscript by that autumn; the book took another year of intense writing to complete. The British edition, titled *The Whale*, came out in October 1851, the American edition one month later, dedicated to Hawthorne.

The plot of *Moby Dick* is deceptively simple. Ishmael, the narrator of the story, recounts his adventures as a young man, an ex-schoolmaster who feels he must leave his quiet life on land and go to sea. Deciding to sign on a whaling ship, he leaves Manhattan for New Bedford where he will find a ship. Overnighting at the Spouter Inn near the waterfront, he is forced to share accommodations with a strange savage of a man, Queequeg, a Maori harpooner also looking for a ship. At first frightened of this native, fearing that he is a cannibal, Ishmael soon makes friends with the man, who proves to be a loyal and trusting individual. They decide to sign on the same ship, *Pequod*, a whaler out of Nantucket. Though they are warned against this ship and its mysterious Captain Ahab, the two go forward with their plans, yet are curious to see this captain about whom so many stories are circulating.

There is, however, no sight of Ahab for several days out to sea. The ship is ably run by two mates, Starbuck and Stubb, with whom Ishmael becomes friends. Finally, one day as the ship is sailing south around the Cape, Ahab makes his appearance. He is a stern looking man, with one missing leg—supplanted by a peg-leg made from the jaw bone of a whale—and a long white scar running down the side of his face. Ishmael later learns that the captain's injuries were caused by a huge albino whale called Moby Dick, which Ahab intends to kill. Early in the voyage, Ahab nails a gold piece to the mast, declaring that the sailor who first spots the white whale shall have the gold. The sailors are enthused by this, but Starbuck deplores the captain's maniacal obsession with Moby Dick.

Ahab plots a course for where he has heard the whale may be, and near the Cape of Good Hope the ship encounters its first school of sperm whales. The crew busy themselves with harpooning the whales and rendering the blubber. Encountering another whaler, Ahab is warned against pursuing Moby Dick, but he will not be deflected from his mission. Encountering more whales, Queequeg harpoons several of them, and more laborious work is at hand to strip the animals of their fat before they are completely devoured by circling sharks. All this keeps the men busy, even as they approach the Indian Ocean where the white whale may be found.

The *Pequod* encounters a British whaler whose captain has lost his arm to the whale, and Ahab ignores more warnings about going after Moby Dick. Ahab also rejects Starbuck's demands to give up the mad pursuit. At this time, Queequeg falls ill, and believing that he is dying, has a coffin fitted for himself in the shape of a canoe, which is the custom of his tribe. In the event, however, he recovers, and uses his coffin as a sea chest. A Parsee named Fedallah who is on board now prophesies that Ahab will die after seeing two strange hearses carrying dead on the sea. Ahab ignores this prediction, as well.

Battling storms and a restless crew, Ahab pushes on, and at length encounters the white whale. They chase the leviathan for three days, with Moby Dick repeatedly turning on the harpooners and wrecking smaller craft pursuing him. On the third day, they see that Fedallah—gone missing the day before—has been bound to the hump of the whale by the coils of a harpoon rope: the Parsee's first prophesy has come true. Then the second comes true, as well, as Moby Dick turns on the *Pequod* and shatters the ship's timbers. Ahab, caught in the rope of his own harpoon, is drowned. The only one saved is Ishmael, who clings to Queequeg's canoe-coffin.

Such is the plot line of the novel, but Melville did not tell it in a straight narrative fashion. Instead he embroidered a "successive layering of literary forms, styles, tones, references, allusions, and particularly the manipulation of language," according to Cohen in *Dictionary of Literary Biography*, to create an allegory of good and evil, of the pursuit of absolute knowledge, of man versus nature, of the costs of a Faustian bargain, and of the inadequacy of human perception. The novel is at once a sea story, a tall tale, an epic quest, a satire, a primer on whaling, and a lyric ode to man's overweening ambition. Melville employs several styles, including fictional narrative, journalism, scientific treatise, and—in sections—the dialogue format of a drama. Laden with symbolism, from the whiteness of the whale to the changing face on the gold doubloon Ahab tacks to the mast, the novel could be read on several levels, and was not just a pure entertainment.

As Cohen noted, "*Moby Dick* brought Melville personal satisfaction but the reviewers, while indicating that they had some grasp of what he was trying out, were not altogether enthusiastic." Henry F. Chorley, for example, writing in the *Atheneum*, called the book "an ill-composed mixture of romance and matter-of-fact." In *Literary World*, Evert A. Duyckinck called the novel "an intellectual chowder," pointing out that there were "evidently two if not three books in Moby Dick rolled into one." An anonymous reviewer in the *Southern Quarterly Review* called all the material apart from the chase and battle with Moby Dick "sad stuff, dull and dreary, or ridiculous," and demanded "a writ of *de lunatico* against all parties."

Not all reviewers at the time were so negative. George Ripley, writing in *Harper's New Monthly*

Magazine, also noted the layers of style, but observed that "Beneath the whole story, the subtle imaginative reader may perhaps find a pregnant allegory, intended to illustrate the mystery of human life." Ripley went on to assert that "the genius of the author for moral analysis is scarcely surpassed by his wizard power of description." William A. Butler, in the *National Intelligencer,* pointed out that Melville's "delineation of character is actually Shakespearean," and dubbed the novel "a prose epic on whaling." In spite of these favorable reviews, the book did not sell well in Melville's lifetime.

So the matter stood for over forty years. *Moby Dick* was a largely forgotten novel until after Melville's death. By 1893, a reviewer for the *Critic* was calling the book "a marvelous odyssey," concluding that the "only wonder is that Melville is so little known and so poorly appreciated." Years later, the American critic Carl Van Doren declared in *The Cambridge History of American Literature* that "the immense originality of *Moby Dick* must warrant the claim of its admirers that it belongs with the greatest sea romances in the whole literature of the world." First published in England, Melville also gained in posthumous stature across the Atlantic. In his *Studies in Classic American Literature,* the author D. H. Lawrence declared *Moby Dick* to be "a great book . . . the greatest book of the sea ever written. It moves awe in the soul." Lawrence also took the critical debate to the symbolic level, calling the whale Moby Dick a symbol of "our deepest blood nature. . . . The last phallic being of the white man." Critical momentum continued to grow for the novel, carrying Melville's entire canon with it.

Symbolic and stylistic conjectures regarding the novel abound: the question as to whether the power embodied in the white whale was that of innocent nature or malevolent evil; the Biblical nature of the book; the sense of Greek tragedy. The book has become everything to everybody, with later criticism even wondering at the possibility of a homosexual friendship between Ishmael and Queequeg. The American novelist William Faulkner called it the book he wished he "had written," and the British novelist E. M. Forster noted its "prophetic song" which "asks for endurance or loyalty without hope of reward." Lewis Mumford, in his *Herman Melville,* announced that "Moby Dick is a poetic epic," and the critic Van Wyck Brooks declared the novel "our sole American epic" in his *Emerson and Others.* Later criticism has dealt with every symbolic and textual nuance ranging from the composition of the novel to the meaning of evil as coded in its pages. A century and a half after publication, *Moby Dick* is considered not only an American classic, but one which belongs to the whole world, to be compared with *Hamlet* and *Paradise Lost.*

The Short Stories and *The Confidence Man*

Melville had no time to read his reviews, too busy was he trying to earn a living from his writing. After the hard work of *Moby Dick,* he immediately set to work on another novel, *Pierre; Or, The Ambiguities,* the first of his novels to be set on land. This partially autobiographical account of his own fortunes as a young man was poorly received, and his family began to worry about the state of his nerves from constant work. Melville, however, kept on working—a family of four children needed supporting. To do this, Melville turned to the short story form, writing pieces for both *Putnam's Monthly Magazine* and *Harper's Monthly Magazine* over a period of four years which were collected in *The Piazza Tales* of 1856. Predominant among these stories are "Bartleby, the Scrivener" and "Benito Cereno."

As Cohen observed in *Dictionary of Literary Biography,* "'Bartleby' is a tragi-comic fable about a man, hemmed in by the walls of society, responding through the force of his passivity." The story takes place mainly in a Wall Street law office where Bartleby has recently found employment. Initially a diligent worker, copying legal documents, Bartleby slowly begins to decline and withdraw, shirking his responsibilities with the continual refrain, "I would prefer not to." Eventually Bartleby stops his copying altogether and merely stares at the wall outside his window. The story's lawyer-narrator tells of Bartleby's withdrawal from society as he himself is forced to move his place of business because Bartleby prefers not even to leave the office. Ultimately Bartleby is jailed for vagrancy, but the lawyer begins to feel responsible for his former clerk and visits him in prison only to discover him dead from self-imposed starvation.

"Bartleby" has received much critical attention over the years, with many diverse interpretations. On one level, as Lee pointed out in *Dictionary of*

Literary Biography, the story is a "quasi-religious fable," with Bartleby a stand-in for Christ. It has also been seen as a clinical account of schizophrenia, or as a depiction of Wall Street "in which this business epicenter of nineteenth-century America is seen as murderous to the human creative spirit." More recent interpretation, such as that of Leo Marx in the *Sewanee Review*, sees Bartleby as a surrogate for Melville himself, perhaps feeling in ways like a lowly scrivener, still reeling from the failure of *Pierre*. "There are excellent reasons for reading 'Bartleby' as a parable having to do with Melville's own fate as a writer," Marx stated. The passive Bartleby has been seen by others as a resister to the pressures of society,

Written in the final years of Melville's life, this story of a sailor who is falsely accused of mutiny was the result of both copious research and a life spent at sea.

and thus a Thoreau-like character, and the work remains as Lee observed, "as sure and consequential a story as any Melville wrote."

With "Benito Cereno," Melville adapted a historical event recorded in the 1817 publication of Amaso Delano, *Narrative of Voyages and Travels*. This story represents, according to Lee, "Melville again at his greatest strength. A chill, tense, and exhilarating novella-length story of slave insurrection off the Chilean coast." The story is told through the eyes of a fictionalized Amaso Delano, a captain sailing out of Duxbury, Massachusetts. Delano attempts to help a Spanish ship in distress, the vessel commanded by Benito Cereno. But the good-natured Delano slowly comes to realize that the Spanish ship is a world turned upside-down, that it is a slave ship whose human cargo—led by Babo—has revolted and actually control the ship, having killed most of the white crew. They play "slaves" when Delano comes aboard, but in so doing take on all the negative attributes of their former masters. The story becomes an allegory of enslavement on many levels. Eventually the charade is exposed and Cereno and his remaining crew saved; Babo and his men are tried and executed.

Lee noted in *Dictionary of Literary Biography* that the story "puts before the reader a complex weaving of language and metaphor, the interplay of references to black, white, and gray," and further explores two of Melville's favorite themes: the deceptiveness of appearances and the dynamics of evil. Lee concluded that of all Melville's tales, "Benito Cereno" "contains his most challenging drama; it is narrative as an inquiry into freedom and revolt, blackness and whiteness, and the denial and liberation of self." John Freeman, in his *Herman Melville*, has called Delano "a Conradian figure," and Mumford noted in his biography that "there is not a feeble touch in the whole narrative." Other critics have agreed, placing "Benito Cereno" among Melville's highest achievements. Another notable story included in *The Piazza Tales* is "The Encantadas," a sequence of narratives about the Galapagos Islands.

Melville's difficult financial situation continued, and there was domestic strain as well. In 1856 he needed a break. Borrowing money from his father-in-law, Melville set out on an extended trip to Europe, visiting Hawthorne also, who was then American consul in Liverpool. Upon his return to

If you enjoy the works of Herman Melville, you may also want to check out the following books and films:

Avi, *The True Confessions of Charlotte Doyle*, 1990.
Daniel Defoe, *Robinson Crusoe*, 1719.
Ernest Hemingway, *The Old Man and the Sea*, 1952.
Theodore Taylor, *Timothy of the Cay*, 1993.
The Caine Mutiny, starring Humphrey Bogart, 1954.

New York, he published *The Confidence Man*, a novel finished just before his departure for Europe and the last work of fiction to appear in his lifetime. Inspired by the steamboat trip he had taken down the Mississippi as a youth, the novel is an extended allegorical satire which takes place aboard the steamboat *Fidele* between dawn and midnight of April Fool's day. Structured as a series of games which take place between various confidence men and their victims, the novel was neither a critical nor a commercial success. Over the years, however, this novel too has gained in stature. Cohen called it Melville's "second masterpiece" in *Dictionary of Literary Biography*, and Lee summed it up as Melville's "final Swiftian vision of the human 'masquerade.'" His tenth book in eleven years, the novel signaled Melville's retreat from literary life.

The Later Years and *Billy Budd*

In the late 1850s Melville was forced to go on the lecture circuit to help his finances, talking about the South Seas and travel in general. He was also becoming increasingly interested in poetry, and spent the next three decades working on verse. In 1860 he traveled on a ship, the *Meteor*, captained by his brother, and with the outbreak of the Civil War attempted to win a naval appointment, though nothing came of it. In 1863 he sold his Pittsfield farm and moved his family back to New York City, where he would reside for the rest of his life. Then in 1866 he took an oath to become an inspector at the customs of the Port of New York, a position he held for nineteen years. The following year his son

Malcolm was found dead of a self-inflicted gunshot wound.

Melville's later publications were mostly poetry: *Battle-Pieces and Aspects of the War*, which was Melville's reaction to the Civil War, *Clarel: A Poem and Pilgrimage in the Holy Land*, a poem inspired by his travels to that region, *John Marr and Other Sailors with Some Sea Pieces*, and *Timoleon Etc.* Melville has increasingly won regard as a poet, but it is as a writer of fiction for which he is remembered. And fiction concerned him in his final days.

Melville worked at the customs house until 1885 when he was sixty-six. An inheritance in part enabled him to retire and devote his final years to his writing. In 1888 he began a poem about a sailor awaiting execution for mutiny, and prefaced it with a headnote. In the event, the preface grew into the short novel *Billy Budd*, discovered among Melville's papers at his death. With the writing of this final novella, Melville went back to research, reading sea narratives and histories, and interweaving these with a lifetime of personal experience. The story uses an actual British naval insurrection as its plot line. The young, handsome sailor Billy Budd is falsely accused of mutiny by the master-of-arms of the *Bellipotent*, John Claggart. As a stutterer, however, Billy cannot protest his innocence. Eventually he kills his accuser with a blow of the fist, is sentenced to death by Captain Edward Vere, and is hung to restore order on board. In death, Billy becomes a martyr to his fellow shipmates, a Christ figure who suffers a new crucifixion for them.

Melville, critics have pointed out, asks more questions with this narrative than he answers, and since its publication in 1924, the novella has won high praise and has been adapted as a play, opera, and movie. The British novelist E. M. Forster called it "a remote unearthly episode," while the French writer and philosopher Albert Camus, in his *Lyrical and Critical Essays*, saw the tale as a "flawless story that can be ranked with certain Greek tragedies." Modern critical appraisal ranks the book with *Moby Dick* as one of Melville's finest achievements, though some continue to wonder if in fact this final narrative was actually finished at the time of Melville's death.

The summer of 1891, Melville began a volume of verse for his wife about the roses and wildflowers to be found around their old farm in Pittsfield. His work was cut short, however, when on September 28 he died of heart failure. Though he died in almost total obscurity, Melville was not to be long forgotten. His literary resurrection began in 1919, the centenary of his birth. A 1921 biography by Raymond W. Weaver, *Herman Melville: Mariner and Mystic*, also helped the process of reassessment of Melville's literary achievements. Two years later, in his 1923 *The Advance of the American Short Story*, Edward J. O'Brien declared that Melville was "one of the greatest visionary artists the world has had since William Blake." It is a judgment that remains equally true today when Melville's novels and shorter work are studied in universities and still inspire readers from around the world.

■ Works Cited

Brooks, Van Wyck, "Notes on Herman Melville," *Emerson and Others*, Dutton, 1927, pp. 171-205.

Butler, William A., review of *Moby Dick; or, The Whale, National Intelligencer*, December 16, 1851, p. 214.

Camus, Albert, "Critical Essays: Herman Melville," *Lyrical and Critical Essays*, Knopf, 1968, pp. 288-94.

Chorley, Henry F., "Reviews: 'The Whale'," *Atheneum*, October 25, 1851, pp. 1112-13.

Cohen, Hennig, "Herman Melville," *Dictionary of Literary Biography*, Volume 3: *Antebellum Writers in New York and the South*, Gale, 1979.

Duyckinck, Evert A., "An Intellectual Chowder," *Literary World*, November 26, 1851, pp. 403-4.

Faulkner, William, "Moby Dick, 'Golgotha of the Heart'," *Chicago Tribune Book Review*, July 1, 1927.

Forster, E. M., "Prophesy," *Aspects of the Novel*, Harcourt, Brace, 1927, pp. 181-212.

Freeman, John, *Herman Melville*, Haskell House, 1974, pp. 148-49.

Greeley, Horace, review of *Omoo: A Narrative of Adventure in the South Seas, Weekly Tribune*, June 23, 1847.

Hawthorne, Nathaniel, review of *Typee: A Peep at Polynesian Life, Salem Adviser*, March 25, 1846.

Lawrence, D. H., *Studies in Classic American Literature*, Viking, 1964, pp. 131-61.

Lee, A. Robert, "Herman Melville," *Dictionary of Literary Biography*, Volume 74: *American Short-Story Writers before 1880*, Gale, 1988, pp. 249-67.

Leyda, Jay, *The Melville Log: A Documentary Life of Herman Melville, 1819-1891*, Harcourt, 1951.

Marx, Leo, "Melville's Parable of the Whale," *Sewanee Review*, Autumn, 1953, pp. 602-27.

Melville, Herman, *Typee: A Peep at Polynesian Life*, Wiley & Putnam, 1846.

Melville, Herman, *Redburn: His First Voyage*, Harper & Brothers, 1849.

Melville, Herman, *Moby Dick; or, The Whale*, Harper & Brothers, 1851.

Melville, Herman, *The Letters of Herman Melville*, edited by Merrell R. Davis and William H. Gilman, Yale University Press, 1960.

Melville, Herman, "Bartleby, the Scrivener," *Great Short Works of Herman Melville*, Harper & Row, 1966.

Review of *Moby Dick; or, The Whale, Critic*, Number 22, 1893, p. 382.

Review of *Moby Dick; or, The Whale, Southern Quarterly Review*, January, 1852, p. 262.

Mumford, Lewis, *Herman Melville*, Harcourt, Brace, 1929, pp. 123-24.

O'Brien, Edward J., "Hawthorne and Melville," *The Advance of the American Short Story*, Dodd, Mead, 1923, pp. 42-64.

Ripley, George, review of *Moby Dick; or, The Whale, Harper's New Monthly Magazine*, December, 1851.

Van Doren, Carl, *The Cambridge History of American Literature*, Volume 1, Macmillan, 1917, p. 322.

Whitman, Walt, review of *Omoo: A Narrative of Adventure in the South Seas, Daily Eagle*, May 5, 1847.

■ For More Information See

BOOKS

Anderson, Charles Roberts, *Melville in the South Seas*, Columbia University Press, 1939.

Arvin, Newton, *Herman Melville*, Sloane, 1950.

Baird, James, *Ishmael: A Study of the Symbolic Mode of Primitivism*, Johns Hopkins Press, 1956.

Bernstein, John, *Pacifism and Rebellion in the Writings of Herman Melville*, Mouton, 1964.

Berthoff, Warner, *The Example of Melville*, Princeton University Press, 1962.

Bewley, Marius, *The Eccentric Design*, Columbia University Press, 1959.

Bickley, R. Bruce, *The Method of Melville's Short Fiction*, Duke University Press, 1975.

Bloom, Harold, editor, *Herman Melville's 'Moby Dick'*, Chelsea House, 1995.

Boswell, Jeanetta, *Herman Melville and the Critics: A Checklist of Criticism, 1900-1978*, Scarecrow, 1981.

Bowen, Merlin, *The Long Encounter: Self and Experience in the Writings of Herman Melville*, University of Chicago Press, 1960.

Branch, Watson G., editor, *Melville, The Critical Heritage*, Routledge & Kegan Paul, 1974.

Braswell, William, *Melville's Religious Thought*, Duke University Press, 1943.

Brodhead, Richard, *Hawthorne, Melville, and the Novel*, University of Chicago Press, 1976.

Bryant, John, editor, *A Companion to Melville Studies*, Greenwood Press, 1986.

Cahoon, Herbert, *Herman Melville: A Check List of Books and Manuscripts in the Collections of the New York Public Library*, New York Public Library, 1951.

Chase, Richard, *Herman Melville: A Critical Study*, Macmillan, 1949.

Chase, Richard, *The American Novel and Its Tradition*, Doubleday, 1957.

Chase, Richard, editor, *Melville: A Collection of Critical Essays*, Prentice-Hall, 1962.

Cohen, Hennig, and James Calahan, *A Concordance of Melville's Moby Dick*, three volumes, Melville Society, 1978.

Concise Dictionary of American Literary Biography: Colonization to the American Renaissance, 1640-1865, Gale, 1988.

Dillingham, William B., *Melville's Short Fiction 1853-1856*, University of Georgia Press, 1977.

Dillingham, William B., *Melville and His Circle: The Last Years*, University of Georgia Press, 1997.

Dryden, Edgar, *Melville's Thematics of Form: The Great Art of Telling the Truth*, Johns Hopkins Press, 1968.

Duban, James, *Melville's Major Fiction: Politics, Theology, and Imagination*, Northern Illinois University Press, 1983.

Feidelson, Charles, Jr., *Symbolism and American Literature*, University of Chicago Press, 1953.

Fiedler, Leslie, *Love and Death in the American Novel*, revised edition, Stein & Day, 1966.

Fisher, Marvin, *Going Under: Melville's Short Fiction and the American 1850s*, Louisiana State University Press, 1977.

Fogle, Richard Harter, *Melville's Shorter Tales*, University of Oklahoma Press, 1960.

Frank, Stuart M., *Herman Melville's Picture Gallery: Sources and Types of the "Pictorial" Chapters of Moby-Dick*, E. J. Lefkowicz, 1986.

Franklin, H. Bruce, *The Wake of the Gods: Melville's Mythology*, Stanford University Press, 1963.

Gale, Robert L., *Plots and Characters in the Fiction and Narrative Poetry of Herman Melville*, Archon Books, 1969.

Gale, Robert L., *A Herman Melville Encyclopedia*, Greenwood Press, 1995.

Gross, Theodore L., and Stanley Wertheim, editors, *Hawthorne, Melville, Stephen Crane: A Critical Bibliography*, Free Press, 1971.

Haul, A. N., *The American Vision: Actual and Ideal Society in Nineteenth-Century Fiction*, Yale University Press, 1963.

Hayes, Kevin J., editor, *The Critical Response to Melville's 'Moby Dick'*, Greenwood Press, 1994.

Hetherington, Hugh W., *Melville's Reviewers, British and American, 1846-1891*, University of North Carolina Press, 1961.

Higgins, Brian, *Herman Melville: An Annotated Bibliography, Volume 1, 1846-1930*, G. K. Hall, 1979.

Hillway, Tyrus, *Herman Melville*, Twayne, 1963.

Hoffman, Daniel, *Form and Fable in American Fiction*, Oxford University Press, 1961.

Howard, Leon, *Herman Melville: A Biography*, University of California Press, 1951.

Humphreys, A. R., *Melville*, Oliver & Boyd, 1962.

Inge, M. Thomas, editor, *Bartleby the Inscrutable: A Collection of Commentary on Herman Melville's Tale "Bartleby the Scrivener,"* Archon Books, 1979.

Lebowitz, Alan, *Progress Into Silence, A Study of Melville's Heroes*, Indiana University Press, 1970.

Lee, A. Robert, editor, *Herman Melville: Reassessments*, Vision Press, 1984.

Lee, A. Robert, editor, *The Nineteenth-Century American Short Story*, Vision Press, 1986.

Levin, Harry, *The Power of Blackness: Hawthorne, Poe, Melville*, Knopf, 1958.

Lewis, R. W. B., *The American Adam: Innocence, Tragedy, and Tradition in the Nineteenth-Century*, University of Chicago Press, 1955.

Marx, Leo, *The Machine in the Garden: Technology and the Pastoral Ideal in America*, Oxford University Press, 1964.

Mason, Ronald, *The Spirit Above The Dust*, John Lehmann, 1951.

Matthiessen, F. O., *American Renaissance: Art and Expression in the Age of Emerson and Whitman*, Oxford University Press, 1941.

Mayoux, Jean-Jacques, *Melville par lui-meme*, Editions de Seuil, 1958, translated by John Ashbery as *Melville*, Grove, 1960.

Metcalf, Eleanor Melville, *Herman Melville: Cycle and Epicycle*, Harvard University Press, 1953.

Miller, Edwin Haviland, *Melville*, Braziller, 1975.

Miller, James E., Jr., *A Reader's Guide To Herman Melville*, Farrar, Straus & Cudahy, 1962.

Miller, Perry, *The Raven and the Whale: The War of Words and Wit in the Era of Poe and Melville*, Harcourt, Brace, 1956.

Minnigerode, Meade, *Some Personal Letters of Herman Melville and a Bibliography*, E. B. Hackett, 1922.

Mushabac, Jane, *Melville's Humor: A Critical Study*, Archon Books, 1981.

Newman, Lea B., *A Readers Guide to the Short Stories of Herman Melville*, G. K. Hall, 1986.

Nineteenth-Century Literature Criticism, Gale, Volume 3, 1983, Volume 12, 1986, Volume 29, 1991, Volume 45, 1994.

Olson, Charles, *Call Me Ishmael: A Study of Melville*, Reynal & Hitchcock, 1947.

Parker, Hershel, editor, *The Recognition of Herman Melville: Selected Criticism since 1846*, University of Michigan Press, 1967.

Parker, Hershel, editor, *Herman Melville: The Contemporary Reviews*, Cambridge University Press, 1995.

Parker, Hershel, *Herman Melville: A Biography*, Johns Hopkins University Press, 1997.

Percival, M. O., *A Reading of Moby-Dick*, University of Chicago Press, 1950.

Pullin, Faith, editor, *Melville: New Perspectives*, Edinburgh University Press, 1978, republished as *New Perspectives on Melville*, Kent State University Press, 1978.

Reference Guide to American Literature, third edition, St. James Press, 1994.

Robertson-Lorant, Laurie, *Melville: A Biography*, Potter, 1995.

Rogin, Michael Paul, *Subversive Genealogy: The Politics and Art of Herman Melville*, Knopf, 1983.

Rosenberry, Edward H., *Melville and the Comic Spirit*, Harvard University Press, 1955.

Rosenberry, Edward H., *Melville*, Routledge & Kegan Paul, 1979.

Rourke, Constance, *American Humor: A Study of the National Character*, Harcourt, Brace, 1931.

Sachs, Viola, *The Game of Creation*, Editions de la Maison des sciences de l'homme, 1982.

Samson, John, *White Lies: Melville's Narratives of Facts*, Cornell University Press, 1989.

Sedgwick, William Ellery, *Herman Melville: The Tragedy of Mind*, Harvard University Press, 1944.

Seelye, John, *Melville: The Ironic Diagram*, Northwestern University Press, 1970.

Short Story Criticism, Gale, Volume 1, 1988, Volume 17, 1995.

Stern, Milton R., *The Fine Hammered Steel of Herman Melville*, University of Illinois Press, 1957.

Stetoff, Rebecca, *Herman Melville*, Messner, 1994.

Stone, Geoffrey, *Melville*, Sheed and Ward, 1949.

Thompson, Lawrance, *Melville's Quarrel With God*, Princeton University Press, 1952.

Weaver, Raymond W., *Herman Melville, Mariner and Mystic*, Doran, 1921.

Wenke, John Paul, *Melville's Muse: Literary Creation and the Forms of Philosophical Fiction*, Kent State University Press, 1995.

Widmer, Kingsley, *The Ways of Nihilism: Herman Melville's Short Novels*, California State Colleges, 1970.

Wilson, Edmund, *The Shock of Recognition, The Development of Literature in the United States by the Men Who Made It*, Farrar, Straus & Cudahy, 1943.

World Literature Criticism, Gale, 1992.

Wright, Nathalia, *Melville's Use of the Bible*, Duke University Press, 1949.

PERIODICALS

American Heritage, December, 1960, p. 110; June-July, 1986.

American History Illustrated, October, 1984, p. 38; October, 1991, p. 20.

American Literature, May, 1952, p. 224; November, 1953, p. 307; January, 1958, p. 463; November, 1971, p. 239.

Humanist, March-April, 1983, p. 29.

New Republic, April 11, 1981, p. 28.

New York Times Magazine, December 15, 1996, p. 60.

Reader's Digest, March, 1965, p. 182.*

—Sketch by J. Sydney Jones

Claude Monet

Personal

Born November 14, 1840, in Paris, France; died December 5, 1926, in Giverny, France; son of a grocer and his wife; married Camille Doncieux, 1870 (died, 1879); married Alice Hoschede, 1892 (died, 1911); children: (first marriage) Jean, Michel (sons). *Education:* Attended Academie Suisse, 1859-60; studied painting under Eugene Boudin, 1856-59, and Charles Gleyre, 1862.

Career

Painter. Exhibited first picture at Salon, Paris, 1865; lived in Argenteuil, 1872-78; moved to Giverny, 1883. *Exhibitions:* Major collections housed in museums in Boston, Chicago, New York City, Paris, d'Orsay, and Marmottan; work exhibited at major galleries throughout the world, including galleries in Berlin, Bremen, Frankfurt, Lisbon, Moscow, Munich, Rouen, Stockholm, Vienna, Cambridge, MA, Dallas, TX, and Washington, DC. *Military service:* Chaussures d'Afrique; served in Algeria, 1860-61.

Sidelights

Associated as much with the inspiration for his art as with his many paintings, Claude Monet is considered by many to be the foremost, as well as the founding, member of the Impressionist school of painting. Concerned with the play of light on the landscape, Monet's works exhibited new uses of both color and brush technique that were considered revolutionary within the art establishment of his day. Today he is best known for the series of "Water Lilies" paintings that he completed later in his life; his gardens in the French town of Giverny have also sparked a great deal of interest among horticulturalists and garden designers due to their sophisticated use of color. As the painter Cezanne is reported to have said, "Monet is only an eye, but, my God, what an eye!"

Monet was born in Paris, France, in November of 1840. The son of a grocer and his wife, Monet moved with his family to the seaside city of Le Havre in 1845, where he would remain for the rest of his childhood. Distracted and undisciplined, the young Monet was dismissed by both his teachers and his parents as not destined to amount to much; the boy's lack of interest in working in his father's grocery business further alienated him from the parental guidance that would have steered him down a structured academic path. His only interest, his art, became visible when Monet reached his teens; the young man gained a repu-

Completed in 1872, *Impression: Sunrise* was the work that inspired the school of Impressionism.

tation for drawing caricatures of prominent persons and friends, a talent he had put to work to make money by the time he was fifteen.

Early Mentor Proves Major Influence

In 1856, when Monet was sixteen, he met the painter Eugene Boudin, who recognized the younger man's talent. Boudin took the young painter under his wing and imbued in him his own passion for painting outside, in *plein air*, where the beauty and intricacy of nature could truly be seen and captured. This love of working outside, coupled with the older painter's fascination with water, would inform all of Monet's works, and can be seen in his first major work, "View from Rouelles," which he painted at sev-

enteen. The accurate, honest depiction of nature would also become one of the main characteristics of the school of painting he would later help to establish. Monet left Le Havre in 1859; he would acknowledge his artistic debt to his friend and mentor by returning repeatedly to visit Boudin throughout the older artist's lifetime.

While Monet had found a kindred spirit in Boudin, the constrictions of Le Havre to a young artist were too much. Paris, then the artistic center of Europe, beckoned, with its creative energies and communities of like-minded people, and Monet arrived there in 1859. The nineteen-year-old painter soon became disillusioned by the conformity to traditions he had not been conditioned to follow. Rejecting many of the formalized programs of study offered to him—including the highly acclaimed l'Ecole de Beaux Arts, a bastion of traditionalism—he eventually enrolled at the Academie Suisse, known for its less-structured atmosphere.

Even in his early work, Monet showed Boudin's influence through his belief in the importance of natural light and positioning. His method of working was to examine a setting at varying times of day and to capture its subtle transition through the seasonal shifts. A pencil sketch would provide the basis for his oil painting; on it not only the objects but the position of light and shadow would be carefully noted. His actual method of painting, which involved a series of sessions as short as fifteen minutes at the same time each day so as to capture similar patterns of light and shadow, has been described by Virginia Spate in her *Monet: His Life and Work:* "Monet laid in the major elements of the composition with broad parallel or criss-cross strokes and long loopy lines.

He covered the entire canvas in a first session of no more than half an hour. Later, Monet smudged the strokes and strengthened the calligraphic lines. . . . [He] must have returned to it again and again, using an extraordinary range of brushstrokes—thick and fat or fine, almost linear ones, scumbles, tiny dabs and even flecks of paint—to build up a surface so dense that some of the paintings' original contours are like sunken channels." He used five pure colors, placing them either side by side or one atop the other, thereby allowing the eye of the viewer, rather than the artist, to create variations of tone within each picture.

Monet was drafted into service for his country and went to Algeria with the Chaussures d'Afrique. Finding himself in a totally new environment, the young artist gained an even deeper awareness of light and landscape through exposure to the African continent, despite the brevity

During the 1890s Monet worked on a series of haystack paintings to improve his use of dimension and color.

of his service: in less than a year Monet had contracted typhoid and was shipped back to France through the intervention of an influential aunt. His aunt's only condition: that he make a committed effort to gain formal schooling in art. Still adamant in his refusal to attend the Ecole des Beaux Arts, Monet opted to join the studio of painter Charles Gleyre, a noted benefactor to struggling young artists that at that time included Pierre-August Renoir. Befriending Renoir as well as students Frederic Bazille and Alfred Sisley, Monet often escaped with the group to the forests of Fontainbleau, where the diverse landscape and the play of sunlight upon the natural vegetation inspired each of the young men.

While his artistic vision and technique broke with the classical and religious themes, dull, muted colors, and clearly defined images then in vogue in the Salon—the Paris art world's annual exhibition—Monet realized that only through the acceptance of his work by the Academie would he be a success as a painter. In conformance with the fashion of the day, he painted several indoor still-lifes. While his smaller paintings met with approval, the textured surface of Monet's larger canvasses invited criticism from artists who aspired to glass-smooth surfaces free of visible brushstrokes. Undaunted, he continued, finally producing "The Woman in the Green Dress" in 1866. This painting, reportedly painted in only four days and which featured the artist's girlfriend, Camille Doncieux, as its model, finally brought Monet the acclaim he had been seeking and gained him recognition in artistic circles in and around Paris. His next goal was admission to the Academie, and he worked diligently for the next year, finally producing "Women in the Garden" in 1866. Despite his efforts, the work was rejected for admission into the Salon.

Meanwhile, the young artist's financial circumstances were deteriorating. Because he was living with his girlfriend, his family ceased providing him with an allowance; furthermore, Camille had become pregnant with the first of the couple's two sons. The pair was forced to separate, Camille remaining in Paris with family while Monet moved in with his aunt, Madame Lecadre. With the outbreak of the Franco-Prussian war in 1870, he finally left France altogether and temporarily moved to London in order to avoid another term in the military. In England, the French artist became familiar with the works of his British coun-

terparts, among them John Constable, who focused on natural scenes of the countryside around his home and whose works were imbued with a fresh awareness of light and shadow, and landscape artist and watercolorist J. M. W. Turner.

Painting Establishes New Trend

Returning to France in 1871, Monet and Camille (whom he had married just months before) settled at La Havre, where he would paint his—indeed, one of modern art's—most significant works. A view of Le Havre harbor viewed from the artist's window, "Impression: soleil levant" ("Impression: Sunrise") was completed in 1872 and exhibited two years later in Paris at the studio of photographer Nadar, sparking the school of art that now bears its name. Impressionism, which as a trend began in the 1860s, is characterized by the painter's attempt to capture the play of sunlight on both the landscape and adults and children engaged in gentle, idyllic pastimes, in stark contrast to the deep, somber tones common in the works of painters in the major studios of the day. Dismissed by one critic as a "formless monstrosity," the subject matter of "Impression: Sunrise" symbolizes the instantaneous aspect of impressionist art, which strives to capture a brief moment in time on canvas.

By now Monet had returned to Paris, where he and his wife and children lived together at Vetheuil, in a house near the Seine. His first few years in Paris had been relatively stable; he had been able to satisfy the creditors that had hounded him during previous years and could now dedicate himself to his painting, often joined by friends Renoir and others of like mind and artistic sensibility. Unfortunately, the 1874 exhibition, which included works by Renoir, Edouard Manet, Degas, Cezanne, Pissarro, and Sisley, proved to be a financial disaster due to the controversial reception of the "impressionist" style. It was only with the help of Manet and the sale of several of his works at the Hotel Drouot that the artist could support his family. He and his family were able to remain together by taking up residency at the home of friends Ernest and Alice Hoschede, where they stayed from 1878 to 1881. After his retail stores went bankrupt, Ernest was forced to flee from France, leaving Alice and six children to fend for themselves, with Monet the sole breadwinner among the two families.

If you enjoy the works of Claude Monet, you may also want to check out the following:

The work of Impressionists such as Pierre-Auguste Renoir ("Le Moulin de la Galette"), Edouard Manet ("Bar at the Folies-Bergère"), Alfred Sisley, Paul Cézanne, Camille Pissarro, Berthe Morisot, and Edgar Degas.

Creates Masterful Gardens at Giverny

Monet's second son, Michel, was born in 1877, and Camille died of tuberculosis two years later. In 1892, after receiving news that Ernest Hoschede had died, Monet married the now-widowed Alice, moving with her, his two sons, and Alice's six children to a cottage on a former apple orchard in the village of Giverny, located to the northwest of Paris, where he would remain until his death in 1926. The impressionist group, which had been initially unified by the criticisms levelled against its young members, gradually dissolved, each artist going on to develop his own style as acceptance toward them grew. Monet had finally established a reputation as an artist of note through adopting a serial approach to landscape paintings, and was now living in comfort. Then forty-three years of age, and now presented with two-and-a-half acres of garden space at his new home, Monet "now could put into practice what previously he had only explored with paint—his perception of dimension, color and atmosphere," according to Vivian Russell in her *Monet's Gardens: Through the Seasons at Giverny*.

The early 1890s found the painter at work on a series of paintings of haystacks; in 1891 he produced a series of twenty-four separate renderings of a poplar grove that lined a stretch of waterway near his home at Giverny. By the following year, the painter was hard at work on a series of oils depicting the cathedral at Rouen, each version reflecting a shift in the natural light due to the changing seasons. His last significant series of painting was "Water Lily Pool," begun in 1900, which depicted a water garden the artist had constructed on his estate. As he would write to friend and critic Gustave Geffroy in 1908, "These land-scapes of water and reflections have become an obsession. They are beyond the powers of an old man, and yet I want to succeed in rendering what I perceive." While this series would eventually become among his most admired by lovers of his art, their creation proved a constant frustration to the elderly artist, who burned several of the canvases (by some accounts, up to five hundred canvases) and remained unconvinced that the remaining pictures were of exhibition quality. Deteriorating sight would cause him further frustration, and many of his final works reflected the distorted color sense that he himself experienced due to changes in his vision. In contrast to the artist's own appraisal of his work, the 1909 exhibit of his "Water Landscapes" would create a groundswell of interest in Monet's works.

Surprisingly, the gardens that the artist would become devoted to during the final decades of his life would be among his most enduringly popular works—in fact, they have drawn millions of tourists to Giverny since the house and grounds were painstakingly restored and opened to the public in September of 1980. While his art was in high favor after the "Water Landscapes" exhibition in 1909, by 1929 Monet's work had dropped from favor again. His style was perfunctorily dismissed by the newly appointed director of New York City's Museum of Modern Art, who wrote in a museum catalogue that "There are few moments in the history of art so removed from esthetic intention and so closely approximating a laboratory experiment as are Monet's series of `Haystacks.'"

Not until the 1950s, when French painter Andre Masson praised Monet's works, did he again find public favor, particularly among the school of abstract expressionists then in vogue. As Jerome Klein noted in *Atlantic*, commenting on the renewed interest in Monet by viewers in the technology-driven late twentieth century, "[Monet's later paintings will most likely be seen], not as the harbingers of a new era in twentieth-century art, but as striking examples . . . of unremitting efforts by the artist to carry on against all obstacles in search of the summit embodied in the water lily murals. In his own words, he sought the 'illusion of an endless whole, of water without horizon or bank; nerves tense from work would relax there . . . the refuge of a peaceful meditation in the center of a flowering aquarium.'"

■ Works Cited

Klein, Jerome, "The Strange Posthumous Career of Claude Monet," *Atlantic*, March, 1981, pp. 46-51.

Russell, Vivian, *Monet's Gardens: Through the Seasons at Giverny*, Stewart, Tabori & Chang (New York City), 1995.

Spate, Virginia, *Monet: His Life and Work*, Rizzoli (New York City), 1992.

■ For More Information See

BOOKS

Gerstein, Marc S., *Impressionism*, Hudson Hill Press (New York City), 1980.

Howard, Michael, *Monet*, Bison Books, 1989.

Mount, Charles Merrill, *Monet: A Biography*, [New York City], 1967.

Rewald, John, *The History of Impressionism*, fourth edition, Museum of Modern Art (New York City), 1973.

Tucker, Paul, *Monet: Life and Art*, Yale University Press (New Haven, CT), 1995.

Tucker, Paul, *Monet in the '90s: The Series Paintings*, Museum of Fine Arts/Yale University Press, 1995.

PERIODICALS

American Magazine of Art, March, 1927.

Art in America, October, 1992, p. 126.

ARTNews, January, 1984, p. 104.

Chicago, July, 1995, p. 68.

Detroit News and Free Press, January 21, 1998, p. D1.

Life, May, 1980, p. 62.

Smithsonian, February, 1980, p. 52.

U.S. News and World Report, August 31-September 7, 1992.

—Sketch by Pamela L. Shelton

Kyoko Mori

writer. *Member:* Modern Language Association of America, Associated Writing Programs.

■ Personal

Born March 9, 1957, in Kobe, Japan; immigrated to the United States, 1977; naturalized U.S. citizen, 1984; daughter of Hiroshi (an engineer) and Takako (a homemaker; maiden name, Nagai) Mori; married Charles Brock (an elementary school teacher, March 17, 1984 (divorced). *Education:* Rockford College, B.A., 1979; University of Wisconsin—Milwaukee, M.A. 1981, Ph.D., 1984. *Politics:* Democrat, feminist. *Hobbies and other interests:* Fiber arts (knitting, spinning, weaving), running, birdwatching.

■ Addresses

Home—De Pere, WI. *Office*—106-A South Broadway, De Pere, WI 54115. *Agent*—Ann Rittenberg, 14 Montgomery Pl., Brooklyn, NY 11215.

■ Career

Saint Norbert College, De Pere, WI, associate professor of English and writer-in-residence, 1984—;

■ Awards, Honors

Editors' Prize, *Missouri Review,* 1992, for poem "Fallout"; American Library Association Best Book for Young Adults, *New York Times* Notable Book, *Publishers Weekly* Editors' Choice, Council of Wisconsin Writers Best Novel, and Elizabeth Burr award for best children's book of the year, Wisconsin Library Association, all 1993, all for *Shizuko's Daughter;* Paterson Poetry Center Best Books for Young Adults, Council of Wisconsin Writers Best Novel, American Library Association Best Book for Young Adults, and Children's Books of Distinction Award, *Hungry Mind Review,* 1996, all for *One Bird.*

■ Writings

Shizuko's Daughter, Holt (New York City), 1993.
Fallout (poems), Ti Chucha Press, 1994.
The Dream of Water: A Memoir, Holt, 1995.
One Bird, Holt, 1995.
Polite Lies: On Being a Woman Caught between Cultures (essays), Holt, 1998.

Contributor of short stories to *Apalachee Quarterly, Beloit Poetry Journal, Crosscurrents, Kenyon Review—New Series, Prairie Schooner,* and *South-East Review.*

Contributor of poems to periodicals, including *Missouri Review, Paterson Review, American Scholar,* and *Denver Quarterly.*

■ **Work in Progress**

A novel; poems.

■ **Sidelights**

In several of her prose works, award-winning novelist and poet Kyoko Mori poignantly describes the devastating pain that haunts a young person who must deal with the death of a beloved parent. After coping with the suicide of her mother when Mori was still a preteen, she was then forced to watch her once secure way of life become drastically altered through the tirades of a selfish, patriarchal, and unfeeling father and an insensitive and equally selfish stepmother. This abiding sense of loss, which deprived Mori of both family and community and which has imbued much of her written work, would eventually prompt her to voluntarily give up yet another tie with her youth: her country. Attending an American college on a scholarship program, she felt more in sync with the relaxed, less emotionally inhibited culture of the United States than she did with the strictures in place in Japanese society. Since her college days, Mori has made her home in the United States, where she has written and published several critically acclaimed novels for young adults, the poignant memoir *The Dream of Water,* and *Polite Lies: On Being a Woman Caught between Cultures,* a book of essays.

Mori was born on the main island of Honshu, in the city of Kobe, Japan, in 1957. Located near both mountains and water, "Kobe is a very beautiful, sophisticated city," she once noted, "but it is also close to nature." The daughter of an engineer and his wife, she was born with both hips displaced, and spent her first year in leg harnesses to correct her gait. Fortunately, that condition was corrected and Mori was soon able to accompany her mother on walks in the mountains and enjoy the visits to the country home of her grandparents that the family made before she began school. She was inspired with an early love of reading and a love of beauty by her mother. A sensitive and creative woman, Takako Mori made a cultured home for her children, reading to both Kyoko and

her younger brother, Jumpei, from the time both children were small. Tragically, Takako would commit suicide when Mori was twelve, a victim of depression and, perhaps, the repressive Japanese society that relegated women to a subservient status in relation to their husbands.

Finds Western Literature Liberating

While, like most Japanese children, Mori had an early exposure to a few English words and phrases, she began a serious study of the language and its literature when she was twelve. She was immediately struck with the emotional content of much Western writing in comparison with the restraint of its Japanese counterpart; English would be her major in college and she now writes exclusively in her adopted language. "In my teenage years I read a lot of English books in English," she explained in an interview for *Authors and Artists for Young Adults* (*AAYA*). "Before then I don't remember that much what I read, because I don't think that in Japan they really have books written for teenagers. You have to read 'literature'—some 'Great Book' by some guy who died fifty years ago or something. And that was fine; I liked some of that. But to be thirteen and to be a girl and to read that is not necessarily a good experience because [much of Japanese literature] was so male and with such different aesthetics than my everyday life." While she was drawn to the beauty of the language she was exposed to in the books she read in school, Western books such as *Jane Eyre* and *Anne of Green Gables* captured her imagination.

In her junior year of high school, Mori was given the opportunity to study at a school in Mesa, Arizona, for a year as an exchange student. "It was a revelation for me," she once commented. "For the first time in my life I was away from the social constrictions of my society. In Japan there is so much pressure from family. You can't do . . . [certain things] because it will bring shame to your family." After returning to her home, Mori decided to intensify her studies in English; during her first two years of college in Japan she majored in the subject. "After my year in the United States, I began to think of English as my writing language. So much of Japanese aesthetics is involved in not saying what you want to. To talk about yourself in Japanese is considered rude. So English became a much better language for me

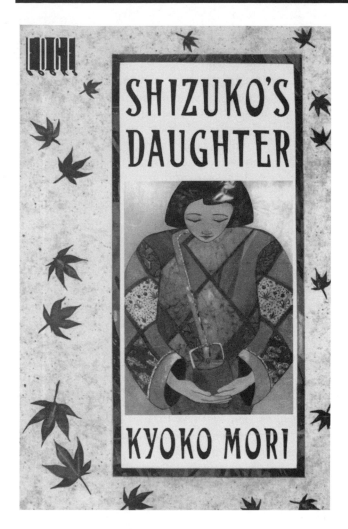

Yuki struggles with the death of her beloved mother and a difficult relationship with her father and new stepmother in Mori's award-winning young adult work.

as a writer." Her focus on writing in English became so intensive that Mori decided to finish her college education in the United States. She earned a scholarship to Rockford College in 1977 and graduated from that school two years later. Since then she has completed her master's degree and Ph.D. and established a career as a writer and educator.

Writes First Two Prose Works

Shizuko's Daughter, Mori's first published book, would be released in 1993. Based on a group of short stories that she wrote for her doctoral dissertation, the book tells the story of Yuki, a young girl who returns from a music lesson one day to discover her mother dead by her own hand. "People will tell you that I've done this because I did not love you," reads the suicide note Shizuko leaves for her daughter. "Don't listen to them. When you grow up to be a strong woman, you will know that this is for the best." During the six years that follow, Yuki must learn to deal with the changes in her life that follow her mother's death: the remarriage of her father, the gradual estrangement of grandparents, and her deep feelings of responsibility and guilt over her mother's unhappiness. Calling the book a "jewel," *New York Times Book Review* contributor Liz Rosenberg felt *Shizuko's Daughter* to be "one of those rarities that shine out only a few times in a generation. It begins and ends with a dream, with a death, yet it is not dreamy or tragic."

Shizuko's Daughter wasn't intended to be a young adult novel to begin with. But as Mori began to revise and edit her initial manuscript with the advice of her editor, she realized that conforming it to certain conventions of the genre ultimately made it a better novel: "Because the way I had it before, I time-skipped around a lot. Straightening that out made it a more straightforward book, which is what it needed to be."

One Bird, which Mori published in 1995, was even more concise than Mori's first book. In the novel, fifteen-year-old Megumi watches as her mother packs her suitcase and leaves the house of her husband, Megumi's father. Unable to go with her mother because to do so would be neither "appropriate" in Japanese society nor financially possible, Megumi is forced to deal with the vacuum left by her mother's abrupt departure, a vacuum that her distant father avoids filling by staying with an out-of-town mistress for long periods of time. During the course of the novel, her emotions and reactions shift from those of a little girl to those of a young woman through the support of a woman veterinarian whom she meets while attempting to care for a small bird. Ultimately, Megumi is able to creatively find a solution to her problem, a solution whereby she and her mother can spend at least part of the year together. "Kyoko Mori's second novel . . . is so lively and affecting that one imagines its readers will be too engaged by its heroine's situation to notice how much—and how painlessly—they are learning about another culture," according to *New York Times Book Review* critic Francine Prose. Noting that the book is filled with "small, radiant schemes and glints of observation," Prose added that *One Bird* shows that teen feelings and attitudes toward life are universal.

Writing for Teens Requires Poet to Adopt New Focus

As Mori noted in her interview with *AAYA*, writing for teens requires that authors rely more on character and plot than on imagery and style. "Both [*Shizuko's Daughter* and *One Bird*] had to be more straightforward, and in a way I think that

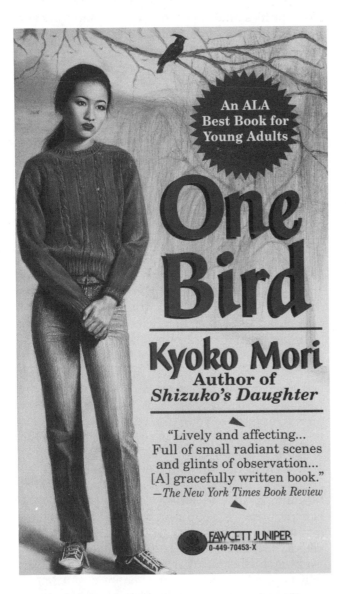

An ALA Best Book for Young Adults

One Bird

Kyoko Mori
Author of
Shizuko's Daughter

"Lively and affecting...
Full of small radiant scenes
and glints of observation...
[A] gracefully written book."
—*The New York Times Book Review*

FAWCETT JUNIPER
0-449-70453-X

With the help of a veterinarian she meets while caring for a bird, Megumi finds the strength to reach out to the mother who left her and her father.

this made them better books, because sometimes it is so easy to rely on your ability to write and, when you get to some crucial moment in the narrative, try to get through it through fine writing and strong imagery. And I see this as something that I am tempted to do because I am also a poet.

"But I think what you do well is also your downfall," Mori added. "And I think that when you're a poet as well as a fiction writer, there is always the temptation to do something poetic at a crucial moment. Writing for teens, you're not allowed to do that. You have to be straightforward and direct in developing the characters and manipulating the plot."

One Bird and *Shizuko's Daughter* are essentially the same story, seen from different points of view, according to Mori. "One is a tragic version of the story about an isolated teenager and the other is a more humorous version," the author explained. "In *One Bird*, I think there is an inherent sense of humor and resilience that Megumi doesn't take herself that seriously, not in the way that the teen in *Shizuko's Daughter* has to take herself seriously." Mori characterizes the books as "two flavors of the same thing," admitting that "maybe I needed to do that to grow up. I think that even though I didn't write those books to grow up, it became a process of that. When I first wrote *Shizuko's Daughter*, it was a way of admitting the pain in my life perhaps. And then when I wrote *One Bird*, it was a way of being able to look at that same story with more irreverence. And humor."

Sabbatical in Japan Results in Memoir

In 1990, with the manuscript for *Shizuko's Daughter* circulating among publishers, Mori decided to go to Japan on sabbatical "because it was the only foreign country where I speak the language," she explained to *AAYA*. She planned to keep a journal, out of which poems normally sprang, and then begin work on a new novel. While she was in Japan, visiting parts of the country that she had never seen as a child and spending time with beloved relatives, she thought to herself, "I'm kind of gathering material and waiting for that novel to form." Finding the time to keep a journal record of her thoughts and reflections was not difficult: "I couldn't sleep in Japan because I was jet-lagged," Mori recalled. "I kept waking up; I couldn't fall asleep,. . . but in a way this was good because it gave me a lot of time to write. In the middle of the night I can't sleep; what else am I going to do? I can only read so much."

After returning to her home in Wisconsin and writing several poems based on her experiences in her native country, Mori realized that an autobiography, rather than a novel, was to be the literary outcome of her trip. "I knew in Japan that the trip was so specific to my family that I couldn't see how I could write it as a novel," the writer explained. "I would be translating these facts in an uncreative way rather than transforming them. So I decided that I would do this as a nonfiction, autobiographical narrative." Mori realized from the start of her new project that she had a wealth of literary models, including *The Woman Warrior* by Maxine Hong Kingston, that read like novels but are nonfiction. The result of her creative efforts was *The Dream of Water: A Memoir*.

In *The Dream of Water*, the reader is drawn into the narrator's reality, but that reality is as compelling as a work of fiction due to Mori's ability to imbue her relatives and her setting with qualities that transcend the mundane and everyday. Each person she meets on her trip is linked to past memories, and past and present interweave on both a physical and emotional plain. Her beloved grandfather is dead, and she is left with only memories and the journals a relative saved for Mori after his death. The house where she lived when her mother committed suicide is gone, replaced by a parking lot, and yet the memories that empty space conjures up render it almost ghostlike. Called "deeply private" by *Booklist* contributor Donna Seaman, Mori's memoir unfolds with "dignity and cathartic integrity, chronicling not only her struggle with grief, anger, and guilt" and her growing understanding of the differences between Japanese and U.S. culture, but the author's ability to ultimately "finally feel at home in both worlds."

A Constant Ambition to Be a Writer

"I always wanted to be a writer," Mori maintained to *AAYA*. "When you're a kid, though, you have all these different aspirations, from the firefighter all the way to the great composer, all at the same time. While I had a series of these dreams, being a writer was always on the list. So every year it

---

If you enjoy the works of Kyoko Mori, you may also want to check out the following books and films:

Sharon Creech, *Walk Two Moons*, 1994.
Amy Tan, *The Kitchen God's Wife*, 1991.
Jacqueline Woodson, *I Hadn't Meant to Tell You This*, 1994.
The Joy Luck Club, based on the novel by Amy Tan, 1993.

---

would be a different list, but the recurring one was that I wanted to be a writer." In grade school she did a lot of writing, but it was actually her mother and grandfather who inspired her to take her writing seriously. "My grandfather wrote journal entries every morning," Mori recalled, looking back at the visits she made to her grandparents' house as a young child. "When I would go and stay with his family, he would get up and write in his diary. And that really inspired me. Writing was a serious thing. It was something my grandfather did every morning." Mori, who now teaches creative writing at Saint Norbert College in De Pere, Wisconsin, considers herself to be a fairly disciplined writer. "I'm not disciplined all the way in my life," she admitted in her interview, "but there are three or four things I'm very disciplined about: running is one of them, and writing. Those are things that I don't have a hard time getting to."

Views on Writing and Teaching Writing

A poet as well as a prose writer, Mori's craft follows certain stages, beginning with thoughts jotted down in journal entries, then poetry, and finally into prose. "I don't see the poems as just a process," she explained; "I see them as finished products. But once I do about ten poems, I start thinking, 'There's something I could do with this.' There's a collective thought that kind of forms in that process that leads me to do a longer prose project." Such is the process that Mori has used with each of her longer prose works. "The only time that I really think about audience is in terms of developing the plot as well as the imagery, so it has more to do with technique in the end than with the story itself," the author added.

Until Mori started teaching creative writing, she believed that anyone could write, on some level at least. "And that's still true," she admitted to *AAYA*. "I think that anyone can write better than he or she is doing *now*. But as I teach more I start thinking that talent really does play a valuable part in this. There are kids who, without trying, write something so much better than the kid who is trying so hard who is a good student. It really has to do with the way they can see.

"But some of the most talented students are not the best disciplined. [While] I think I can motivate them to be disciplined because they have something to work with, they have to put something out there before I can give them direction." She maintains that the better English majors, those who "read and analyze things and write clearly in an expository manner," don't always write the best stories or poems. "They just don't seem to have the 'eye,'" she surmises. "And that, to me, is much more frustrating than working with a talented but undisciplined student whom I have to nag by saying, 'Your rewrite is due in a week,' because I can usually get that student to do it. And if it's two days late, it's okay."

In addition to an active teaching schedule and a daily schedule given structure by her disciplined attitude towards running and writing, Mori continues to produce books, poems, and short stories. In 1998, she published a series of twelve essays wherein she contrasts living in the Midwest and living in Japan, titled *Polite Lies: On Being a Woman Caught between Cultures*. She is also working on another novel.

■ Works Cited

Mori, Kyoko, *Shizuko's Daughter*, Holt, 1993.
Mori, Kyoko, in a telephone interview conducted by Pamela Shelton for *Authors and Artists for Young Adults*, March 3, 1998.
Prose, Francine, review of *One Bird*, *New York Times Book Review*, November 12, 1995, p. 50.
Rosenberg, Liz, review of *Shizuko's Daughter*, *New York Times Book Review*, August 22, 1993, p. 19.
Seaman, Donna, "Poets Remembered," *Booklist*, January 1, 1995, p. 794.

■ For More Information See

BOOKS

Something about the Author, Volume 82, Gale, 1995.
Something about the Author Autobiography Series, Volume 26, Gale, 1998.

PERIODICALS

Bulletin of the Center for Children's Books, May, 1993, p. 291; January, 1996, p. 161.
English Journal, September, 1994, p. 87.
Horn Book, May, 1993, p. 291.
Kirkus Reviews, November 1, 1997, p. 1628.
Los Angeles Times Book Review, April 9, 1995, p. 6.
New York Times Book Review, February 5, 1995, p. 13; March 8, 1998, p. 19.
Publishers Weekly, January 25, 1993, p. 87; November 7, 1994, p. 54.
Voice of Youth Advocates, October, 1993, p. 217; February, 1996, p. 374.
Wilson Library Bulletin, January, 1994, p. 117.

—Sketch by Pamela Shelton

Marcia Muller

■ Personal

Born September 28, 1944, in Detroit, MI; daughter of Henry J. (a marketing executive) and Kathryn (Minke) Muller; married Frederick T. Guilson, Jr. (in sales), August 12, 1967 (divorced, 1981), married Bill Pronzini (a writer), 1992. *Education:* University of Michigan, B.A., 1966, M.A., 1971.

■ Addresses

Home—P.O. Box 2356, Petaluma, CA 94953-2536. *Agent*—Sonia Barber, 44 Greenwich Ave., New York, NY 10011.

■ Career

Sunset (magazine), Menlo Park, CA, merchandising supervisor, 1968-69; University of Michigan Institute for Social Research, Ann Arbor, MI, field interviewer in the San Francisco Bay area, 1971-73; freelance writer and novelist, 1973—. *Member:* Mystery Writers of America, Sisters in Crime, Women in Communications.

■ Writings

NOVELS

Edwin of the Iron Shoes, McKay, 1977, Mysterious Press, 1990.
Ask the Cards a Question, St. Martin's, 1982.
The Tree of Death, Walker, 1983.
Leave a Message for Willie, St. Martin's, 1984, Mysterious Press, 1990.
Games to Keep the Dark Away, St. Martin's, 1984.
(With Bill Pronzini) *Double,* St. Martin's, 1984.
There's Nothing to Be Afraid Of, St. Martin's, 1985.
The Legend of the Slain Soldiers: An Elena Oliverez Mystery, Walker & Company, 1985.
(With Bill Pronzini) *Beyond the Grave,* Walker & Company, 1986.
(With Bill Pronzini) *The Lighthouse,* St. Martin's, 1987.
Eye of the Storm, Mysterious Press, 1988.
There Hangs the Knife, St. Martin's, 1988.
The Cavalier in White, Harlequin, 1988.
Dark Star, St. Martin's, 1989.
The Shape of Dread, Mysterious Press, 1989.
There's Something in a Sunday, Mysterious Press, 1989.
The Cheshire Cat's Eye, Mysterious Press, 1990.
Trophies and Dead Things, Mysterious Press, 1990.
Where Echoes Live, Mysterious Press, 1991.
Pennies on a Dead Woman's Eyes, Mysterious Press, 1992.
Wolf in the Shadows, Mysterious Press, 1993.
Till the Butchers Cut Him Down, Mysterious Press, 1994.

The McCone Files, Crippen & Landru, 1995.
A Wild and Lonely Place, Mysterious Press, 1995.
The Broken Promise Land, Mysterious Press, 1996.
Both Ends of the Night, Mysterious Press, 1997.

COLLECTIONS EDITED WITH BILL PRONZINI

The Web She Weaves: An Anthology of Mysteries and Suspicious Stories by Women, Morrow, 1984.
Child's Play, Macmillan, 1984.
Witches' Brew, Macmillan, 1984.
Kill or Cure: Suspense Stories about the World of Medicine, Macmillan, 1985.
She Won the West: An Anthology of Western and Frontier Stories by Women, Morrow, 1985.
Dark Lessons: Crime and Detection on Campus, Macmillan, 1985.
Chapter and Hearse: Suspense Stories about the World of Books, Morrow, 1985.
The Deadly Arts: A Collection of Artful Suspense, Arbor House, 1985.
1001 Midnights: The Aficionado's Guide to Mystery and Detective Fiction, Arbor House, 1986.
The Wickedest Show on Earth, Morrow, 1986.
(Also with Martin H. Greenberg) *Lady on the Case*, Bonanza, 1988.
Detective Duos, Oxford University Press, 1997.

OTHER

(Author of preface) *Hard-Boiled Dames: A Brass-Knuckled Anthology of the Toughest Women from the Classic Pulps*, St. Martin's, 1986.
(Author of introduction) *Spadework: A Collection of "Nameless Detective" Stories*, Crippen and Landru, 1996.
(Contributor) *Great Stories of the American West II*, D. I. Fine Books, 1996.

■ **Sidelights**

Mystery writer Sue Grafton has described Marcia Muller, the creator of the popular "Sharon McCone" detective series, as "the founding mother of the contemporary female hardboiled private eye." Most readers would agree, for when Muller introduced her signature character in the 1977 book *Edwin of the Iron Shoes*, she changed the genre forever. In the years since, Muller has quietly built the McCone mysteries into one of the most successful and popular series of its type. However, she remains less well known than some of her female peers. "Still less celebrated than Sue Grafton or Sara Paretsky, Muller quietly keeps getting better and better," Charles Champlin noted in the *Los Angeles Times Book Review*.

Marcia Muller, who was born and raised in a middle-class home in Detroit, became interested in the world of books and writing at an early age. "Ever since I could read, I'd wanted to write fiction," Muller told Bruce Taylor of the *Armchair Detective* in a 1990 interview. She persisted in her dream while studying at the University of Michigan for a bachelor's degree in English. Muller pursued creative writing as a hobby until one of

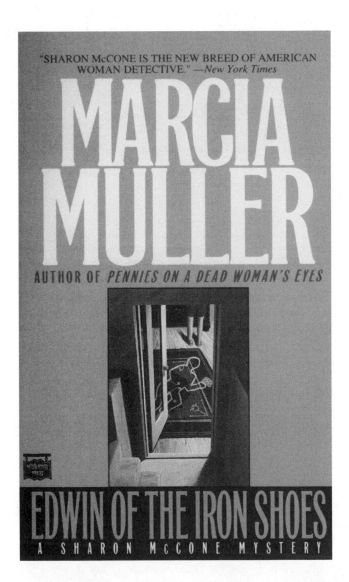

Muller transformed the mystery genre when she first introduced Sharon McCone in this 1977 work centering on a mannequin that hides a deadly secret.

her professors advised her that she had no future as a writer. "He told me I had nothing to say, which of course, at 19, was true. It was devastating and I backed off completely," Muller recalled in a 1994 interview with Dulcy Brainard of *Publishers Weekly*.

A Rough Start

In 1967, following her first marriage, Muller and her husband moved to California. There she worked for two years as the merchandising supervisor at a local magazine. She returned to the University of Michigan in 1971 for a year to finish a journalism degree. Afterward, it did not take long for her to realize she was *not* a good reporter. "I was always putting quotes into people's mouths," she told Brainard.

Muller returned to San Francisco, where she spent the next six years toiling at a variety of dead-end jobs. From 1971 to 1973 she conducted field interviews for the University of Michigan Institute of Social Research. This experience proved to be invaluable training for her future literary career. "[It] required writing very detailed character sketches and descriptions of living conditions," Muller told Brainard. "It got me into parts of San Francisco and the Bay area where I never would have gone, and meeting people whom I never would have met."

It was during this period that Muller began writing again. She did freelance articles and also read voraciously. When Muller chanced to pick up a novel by Ross Macdonald, it changed her life. She got hooked on mystery stories. Muller subsequently discovered the works of such masters of the genre as Raymond Chandler, Dashiell Hammett, Christie Sayers, Ngaio Marsh, and P. D. James. "I also read a lot of American women [writers], two in particular, Dorothy Uhnak and Lillian O'Donnell, who were doing police procedural series with very strong women characters," Muller said in her interview with Brainard. "I had finally found the form I wanted to write."

At that time, there were no recurring female detective characters in American crime fiction. The few homegrown novels that featured women protagonists had been written by men, and Muller felt their efforts were not very good; she also decided that she could do better. In 1972, Muller

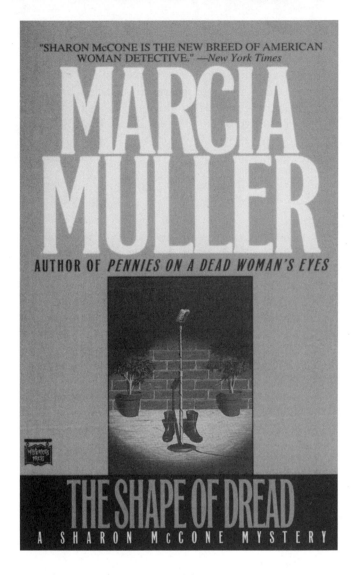

Humor and death mingle when a comedy club employee confesses to the murder of a star comedian in this Sharon McCone mystery.

began work on her first Sharon McCone mystery. From the beginning, she intended it to be the first book in a series. "As for the character being a woman, that came out of the old business of 'write what you know.' I knew what it was like to be a woman, and I could imagine what it was like to be a detective," Muller told Bruce Taylor. She went on to explain the origin of Sharon McCone's name: the former is one of Muller's favorite given names; the latter is an "in-joke" because it was borrowed from a former director of the Central Intelligence Agency. Asked by Taylor how much of herself there is in the McCone character, Muller admitted, "There is a great deal of me in her. We are alike in a lot of our attitudes, likes, and dislikes. We are also very different in a number of respects: she is much braver than I. She is more outgoing and social. In developing her, I chose to make her background and living circumstances different from mine because I needed to keep an objective distance between us."

To Muller's disappointment, her first Sharon McCone novel proved to be unpublishable. Undaunted, she continued to write. Then one day she spotted an advertisement in *Writer's Digest* magazine, placed by a literary agent who was seeking new clients. Michele Slung of the David McCay Company rejected the first novel that Muller sent her, but she asked to see other writings about the McCone character. Muller sent Slung a draft for a novel called *Edwin of the Iron Shoes*. That book, which became the first in the "Sharon McCone" series, caused little stir despite the fact it was chosen as the December 1977 main selection of the Mystery Guild. Apart from Muller, few people felt that *Edwin of the Iron Shoes* was in any way special or different. "No new ground here, and all situations are predictable, but the plotting is competent and the writing lively," wrote Newgate Callendar in the *New York Times Book Review*. A reviewer for *Publishers Weekly* echoed that praise, describing the book as "entertaining" and concluding that "one looks forward to Muller's future mysteries."

The irony in those words quickly became apparent when Muller's agent decided to stop representing mystery writers. A new agent tried unsuccessfully for four years to find a publisher for a second Sharon McCone novel. Muller's luck changed when she switched agents and met mystery writer Bill Pronzini, the creator of the "Nameless Detective" mystery series. Muller and Pronzini became involved both romantically (they married in 1992) and creatively. Pronzini gave Muller's career a vital boost when he introduced her to Tom Dunne, an editor at St. Martin's Press. Dunne liked Muller's writing and decided to publish a novel called *Ask the Cards a Question*. Ironically, just a year earlier another editor at St. Martin's had rejected the same book.

The reviews for this second Sharon McCone novel were also indifferent. "Sharon [McCone] remains a tepid heroine, not much helped here by plot and

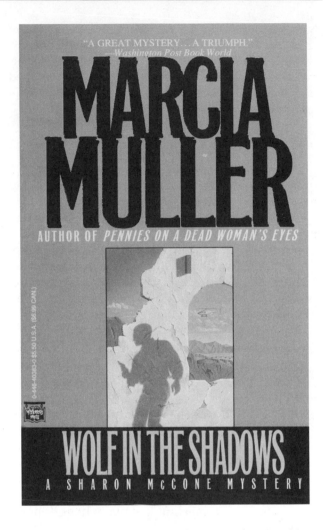

McCone's personal life comes into play in this 1993 work, which finds the private eye determined to track down her lover, who has disappeared.

characters that are mildly interesting at best," wrote a critic in *Kirkus Reviews*. Nick B. Williams of the *Los Angeles Times Book Review* was even less complimentary, musing that "[Muller's] second mystery . . . makes me wonder what could have been so good about her first." Newgate Callendar of the *New York Times Book Review* offered mild praise when he wrote, "It's all neighborhood stuff—the corner grocer, a blind man, a fortuneteller, the middle class of the city—written in a snappy prose and nicely worked on."

Fortunately for Muller, enough copies of her first two books were sold that Dunne became convinced that it was only a matter of time until her mysteries found their audience. Between 1982 and 1988, Dunne edited six Sharon McCone novels.

If you enjoy the works of Marcia Muller, you may also want to check out the following books and films:

The suspense thrillers of Patricia D. Cornwell, including *Postmortem*, 1990.
The works of Sue Grafton, including *A Is for Alibi*, 1982, and *I is for Innocent*, 1992.
The Long Goodbye, directed by Robert Altman, 1973.

With each one, Muller matured as a writer and her sales increased. "Back then, you could learn to write while making a living at it," she explained to Dulcy Brainard. "It's not as easy for new writers now. Publishers aren't willing to bring people along slowly, the way I developed. I think if I'd had more and tougher editing then, I'd have come along a lot faster. But St. Martin's allowed me to learn to write." Muller's progress was reflected in the increasingly favorable reception for her books. Nick B. Williams of the *Los Angeles Times Book Review* praised her 1984 novel *Leave a Message For Willie* as "one of the niftiest crime yarns this year." The following year, Callendar of the *New York Times Book Review* lauded Muller's literary talents, observing that although *There's Nothing to Be Afraid Of* was not the best book in the "Sharon McCone" series, the writing was nonetheless "crisp, fluent, [and] neat. There is no extraneous material." Jo Ann Vicarel of *Library Journal* agreed, commenting that "[Sharon McCone] becomes more real with each book."

Begins Two New Series

Throughout the 1980s, Muller worked at broadening her literary range. In 1984, she collaborated with her partner Bill Pronzini on the novel *Double*, which teamed the Sharon McCone and Nameless Detective characters; Muller and Pronzini plotted the book, then wrote alternating chapters. The pair also coauthored a 1987 "straight suspense novel" entitled *The Lighthouse*, and they co-edited various anthologies. In addition, Muller took her own career in fresh directions by devising two new mystery series. One involved an Hispanic museum curator named Elena Oliverez, the other a character named Joanna Stark, who works in the San Francisco securities industry.

The debut book in the "Elena Oliverez" series, *The Tree of Death*, was published in 1983. Kathleen Maio of the *Wilson Library Bulletin* praised the novel as "a promising series premiere." The second Elena Oliverez adventure, *The Legend of the Slain Soldiers*, came out two years later. Reviewer Connie Fletcher of *Booklist* liked it, stating that "The exciting action is spiced with fascinating information on Depression-era labor struggles and the *los ranchos grandes* period of California history." However, Fletcher's opinion proved to be in the minority; other reviews were less complimentary.

The third—and final—Elena Oliverez mystery, *Beyond the Grave*, was published in 1986. For that

"MULLER HAS US HOOKED."—*New York Times Book Review*

MARCIA MULLER

A Sharon McCone Mystery

TILL THE BUTCHERS CUT HIM DOWN

WARNER BOOKS 60302 3 $5 99 U.S.A. ($6 99 CAN.)

A shady client leads McCone into a series of dangerous situations in this action-packed thriller.

book, Muller once again teamed with Pronzini to good effect. Bernard Drew of the *Armchair Detective* described the novel as "fascinating reading," while a *Publishers Weekly* critic lauded it as an "exciting, colorful tale of historic and modern times in Baja, California." Despite the book's success, Muller's enthusiasm for the Oliverez character by now had waned, and she decided to end the series. "After a while, it became difficult to relate to that character," Muller told Bruce Taylor. "It was because she was so young, not just in years, but in attitude, and finally I found I just didn't share her concerns and problems."

Joanna Stark, Muller's other new fictional creation, debuted in a 1988 novel entitled *There Hangs the Knife*, and she returned in *The Cavalier in White* and *Dark Star*. Reviewing *There Hangs the Knife*, a writer for *Publishers Weekly* predicted, "Muller may not be able to get as much mileage out of this detective as she has out of her deservedly successful Sharon McCone." That assessment proved correct, for Muller shelved the Stark character in 1989. "Joanna Stark was intended to be a long-running series until I wrote the first book and realized that what I was writing was a personal story that couldn't extend beyond three books," Muller explained to Taylor.

McCone Series Endures

After abandoning both the Elena Oliverez and Joanna Stark characters, Muller again focused her creative energies on her trademark "Sharon McCone" series. New books have appeared at a rate of almost one per year throughout the 1990s and have earned positive reviews. The 1994 work *Till the Butchers Cut Him Down*, in which McCone becomes reacquainted with a figure from her past, a former drug peddler turned corporate wheeler-dealer named T. J. (Suitcase) Gordon, "shows both Marcia Muller and Sharon McCone at the top of their form," according to Ronald C. Miller in the *Armchair Detective*. And a 1996 thriller, *The Broken Promise Land*, about a country-music star whose life is in danger, was described as a "superbly plotted, briskly paced mystery" by Benjamin Segedin in *Booklist*.

Reviewing the 1993 Sharon McCone novel *Wolf in the Shadows*, Chicago *Tribune Books* columnist Dick Adler predicted this "may be Muller's breakthrough book—the one that finally pushes her into the household icon realm." As yet, that "breakthrough" still has not happened. Nonetheless, Muller seems to have found her literary niche; her readership remains loyal and the critics continue to applaud her work. Reviewer Bill Ott of *Booklist* has described her as "a veteran who knows all the tricks."

■ Works Cited

Adler, Dick, "Trouble in L.A.'s Chinatown and—Alas!—Death in Venice," *Tribune Books* (Chicago), September 4, 1993, p. 5.

Review of *Ask the Cards a Question*, *Kirkus Reviews*, April 15, 1982, p. 520.

Review of *Beyond the Grave*, *Publishers Weekly*, September 12, 1986, p. 84.

Brainard, Dulcy, "Marcia Muller: 'The Time Was Ripe,'" *Publishers Weekly*, August 8, 1994, pp. 361-62.

Callendar, Newgate, review of *Edwin of the Iron Shoes*, *New York Times Book Review*, November 27, 1977, p. 36.

Callendar, Newgate, review of *Ask the Cards a Question*, *New York Times Book Review*, November 7, 1982, p. 39.

Callendar, Newgate, review of *There's Nothing to Be Afraid Of*, *New York Times Book Review*, October 6, 1985, p. 35.

Champlin, Charles, review of *Till the Butchers Cut Him Down*, *Los Angeles Times Book Review*, October 7, 1994, p. 8.

Drew, Bernard A., review of *Beyond the Grave*, *Armchair Detective*, summer, 1987, p. 300.

Review of *Edwin of the Iron Shoes*, *Publishers Weekly*, October 10, 1977, p. 60.

Fletcher, Connie, review of *The Legend of the Slain Soldiers*, *Booklist*, August, 1985, p. 1635.

Maio, Kathleen, review of *The Tree of Death*, *Wilson Library Bulletin*, January, 1984, p. 361.

Miller, Ronald C., review of *Till the Butchers Cut Him Down*, *Armchair Detective*, fall, 1994, pp. 494-95.

Ott, Bill, review of *Both Ends of the Night*, *Booklist*, May 1, 1997, p. 1462.

Segedin, Benjamin, review of *The Broken Promise Land*, *Booklist*, April 1, 1996.

Taylor, Bruce, "The Real McCone" (interview), *Armchair Detective*, summer, 1990, pp. 260-69.

Review of *There Hangs the Knife*, *Publishers Weekly*, May 6, 1988, p. 96.

Vicarel, Jo Ann, review of *There's Nothing to Be Afraid Of*, *Library Journal*, September 1, 1985, p. 216.

Williams, Nick B., review of *Ask the Cards a Question, Los Angeles Times Book Review,* October 10, 1982, p. 7.

Williams, Nick B., review of *Leave a Message for Willie, Los Angeles Times Book Review,* November 4, 1984, p. 11.

■ For More Information See

PERIODICALS

Armchair Detective, fall, 1989, p. 434; fall, 1995, p. 383; winter, 1996, pp. 119-20.

Booklist, May 15, 1992, p. 1666.

Globe and Mail (Toronto), December 7, 1985; April 11, 1987.

Kirkus Reviews, May 15, 1993; June 15, 1995, pp. 817-18; May 1, 1996; June 1, 1997; August 15, 1997.

Library Journal, October 1, 1977; May 1, 1993; May 1, 1996.

Los Angeles Times, August 14, 1985; June 6, 1986.

Los Angeles Times Book Review, February 12, 1989, p. 6; July 12, 1992, p. 8; August 11, 1992, p. 5; July 11, 1993, p. 8.

New York Times Book Review, March 12, 1989, p. 24; December 24, 1989, p. 23; November 4, 1990, p. 30; August 9, 1992, p. 20; July 18, 1993, p. 17; August 7, 1994, p. 16; September 3, 1995, p. 15.

Publishers Weekly, May 26, 1989, p. 58; September 7, 1990, p. 77; May 24, 1991, p. 49; May 17, 1993; April 22, 1996; May 27, 1996; May 5, 1997.

Tribune Books (Chicago), July 7, 1991, p. 6; July 3, 1994, p. 4.

USA Today, July 27, 1987.*

—*Sketch by Ken Cuthbertson*

Donna Jo Napoli

guistics professor, 1980-87; Swarthmore College, Swarthmore, PA, linguistics professor, 1987—. *Member:* Society of Children's Book Writers and Illustrators, Authors Guild, Authors League of America, Linguistic Society of America, Societa linguistica italiana.

■ Personal

Born February 28, 1948, in Miami, FL; daughter of Vincent Robert and Helen Gloria (Grandinetti) Napoli; married Barry Ray Furrow (a law professor), December 29, 1968; children: Elena, Michael Enzo, Nicholas Umberto, Eva, Robert Emilio. *Education:* Harvard University, B.A., 1970, Ph.D., 1973.

■ Addresses

Office—Linguistics Dept., Swarthmore College, Swarthmore, PA 19081. *Agent*—Barry Furrow, Widener University School of Law, Wilmington, DE 19803.

■ Career

Writer. Smith College, Northampton, MA, lecturer in philosophy and Italian, 1973-74; University of North Carolina, Chapel Hill, lecturer in mathematics and Italian, 1974-75; Georgetown University, Washington, DC, assistant professor of linguistics, 1975-80; University of Michigan, Ann Arbor, lin-

■ Awards, Honors

One Hundred Titles for Reading and Sharing selection, New York Public Library, 1992, Children's Book of the Year, Bank Street Child Study Children's Book Committee, 1993, and New Jersey Reading Association's Jerry Award, 1996, all for *The Prince of the Pond: Otherwise Known as De Fawg Pin*; Best Book selection, *Publishers Weekly*, and Blue Ribbon Book designation, *Bulletin of the Center for Children's Books,* both 1993, and Best Book for Young Adults selection, Young Adult Library Services Association (YALSA), 1994, all for *The Magic Circle;* Children's Books of the Year, Bank Street Child Study Children's Book Committee, 1995, for *When the Water Closes over My Head,* and 1996, for *Jimmy, the Pickpocket of the Palace;* Leeway Foundation Prize for excellence in fiction, 1995; Pick of the List, American Booksellers Association, 1996, for *Zel* and *Song of the Magdalene;* Best Book selection, *Publishers Weekly* and *School Library Journal,* and Blue Ribbon Book designation, *Bulletin of the Center for Children's Books,* all 1996, all for *Zel;* Hall of Fame Sports Book for Kids, Free Library of Philadelphia, 1996, for *Soccer Shock.*

Napoli has also held grants and fellowships in linguistics from the National Science Foundation, the National Endowment for the Humanities, the Mellon Foundation, and the Sloan Foundation.

■ **Writings**

JUVENILE FICTION

The Hero of Barletta, illustrated by Dana Gustafson, Carolrhoda Books, 1988.

Soccer Shock, illustrated by Meredith Johnson, Dutton, 1991.

The Prince of the Pond: Otherwise Known as De Fawg Pin, illustrated by Judith Byron Schachner, Dutton, 1992.

The Magic Circle, Dutton, 1993.

When the Water Closes over My Head, illustrated by Nancy Poydar, Dutton, 1994.

Shark Shock, Dutton, 1994.

Jimmy, the Pickpocket of the Palace, illustrated by Judith Byron Schachner, Dutton, 1995.

The Bravest Thing, Dutton, 1995.

Zel, Dutton, 1996.

Song of the Magdalene, Scholastic, Inc., 1996.

Trouble on the Tracks, Scholastic, Inc., 1997.

On Guard, Dutton, 1997.

Stones in Water, Dutton, 1997.

Sirena, Scholastic, Inc., 1998.

For the Love of Venice, Delacorte, 1998.

Changing Tunes, Dutton, 1998.

ADULT NONFICTION

(Editor) *Elements of Tone, Stress, and Intonation*, Georgetown University Press, 1978.

(With Emily Rando) *Syntactic Argumentation*, Georgetown University Press, 1979.

(Editor with William Cressey) *Linguistic Symposium on Romance Languages: Nine*, Georgetown University Press, 1981.

Predication Theory: A Case Study for Indexing Theory, Cambridge University Press, 1989.

(Editor with Judy Anne Kegl) *Bridges between Psychology and Linguistics: A Swarthmore Festschrift for Lila Gleitman*, L. Erlbaum, 1991.

Syntax: Theory and Problems, Oxford University Press, 1993.

(With Stuart Davis) *Phonological Factors in Historical Change: The Passage of the Latin Second Conjugation into Romance*, Rosenberg & Sellier, 1994.

Linguistics: Theory and Problems, Oxford University Press, 1996.

Also contributor to and editor of poetry books, including *The Linguistic Muse, Meliglossa, Lingua Franca,* and *Speaking in Tongues.* Author of numerous professional articles on linguistics. Also author of two short stories, "Sweet Giongio" and "Little Lella," both in collections compiled and illustrated by Diane Goode and published by Dutton in 1992 and 1997.

■ **Work in Progress**

Albert, illustrated by Jim LaMarche, for Harcourt.

■ **Sidelights**

Donna Jo Napoli has never forgotten the refuge from difficult situations that she found in the world of language—it's a thrill she tries to convey to her young adult and middle-school readers, as well to as those who only know her as an accomplished linguistics professor. Whether she's writing historical fiction, spinning new versions of fairy tales, or detailing the complications of life on the brink of adulthood, Napoli brings humor and great respect for language to every book. In an essay in the *Junior Library Guild*, Napoli wrote: "When I write, I say the words out loud. All my books are meant to be read aloud. I try to talk to my reader. I want my books to be my readers' friends—just as books were my friends in my childhood and remain so today."

Born in Miami, Florida, Napoli was the youngest of four in a family that moved often—thirteen times by her thirteenth birthday. Her contractor father built several houses at once, settling the family in one until it sold and then moving on. In an essay in *Something about the Author Autobiography Series (SAAS)*, Napoli describes herself as an "outsider." The family's constant uprooting and sometimes precarious financial situation kept her a little isolated from her peers, so, initially at least, school was a struggle. But by the second grade, Napoli learned to read, delighting in the seemingly endless supply of books in the school library. Although she remembers her father read the newspaper, Napoli wrote in *SAAS* that "We had no books in our house. None whatsoever. . . . I'm not sure I ever saw my mother read at all." Even with her enthusiasm for reading, Napoli didn't shine academically until a few years later, her progress stunted by her severe myopia. When her vision problems were finally diagnosed and treated, Napoli began to excel at her schoolwork. She was voted "best all around" by the time of her high school graduation in 1966, with special proficiency in math, French, and Latin.

The full scholarship she earned to Radcliffe College, then the women's college affiliated with Harvard University, became a turning point for Napoli. As she wrote in *SAAS*, "the world of ideas I had yearned for in the books I read and gotten a hint of in my high school honors classes opened up to me at last." She got her undergraduate degree in math but switched to Romance linguistics for graduate school. Academically serious, Napoli also made an early commitment in her personal life, marrying in her junior year. She took an expository writing class in college, a required course. When her impressed instructor advised her to continue with writing, she described herself as "momentarily dazzled." She continued in her *SAAS* entry, "I didn't want to be a poor writer. I wanted to earn money and never have to make my family move and never have to make my children worry about whether there would be food on the table. I was practical."

Napoli worked as a lecturer and assistant professor after finishing her doctorate, teaching at Smith College, the University of North Carolina, and Georgetown University. When she got pregnant with her first child in 1974, Napoli and husband Barry Furrow adjusted their lives to center on the family: he left private practice to teach law, she focused on gaining a tenured full professorship. Between her first and second children, Napoli suffered a miscarriage. She worked out her considerable grief in a series of letters to a friend, writing sometimes two and three times daily. When Napoli eventually got pregnant again, her friend returned her letters, all saved, and told her she'd written a novel. "He was wrong," Napoli states in *SAAS*, "Epistolary novels . . . are carefully shaped." But she made an important realization: "Writing transported and absorbed me." Recognizing that writing allowed her to express much of what she couldn't say otherwise, Napoli embarked on her writing career.

A Giant Opens the Door to Publishing

As she moved from Georgetown to the University of Michigan and from there to Swarthmore College, Napoli's academic career flourished. For a few years the writing lagged a little further behind, but Napoli remained undaunted by the several rejections she received. Her perseverance paid off in 1988 when Carolrhoda Press in Minnesota published *The Hero of Barletta*, her version of an Italian folktale in which a giant keeps his town from being conquered by an army. A second work stayed closer to home, drawing on her son's experiences with soccer. In *Soccer Shock*, the ten-year-old hero has magic freckles that can both see and talk. An agent to whom Napoli submitted the book dismissed this idea as too "dopey." Convinced by her own children and other young readers, Napoli submitted the manuscript—with freckles intact—to Dutton, where it was accepted. A *Kirkus Reviews* critic credited the freckles with "stealing the show," but also found the book "a well-written story with an affectionate, tolerant cast." In *School Library Journal*, Denise Krell deemed the freckles "far-fetched" but concluded that this "lighthearted novel succeeds with genuine characters in a believable setting."

Napoli followed with several books for younger readers: *The Prince of the Pond*, a different take on the frog-prince fairy tale, whose popularity inspired a sequel, *Jimmy, the Pickpocket of the Palace*. Typical of the critical praise for her ingenuity was the *Kirkus Review* critic who liked the "astonishing amount of in-depth natural history cleverly enmeshed in its endearing, screwball charm" found in *The Prince of the Pond*. In *SAAS*, Napoli credited her own childhood with much of the stories' inspiration. "Though I was a loved child, I was never taken seriously. . . . The family problems were so huge that my own life within it was dwarfed. The only one who took me seriously, as a result, was me. . . . And when I write for children, I am dead serious."

In her first novel for young adults, Napoli applied her ability to delve beyond the obvious with another well-known tale. Narrated by *Hansel and Gretel*'s evil witch, *The Magic Circle* sympathetically explains what drove the witch to such cruelty. Originally a healer, the sorceress succumbs to the temptation of evil spirits. Eating a child, which she feels compelled to do, will condemn her to eternal damnation. She therefore removes herself from society, until Hansel and Gretel happen to arrive at her doorstep. Pam Nealon-LaBreck, writing in *Kliatt*, lauded the "compelling and complex historical background" Napoli manages to create for "one of the archetypal characters in literature." *Voice of Youth Advocates* critic Rosie Peasley stated that with the author's "beautifully and sensitively written" novel, she "presents a powerful, effective alternative to the traditional tale." A reviewer in *Southern Book Trade* noted Napoli's "skill and grace" in creating "powerful emotion" in a work "filled with intensity, beauty and terror." Ann Waldron, of the *Philadelphia Inquirer*, found *The Magic Circle* "fantastic, yet entirely credible in the world of medieval superstition and evil that Napoli has created." Several reviewers agreed with Marc Silver's assessment in *U.S. News & World Report* that "parents and children might wind up fighting about who gets to read the book first."

Using Personal, Biblical, and Political History

After *The Magic Circle*, Napoli planned a series of amplifications and reinterpretations of fairy tales. Her next installment, in 1996, was *Zel*, a reworking of *Rapunzel*. Alternating her narrative among Zel, the prince, and the witch, Napoli's version allowed the reader sympathy with the witch and deep psychological insight into the motivations of all the characters. A reviewer in *Publishers Weekly* contended that "the genius of this novel lies not just in the details but in its breadth of vision." The critic declared: "Its shiveringly romantic conclusion will leave readers spellbound." *Horn Book* contributor Roger Sutton found the writing "although always sensuous in description and perceptive in shading character . . . less concentrated" than in Napoli's earlier work. Despite his objections to some vagueness and "a telescoped last chapter," Sutton approved the book's ability to "transform . . . myth without flippancy, honoring the power of its roots." Bruce Ann Shook, writing in *School Library Journal*, admired that this "story realistically portrays the dismal effects of isolation on [Zel's] mind and spirit. . . . This version, with its Faustian overtones, will challenge readers to think about this old story on a deeper level." In *Voice of Youth Advocates*, Sarah Flowers pronounced *Zel* "exceptional," and a "moving exploration of the age-old question: 'What will I do—and what will I give up—to achieve my heart's desire?'" Citing the mother-daughter conflicts that inform much of *Zel*, Katie O'Dell Madison, writing in *School Library Journal*, found that the "captivating" novel "though extreme in nature . . . represents many modern parent-child relationships."

If you enjoy the works of Donna Jo Napoli, you may also want to check out the following books and films:

Carol Matas, *After the War*, 1996.
Jennifer Roberson, *Lady of the Forest*, 1992.
Jane Yolen, *Briar Rose*, 1992.
The Princess Bride, directed by Rob Reiner, 1987.

Turning away from folklore, Napoli embarked on historical fiction with *Song of the Magdalene*. Set in Magdala in the Palestine of the first century and based on Mary Magdalene's life, the novel offers an interpretative biography that traces her girlhood as the daughter of a wealthy Jewish widower to her life with Jesus. In *SAAS*, Napoli wrote that the research alone "took most of a year. And a lot of my misery over the loss of my baby is built into the center of this story." A *Kirkus Reviews* contributor noted that the tale's "length, stiff prose, . . . and deliberate pace" might keep readers from "appreciating the intelligence with which Napoli develops her themes and characters." A *Publishers Weekly* reviewer had trouble with the book, criticizing the pacing as "clotted around too many climactic moments," but also felt that "readers may come away with new thoughts about a different era." Writing in *Voice of Youth Advocates*, Libby Bergstrom was more enthusiastic about "the power of Napoli's investigation into the human psyche [to] draw YA readers; Miriam [Mary] is a character they will not soon forget."

Napoli incorporates many of her own experiences into her novels, particularly the extensive travelling she has done with her family in Europe, Australia, and South Africa. Her 1997 novel, *Trouble on the Tracks*, details the adventures of Zach and his younger sister, Eve, who wind up alone on Australia's famous train, The Legendary Ghan. Dastardly smugglers and a lengthy separation from their parents lead the brother and sister into all sorts of adventures. Stevenson, critiquing the work in the *Bulletin of the Center for Children's Books*, found the story a "traditionally unlikely middle grades adventure" and a bit contrived. But she liked the siblings' relationship, finding their "dialogue authentic and the characterization . . . credible."

Combining both a sense of place and historical perspective, Napoli set *Stones in Water* in Europe during World War II. Based in part on the memories of a real survivor, the novel tells of Roberto, a thirteen-year-old Venetian who, along with his best friend Samuele (who happens to be Jewish), is seized by German soldiers and sent to a labor camp near Munich. His loyalty to his friend and his ability to survive are put to the test. In *Horn Book*, Kitty Horn admired "Napoli's detailed and gripping descriptions [that] bring the incomprehensible tragedy to life for readers." She found the perspective "unique" and deemed this "an affecting coming-of-age novel with a vivid and undeniable message about the human costs of war." For a *Publishers Weekly* reviewer, *Stones in Water* was a "gripping, meticulously researched" story that "portrays a war in which resisters and deserters are the real heroes." The reviewer concluded that "children will be riveted by Roberto's struggle to stay alive—and to aid others along the way—against enormous odds. And adults may never view WWII the same way again." A *Kirkus Reviews* contributor found this a "memorable survival story" in which the protagonist moved from "victim to hero, seizing control of his life for a noble cause."

In addition to her books for young adults, Napoli has written both picture books for very young readers and mysteries and nonfiction for adults. As she noted in *SAAS*, "I found that writing helped me through difficult times in my life. I'm happy when I write. Very." She divides her time nearly evenly between her academic and literary careers, though fiction gets a little more attention. As a working mother, Napoli finds ways to do more than one thing at once, often combining mundane housework such as laundry with her composition of a manuscript (she usually has several in progress at once).

With what *Bulletin of the Center for Children's Books* contributor Betsy Hearne termed her "proven talent for unexpected viewpoints," Napoli constantly reminds her readers that things are rarely as they seem—in fairy tales *or* real life. Rather than shedding her "outsider" point of view, she has incorporated it into all her work. In the *ALAN Review*, Napoli talked about the fact that "maybe one of the defining characteristics of adolescence is that for some significant period of time between the ages of twelve and eighteen most of us feel like outsiders. . . . For some of us, being an outsider is not just a certain perspective on life—it is not something that naturally changes with time—but, instead, is a lifelong characteristic. We are simply different." She encourages anyone who feels the urge to write not to ignore it, positing three matter-of-fact rules: to write what you know (or what you can find out through your own reading); to write about something that matters to you; and to use good language. Napoli has written of the hard work that writing is, the learning and relearning of ways to deal truthfully with characters. "Maybe that's why I love writing," she noted in *SAAS*, "it keeps my head running."

■ Works Cited

Bergstrom, Libby, review of *Song of the Magdalene*, *Voice of Youth Advocates*, February, 1997, p. 331.

Flowers, Sarah, review of *Zel*, *Voice of Youth Advocates*, April 1, 1997.

Hearne, Betsy, review of *The Magic Circle*, *Bulletin of the Center for Children's Books*, April, 1993, p. 260.

Horn, Kitty, review of *Stones in Water*, *Horn Book*, January/February, 1998, pp. 77-78.

Krell, Denise, review of *Soccer Shock*, *School Library Journal*, April, 1992, p. 118.

Madison, Katie O'Dell, "Our Daughters in Danger," *School Library Journal*, January, 1998, pp. 40-41.

Review of *The Magic Circle*, *Southern Book Trade*, June, 1995.

Napoli, Donna Jo, essay in *Junior Library Guild*, April-September, 1995, p. 30.

Napoli, Donna Jo, essay in *Something about the Author Autobiography Series*, Volume 23, Gale, 1997, pp. 161-78.

Napoli, Donna Jo, "Fairy Tales, Myths, and Religious Stories," *ALAN Review*, fall, 1997, pp. 6-9.

Nealon-LaBreck, Pam, review of *The Magic Circle*, *Kliatt*, November, 1995, p. 18.

Peasley, Rosie, review of *The Magic Circle*, *Voice of Youth Advocates*, August, 1993, p. 169.

Review of *The Prince of the Pond*, *Kirkus Reviews*, October 1, 1992, p. 1259.

Shook, Bruce Ann, review of *Zel*, *School Library Journal*, September, 1996.

Silver, Marc, "Kids' Books for Adults?," *U.S. News & World Report*, December 20, 1993.

Review of *Soccer Shock*, *Kirkus Reviews*, September 15, 1991, p. 1225.

Review of *Song of the Magdalene*, *Kirkus Reviews*, September 1, 1996.

Review of *Song of the Magdalene, Publishers Weekly,* November 4, 1996, p. 77.

Stevenson, Deborah, review of *Trouble on the Tracks, Bulletin of the Center for Children's Books,* February, 1997, p. 217.

Review of *Stones in Water, Kirkus Reviews,* October 15, 1997, p. 1585.

Review of *Stones in Water, Publishers Weekly,* September 1, 1997, p. 106.

Sutton, Roger, review of *Zel, Horn Book,* September/October, 1996, p. 603.

Waldron, Ann, review of *The Magic Circle, Philadelphia Inquirer,* August 8, 1993.

Review of *Zel, Publishers Weekly,* June 17, 1996, p. 66.

■ For More Information See

PERIODICALS

Booklist, January 15, 1993, p. 909; July, 1993, p. 1957; January 1, 1994, p. 827; October 15, 1994, p. 427; March 15, 1995, p. 1331; October 1, 1995, p. 317.

Bulletin of the Center for Children's Books, January, 1993, p. 153; September, 1994, p. 21; June, 1995, p. 355; October, 1995, p. 64; January, 1997, p. 182; March, 1997, p. 253; February, 1998, pp. 214-15.

Kirkus Reviews, June 15, 1993, p. 789; January 1, 1994, p. 72; May 1, 1995; January 15, 1997, p. 144; April 15, 1998, p. 584.

Publishers Weekly, January 27, 1992, p. 98; November 16, 1992, p. 64; June 14, 1993, p. 73; February 21, 1994, p. 255; June 12, 1995, p. 61; July 3, 1995, p. 62; October 30, 1995, p. 62; March 23, 1998, p. 101.

School Library Journal, August, 1988, p. 84; October, 1992, p. 118; August, 1993, p. 186; March, 1994, p. 223; January, 1995, p. 109; June, 1995, p. 112; October, 1995, p. 138.

Voice of Youth Advocates, February, 1998, pp. 387-88.*

—Sketch by C. M. Ratner

Theresa Nelson

80; St. Mary's School, Katonah, NY, glee club director, 1983-90. *Member:* Authors Guild, Authors League of America, Society of Children's Book Writers and Illustrators, Southern California Council on Literature for Children and Young People.

■ Personal

Born August 15, 1948, in Beaumont, TX; daughter of David Rogers, Jr. (an insurance executive) and Alice Carroll (a real estate agent; maiden name, Hunter) Nelson; married Kevin Cooney (an actor), September 26, 1968; children: Michael Christopher, Brian David, Errol Andrew. *Education:* University of St. Thomas, B.A. (magna cum laude), 1972. *Politics:* Democrat. *Religion:* Roman Catholic. *Hobbies and other interests:* "Singing, dancing, playing the piano. Most of all I love reading and going to movies and plays."

■ Addresses

Home—3508 Woodcliff Rd., Sherman Oaks, CA 91403.

■ Career

Writer, 1983—; speaker in schools, libraries, and literary groups. Theatre Under the Stars, Houston, TX, actor and teacher of creative dramatics, 1971-

■ Awards, Honors

Best Book of the Year citation, *School Library Journal*, 1986, and Washington Irving Children's Choice Award, 1988, for *The Twenty-Five Cent Miracle*; Notable Children's Trade Book in the Field of Social Studies citation, National Council for the Social Sciences-Children's Book Council, 1987, for *Devil Storm*; Notable Children's Book citation and Best Book for Young Adults citation, American Library Association, Best Book of the Year citation, *School Library Journal*, Editor's Choice citation, *Booklist*, Fanfare citation, *Horn Book*, Pick of the Lists citation, *American Bookseller*, Books for Children citation, Library of Congress/Children's Literature Center, Teacher's Choice citation, International Reading Association, Books for the Teen Age citation, New York Public Library, Notable Children's Trade Book in the Field of Social Studies citation, National Council for the Social Sciences-Children's Book Council, all for *And One for All*; Notable Children's Book citation and Best Book for Young Adults, American Library Association, Best Book of the Year citation, *School Library Journal*, Fanfare citation, *Horn Book*, Books for the Teen Age citation, New York Public Library and Children's Literature Center, Books for Children citation, Library of Congress, all for *The Beggars' Ride;* Best Book of the Year citation, *School Library Journal,* 1994, Books for the Teen Age citation, New York Public Library, Child Study Children's Book Award, Child Study Book Committee at Bank Street College of Education, 1994, Honor Book selection, *Boston Globe-Horn Book Awards,* 1995, Award for Distinguished Fiction, Southern California Council on Literature for Children and Young Adults, 1995, Best Book for Young Adult, Quick Picks for Young Adults, and Notable Book citations, American Library Association, all for *Earthshine.*

■ Writings

The Twenty-Five Cent Miracle, Bradbury, 1986.
Devil Storm, Orchard, 1987.
And One for All, Orchard, 1989.
The Beggars' Ride, Orchard, 1992.
Earthshine, Orchard, 1994.
The Empress of Elsewhere, DK Ink, 1998.

Contributor of story, "Andrew, Honestly," in *Don't Give Up the Ghost,* Delacorte, 1993.

■ Sidelights

It was just luck—the first letter of his last name—which sent Theresa Nelson's draftee husband to Korea instead of Vietnam. One of the couple's friends was not so fortunate; he was sent to fight in the war in Vietnam. Nelson's husband, Kevin Cooney, and his friend exchanged letters until the day that one of Cooney's letter came back with a stamped notice that the addressee was deceased. Cooney and Nelson soon learned that their friend had been killed in the fighting. Nelson, barely out of her teens and newly married, did not know how to deal with the war, or the death of her husband's friend. "We didn't know anything about life and death," she recalled in an interview with *Authors and Artists for Young Adults (AAYA).* She added, "it was easy enough to pretend" that the war "wasn't there." But some twenty years later, when Nelson, an accomplished author, observed that her own son was receiving letters from various branches of the armed forces urging him to enlist, her feelings about Vietnam surged back. Nelson began to write the book which would be described as "powerful" by a *New York Times Book*

Review critic, and which would win several citations: *And One for All.* For this book and others, Nelson has received praise for her complex portrayal of young characters, her intensely detailed settings, and her treatment of difficult issues.

Nelson was born in 1948 in Beaumont, Texas, to a family which eventually included eleven children altogether. Her father was a former Junior World Champion calf roper, a tap dancer, and a World War II veteran as well as an insurance executive; her mother was a ballerina, story teller, and real estate agent. As a small child, Nelson loved to hear her mother read books and tell stories (especially about the pirates that were supposed to have buried treasure on the Gulf Coast). When she grew older, she enjoyed family trips to the library. Nelson wrote her own stories, poems, and plays, and with the goal of becoming a stage performer, she took singing, piano, and dancing lessons.

Nelson explained to *AAYA* that her childhood memories provide inspiration and material for her work as a writer: "Everyday when I work I'm digging into my past." Although Nelson recalled a "very happy childhood," she felt that "even the happiest childhood can be pretty traumatic—the years eleven to thirteen can be tough for anybody." Nelson's own memories of those years are "vivid." "Even in a big happy family I think you are just so beset by doubts. It's that time of self discovery," she continued. "You think the world's looking at you. . . . You feel so different from everyone else." Nelson's books continue to feature protagonists from eleven to thirteen years old because "I just keep feeling drawn to the intense emotion—the conflict and comedy and tenderness of those years."

Nelson attended college at the University of St. Thomas in Houston. There, she was active in theatre and involved in numerous plays. She met Cooney, her future husband, in one of these plays. The couple married in 1968, and their first son, Michael, was born the next year. While Nelson continued her studies at the university, she worked as both as an actress and a creative dramatics teacher at the Theatre Under the Stars. Nelson graduated with a bachelors degree in 1972, and gave birth to two more sons, Brian and Errol. After taking a tour around the country as actors, the family made Katonah, New York, home for several years. It was there that Nelson, while working as a glee club director at a private school, began to write seriously.

A First Novel Brings Nelson Attention

Traveling—and finding herself far from home—positively affected Nelson's creativity. When Nelson began writing, she thought that she would write about her family's travels, but she began instead to write about a young girl living a small town just like the one in which she grew up (renamed Calder and rearranged geographically). The resulting book, *The Twenty-Five Cent Miracle*, features Elvira Trumbull, whose unemployed and alcoholic father provides her with little comfort or guidance. Elvira spends much time in the library and develops a friendship with the librarian, Miss Ivy. Rather than go peacefully to live with an aunt, Elvira plays matchmaker, and tries to set up her father and the librarian; when this plan fails, she attempts to run away. By the end of the novel, however, Elvira begins to appreciate her father's love for her, and he begins the process of reforming his life. Nelson's first novel received a Washington Irving Children's Choice Award, as well as a place on *School Library Journal*'s Best Book of the Year List.

Nelson was pining for Texas when she remembered a story her mother had told her long ago. The story—which gave Nelson goosebumps as a girl—was about a mysterious tramp who saved some children during a storm. Still fascinated with the story, Nelson did some research in the Galveston library about the tramp, and about the storm in Galveston which killed six thousand people. Nelson found that there was no information about the strange tramp, and this knowledge "freed" her to create her own character. Nelson was nevertheless very careful to learn all she could about life in Galveston before the storm, as well as about the storm itself and the devastation it caused, by reading newspapers and interviews with survivors. One of those newspaper stories told of a crazy, wild roamer who boasted of sailing with the legendary pirate Jean LaFitte. Nelson put two and two together, and asked herself "what if this old man is the illegitimate son of Lafitte and a slave girl, or what if this is at least the rumor, and this man is looking for his father's buried treasures?" Asking what if, and adding some personal memories, Nelson turned a historical event into an exciting and mysterious story for young adults, *Devil Storm*.

Devil Storm is set on the Gulf Coast of Texas in 1900. The novel begins the story of a fictional, watermelon-farming family, the Carrolls, after the death of their youngest child. Thirteen-year-old Walter and Alice, a bit younger, are the eldest in the Carroll family. Although they usually obey their parents, they make an exception to befriend a wanderer known as Tom. Tom is a mysterious figure; the people in the community think he is a madman, the son of a pirate named Jean Lafitte. Walter and Alice come to love Tom's stories, and they care for him; they warn him after they learn that he is suspected of stealing chickens. When

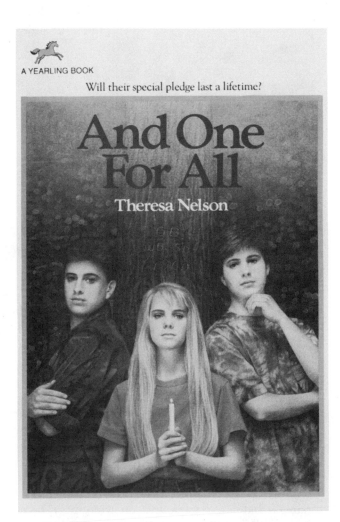

A YEARLING BOOK

Will their special pledge last a lifetime?

And One For All
Theresa Nelson

Having pledged an oath of loyalty to one another years ago, two teenagers in the late 1960s find themselves on opposite sides of the fence regarding the Vietnam War.

the devastating storm arrives, the father of the Carroll family is away in Galveston, and it is Tom who rescues the family. He disappears after leaving Alice his mother's locket.

Devil Storm met with approval from critics. According to Barbara Chatton of *School Library Journal*, "the book builds to a fever pitch of intensity as the story parallels the rising waters of the storm and flood." Ann A. Flowers of *Horn Book* wrote, "the author has a light but accurate hand with the local dialect and culture." In the words of a *Publishers Weekly* critic, Nelson "offers readers a look at a little-known corner of the nation's past."

Recalling the Past in *And One for All*

Nelson returned to the memories of her early adulthood while utilizing Katonah as the setting in *And One for All*. The story opens in 1968, as Geraldine rides on a bus towards Washington, D.C. Readers are then taken back to upstate New York in 1966, and introduced to Geraldine's brother Wing, and his friend, Sam. Geraldine's family life is relatively peaceful until the talk about war in Vietnam intensifies. While Sam, whose father was killed in the Korean war, decides to protest, Wing quits school and joins the Marines. As Geraldine's family worries about Wing, they distance themselves from Sam. Geraldine is saddened and confused, but when her family is informed of her brother's death, she blames Sam. After taking the bus to the capital, she finds Sam at an anti-war demonstration at the Washington Monument and confronts him. As Gerry Larson of *School Library Journal* observed, Geraldine finally understands "that Sam was always on Wing's side in trying to end the war," and she convinces her family to share the same perspective.

In a review of *And One for All*, Betsy Hearne of *Bulletin of the Center for Children's Books* found that "[p]lot, dialogue, and setting are effortlessly authentic" and referred to the book as "a thought-provoking probe of the past." "Nelson has written a touching story, which will probably provoke middle graders to think about war and its consequences," concluded Frances Ruth Weinstein in *Voice of Youth Advocates*. According to Phillis Wilson of *Booklist*, the novel is "heartening in its integrity and wrenching in its effect."

In this 1994 work, two girls, each of whom has a parent with AIDS, journey to the mountains in search of a miracle cure.

Nelson's next book, published in 1992, emerged from her fascination with Atlantic City. The family lived in Atlantic City for a short time while Cooney worked as an actor in a play there. Their basement apartment, hurriedly procured, was usually empty—Nelson and her sons were often out exploring the boardwalk and the streets with names that are now found on Monopoly boards. Nelson thought it would be interesting to write a book set on this life-size predecessor to the Monopoly board. Also, as she told *AAYA*, Nelson was struck by the sight of "people living in the most terrible poverty" she had ever seen, suffering so close to all the "glitz and glamour," and to all the money changing hands in the casinos.

A couple of years later, Nelson was invited to tell stories for visiting children at a women's prison. Nelson recalls the experience as a strange one: although she heard the gates of the prison shutting behind her, and knew she was in a prison, the room, and the children, were completely normal. Nelson noticed a girl in the audience who obviously "thought she was way too cool" to be listening to children's stories. The girl, some twelve years old, was dressed like a punk rocker with high heels, a short tight skirt, makeup and costume jewelry, and she was chewing gum. Nelson saw beyond the girl's costume to understand that she was "just like me when I was twelve years old." This girl had just lived in more difficult circumstances. Later, trying to write, Nelson found an image of the girl emerging in her mind. The girl was in Atlantic City, walking into a group of teenage runways. "I started asking myself questions, why is she there, what is she doing?"

The result of this careful questioning of her own imagination was *The Beggars' Ride*. Just twelve years old, the protagonist in this novel, Clare, has been sexually abused by her alcoholic mother's boyfriend. Thinking that she can contact her mother's ex-boyfriend Joey, she runs away to Atlantic City. Yet when Clare arrives, Joey is gone, and an elderly man named A. J. is living at Joey's address. Clare takes up with a group of children who, like Clare, are homeless. Savvy and streetwise, they show her how to live without parental support. The children are forced to rely on A. J. when the leader of the gang is stabbed. As Stephanie Zvirin of *Booklist* explained, A. J. flies them "to temporary safety in his old plane" and "begins a new cycle of adult-child trust." Maeve Visser Knoth of *Horn Book* observed that the author treats several "somber issues . . . but balances them with wry humor and hope in a poignant, effective novel." Jacqueline C. Rose of *Kliatt* noted that "the story is rich with feelings—of anger, fear, mistrust, and love. . . ."

Writing *Earthshine* Is a Joy

Earthshine evolved after one of the Nelson family's friends, an actor, died of AIDS. He was "an amazing actor, writer, comedian, musician—the star of

every show. We all loved him. . . . He was the last person in the world you could imagine dying." Nelson recalled that this man had a daughter, whom she had not seen in years, but she remembered her watching her father perform from backstage, with her "eyes lit up." Nelson could not stop thinking of the girl, and what she had been through during her father's illness and death. Nelson scribbled some notes, as much to sort through her own feelings as to begin a story about a girl living in Los Angeles with a beloved father dying of AIDS. Nelson did not write anything she liked until she heard the character that became Isaiah talking in her mind. After that, revealed Nelson, writing *Earthshine* was a "joyful experience." "I feel sure my friend was around."

As Margery Grace, or "Slim," the female protagonist in *Earthshine*, prefers to live in Hollywood with her father, a television actor, she keeps the seriousness of his condition away from her mother. She joins a children's support group and meets Isaiah, whose father has died of AIDS and whose pregnant mother also has the AIDS virus. Together, twelve-year-old Slim and eleven year-old Isaiah ponder life and death; Slim benefits from Isaiah's optimism. She finally agrees to go with Isaiah to visit Hungry Valley in search of a miracle. In a concluding scene featuring fog and flowers, the children, in some respects, find what they need.

Earthshine, like Nelson's other books, won praise from many critics. The book is as "much about a parent's dying as it is about gay themes," explained Mary Harris Veeder in *Booklist*. "This special book should find a wide audience," wrote Amy Kellman in *School Library Journal*. According to a *Voice of Youth Advocates* critic, Nelson's work "makes AIDS a little more understandable to preteens." "Few juvenile books set in Southern California give such a sense of place," commented Linda Perkins in *Wilson Library Bulletin*.

Nelson's sixth book began with an image of a mansion the author recalled from her childhood. The mansion belonged to a wealthy family beset by tragedy. Nelson's aunt had married into the family, and although Nelson was invited to swim in the outdoor swimming pool, she was never invited inside the house. She was also never allowed to touch the family's pet monkey. Nelson was busy with another story when she "heard a little kid talking." In her mind, she pictured this

If you enjoy the works of Theresa Nelson, you may also want to check out the following books and films:

Peter Abrahams, *Hard Rain*, 1988.
M. E. Kerr, *Night Kites*, 1986.
Marsha Qualey, *Hometown*, 1995.
In Country, starring Bruce Willis and Emily Lloyd, 1989.

child, a boy, standing at the gates to the mansion, and looking in at a girl who was angry and wanted out. "And then I saw the monkey run over the gate." Nelson developed the image into a story in *The Empress of Elsewhere*.

The Empress of Elsewhere is about a girl whose father is dead (readers aren't told what has happened to her mother in the beginning of the book) and who has gone to live with her paternal grandmother. The grandmother never leaves the mansion, and she does not allow the girl to leave it, either. When a monkey escapes from the mansion's gated yard, the boy and his little sister return it and meet the girl. The grandmother enlists the boy and his sister to babysit the monkey, and they develop a relationship with the girl as well. Gradually, the mystery of the monkey's presence, and of the girl's family, is revealed. "Everybody in this book is trying to escape—the whole book is about people trying to break free from whatever their cages are," Nelson stated.

Nelson Reveals How She Writes

Nelson told *AAYA* how she writes her books. While the process of creating each of her books has been different, she explained: "mostly I start up all my stories sitting down with an old . . . spiral notebook," jotting down ideas and memories. "Stuff just turns up. I never really plan that—you never know what or why or where some particular thing sticks with you." Sometimes, the bits and pieces turn into a story, and "sometimes nothing happens." It is a good sign, however, when "characters start talking to me." From that point on, Nelson is not quite sure what will happen in the story. She makes "tentative outlines, but then I never ever follow them. I know who the people are, and let them talk. And its not just

character description, it's seeing what they do—you can't really separate character and action, or character and plot. It's so interwoven. Sometimes you don't know who a person is until you see him doing something."

Many of Nelson's most important characters are inspired by people she has known. Like the mother in *Devil Storm*, Nelson's grandmother "lost her son William and never got over it, even after raising six other children. He was a force in my life and my mother's, though neither of us ever knew him. In my book the mother in that story can't . . . go on with her life." Geraldine from *And One for All* is "very much" Nelson herself. "She's just as torn as I was in those days." Wing is a composite of family members: Nelson's older brother, her younger brothers, her father (who joined the marines at a young age) and her first two sons. The little brother in *And One for All* was "based on my youngest son at that age; we called him 'The Captain' just like in the book." There is also "quite a bit" of Nelson's husband in the character of Slim's father in *Earthshine*.

Place, as well, is very important to Nelson. Instead of recreating the places she remembers, however, she adjusts them as she sees fit. Her settings are often "dream versions" of actual places, "slightly skewed." Sometimes she takes a place she has seen and develops it. For example, the scene in *Earthshine,* in which a field of poppies is revealed as the fog lifts is based on a sight Nelson and her son witnessed as she drove him to college. Nelson also often writes about places she is living in at the time. The view out of Slim's windows in *Earthshine* is Nelson's view, and the deer that visit Slim's backyard are those that visit Nelson's.

Once Nelson knows her characters, has her setting, and is into her story, she writes and rewrites until she is satisfied. Nelson has had to throw out beginnings and endings, switch perspectives, and even eliminate characters. "The answers don't come right away," she acknowledges.

Nelson, who continues to write for children, lives in Southern California with Cooney. (Cooney has appeared on many television series, including *Law and Order, NYPD Blue,* and *The Fresh Prince of Bel Air,* and in a number of films, including *Primary Colors*). Her children have grown up: Michael is teaching and attending graduate school, Brian is an inventory analyst and a "filmmaker at heart," and Errol is a jazz guitarist.

■ Works Cited

Review of *And One For All*, *New York Times Book Review*, October 22, 1989, p. 35.

Chatton, Barbara, review of *Devil Storm*, *School Library Journal*, June-July, 1987, pp. 111-12.

Review of *Devil Storm*, *Publishers Weekly*, June 26, 1987, p. 73.

Review of *Earthshine*, *Voice of Youth Advocates*, October, 1994.

Flowers, Ann A., review of *Devil Storm*, *Horn Book*, November, 1987, pp. 737-38.

Hearne, Betsy, review of *And One For All*, *Bulletin of the Center for Children's Books*, January, 1989, p. 130.

Kellman, Amy, review of *Earthshine*, *School Library Journal*, September, 1994, p. 241.

Knoth, Maeve Visser, review of *The Beggars' Ride*, *Horn Book*, November/December, 1992, pp. 729-30.

Larson, Gerry, review of *And One For All*, *School Library Journal*, February, 1989, p. 102.

Nelson, Theresa, interview with R. Garcia-Johnson for *Authors and Artists for Young Adults*, March 2, 1998.

Perkins, Linda, review of *Earthshine*, *Wilson Library Bulletin*, March, 1995, pp. 105-6.

Rose, Jacqueline C., review of *The Beggars' Ride*, *Kliatt*, July, 1994, p. 10.

Veeder, Mary Harris, review of *Earthshine*, *Booklist*, September, 1994, p. 35.

Weinstein, Frances Ruth, review of *And One For All*, *Voice of Youth Advocates*, April, 1989, p. 30.

Wilson, Phillis, review of *And One For All*, *Booklist*, March 15, 1989, p. 1302.

Zvirin, Stephanie, review of *The Beggars' Ride*, *Booklist*, November 1, 1992, p. 504.

■ For More Information See

PERIODICALS

Booklist, April 15, 1986, p. 1226.

Bulletin of the Center for Children's Books, September, 1987, pp. 14-15.

Horn Book, March, 1989, p. 218.

Kirkus Reviews, October, 1994.

Los Angeles Times, March, 1988, p. 319.

New York Times Book Review, April 9, 1995, p. 25.

Publishers Weekly, October 13, 1989, p. 56.

—Sketch by R. Garcia-Johnson

James Patterson

■ Personal

Born March 22, 1947, in Newburgh, NY; son of Charles (an insurance broker) and Isabelle (a teacher and homemaker; maiden name, Morris) Patterson. *Education:* Manhattan College, B.A., 1969; Vanderbilt University, M.A., 1970.

■ Addresses

Home—760 West End Ave., New York, NY 10025. *Office*—J. Walter Thompson Co., 466 Lexington Ave., New York, NY 10017. *Agent*—Arthur Pine Associates, Inc., 250 West 57th St., Suite 417, New York, NY 10019.

■ Career

J. Walter Thompson (JWT) Company, New York City, junior copywriter, beginning 1971, JWT/U.S.A. Company, named vice president and associate creative supervisor, 1976, JWT/New York, named senior vice president and creative director, 1980, JWT/U.S.A. Company, named executive creative director and member of board of directors, 1984, chairman and creative director, 1987, and chief executive officer, 1988, chairman of JWT/North America, 1990—.

■ Awards, Honors

Edgar Award for best first mystery novel, Mystery Writers of America, 1977, for *The Thomas Berryman Number.*

■ Writings

FICTION

The Thomas Berryman Number, Little, Brown, 1976.
The Season of the Machete, Ballantine, 1977.
The Jericho Commandment, Crown, 1979, new edition published as *See How They Run,* Warner Books.
Virgin, McGraw, 1980.
Black Market, Simon and Schuster, 1986.
The Midnight Club, Little, Brown, 1989.
Along Came a Spider, Little, Brown, 1993.
Kiss the Girls, Little, Brown, 1995.
Hide and Seek, Little, Brown, 1996.
Jack and Jill, Little, Brown, 1996.
(Coauthor with Peter de Jonge) *Miracle on the 17th Green,* Little, Brown, 1996.
Cat and Mouse, Little, Brown, 1997.

NONFICTION

The Day America Told the Truth, Prentice-Hall, 1991.
(Coauthor with Peter Kim) *The Second American Revolution,* Morrow, 1994.

■ **Work in Progress**

Pop Goes the Weasel and *When the Wind Blows.*

■ **Adaptations**

Kiss the Girls was adapted for a film starring Morgan Freeman as Alex Cross and also starring Ashley Judd, Paramount, 1997; *Along Came a Spider* has been optioned for film.

■ **Sidelights**

An accomplished advertising executive and best-selling writer, James Patterson has proven again and again that he understands how to please his audience. Concentrating on thrillers and suspense stories, he has fostered a loyal following of readers, particularly for his several books that feature Alex Cross, a psychologist-turned-detective who is African American, though Patterson himself is not. His books combine grisly detail with complicated plots and sell in the hundreds of thousands of copies all over the world. While balancing two successful careers is not easy, as Patterson told *People*'s Maria Speidel, "I like to go inside myself, but I also need to go outside and meet other people, and I like the ad work." The contrasts—he is boss to more than a thousand employees and a disciplined writer—seem to fuel Patterson's fundamental need to communicate with people at many levels.

Patterson was born in 1947 in Newburgh, New York. His mother was a teacher, his father an insurance executive: together they provided a comfortable home for Patterson and his three younger sisters. Although he graduated class valedictorian in 1965 from St. Patrick's, a Christian Brothers school, Patterson told Andre Bernard and Jeff Zaleski of *Publishers Weekly* that as a teenager he read reluctantly; perfunctory teaching of required texts such as *Silas Marner* "crushed the life out of books," depriving him of the pleasures of reading until later in his life.

He majored in English at Manhattan College, and worked the first summer as an aide at McLean Hospital, a mental institute near Boston. Patterson began to read on the night shift, his new interest bolstered by a friendship with the poet Robert Lowell, who was under treatment for depression at McLean at the time. Lowell read aloud to his fellow patients and talked to Patterson about writing. Over that summer, Patterson began writing his own works and aimed to get a job in academia. Patterson entered the graduate program at Vanderbilt University but soon discovered that teaching was not for him. Instead of the usual literary analysis, he submitted a novel for his master's thesis in 1970.

Never Planned To Be A Writer

The next year, he had told Bernard and Zaleski that he had "a pivotal experience" when he began reading commercial fiction, including such popular novels as *The Exorcist* and *The Day of the Jackal*. Suddenly, Patterson's own writing had a focus: suspense and excitement. "I never thought of making it as a writer," he recalled in the *Publishers Weekly* interview. "That seemed presumptuous to me." Instead, he landed a job as a junior copywriter at J. Walter Thompson advertising agency. But he also kept writing and completed a novel in his off-hours.

The Thomas Berryman Number, Patterson's debut work, is the story of an investigative reporter seeking the assassin of the popular black mayor of Nashville, Tennessee. A *Library Journal* reviewer heralded the novel as "an encouraging change from the usual thriller, brilliantly written with a faultless ear for real speech and an accurate eye for real people." Alice Cromie of *Booklist* found the story "gripping," with "superb suspense and magnificent narration." *The Thomas Berryman Number* earned Patterson an Edgar Award in 1977. "The thrill of winning the Edgar was mind-boggling; it was great," Patterson stated in an online interview with Time Warner Electronic Publishing. Three more novels, *The Season of the Machete, The Jericho Commandment* (later re-published as *See How They Run*), and *Virgin,* soon followed.

Patterson's personal life took an unfortunate turn in 1981. Jane Blanchard, his companion of seven years, was diagnosed with a brain tumor. He devoted himself to her until her death in 1984. Anxious to quell his grief, Patterson put his energy into his work. "I wanted to have something to do to escape," he told Maria Speidel of *People.* "That's when I took off in advertising." Four years later, at age thirty-nine, he became CEO; then in 1990 he became chairman. By 1994, he was Worldwide Creative Director at J. Walter Thompson Company.

Detective Alex Cross (Morgan Freeman) with kidnapping victim Dr. Kate Mctiernan (Ashley Judd) in the 1997 movie *Kiss the Girls*.

In *Black Market*, Patterson's 1986 novel, a group of Vietnam veterans firebomb Wall Street, paralyzing world finance with their terrorism. The critics were less kind to this book than to Patterson's earlier efforts. In the *New York Times*, Newgate Callendar found the book "ambitious" but "written in a superheated prose very heavy on the italics," concluding that "the entire scenario is artificial and unbelievable." Ronald C. Miller, writing in *Armchair Detective*, found the novel "complex and suspenseful," but wondered if "perhaps the immense scope of the plot for *Black Market* has prevented Patterson from fleshing out the details . . . that would have made this book must reading."

The protagonist of *The Midnight Club*, Patterson's next novel, is a wheelchair-bound policeman eager to nab the culprit who caused his affliction, a psychopathic drug dealer. When the criminal is murdered in a Manhattan brothel, the policeman joins with the female writer of a best-selling series of crime novels to crack the network of corruption and murder his nemesis once headed. "Sleek, fast, skillful, and larger than life," was Charles Champlin's assessment in the *Los Angeles Times Book Review*. Though Robert Minkoff, writing in the *New York Times Book Review,* found that the characters "suffer from clumsy characterizations and the novel's lapses into the shorthand banalities of a screenplay," he conceded that *"The Midnight Club* still holds one or two surprises and a fair degree of excitement." A critic in *Publishers Weekly* noted that the book had "plenty of gore, many plot twists—some quite murky—and a little sex [to] keep readers turning pages up to the melodramatic, rather unlikely ending."

Alex Cross Debuts

Patterson's first novels enjoyed only modest success. It was his 1993 work *Along Came a Spider* that put him squarely on the best-seller roster. He told Bernard and Zaleski that his popularity had to do with changing his writing over time, shifting from an emphasis on the writing itself to conveying his stories as clearly as possible. "What I've learned over time is telling stories," he acknowledged. "At this point, I'm much heavier into the telling of the story, and a little less careful with the writing of good sentences." *Along Came a Spider* introduced Alex Cross, a black psychologist on the Washington, D.C., detective force, a character Patterson has returned to in several subsequent books. He told Bernard and Zaleski that he named the character after a woman who took care of him as a child: "I remember when she left and went back to Detroit. I was around eight, and it was devastating."

In his online interview, Patterson described the character of Alex Cross as "extremely human and very sensitive. He is raising . . . two kids by himself; he has this terrific relationship with his grandmother. He chooses to live in a tough part of town, even though he doesn't have to. He's raised himself up and has gotten a very good education. He's also larger than life in being this swashbuckling heroic kind of guy, and he's genuinely a good person, too."

In *Along Came a Spider,* a serial killer kidnaps two children, forcing Cross to mesh his personal and private lives when he teams up with Secret Service agent and romantic interest Jezzie Flanagan. Critics were divided on the merits of the novel. Among those who praised the work was Will Hepfer of *Library Journal,* who found the psychotic serial killer "effectively nightmarish" and believed that Patterson's use of "shifting viewpoint add[s] brisk pacing and genuine suspense." Chris Petrakos, writing in the Chicago *Tribune Books,* declared that Jezzie Flanagan is "a woman who's considerably more than window dressing." Other reviewers were less enchanted: Marilyn Stasio of the *New York Times Book Review* felt that partway into the novel "the juices have all but run out of this far-fetched thriller." She concluded that "the erratic plot convulsions make us edgy, without delivering a real charge." A *Publishers Weekly* reviewer noted that "If a contemporary would-be nail-biter is to thrill as it should, it urgently needs stronger connections to reality than this book has." Regardless of the critics' opinions, the reading public turned *Along Came a Spider* into a blockbuster hit for its author, propelling him onto the best-seller lists, where he has become a fixture.

A pair of serial murderers taunt Cross in *Kiss the Girls.* Living on opposite sides of the country—one in Los Angeles, the other in North Carolina—the killers vie with each other to commit the "perfect" crime. When his niece falls into their hands, Cross tackles the case. The novel found success with readers and reviewers alike and was adapted for a 1997 film starring Morgan Freeman and Ashley Judd. Though Patterson was concerned that his book might receive poor treatment in Hollywood, he stated in his online interview that the "movie is really terrific," adding, "The film moves along, it's suspenseful, and I think it'll do well. . . ."

Maggie Bradford, the protagonist of *Hide and Seek,* is a successful singer-songwriter whose self-defense

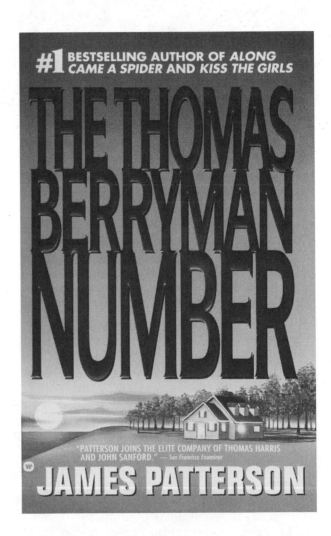

Patterson received a 1977 Edgar Award for his first book, which concerns the murder of a popular black mayor in Tennessee.

murder of her first husband gets her locked up on suspicion of having killed her second. The novel received mixed reviews. A *Publishers Weekly* contributor found the novel's two murder trials not "quite riveting," adding that the book's finale "will only surprise those fresh to the thriller genre. Still, . . . various loose threads will probably not bother readers swept along by this lightweight pop fiction." For Stacie Browne Chandler, writing in the *Library Journal*, the novel "delivers a solid punch, complete with a surprise ending. Patterson . . . offers a vivid, emotionally revealing tale."

Detective Cross returned in *Jack and Jill*, plagued by a bevy of serial killers, including a duo from whom the book takes its title. The trail leads straight to the White House, where the killers' ultimate target appears to be the President of the United States. *Booklist*'s Mary Frances Wilkens stated that Patterson again makes the reader's "stomach queasy with his latest graphic 'nursery rhyme.'" Wilkens noted the tension between Cross's sense of duty to his family and to his country and deemed the book "a fast-paced, electric story that is utterly believable." Rebecca House Stankowski of *Library Journal* appreciated the "breakneck pacing . . . followed by a truly surprising ending," and a *Publishers Weekly* reviewer found that "Patterson grabs readers from the beginning and sweeps them along toward riveting double climaxes. . . . It's fine, full-blooded entertainment from start to finish."

Golf Novel Not Par For The Course

In a change of pace, Patterson published a 1996 work titled *Miracle on the 17th Green*, which he coauthored with journalist Peter de Jonge. This Christmas tale concerns a fifty-year-old advertising executive who finds himself laid off. Teeing off on a Christmas morning golf outing, he realizes he has acquired the ability to make perfect shots and decides to turn professional. A critic in *Kirkus Reviews* found *Miracle on the 17th Green* "quite entertaining," and a *Publishers Weekly* reviewer felt the authors "succeed admirably in creating a winning character who is enough of a child to believe in his dreams and is also mature enough to offer some gently humorous reflections on our national obsession with an engaging sport."

Patterson returned to suspense thrillers with the 1997 work Cat and Mouse. He told Bernard and

If you enjoy the works of James Patterson, you may also want to check out the following books and films:

Patricia D. Cornwell, *All That Remains*, 1992.
A. J. Holt, *Watch Me*, 1995.
John Saul, *Black Lightning*, 1995.
Seven, starring Morgan Freeman and Brad Pitt, 1995.

Zaleski that "the Cross books in particular are about nightmares that I have—not literal nightmares but nightmares that I have about the world. And one of those is of domineering men." In *Cat and Mouse* the detective is confronted not only with his nemesis from *Along Came a Spider*, the serial killer he thought he had put away for good, but another madman as well. "James Patterson has such a seething imagination," wrote *New York Times Book Review* critic Marilyn Stasio, that "it's too bad this . . . writer can't rent out his ideas to authors with more polished literary skills." Charles Michaud of the *Library Journal*, however, assured readers that the "driving plot will distract you from thinking about its implausibilities and keep you turning pages to the last, when you'll find yourself impatiently awaiting the arrival of the next Cross novel." *Booklist*'s Emily Melton lauded the "take-no-prisoners suspense," and predicted that the "darkly explosive ending will have readers lining up, eager to claim their copy of Patterson's latest sure-to-be-a-hit page-turner."

In *Cat and Mouse*, Patterson took a different approach to his writing, hoping to avoid the repetition that can occur when an author pens a continuing series: "So I challenged myself to do something really adventurous," he stated in his online interview, later adding, "I did something completely different, which was to introduce a second narrator, a second first-person narrator. . . . It really got me pumped up about what I can pull off in a work of fiction."

Despite his success in advertising—"I'm a Toys R Us kid" and "Aren't you hungry for a Burger King now?" are two of the slogans he dreamed up—Patterson has said that he never thought of himself as having had a career. As in writing, he has gone after what interested him. He told Bernard and Zaleski, "I think that's the key thing, doing something you love. It's so hard to find meaning today. Be it ever so simple-minded, I really do find meaning in creating these entertainments that divert, distract and please millions of people for a short time." Or, as he summed up to Speidel, "When people think of my books, I want them to say, 'I can't put those down.'"

■ Works Cited

Review of *Along Came a Spider*, *Publishers Weekly*, November 2, 1992, p. 48.

Bernard, Andre, and Jeff Zaleski, "James Patterson: Writing Thrillers Is Not His Day Job," *Publishers Weekly*, October 21, 1996, pp. 58-59.

Callendar, Newgate, review of *Black Market*, *New York Times*, July 20, 1986, p. 20.

Champlin, Charles, "Bloody Sunday," *Los Angeles Times Book Review*, January 1, 1989, p. 9.

Chandler, Stacie Browne, review of *Hide and Seek*, *Library Journal*, December, 1995, p. 158.

Cromie, Alice, review of *The Thomas Berryman Number*, *Booklist*, May 1, 1976, p. 1322.

Hepfer, Will, review of *Along Came a Spider*, *Library Journal*, December, 1992, p. 187.

Review of *Hide and Seek*, *Publishers Weekly*, October 30, 1995.

House, Rebecca, review of *Jack and Jill*, *Library Journal*, August 1, 1996, p. 114.

Review of *Jack and Jill*, *Publishers Weekly*, August 5, 1996, p. 430.

Melton, Emily, review of *Cat and Mouse*, *Booklist*, September 1, 1997, p. 8.

Michaud, Charles, review of *Cat and Mouse*, *Library Journal*, October 1, 1997.

Review of *The Midnight Club*, *Publishers Weekly*, November 4, 1988, p. 74.

Miller, Ronald C., review of *Black Market*, *Armchair Detective*, Winter, 1988, pp. 89-90.

Minkoff, Robert, review of *The Midnight Club*, *New York Times Book Review*, May 14, 1989, p. 22.

Review of *Miracle on the 17th Green*, *Kirkus Reviews*, September 1, 1996, p. 1269.

Review of *Miracle on the 17th Green*, *Publishers Weekly*, September 16, 1996, p. 68.

Patterson, James, online interview with Time Warner Electronic Publishing at http://www.pathfinder.com/twep/little_brown/authors.

Petrakos, Chris, "Amid the Most Macho of Genres, Intriguing Woman Emerge," *Tribune Books* (Chicago), February 21, 1993, p. 7.

Speidel, Maria, "A Killer at Thrillers," *People*, March 20, 1995, pp. 83-84.

Stasio, Marilyn, review of *Along Came a Spider*, *New York Times Book Review*, February 7, 1993, p. 19.

Stasio, Marilyn, review of *Cat and Mouse*, *New York Times Book Review*, November 23, 1997, p. 44.

Review of *The Thomas Berryman Number*, *Library Journal*, March 1, 1976, p. 742.

Wilkens, Mary Frances, review of *Jack and Jill*, *Booklist*, May 15, 1996.

■ For More Information See

PERIODICALS

Booklist, September 15, 1992; November 1, 1995.

Entertainment Weekly, January 20, 1995, pp. 46-47.

Kirkus Reviews, November 15, 1992; October 1, 1994, p. 1299; January 3, 1996; July 15, 1996, p. 998; September 1, 1997, p. 1334.

Library Journal, October 1, 1996.

Los Angeles Times, April 10, 1989.

New York Times Book Review, December 8, 1996, p. 102.

Publishers Weekly, April 25, 1986, p. 65.

Tribune Books (Chicago), December 17, 1995, p. 6.*

—Sketch by C. M. Ratner

Marc Talbert

■ Personal

Born July 21, 1953, in Boulder, CO; son of Willard L. (a physicist) and Mary A. Talbert; married Moo Thorpe (a real estate broker and contractor); children: Molly, Jessie. *Education:* Attended Grinnell College, 1971-73; Iowa State University, B.S., 1976.

■ Addresses

Home—P.O. Box 847, Santa Fe, NM 87504.

■ Career

Marshalltown Public Schools, Marshalltown, IA, teacher of fifth and sixth grade, 1976-77; Ames Public Schools, Ames, IA, teacher of fifth grade, 1977-81; Los Alamos National Laboratory, Los Alamos, NM, writer and editor, 1981-86; speech writer for National Science Foundation, 1984-85; writer. University of New Mexico, part-time instructor in children's literature. *Member:* PEN, Society of Children's Book Writers and Illustrators, Authors Guild, Children's Literature Assembly.

■ Awards, Honors

Best Books for Young Adults award, American Library Association, 1985, shortlisted for British Children's Book Group award, 1986, West Australian Young Readers' Book Award, Library Association of Australia, 1988, all for *Dead Birds Singing; Toby* was named a Notable Children's Book in the Field of Social Studies, National Council on Social Studies, 1987; Owl of the Month Prize, *The Bulletin of Youth and Literature,* 1989, for *The Paper Knife;* Américas Award, Consortium of Latin American Studies Program (CLASP), honorable mention for *Heart of the Jaguar* and commended list for *A Sunburned Prayer,* both 1995.

■ Writings

JUVENILE

Dead Birds Singing, Little, Brown, 1985.
Thin Ice, Little, Brown, 1986.
Toby, Dial Books for Young Readers, 1987.
The Paper Knife, Dial Books for Young Readers, 1988.
Rabbit in the Rock, Dial Books for Young Readers, 1989.
Double or Nothing, Dial Books for Young Readers, 1990.
Pillow of Clouds, Dial Books for Young Readers, 1991.

The Purple Heart, HarperCollins, 1992.
A Sunburned Prayer, Simon and Schuster, 1995.
Heart of a Jaguar, Simon and Schuster, 1995.

SHORT STORIES

"Fountain of Youth," in *Trapped,* edited by Lois Duncan, Simon and Schuster, 1998.

OTHER

Columnist for *Daily Tribune,* Ames, IA, *Cedar Valley Times,* Vinton, IA, and *Iowa State Daily,* Ames, IA.

■ Work in Progress

Star of Luís, a novel for Clarion, 1999; a series of six novels about search-and-rescue teams.

■ Sidelights

Marc Talbert follows a unique philosophy in writing books for children and young adults. Whereas many authors create stories for a specific age group and others focus on a popular type of fiction, Talbert writes for his characters. In an interview with *Authors and Artists for Young Adults (AAYA),* the writer explained: "My stories have to remain true to the characters I've created. If they don't, then I feel I've betrayed the characters and I haven't fulfilled my purpose as a novelist." In keeping with this perception of his role, Talbert conducts meticulous research for all of his books. He reads extensively, talks with experts, observes human behavior, and even tries new and unusual experiences to gain insight into his characters. Talbert's approach clearly has worked. He currently ranks among the foremost writers of social-issue novels for younger readers, and critics consistently praise his complex, realistically drawn characters.

Although Talbert decided to become a writer during college, he began cultivating his talent at an early age with a fascination for words. He told *AAYA,* "I can't remember a time I wasn't in one way or another intrigued by words. My interest in story began with my interest in words—how they sounded, how they could capture, how they could describe, something. I was forever walking around with scraps of paper as soon as I could

write anything at all, trying to come up with words to describe things I was seeing when we traveled as a family or when I was walking through the town I grew up in. If I couldn't come up with a word I knew, then I would just make one up." He recalled, too, an early love of reading. "There wasn't a time that I wasn't interested in reading also. As soon as I was able to read anything on my own I was poring over magazines, making up stories if I didn't know the words from the pictures I saw." When Talbert was a small child his mother read to him from Golden Books. Among his favorites were *The Brown Bunny* and *The Little Engine That Could,* as well as Margaret Wise Brown stories illustrated by Garth Williams. Today, Talbert has those books in his own library and he reads them to his daughters, Molly and Jessie.

"I remember a lot of the Greek myths, too, from the Childcraft Books," Talbert stated in the interview. "They were wonderful—they were always bordering on being naughty because of what the gods got away with and all the games they played, how nasty they were, and how they were actually grown-up people. It was interesting to see Zeus with his beard and all the other gods doing very childish things." The author acknowledged that these myths almost certainly influenced his work as a novelist. "I think that myth and myth-like stories boil the basic human issues down and make them accessible. . . . Myths try to confront fear, unfairness, cruelty, and death." Talbert also noted the value of fairy tales in clarifying life for young readers: "I can't think of anything more direct in showing kids all these different things than the Grimm fairy tales. You don't just kill the witch once. You kill her and then you boil her in oil, then you chop her into bits. You kill her many times. There weren't always happy endings." Talbert continued, "Although these stories make the world scary for kids, they are also very comforting because at least they bring out in the open issues kids find themselves wrestling with privately. It helps them do their wrestling in a more public way and with the support of an adult."

A Troubled Reader

Yet the award-winning novelist revealed that throughout his life words have been a problem, too. "Although I was always attracted to stories and I was always attracted to words and writing as far back as I can remember, I suffered greatly from learning problems while growing up," Talbert revealed to *AAYA*. "I am also an extremely slow reader and I'm a horrible speller. Why I was attracted to words, to books, and to stories when I couldn't spell very well and when I read very slowly, I really don't know. Those are two things I've carried with me into my professional life. I've worked extremely hard at covering up that fact." During his school years Talbert's teachers were frustrated that he was obviously bright and intelligent—they always placed him in advanced learning groups—but he did not excel in reading and spelling. "I was a fairly bright kid, but I was labeled as a bright kid who would not concentrate on his reading," he recalled. His own frustration was even more intense because of the social pressure of his parents being well educated (his father is a nuclear physicist) and his growing up in a university town. Nevertheless, Talbert was an avid reader. "In spite of being a slow reader," he commented, "I carried books around with me all the time." But at that time in his life he did not consider pursuing a fiction writing career. "I was never encouraged to be a writer," he recalled. "I never even contemplated doing that when I grew up."

Talbert continues to be a slow reader, and spelling remains a challenge, which is a curious situation for a writer. "When I worked as a journalist, if I didn't know how to spell a word I'd use another word," he confessed. "In my novel writing I don't compromise that way, but when I was writing as a journalist and meeting deadlines that's what I'd do. Of course journalism wants you to use the simplest word, anyway." Talbert told *AAYA* he refuses to use the spell-checker on his computer, however, choosing instead to consult a dictionary. He regards looking up a word as an adventure that offers intriguing sidetrips to the discovery of other words. The spell-checker, on the other hand, thwarts curiosity. "It removes me from the words I wrestle with, the tools of my trade," he contended. "I think it makes me lazy in this struggle I have with words. If I get lazy they're going to end up mastering me and not the other way around. Using a spell-checker is like throwing a pot on a wheel using garden gloves."

After graduating from high school, Talbert entered Grinnell College, where he majored in English. Soon he realized he did not enjoy the academic approach to literature, which neglected any consideration of an emotional connection between writer and reader. After two years he transferred to Iowa State University, graduating with a major in elementary education and a minor in journalism. Talbert's trouble with spelling resurfaced when he received his college diploma. His mother was "incensed" to see that his middle name, Allan, was spelled *Alan*. Only then did Talbert realize he had been spelling his own name wrong all his life. (His middle name is now officially "misspelled" Alan.)

> "My stories have to remain true to the characters I've created. If they don't, then I feel I've betrayed the characters and I haven't fulfilled my purpose as a novelist."
> —Marc Talbert

During summers between college terms Talbert had worked as a tennis instructor and waterfront director at a camp near Cleveland, Ohio, for children with diabetes and cystic fibrosis. This experience led to him to discover that he "loved working with kids" and thus to specialize in elementary education. After college Talbert taught a combined fifth and sixth grade class in Marshalltown, Iowa. Then he worked as a journalist while teaching fifth grade at the school he himself had attended in Ames. After meeting his wife, Moo Thorpe, he moved to New Mexico, where his wife had grown up. At that time he switched careers, becoming a writer and editor at the Los Alamos National Laboratory, where his father also worked. Two years later Talbert and his wife moved to Washington, D. C., so he could take a job as the speech writer for the Director of the National Science Foundation.

Teaching Career Influences Novels

All of these experiences provided Talbert with material for his books. The first direct influence, however, came when he was teaching the fifth grade class in Ames, and one of his students died in an automobile accident. Finding few books that could help young people cope with the death of a friend, Talbert decided he would someday write a book to fill that gap. He finished the book, *Dead Birds Singing,* while he was living in Washington. Within two weeks of submitting the manuscript to Little, Brown and Company, he received a contract. The work, which earned Talbert immediate recognition as a serious novelist for young adults, went on to win several prestigious awards.

Dead Birds Singing features seventh-grader Matt Smythe, whose mother and sister are killed in an automobile accident by a drunken driver. Now an orphan, Matt is adopted by the Fletchers, the family of his best friend. The story takes place during the four months following the crash as Matt confronts questions about life and death. In the *New York Times Book Review,* Otto R. Salassi observed that this "seriously intense first novel" effectively portrays Matt's struggle. Yet the reader can only give the boy "a pat on the shoulder and wish him good luck," Salassi noted. "There's not much else we feel we can say or do, and maybe there's not supposed to be."

After writing *Dead Birds Singing,* Talbert and his wife moved back to New Mexico, settling in an adobe house near Santa Fe. Although Talbert had returned to his Los Alamos job, he spent more and more time writing. Little, Brown gave him an advance and he began working on *Thin Ice,* a book about a young boy whose parents are separated. Like *Dead Birds Singing, Thin Ice* was inspired by Talbert's students. The author told *AAYA,* "When I was a teacher I was astonished to learn that a quarter to a third of all the kids in every class I taught came from divorced, remarried or redefined families. In an upper-middle-class, highly educated community like Ames, Iowa, I thought that was astonishing. It was something that as a teacher I addressed every single day in one way or another. . . . Fanny, the girl in that book, was diabetic, and that was inspired by working with kids at Camp Ho Mita Koda."

Ten-year-old Martin Enders, the main character in *Thin Ice,* is confused about his place in the world. He is "skating on thin ice" as he tries to adjust to his parents' recent divorce while his life spins out of control. Not only does he have the stress of helping care for his diabetic sister Frannie, but he also loses his best friend Barney and his school work goes into a steady decline. Martin reaches a crisis point when his mother starts dating his

fifth-grade teacher, Mr. Raven—a development that Martin considers to be a profound betrayal. Commenting on the character of Mr. Raven, Talbert said, "The idea of the mother dating the teacher was pure whimsy, it was almost a challenge to the audience—What would *you* do in this situation?" *Voice of Youth Advocates* reviewer Jane Van Wiemokly called *Thin Ice* "a thought provoking, touching story" that has "added relevance" for young adults facing similar family problems. A *Publishers Weekly* reviewer described it as a "beautifully written book," and a critic in the *Junior Bookshelf* praised the novel's "freedom from exaggeration," further noting that "we get to know [Martin] intimately, warts and all."

"Sometimes I cringe when people say I have written problem novels. We all have problems, and there are always problems in novels. You don't write a novel about a world that is perfect—you portray a problem that needs to be solved or overcome. I would like to think that if there are problems in my books that they're more than just the surface problem that is being dealt with."

—Marc Talbert

Talbert told *AAYA* that his third novel, *Toby,* was actually his second novel. Following the success of *Dead Birds Singing,* he mentioned to Little, Brown, that he had an idea for a book about a boy whose parents are mentally retarded. An editorial board member did not approve of the subject for personal reasons, however, so Talbert wrote *Thin Ice* instead. When that book was completed he moved to Dial. His editor at Dial accepted the proposal for *Toby,* which is based on the experiences of one of Talbert's former students. "Toby was inspired by a student in my class the first year I taught, whose parents were retarded," Talbert said. "He was a very bright boy, he was a very clever boy. He was my favorite student." The novel depicts the prejudices, conflicts, and misunderstandings encountered by the title character, whose parents are illiterate and mentally slow. *Toby* was named a Notable Children's Book in the Field of Social Studies by the National Council of Social Studies.

Tackles Sensitive Subjects

In *The Paper Knife* Talbert addresses the sensitive subject of sexual abuse. Discussing the novel in the *AAYA* interview, Talbert stressed that he himself has never been sexually abused. He went on to say that the story was born of his observations as a teacher. "The first year I taught a girl was transferred into my classroom across Marshalltown," he recalled. "She was transferred into my class because I was a male teacher and her father had been put in the county jail for not only sexually abusing her and her sister but making her older sister pregnant. It was the first time I had ever been confronted with the fact that this really and truly happened to people, to kids." Yet this girl's experience was not unusual. "In every class I taught it became obvious down the road that at least one, sometimes two, of the kids, and it wasn't always girls—were being confronted with various levels of sexual abuse. I began to realize it was a fairly common problem that nobody was talking about," Talbert continued.

While doing research for *The Paper Knife* the author met two young boys who were victims of molestation. "I went to the state hospital in Las Vegas, New Mexico, where there is a lock-up facility for troubled children," he recalled. "I talked to the people there, gained their confidence, and then spent time with two boys who were there not only for being sexually abused but also for being sexual abusers. Many of the things I discovered from them ended up in the book. . . . One of them—a fifteen-year-old—escaped a couple of months before the book came out (and I wish this hadn't happened). He had asked a number of friends to get in contact with me because he wanted to see a copy of my book. He completely disappeared and I'm afraid something horrible must have happened to him."

Although *The Paper Knife* could be considered controversial, Talbert has never received adverse reactions from young readers, teachers, or librarians. In fact, he told *AAYA,* when he visits schools students thank him for the honest portrayal of a painful topic that mirrors their own experiences. *The Paper Knife* is the story of Jeremy Johnson, whose mother, Ginny, has been mistreated by her boyfriend George. As the book opens, Ginny has taken Jeremy to live with George's parents, the Hayeses, in the small town of Clifton. Although Ginny has found a safe haven, Jeremy fears that George will find them. Soon it becomes apparent that Jeremy has been sexually abused by George, who made him swear not to tell anyone. When George calls to remind Jeremy about the vow of silence, the boy realizes he can use the truth as a weapon. So he decides to "write those things down." He tells himself, "I'll write them down on a piece of paper, and I'll carry that paper around with me like my knife." Then in a chaotic series of events the paper knife is stolen, and Ginny and Mrs. Hayes wrongly accuse Jeremy's teacher of abusing the boy. After being transferred to a new school, Jeremy must confront the consequences of his silence. In a riveting conclusion, he is finally able to tell the truth to Mr. Hayes.

Wilson Library Bulletin reviewer Frances Bradburn observed that in "the ideal world there would be no need for *The Paper Knife*. But in today's world there is." Jeremy is "a beacon for all sexually molested children," Bradburn wrote, and the book is "an honest assessment of how hard taking control over one's life really is for a child. . . . His story deserves to be shared." In *Bulletin of the Center for Children's Books* Zena Sutherland praised Talbert for taking *The Paper Knife* beyond the "problem novel." The author deals "perceptively with . . . other facets of Jeremy's life," Sutherland stated, for "he sees children as people, avoiding either condescension or evasion in depicting them." Denise Wilms noted in *Booklist* that *The Paper Knife* succeeds in "showing how to get help if one is a victim."

Reviewers frequently label Talbert a "problem novelist" because of the subjects he portrays in his books. Yet the writer refuses to accept such a narrow interpretation of his work. "Sometimes I cringe when people say I have written problem novels," he revealed in the interview with *AAYA.* "We all have problems, and there are always problems in novels. You don't write a novel about a world that is perfect—you portray a problem that needs to be solved or overcome. I would like to think that if there are problems in my books that they're more than just the surface problem that is being dealt with." Talbert went on to point out that in the *Paper Knife*, for instance, "the problem, from a 'problem novel' point of view, is sexual abuse. But I think it's more universal than that. I think it has to do with deep, dark, horrible secrets," he asserted. "I think it has to do with injuries to the part of you that is deep and inaccessible, not only to other people but even to yourself. Sexual abuse is an example of that, which can be made more universal. So it's not just a book for kids who have been sexually abused, or for adults who work with them," Talbert concluded. "It's for anybody who has a deep, dark, horrible secret, or some grinding kind of guilt or some huge fear."

Talbert described his next novel, *Rabbit in the Rock*, as his "fun book." A distinct departure in subject matter from *The Paper Knife*, it tells the story of Bernie, a teenager who lives on her family's dude ranch in New Mexico. Talbert told *AAYA* the character of Bernie is based on his wife, whose family owns a resort ranch in New Mexico. "And there really is a rabbit in the rock," he announced. "There is a rock formation in the canyon on the resort that looks exactly like a rabbit, and when it rains it disappears. It's peeking out from a little canopy of rock. The first time it was ever noticed was when a seven- or eight-year-old girl came back from horseback riding and went to the chef at the restaurant and asked for carrots. He asked, 'Why do you want carrots?' and she said, 'For the rabbit in that canyon over there.' So she took the carrots and was amazed to find it wasn't a real rabbit but a rock." Talbert added that the rabbit is not visible to most observers, "but it's perfect from the perspective of a seven-year-old on a horse."

Rabbit in the Rock opens as Bernie is riding her horse in the hills near her parents' ranch. She happens upon Sean Raven, a rock star and former member of a successful band called the Supersonics. Tired of the music business, he is seeking refuge in the hills. Bernie begins sneaking food and clothing to Sean, and soon they concoct a bogus kidnaping plot that involves sending ransom notes to his father—also a member of the Supersonics—whom he hates. But the scheme backfires when the FBI intercepts the notes and set out in search of the pair. After spending several days and nights roaming the area, Bernie and Sean are discovered by Bernie's brother Carlton. When Carlton breaks his leg, Sean and Bernie rescue him, an act that forces them to turn themselves in.

Talbert returned to family relationships in *Pillow of Clouds*. Chester, the main character, is faced with a difficult dilemma: According to his parents' divorce settlement, he must choose a permanent home with one of them when he turns thirteen. After he decides to join his father in Santa Fe,

> *"Life is an adventure. When you're confronted with the kinds of things that Chester is or Matt is or any of the other characters in my books, it almost becomes life-or-death adventure, at least in an emotional sense. Those are the most exciting adventures to read."*
>
> —Marc Talbert

his alcoholic mother, who lives alone in a small Iowa town, attempts suicide. A private and sensitive young boy, Chester writes poetry in an effort to come to terms with his guilt over hurting his mother. Critics praised *Pillow of Clouds*. Susan Oliver described it as a "moving, thought-provoking novel" in *School Library Journal*, and *Voice of Youth Advocates* reviewer James E. Cook found the book to be "first-rate." Cook noted especially the "positively portrayed" Hispanic family as well as the realistic ending, which does not conveniently resolve Chester's problems. Randy Meyer concluded in *Booklist* that "In a society nearly as quick to divorce as it is to marry, [Chester's] search for friendship and stability will be familiar and rewarding."

Equally well received was *The Purple Heart*, which reviewer *School Library Journal* critic Gerry Larson described as a portrayal of "believable characters" and "a positive statement on the healing power of family love." When Luke Canvin's father comes home from the Vietnam war, Luke is puzzled to see a brooding, worn-out shell of a man instead of a triumphant hero. Finally learning that his father won a Purple Heart but had concealed it in a trunk, Luke sneaks the medal into his pocket and carries it around with him. As a tornado hovers over the Canvins' midwestern town, the boy loses the Purple Heart in a silly prank. Through a culminating rush of events that mirror the storm, Luke learns the true facts of his father's injury and gains a deeper understanding of genuine courage.

Talbert told *AAYA* that he drew *The Purple Heart* from his own experience. "I grew up with Vietnam. While I was a freshman at Grinnell I was not only wrestling with English instructors, I was also part of the second or third to the last of the draft lotteries. My number was five in a year when people were sent to Vietnam with numbers up to the nineties and into the hundreds," he recalled. "So I spent most of my freshman year and part of my sophomore year earning my conscientious objector papers, after the fact, not using religious grounds, which I did not believe in, or taking testimonials. It was sheer determination on my part. I got them but the bittersweet thing about that was that it put me in a camp that alienated me from a lot of the people I'd grown up with who went to Vietnam or were for the war. It also meant that if I didn't go someone else had to. Whatever happened to 'him' I don't know. So from that very personal point of view I wanted to explore the Vietnam War and what it's impact would be on a boy whose father came back a hero with injuries and a Purple Heart, but he wasn't talking."

Talbert wanted to get as close as possible to the character. "I borrowed a friend's Purple Heart and I walked around with it and the story just started coming," he revealed. He also read books by Tim O'Brien, who recounted his own experiences in Vietnam, and he researched CBS-TV news clips from the Vietnam Era. Young readers had positive responses to *The Purple Heart*. "A school in New Jersey used this book as part of their study of the war," the author told *AAYA*, "and then they invited veterans to come in and talk to them about the war and have a Vietnamese meal. Some of them had read my book and talked about many of the things I talked about in my book. Many of the kids couldn't believe I'd gotten so much of it right, not having been there." A *Publishers Weekly* reviewer stated that Talbert "creates a compelling, resonant tale. . . ." A critic in *Kirkus Reviews* noted that the author effectively presents an "ironic contrast" between war games Luke plays with a friend and the "heavy reality and evident cost of his father's experience."

Explores Mexican Culture

Two other Talbert novels, *A Sunburned Prayer* and *Heart of a Jaguar*, are both products of the author's extensive research into Mexican culture. Set in contemporary New Mexico, *A Sunburned Prayer* portrays the story of a boy named Eloy who goes on a Good Friday pilgrimage to the shrine of the Santaurio de Chimayó. Talbert told *AAYA* that, in preparation for writing the book, he walked the route himself not once but twice. The first time he wanted to learn how Eloy would feel as he

traveled the seventeen miles to the church on foot with hundreds of other pilgrims. Talbert made the second trip after completing the novel, to make sure he had the details right. The author went on to say that not only did he gain insight into the character he was creating but he was also able to immerse himself more deeply in New Mexican traditions. He told *AAYA* that, as one of the few blond Anglo-Americans in the group, on each pilgrimage he had the curious sensation of being both an insider and an outsider.

> *"The physical journey almost perfectly matched the emotional journey, and that when you're the most physically tired the terrain gets the most austere, most difficult to walk. Usually that time of the day is the hottest. That part of it was a wonderful coincidence."*
>
> —Marc Talbert, on the pilgrimage he took while researching *A Sunburned Prayer*

Talbert said he got the idea for *A Sunburned Prayer* when he saw people walking toward Chimayó on Good Friday as he drove to work at Los Alamos. "Many of them looked like they had no business walking a distance any longer than from their house to the mailbox," he noted. "Some of them were carrying heavy wooden crosses, some of them were using crutches, and there were some wheelchairs. It was always very moving and it would bring tears to my eyes as I was driving. Having grown up white Anglo-Saxon Protestant middle-class in Iowa, I just wondered at the faith people must have that would compel them to walk sometimes as far away as from Albuquerque, which would be seventy-five miles to Chimayó. The seed for the story, then, was what kind of faith would compel people to do this. When, finally, I couldn't stand it any longer, I decided I would have to do the pilgrimage myself and find out from observing people and observing myself to find out exactly what went on during a pilgrimage."

Talbert also did research at the archdiocese offices in Santa Fe, and he spent considerable time with the priest at the Santaurio de Chimayó. "There I got a feel for the historical perspective as well as the current perspective," the author said. Next, he took the pilgrimage from his house, a distance of seventeen miles. Although Talbert is a long-distance runner, he found "it was torture to walk." He did discover, however, that "the physical journey almost perfectly matched the emotional journey, and that when you're the most physically tired the terrain gets the most austere, most difficult to walk. Usually that time of the day is the hottest. That part of it was a wonderful coincidence." For the first time in his writing career, Talbert recalled, he "began the book not knowing how it was going to end. . . . So I wrote this book about faith on faith that it would work its way out." He took the second walk in memory of his father-in-law, who had recently died and to whom he dedicated *A Sunburned Prayer*.

In the book Talbert again portrays complex family dynamics. Eleven-year-old Eloy has disobeyed his parents by going to Chimayó. The boy believes that if he can taste some of the Santuario's holy soil, his dying grandmother will be cured of cancer. Tired and hungry from fasting on Good Friday, Eloy meets a stray dog who accompanies him the rest of the way. When they reach Chimayó, Eloy discovers that his brother Benito has already taken their grandmother to the church in his car. She assures Eloy, however, that he has brought her peace by making the pilgrimage.

After they return home, Eloy is forgiven by his parents and is allowed to keep the dog as a pet. Later, his grandmother's words help him come to terms with his grief after her death, making him understand that "Sometimes we ask God for one thing and He gives us some other things we might need instead. And sometimes He takes things away. He knows what He's doing." *A Sunburned Prayer* received tremendous praise from critics. In *School Library Journal* Jack Forman asserted that it is "one of Talbert's most moving and meaningful novels to date." He also commended the author for including a glossary of Spanish words at the end of the book. *Booklist* reviewer Mary Harris Veeder noted Talbert's success in telling an engrossing story through interior monologues that explore Eloy's feelings. And, she added, "readers will find the portrait of [Benito], who is certainly no saint, rich in realistic detail."

Talbert told *AAYA* that the idea for his next book, *Heart of a Jaguar*, came to him after a trip to the Yucatán with his wife. "I couldn't believe how moved I was by the Mayan culture I saw—the living Mayan culture as well as the great ruins. It was eye-opening to me that there was this magnificent culture in a horrendous climate on a flat-as-a-pancake peninsula and that there was so much blood involved in their day-to-day lives. That was the beginning of my interest in the Mayans." Although he had not been aware of it, there was a direct connection between *Heart of a Jaguar* and *A Sunburned Prayer*. As Talbert related in the *AAYA* interview, "The old statue of the Cristo Negro at the Santaurio de Chimayó came from Guatemala and is the statue of a Mayan saint, a king who surrendered instead of allowing his people to be massacred by the Spaniards and was made into a saint because of this gesture. Why or how the Cristo Negro made it to Chimayó nobody knows. That connection is uncanny and it's something I didn't consciously realize until I was most of the way through *Heart of a Jaguar*."

Two years later he and his family made a return visit to the area around the ruins of the ancient Mayan cities of Chichén Itzá and Uxmal, where he conducted extensive research. While he was there, he said, he became aware that many Mexicans see their history from the socialist perspective. Intrigued by this perspective, Talbert decided to write his story about common people instead of the aristocracy. Still, he was not ready to start writing, so he read dozens of books about Mayan history and culture. Talbert said that, altogether, the research for *Heart of a Jaguar* "probably took ten months to a year and then it took another six months to write the book. Writing the book was a wonderful experience. I saw everything through Balam's [the main character's] eyes and I became an extension of him." Regarded by critics as one Talbert's best works, *Heart of a Jaguar* won the 1995 Américas Award honorable mention.

Heart of a Jaguar is set in a village near Chichén Itzá during the thirteenth century. Fourteen-year-old Balam is approaching manhood as villagers try to cope with a serious drought. Hoping to receive rain so they can plant the corn they need for survival, leaders make blood sacrifices to the gods. With exquisite attention to detail, Talbert traces the sights, smells, sounds, and sensations of Balam's daily life among the villagers. *School Library Journal* David N. Pauli called the book a "fascinating and worthwhile read." Patty Campbell

If you enjoy the works of Marc Talbert, you may also want to check out the following books and films:

Eve Bunting, *The Hideout*, 1991.
James Duffy, *Missing*, 1988.
Ann Grifalconi, *Not Home*, 1995.
P. J. Petersen, *How Can You Hijack a Cave?*, 1988.
Gary Soto, *Jesse*, 1994.
This Boy's Life, starring Leonardo DiCaprio, 1993.

was even more laudatory in her *Horn Book* review, hailing *Heart of a Jaguar* as a "tour de force." She noted that Talbert immerses the reader in Mayan culture through Balam's daily experiences while at the same time making the boy "an adolescent recognizable in contemporary terms, with all his poignant striving for the dignity of adulthood." But, Campbell continued, "Talbert plays tricks with this, lulling the reader into perceiving him as a familiar young adult protagonist, and then jarring us with the shock of cultural difference."

The author uses this technique throughout the novel, building to a conclusion that the reader may find shocking. Yet it is consistent with Mayan traditions—and with the character of Balam as Talbert has created him. According to Campbell, "*Heart of a Jaguar* is a breakthrough novel, but not because it contains . . . unprecedented scenes. While many historical novels for young adults settle for fancy dress and a protagonist who moves through past times with a twentieth-century mindset, Marc Talbert has had the courage to anatomize a profoundly exotic physicality and mentality without sentimentalizing it for easy consumption." Talbert revealed to *AAYA* that Balam is still with him almost daily. He added that he feels he has been true to Balam if *Heart of a Jaguar* moves the reader to think of the character as a living, breathing person.

Since the publication of *Heart of a Jaguar*, Talbert has been working on several other projects. *Star of Luís* is a novel about Crypto-Judaism in northern New Mexico. Talbert described the background of the book in the *AAYA* interview: "Dating back to the Inquisition, Jews in Spain were told either to convert, leave, or die, and many of them con-

verted on the surface and continued to practice Judaism privately at risk of their lives. Then the first chance they got they left Spain for North Africa or Portugal or Turkey sometimes, or for Mexico. When the Inquisition followed these Crypto-Jews—these secret Jews—to Mexico, many of them moved up into northern New Mexico into little mountain villages where the long arm of the church couldn't reach. Many people are now discovering they have Jewish roots they didn't know anything about."

Talbert said *Star of Luís* begins on January 7, 1941—Pearl Harbor Day—in East Los Angeles, "which at the time was very Jewish and becoming Mexican, as they say in Los Angeles. It involves a boy who is at an age where he is very attracted to his Catholicism and even thinking of being a priest. Then he discovers that he is Jewish. The reason his mother and father moved from northern New Mexico to East Los Angeles was that she came from a Crypto-Jewish family that did not approve her marriage outside the Crypto-Jewish community in their small northern New Mexico town. When the boy's father joins the army after the bombing of Pearl Harbor, his mother and he move back to help her ailing father. There is a collision between secrets and reality, and a reconciliation of sorts."

Talbert has also completed the first in a series of six novels about search-and-rescue teams, which will each feature sixteen-year-old protagonists. The books are based on actual search-and-rescue programs for young people aged sixteen and up at St. Johns College in Santa Fe and the Armand Hammer United World College in Las Vegas, New Mexico. In addition, Talbert is finishing a book about coyotes, which is intended for newspaper serialization in 1998. Drawn from an incident that took place in the writer's own family three years ago, the novel depicts a girl who loses a cat to a coyote. Like Talbert, she will at first want "to kill every single coyote in the entire world," then she will end up "admiring them."

Talbert's works involve his readers emotionally, something he strives for in his writing. "Life is an adventure," he told *AAYA*. "When you're confronted with the kinds of things that Chester is or Matt is or any of the other characters in my books, it almost becomes life-or-death adventure, at least in an emotional sense. Those are the most exciting adventures to read."

■ Works Cited

Bradburn, Frances, review of *The Paper Knife, Wilson Library Bulletin*, December, 1988, pp. 90-91.

Campbell, Patty, review of *Heart of a Jaguar, Horn Book*, January/February, 1996, pp. 110-14.

Cook, James E., review of *Pillow of Clouds, Voice of Youth Advocates*, April, 1991, p. 37.

Forman, Jack, review of *A Sunburned Prayer, School Library Journal*, July, 1995, p. 82.

Larson, Gerry, review of *The Purple Heart, School Library Journal*, February, 1992, pp. 89-90.

Meyer, Randy, review of *Pillow of Clouds, Booklist*, March 1, 1991, p. 1378.

Oliver, Susan, review of *Pillow of Clouds, School Library Journal*, March, 1991, p. 218.

Pauli, David N., review of *Heart of a Jaguar, School Library Journal*, November, 1995, p. 122.

Review of *The Purple Heart, Kirkus Reviews*, December 15, 1991, p. 1599.

Review of *The Purple Heart, Publishers Weekly*, December 6, 1991, pp. 73-74.

Salassi, Otto R., review of *Dead Birds Singing, New York Times Book Review*, May 12, 1985, p. 16.

Sutherland, Zena, review of *The Paper Knife, Bulletin of the Center for Children's Books*, January, 1989, p. 137.

Talbert, Marc, *The Paper Knife*, Dial Books for Young Readers, 1988.

Talbert, Marc, *A Sunburned Prayer*, Simon and Schuster, 1995.

Talbert, Marc, interview with Peggy Saari in *Authors and Artists for Young Adults*, December, 1997.

Review of *Thin Ice, Junior Bookshelf*, December, 1987, pp. 289-90.

Review of *Thin Ice, Publishers Weekly*, December 12, 1986, p. 54.

Van Wiemokly, Jane, review of *Thin Ice, Voice of Youth Advocates*, February, 1987, p. 287.

Veeder, Mary Harris, review of *A Sunburned Prayer, Booklist*, August, 1995, p. 1950.

Wilms, Denise, review of *The Paper Knife, Booklist*, March 1, 1989, p. 1197.

■ For More Information See

BOOKS

Seventh Book of Junior Authors and Illustrators, edited by Sally Holmes Holtze, H. W. Wilson, 1996, pp. 313-15.

PERIODICALS

Booklist, November 15, 1989, p. 653; September 15, 1995, p. 154.

Children's Book Review Service, August, 1991, p. 168.

English Journal, September, 1992, p. 95.

Horn Book, July/August, 1985, p. 459; January/February, 1991, pp. 71-72.

Kirkus Reviews, September 1, 1989, pp. 1333-34.

Publishers Weekly, September 9, 1988, p. 138; October 13, 1989, p. 55; August 31, 1990, p. 68; March 15, 1991, p. 218; April 17, 1995, p. 61; September 18, 1995, p. 133.

School Library Journal, January, 1987, p. 80; November 27, 1987, pp. 82-83; January, 1988, p. 77; October, 1988, pp. 148-49; January, 1990, p. 108; November, 1990, p. 119.

Voice of Youth Advocates, August, 1985, p. 190.

Wilson Library Bulletin, November, 1989, p. S11.

—Sketch by Peggy Saari

Eleanora E. Tate

■ Personal

Born April 16, 1948, in Canton, MO; daughter of Clifford and Lillie Mae (Douglas) Tate (raised by her grandmother, Corinne E. Johnson); married Zack E. Hamlett III (a photographer), August 19, 1972; children: Gretchen R. *Education:* Drake University, B.A. (journalism), 1973.

■ Addresses

Office—P.O. Box 3581, Morehead City, NC 28557. *Agent*—Charlotte Sheedy, Charlotte Sheedy Literary Agency, 65 Bleecker St., New York, NY 10024.

■ Career

Full-time writer, 1983—. *Iowa Bystander*, West Des Moines, news editor, 1966-68; *Des Moines Register* and *Des Moines Tribune*, Des Moines, IA, staff writer, 1968-76; *Jackson Sun*, Jackson, TN, staff writer, 1976-77; Kreative Koncepts, Inc., Myrtle Beach, SC, writer and researcher, 1979-81; Positive Images, Inc., Myrtle Beach, president and co-owner (with husband, Zack E. Hamlett III), 1983-93; media consultant, Tate & Associates, 1993.

Contributor to Black history and culture workshops in Des Moines, 1968-76; guest author at schools, libraries, and conferences, 1968—; giver of poetry presentations, including Iowa Arts Council Writers in the Schools program, 1969-76. *Member:* National Association of Black Storytellers, Inc. (life conferences, 1968—; member of the board, 1988—; national president, 1991-92), North Carolina Writers' Network (board member, 1996), Concerned Citizens Operation Reach-Out Organization of Horry County (SC).

■ Awards, Honors

First place, college division, poetry, Iowa Poetry Association, 1970 and 1971; finalist, fifth annual Third World Writing Contest, Council on Interracial Books for Children, 1973; Unity Award, Lincoln University, 1974, for newspaper educational reporting; Community Lifestyles Award, Tennessee Press Association, 1977; Mary Louise Kennedy—*Weekly Reader* Children's Book Club Fellowship, for *Just an Overnight Guest;* Bread Loaf Writer Conference Fellowship, 1981; "Selected Films for Young Adults" selection, American Library Association, 1985, for film adaptation of *Just an Overnight Guest;* Parents' Choice Gold Seal Award, Parents' Choice Foundation, 1987, list of top ten recommended books for adolescents, *USA Today,* 1991, and California Young Reader Medal Award

Nominee, 1991-92, all for *The Secret of Gumbo Grove*; Presidential Award, National Association of Negro Business and Professional Women's Clubs, Georgetown (SC) Chapter, 1988; second place, Grand Strand Press Association Award for Social Responsibilities and Minority Affairs (reporting), 1988; Notable Children's Trade Book in the Field of Social Studies, National Council for the Social Studies/Children's Book Council, and "Children's Book of the Year," Child Study Book Committee, both 1990, Maryland Black-Eyed Susan Children's Book nominee, and South Carolina School Librarians Children's Book nominee, both 1992-93, all for *Thank You, Dr. Martin Luther King Jr.!*; Resolution, South Carolina House of Representatives, June 9, 1990, for literary and community efforts in South Carolina; "Pick of the Lists," American Bookseller, for *A Blessing in Disguise* and *Front Porch Stories at the One-Room School*; "Distinguished Woman of the Year, Arts" selection, Carteret County (NC) Council, 1993; Indiana Young Hoosier and Sequoyah (Oklahoma) Children's Book Nominee, North Carolina Children's Junior Book Award nominee, and List of Recommended Books for Summer Reading, *This Morning* (CBS-TV), 1994, all for *Front Porch Stories at the One-Room School*; named 1998 North Carolina Kidfest Festival Author; various other awards for journalism and community service.

■ Writings

FICTION FOR YOUNG PEOPLE

Just an Overnight Guest, Dial, 1980, Just Us Books, 1997.
The Secret of Gumbo Grove, F. Watts, 1987.
Thank You, Dr. Martin Luther King, Jr.!, F. Watts, 1990.
Front Porch Stories at the One-Room School, illustrated by Eric Velasquez, Bantam/Skylark, 1992.
Retold African Myths (short stories), illustrated by Don Tate II, Perfection Learning Corporation, 1992.
A Blessing in Disguise, Delacorte, 1995.
Don't Split the Pole: Tales of Down-Home Folk Wisdom (short stories), illustrated by Cornelius Van Wright and Ying-Hwa Hu, Delacorte, 1997.

CONTRIBUTOR

(With photos by husband, Zack E. Hamlett III) *Eclipsed* (poetry), privately printed, 1975.

(And editor) *Wanjiru: A Collection of Black-womanworth* (chapbook), privately printed, 1976.

Also contributor of "I'm Life," *Children of Longing,* edited by Rosa Guy, Holt, Rinehart and Winston, 1970; "An Ounce of Sand" (short story), *Impossible?*, Houghton, 1972; "African Madness, Part IV: Feet," *Broadside Annual 1972* (poetry), Broadside Press, 1972; *Communications* (poetry), Heath, 1973; "Bobby Griffin" (short story), *Off-Beat,* Macmillan, 1974; *Sprays of Rubies* (poetic prose), Ragnarok, 1975; *Valhalla Four* (poetry), Ragnarok, 1977; "Daddy and the Plat-Eyed Ghost" (short story), *Talk That Talk: An Anthology of African American Storytelling,* edited by Linda Goss and Marian Barns, Simon and Schuster, 1989, and *The Headless Haunt and Other African American Ghost Stories,* edited by James Haskins, HarperCollins, 1994; "Hawkeye Hatty Rides Again" (short story), *Success Stories,* Institute of Children's Literature, 1993; "Momma's Kitchen Table" (essay), *In Praise of Our Fathers and Our Mothers: A Black Family Treasury by Outstanding Authors and Artists,* Just Us Books, 1997; (author of foreword) Ronald Daise, *Lil Muddy Waters* (picture book), GOG Enterprises, 1997.

Contributor of "Hawkeye Hatty Rides Again," *American Girl,* February, 1993; contributor of "Tracing the Trilogy" (essay), *African American Review,* Spring, 1998. Contributor of poetry and fiction to periodicals, including *Journal of Black Poetry, Des Moines Register, Picture Magazine, Goldfinch,* and *Scholastic Storyworks.*

■ Adaptations

Just an Overnight Guest was adapted as a film starring Fran Robinson, Tiffany Hill, Rosalind Cash, and Richard Roundtree, directed by Gina Blumenfeld, and with Barbara Bryant as executive producer, Overnight Productions, Phoenix/B.F.A. Films & Video, 1983, broadcast on the Wonderworks Series (PBS) and Nickelodeon. *The Secret of Gumbo Grove* was adapted for audiotape, Recorded Books, Inc., 1997.

■ Work in Progress

A biography, *African American Musicians,* for the "Black Stars" biography series, with James Haskins as senior editor, for John Wiley and Sons.

■ Sidelights

If you visit Morehead City, North Carolina, you may encounter writer Eleanora E. Tate—five feet, five and three-fourths inches tall, with dark skin like actress Whoopi Goldberg, and bifocals—driving her old car, enjoying a festival with her husband, fishing, or just enjoying the view of her pond in her backyard at the edge of town. Coming up on her fiftieth birthday, Tate is taking some time to savor her accomplishments and to set new goals. Tate has devoted most of her adult life to the presentation of African Americans with positive images of themselves, and to helping children of all backgrounds feel good about themselves.

With her photographer husband Zack E. Hamlett III, Tate has used her talents as a journalist to publicize stories and events that bring pride to the Black community from Myrtle Beach, South Carolina to Horry County, South Carolina, and beyond. In her books for middle-graders, including the trilogy begun with *The Secret of Gumbo Grove*, Tate has encouraged young readers to understand their identities and to appreciate their heritage as well as their varied skin colors. She has challenged them, in her books and in talks around the country, to research the local histories of the communities in which they live, and to listen to the stories that people in their neighborhoods can share. With the publication of books like the humorous *Front Porch Stories at the One-Room School*, Tate herself has grown as a literary storyteller, sharing the tales she picked up as a child growing up in Canton, Missouri.

Viewing herself as an "American woman of African descent who writes," Tate believes that her books are for all children. While they may help African American children take pride in their heritage, they may also provide other children with important insights. "If you don't offer students that opportunity, they will go out (of the home and classroom) with the same set of values about other ethnic groups that they went in with, which might, unfortunately, be very limited." Tate's work deals with the issues of a child's need to belong and to feel appreciated, among others. In an interview with *Authors and Artists for Young Adults* (*AAYA*), she explained that she writes about "the attempt of characters to bring forth their own identities and to feel comfortable with who they are" as individuals. "With kids, there is so strong a desire to run with the crowd, to be acceptable.

It is awful to be left behind, outside." A careful observer of children, Tate sees many who get "ostracized because of their . . . lack of academic smarts. They get labeled, or they're considered minorities, which means 'less than.' But these are all good kids, and I want to help them tell their stories, too."

Tate was born in Canton, Missouri, and raised by her grandmother in a time when segregation separated Black people from whites. Her first grade year was spent in a one-room school for "colored" children, with one teacher instructing some fifteen children in the first through eighth grades: "It was an excellent learning environment for me." While Tate believes that "Americans these days tend to talk too much about what should really be private," and for that reason does not "like to point too much" to her childhood, she does reveal that being cared for in an extended family made her childhood in Canton a happy one, "a successful" one. She also remembers enjoying the conversations of her family and friends, especially outside on hot summer nights, and with no television to distract her.

Just An Overnight Guest

Tate began a career in journalism at the *Iowa Bystander* newspaper, an African American weekly located in Des Moines, Iowa. She also won a full, four-year journalism scholarship to attend Drake University from the *Des Moines Register* and *Des Moines Tribune* company. She worked as a journalist during her years in college, married, and graduated from Drake with a bachelor's degree in journalism. She worked as a staff writer at the *Des Moines Register*, the *Des Moines Tribune*, and the *Jackson Sun* newspaper in Jackson, Tennessee, before she went on to Myrtle Beach, South Carolina, in 1978. Then Tate, who had won writing awards in college and had published stories and poems, saw her first book for children published, *Just an Overnight Guest*.

Just an Overnight Guest was written to help children who somehow do not quite fit in, and to celebrate extended families. "I see children trying to find a place, overcoming obstacles, searching for identity, trying to get on path for survival, regardless of race or color," she told *AAYA*. Often these children, who must rely on their own "ingenuity to get along," are cared for and assisted by an extended family. "At the time, this had not been written about a lot."

Just an Overnight Guest, set in Nutbrush, Missouri (based on Tate's hometown, Canton), tells the story of nine-year-old Margie Carson and Ethel Hardisen, the little girl who is dropped off at Margie's house "just for overnight," as Margie's mother explains. Margie is horrified. Ethel, a half-white, half-Black four-year-old, is dirty, ill-behaved, and demanding. Margie is even more upset with the "trashy little kid" when Ethel's stay is extended indefinitely. Although she knows that Ethel has experienced neglect and abuse, Margie resents the fact that Ethel gets so much attention from her own mother, and that she has to share her bed with her. To make matters worse, Ethel, as Celia H. Morris of *Horn Book* noted, "wet Margie's bed, broke all her shells," and even "strutted around in Margie's old Sunday school dress." Margie's only hope is that her father, who works as a truck driver, will return and send Ethel away. When he returns, however, he's had a change of heart about Ethel and accepts her. He explains to Margie that Ethel is her cousin. In the words of Judith Goldberger in *Booklist,* Margie "finds sufficient inner resources to cope on a lasting basis."

Just an Overnight Guest earned a warm reception from many critics. According to Zena Sutherland of *Bulletin of the Center for Children's Books,* Tate's work "gives an effective picture of a loving black family." Gloria Rohmann of *School Library Journal* wrote: "Contemporary small-town life is evoked with loving detail." One critic, however, Beryle Banfield, lamented in *Interracial Books for Children Bulletin* that the story carried confusing and "negative color messages." *Just an Overnight Guest* went on to become an award-winning film. Pleased that the work had been reprinted in 1997, Tate stated, "I stand by everything I wrote in the book."

The "Gumbo Grove" Books

In 1983, Tate and her husband, Zack, started their own business in Myrtle Beach. Positive Images, Inc., according to Tate, was a "mom and pop public relations agency" which presented positive stories and images neglected by the mainstream press (which tended to negatively portray Black people or to ignore them altogether). The stories and images that emerged from Positive Images had the potential to help the area's Black and

white community to become more aware of Black history and prouder of the Black community's contemporary identity.

Tate considers their efforts a success. "We did a lot of work, poked a lot of information about African Americans into a lot of northeastern South Carolina minds. Ours was the first Black licensed syndicated news service from Myrtle Beach in the state. We wrote stories in a positive light about the local African American community, that didn't get into white papers on a regular basis. We sent our stories to Black presses around the state." Importantly, noted Tate, "one could actually 'see' Black people in Zack's photos because he knew how to correctly use a camera. Black people

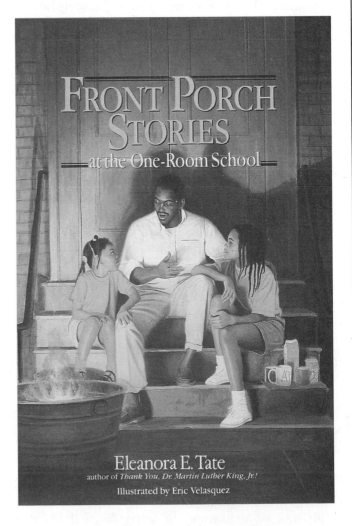

This sequel to *Just an Overnight Guest* finds Margie's father telling stories about his childhood, other members of the family, and the life of the town.

weren't just dark dots in the pictures. So that was another way that people could 'see' themselves, visually, literally, in a positive light."

Tate's next book emerged from her continued concern for positive images of African Americans, her love of history, and her public relations business. She researched and wrote a series of stories about a Myrtle Beach African American cemetery that was published in the *Charleston Chronicle* newspaper and then picked up and published by newspapers around the country. The series served as the basis for *The Secret of Gumbo Grove*. Tate had other incentives to write the book. "When I was living in Myrtle Beach doing research about the community, the children didn't seem to know much about their own community and local African American heroes. I kept getting blank stares."

She also told *AAYA*: "I decided to write *The Secret of Gumbo Grove*" to demonstrate the "importance of local history," to help children "celebrate neighborhoods and communities." Tate explained that children will not know what has come before them "unless they are told" by someone who knows. The oral tradition, in which information (about the community, past events, and lost ways of living) is passed from older people to children is very important. Tate explained that family conversations often "use colloquialisms and sayings as morality tales. These conversations can serve to educate kids because they give children a window into the lives that go on around them beyond their own." Older relatives often play an important role in this process simply because they've witnessed the events and know the history.

To create *The Secret of Gumbo Grove*, Tate developed a setting based on the Myrtle Beach and Horry County area. Then, explained Tate, "the 'what if' factor came in." She posed a character—a "little girl full of life," who is "popular and dark-skinned like Whoopi Goldberg," and asked what the character would do if she could not find any information about African Americans and her hometown history at school. What if she went to the church secretary to ask for information? What if, to get more information, the girl has to go to the graves of the dead?

The Secret of Gumbo Grove features a eleven-year-old girl named Raisin Stackhouse. Raisin is eager to learn about history, dismayed by her teacher's stereotypical portrayal of Black history, and frustrated with her attempts to gain information about the history of her own town. Miz Effie Pfluggins, Raisin's elderly church secretary, guides Raisin by leading her to restore the town's neglected Black cemetery. Raisin learns some exciting secrets as she cleans tombstones and goes through church records. Nevertheless, many people in Gumbo Grove—including her parents and church members—do not want to hear about the secrets. Gradually people respond to Raisin's work, especially the news of the location of Gumbo Grove's founder's grave. Raisin is awarded by the community for her efforts. Raisin learns that the "interlocking connections" shared by families "make people both fearful and proud," as Betsy Hearne observed in the *Christian Science Monitor*.

A *Kirkus Reviews* critic referred to *The Secret of Gumbo Grove* as "A vividly evoked piece of Americana that should be widely enjoyed." The story is "vigorously and affectionately characterized," explained Denise M. Wilms of *Booklist*. "*The Secret of Gumbo Grove* is highly recommended, both as pleasure reading and as an excellent supplement to the study of U.S. history," remarked Lisa Firke in *Kliatt*. Pam Spencer wrote in *School Library Journal* that Raisin is "[o]ne of the most engaging characters in recent years." *The Secret of Gumbo Grove* won a Parents' Choice Gold Seal Award in 1987. Tate herself is pleased with the book, which she believes helps everyone get excited about local history. She noted in her interview with *AAYA* that when she visits schools, and asks what the school's name is and the history behind the name, or the history behind the name of the street where the school is located, many times students (and some teachers) do not know. That opens the way for school projects, and teachers develop lesson plans around the book and their own community. Tate added, "I would love to see it as a movie."

Thank You, Dr. Martin Luther King, Jr.!, also takes place in Gumbo Grove. Mary Elouise Avery, the fourth-grade protagonist of the story, is having a difficult year at school and at home. "She's shy," explained Tate for *AAYA*, and "she has a hard time reading for several reasons. It's not just that academically she has a problem. . . . She tries to blank out words like slavery, Africa, lynching, or Martin Luther King," because "they call up images that have been images of scorn from the dominant society and her teacher. . . . She also

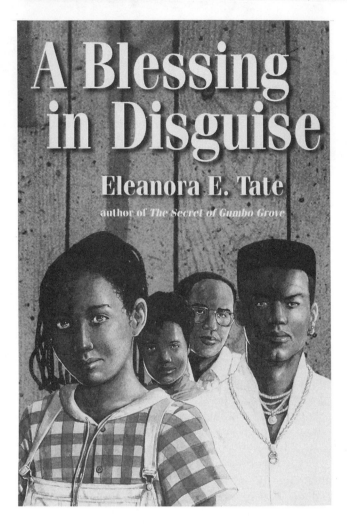

Zambia faces the truth about her flashy father when his new nightclub brings crime to her quiet southern community.

has to find a place in family as well as the classroom." Mary Elouise reacts by attempting to develop a friendship with a rich, snobby, white girl. Mary Elouise laments her own dark skin and neglects her Black doll in favor of white ones. She also disdains her role as a narrator in the school's Black history segment of its President's Month play. Yet, inspired by her grandmother and a Black storyteller, Mary Elouise begins to change her attitude about being a dark-skinned African American. Her grandmother's attention and information, and the President's Month play at school, also help her realize that she has a great deal to be proud of.

Tate also wanted to bring up the issue of "intraracial relations." She explained to *AAYA*: "As long

as the dominant society continues to have a preference that favors and awards lighter skin color, there will continue to be inequities. Because of the history of that preference, a subtle prejudice remains within the African American community. This has been drummed into our society. Darker skinned people face the results of that preference. I write about Mary Elouise's struggles in *Thank You, Dr. Martin Luther King, Jr.!* so that dark-skinned children won't need to feel they are inferior. It's due to that unequal standard of beauty being based on having white skin. Light-skinned African American children, some of whom feel discriminated against, too, and white children—and adults of all kinds, because that's where kids get biased attitudes from—need to be more aware that beauty is beauty, regardless of the shade of one's skin."

"Tate tackles a sensitive issue, taking pains to keep characters multidimensional and human," asserted Wilms in *Booklist*. The work, pointed out Zena Sutherland in *Bulletin of the Center for Children's Books*, demonstrates that "there is bias in both races, just as there is understanding in both." Another critic, Gerry Larson, wrote in *School Library Journal* that the novel "conveys the challenge of maintaining ethnic pride in a society dominated by whites." However, according to a *Kirkus Reviews* critic, Tate's "didactic purpose" "weighs down" the story. *Thank You, Dr. Martin Luther King, Jr.!*, was a 1990 Notable Children's Trade Book in the Field of Social Studies as well as a Child Study Book Committee "Children's Book of the Year."

The story in *A Blessing in Disguise* also takes place in the setting introduced in *The Secret of Gumbo Grove*. According to *Publishers Weekly* critics Elizabeth Devereaux and Diane Roback, its narrator, Zambia Brown, has a "witty and sassy voice" which "instantly grabs readers' attention." Zambia, twelve years old, lives with her aunt, uncle, and cousin in Deacon's Neck. Her alcoholic, drug addicted-mother has been in the hospital for years, and her father, a nightclub owner and drug dealer, lives with his second wife and his two teenaged daughters in Gumbo Grove. Zambia longs to live with her father, who seems sophisticated and glamorous to her. But the new club that her father opens in Deacon's Neck on Zambia's own street brings crime along with it. After Zambia is almost killed in a shooting that takes the life of one of her half-sisters, Zambia learns that, as

Becky Kornman observed in *Voice of Youth Advocates*, "it is possible to love her father, but hate the things he does." While Roger Sutton of *Bulletin of the Center for Children's Books* wrote that the novel presents a much "bleaker theme and atmosphere" than those found in Tate's other "Gumbo Grove" books, he also stated that it frankly shows how an "African-American community can be threatened from within."

Telling Stories and Other Pursuits

Tate is also the author of short stories, like *Retold African Myths*. And in her novel *Front Porch Stories at the One-Room School*, she uses short stories to tell the saga of what has happened three years after Ethel Hardisen arrived in the Carson family first presented in *Just an Overnight Guest*. In *Front Porch Stories,* Margie and Ethel are bored on a hot summer night, so Margie's father, Matthew J. Cornelius Carson, takes them to an old one-room school that used to educate African American children, including himself. Sitting on the porch steps, he relates stories to them. The stories include tales from his experiences at the one-room school, a yarn about the time his Aunt Daisy tried to do the wash on Sunday (and a shadow chased her), and a tale about Great-Grandpa Wally's return from the grave. Mr. Carson also tells about the time Eleanor Roosevelt came to visit Nutbrush. The girls tell stories, too. Ethel's story moves Margie a little closer to understanding Ethel. A *Reading Teacher* critic found that the stories are "superbly written." As a *Kirkus Reviews* critic concluded, "readers may be moved to find comparable stories in their own lives."

Don't Split the Pole: Tales of Down-Home Folk Wisdom is a collection of seven short stories that Tate wrote by wrapping the stories around common, everyday sayings. Published in 1997, it includes the story "You Can't Teach an Old Dog New Tricks," about a sea-going basset hound and a one-footed seagull; in "A Hard Head Makes a Soft Behind," a boy goes handfishing for catfish over the objections of his uncle; and in "Never Leave Your Pocketbook on the Floor," a girl ignores the rules against chewing gum in school. In another story, "What Goes Around Comes Around," two girls engage a "psychic" in an effort to get one girl a boyfriend. In "Don't Split the Pole," the book's signature story, two skateboarders invade an abandoned lot only to face the danger pre-

If you enjoy the works of Eleanora E. Tate, you may also want to check out the following books and films:

Virginia Hamilton, *The People Could Fly: American Black Folk Tales*, 1985.
Angela Johnson, *Toning the Sweep*, 1993.
Walter Dean Myers, *Somewhere in the Darkness*, 1992.
Sounder, based on the novel by William Armstrong, 1972.

sented by a lingering curse. The collection won the admiration of many critics. "'Don't Split the Pole' is a wonderful celebration of superior storytelling that can be enjoyed by the entire family," wrote an *About . . . Time* critic.

Tate and her husband ended their work at Positive Images, Inc. in 1993 following their move to Morehead City, North Carolina, in 1992. While she remains proud of the business, she commented, "I don't think I miss it, because I want to concentrate on books." Tate told *AAYA* that she less frequently visits schools for the same reason, but still lectures on creative writing. "I need to start going into elementary schools again to keep me fresh," she added. When Tate is involved in a writing project, she also likes to read computer magazines. "Oddly enough, it refreshes me," she explained. Tate's other hobbies include freshwater and saltwater fishing, hiking, gardening, eating chocolate cake, listening to stories, and attending festivals. Tate's best friend is her husband, Zack. She says she also loves animals, and enjoys the raccoons, cormorants, herons, egrets, and cardinals that visit their yard. (She even appreciated, if not enjoyed, the seven-foot black snake that came to call one day).

Tate is considering what to do next. She revealed to *AAYA* that she was thinking of earning a master's degree or doctorate, or an MFA degree, or becoming a librarian. She also confided, "I want to get closer to God. . . . God has been my refuge and my everything now that I have recognized who God is. God has made it possible to write, and I really look for that spiritual guidance when I write." Tate may also, someday, publish a book for adults that she has been working on for years: "Its heroine has gone from her twenties to her forties" as Tate herself has aged.

In any case, Tate intends to continue writing for children. "I try to offer an experience of life that can resonate in reader's minds long after the book has been replaced on the shelf, or that makes them remember so vividly that they pull that book off the shelf so that they can read it again." And if Tate's books are "preachy," as she thinks they are—that's just fine. "My culture, which is based on oral tradition, is didactic and preachy. If it wasn't for that we'd be in bad shape. There must be messages in books because some kids are not going to get them any other way."

■ Works Cited

Banfield, Beryle, review of *Just an Overnight Guest*, *Interracial Books for Children Bulletin*, Number 2, 1981, pp. 21-22.

Devereaux, Elizabeth, and Diane Roback, review of *A Blessing in Disguise*, *Publisher Weekly*, December 5, 1994, p. 77.

Review of *Don't Split The Pole: Tales of Down-Home Folk Wisdom*, *About . . . Time*, November-December, 1997, p. 24.

Firke, Lisa, review of *The Secret of Gumbo Grove*, *Kliatt*, April, 1989, p. 18.

Review of *Front Porch Stories at the One-Room School*, *Kirkus Reviews*, July 15, 1992, p. 926.

Review of *Front Porch Stories at the One-Room School*, *Reading Teacher*, February, 1994, pp. 404-5.

Goldberger, Judith, review of *Just an Overnight Guest*, *Booklist*, November 1, 1980, p. 408.

Hearne, Betsy, review of *The Secret of Gumbo Grove*, *Christian Science Monitor*, May 1, 1987, pp. B3-B4.

Kornman, Becky, review of *A Blessing in Disguise*, *Voice of Youth Advocates*, April, 1995, p. 28.

Larson, Gerry, review of *Thank You, Dr. Martin Luther King, Jr.!*, *School Library Journal*, March, 1990, pp. 220-21.

Morris, Celia H., review of *Just an Overnight Guest*, *Horn Book*, December, 1980, pp. 643-44.

Rohmann, Gloria, review of *Just an Overnight Guest*, *School Library Journal*, October, 1980, p. 151.

Review of *The Secret of Gumbo Grove*, *Kirkus Reviews*, March 1, 1987, p. 380.

Spencer, Pam, review of *The Secret of Gumbo Grove*, *School Library Journal*, March, 1992, pp. 163-67.

Sutherland, Zena, review of *Just an Overnight Guest*, *Bulletin of the Center for Children's Books*, October, 1980, p. 42.

Sutherland, Zena, review of *Thank You, Dr. Martin Luther King, Jr.!*, *Bulletin of the Center for Children's Books*, June, 1990, p. 254.

Sutton, Roger, review of *A Blessing in Disguise*, *Bulletin of the Center for Children's Books*, February, 1995, p. 216.

Tate, Eleanora, interview with R. Garcia-Johnson for *Authors and Artists for Young Adults*, February 24, 1998.

Review of *Thank You, Dr. Martin Luther King, Jr.!*, *Kirkus Reviews*, February 1, 1990, p. 186.

Wilms, Denise M., review of *The Secret of Gumbo Grove*, *Booklist*, Mary 15, 1987, pp. 1450-51.

Wilms, Denise M., review of *Thank You, Dr. Martin Luther King, Jr.!*, *Booklist*, April 15, 1990, p. 1636.

■ For More Information See

BOOKS

Rollock, Barbara T., *Black Authors and Illustrators of Children's Books: A Biographical Dictionary*, Garland, 1988, p. 115.

PERIODICALS

Des Moines Register, March 1, 1981.
Essence, December, 1992, p. 108.
Horn Book, Fall, 1995, p. 305.
Kirkus Reviews, October 15, 1997, p. 1589.
Myrtle Beach Sun News, November 23, 1980.
New York Times Book Review, February 8, 1981, p. 20.
Publishers Weekly, October 6, 1997, p. 84
Washington Post Book World, May 10, 1981.

—Sketch by R. Garcia-Johnson

Rob Thomas

■ Personal

Born August 15, 1965, in Sunnyside, WA; son of Bob and Diana Thomas. *Education:* University of Texas, BA. *Hobbies and other interests:* Performing with rock bands, playing sports.

■ Addresses

Home—636 North Courtney Ave., Los Angeles, CA 90046. *Agent*—Jennifer Robinson, Peter Miller & Association Literary and Film Management, Los Angeles, CA. *Electronic mail*—DartsKeith@aol.com.

■ Career

High school journalism teacher and author. Writer for *Space Ghost: Coast to Coast*, Cartoon Network, 1996; *Dawson's Creek*, WB Television Network, 1997-98; and *Cupid* (television pilot), ABC-TV. Adviser to University of Texas student magazine, *UTmost.* Channel One (news network for teenage students), Los Angeles, CA, staff member. *Member:* Society of Children's Book Writers and Illustrators, Austin Writers' League.

■ Awards, Honors

Best Books for Young Adults citation, Top Ten Books for Young Adults citation, and Quick Picks for Young Adults citation, all American Library Association, all 1997, and Austin Writers' League Violet Crown Award for best fiction, all for *Rats Saw God*; Best Books for Young Adults citation, and Quick Picks for Young Adults citation, both American Library Association, both 1998, both for *Doing Time: Notes from the Undergrad.*

■ Writings

Rats Saw God, Simon & Schuster, 1996.
Slave Day, Simon & Schuster, 1997.
Doing Time: Notes from the Undergrad (short stories), Simon & Schuster, 1997.
Satellite Down, Simon & Schuster, 1998.

Contributor to *Seventeen* magazine.

■ Work in Progress

Seattle and Back, for Simon & Schuster.

■ Sidelights

Rob Thomas writes novels that blur the distinction between young adult and adult fiction. His novels have a high degree of literary realism and formal sophistication. The writing techniques students may study in an American literature class parallel the ones Thomas employs in his novels.

But in fact, Thomas did not write *Rats Saw God*, his debut novel, with a teenage audience in mind. Rather, he wanted a book about a teenage boy that his peers (he was twenty-eight at the time) would find appealing. His novels have scenes rendered in precise details readers can easily visualize. Especially adept at writing dialogue, Thomas's ear for the way teenagers talk adds to each book's authenticity. As a former high school journalism teacher who now writes full time, Thomas has a sure understanding of the teen world. His books are socially aware, treating broad themes such as drugs, sex, divorce, and racism. More personal themes, such as love or identity, give the novels an emotional immediacy.

Thomas wrote *Rats Saw God* to prove to himself he could write a book. The process by which he ended up as a young adult novelist is not a typical one, he explained in an interview with Jon Saari for *Authors and Artists for Young Adults* (*AAYA*): "I had an option on writing on anything in the world. *Rats Saw God* was just a story I had in me that happened to be about an eighteen year old. I don't think I made a conscious decision to write a young adult novel. I wrote a story about an eighteen year old, and I didn't temper myself when I was writing it. I never thought, 'Oh, you're writing for a genre. You better edit yourself as you write.' I wrote the story as I saw it, and once I had a book deal, it was for young adult novels."

Never Be Lazy

After playing in a rock band for nine years, Thomas, who had planned to be a magazine journalist, underwent an experience that sent him in a new direction: "I can remember playing in a show on my twenty-first birthday. We were in Knoxville, Tennessee, 1,500 miles from home. The college radio station there had been playing our record. There were all these people in the audience who were singing these words that I had written in Texas. I had this epiphany on the stage: I want to write my own stuff. I don't want to write about what other people are doing or I don't want to cover the local city hall meeting or whatever. I just wanted to pour something out on the page," Thomas said in the *AAYA* interview.

He was forced to leave the band when he was hired by Channel One. "Suddenly, I had this huge

creative void in my life. I wasn't doing anything, so I started writing *Rats Saw God:* a page a day that filled that hole in my life. Once I learned the discipline of that, I became what I wanted to be. I was a pretty mediocre bass player, and I had beat my head against the wall for nine years trying to make it in the band. It happened very quickly for me as a writer. It was a matter of finding the right niche," he told Saari.

Thomas admits that his success happened quickly, using a methodical approach to writing the book, finding an agent, and then getting his first novel published. For *Rats About God*, he completed one page a day, writing from 5:00 A.M. to 9:00 A.M. daily before work, eventually finishing the novel within ten months. "Once I had the book in my

A troubled teenager uses a one-hundred-page writing assignment to resolve the difficulties in his life in Thomas's well-received debut novel.

hand, I thought, 'Maybe I should try to get this published.' I read a bunch of books [about publishing]; getting published is the only thing I have studied hard in my life," he stated. Thomas sent out query letters to thirty-three young adult book agents and received replies from eleven who agreed to read his novel: "The fourth one I heard back from is the agency that represented me, and whom I am still with." An agency representative had seen a magazine article about publishers "looking for edgier, male-centered young adult novels," and she sent Thomas's manuscript to a Simon & Schuster editor who read the work over a weekend. The result was an offer the following Monday.

Thomas credits Russell Smith, a friend and "just a fantastic guy with words" for mentoring him through the writing of *Rats*. "I can remember the early chapters he would send back to me. They would have such extensive notes they would be frightening. He had enough respect for me to not to worry about offending me or upsetting me. I would have a cliché in the text, and I would get a note, 'Enroll in court reporting school today.' That was pretty typical of him," said Thomas in the *AAYA* interview. Thomas learned two things from Smith that have guided his writing. One was pacing, adding in the right amount of detail: "With *Rats Saw God* I wrote the first fifty pages a dozen times because that was such a problem. When I started pacing was the most difficult aspect, but by the end of the novel I had learned it." The other lesson was "the most important: Just never be lazy, never be satisfied with a sentence that is dull, that doesn't give you anything, that doesn't add anything," Thomas explained to Saari.

A Talent for Dialogue

Identity, divorce, and teenage infidelity drive the plot of *Rats Saw God*, which charts the problems of Steven York, a smart student acting against his best personal interests. When a guidance counselor offers Steve a chance to make up a half-credit by completing a one-hundred-page writing assignment, Steve's narrative provides a frame for his disillusionment. Steve's troubles begin when his parents divorce, for which he blames his demanding father, an astronaut (Steve even refers to his father as "the astronaut"). His mother and sister move to California, with Steve remaining behind with his father.

The two male Yorks do not communicate. Steve rejects the social activities of high school his father endorses, yet the son maintains a 4.0 average. "I purposely made Steve York my opposite," Thomas acknowledged to Joel Shoemaker in *Voice of Youth Advocates*. "First of all, Steve was, and possibly is, much smarter than me. He would have loathed me. I dug high school. I was a jock. I was involved in all sorts of clubs and activities. I got along terrifically with my parents. I didn't drink or smoke." Steve and his best friend, Doug, take refuge in a club they form: GOD—the Grace Order of Dadaists (a radical European art and literature movement founded by Tristan Tsara in 1916; dada is a child's cry meaning "nothing"). Through the club, Steve meets Dub, another nonconformist, with whom he falls in love. Everything is fine until Steve discovers Dub is having an affair with Mr. Waters, a.k.a. "Sky," their teacher and mentor. The discovery crushes Steve, who loses interest in school and starts smoking marijuana.

With the conclusion of his junior year, Steve flees Texas to California where his descent continues. His chance to fix his young life comes through the writing assignment. DeMouy, the counselor at Steve's new school, assigns him to make up a half-credit Steve needs to graduate. Steve chooses a topic he knows something about: himself. The writing project is part of the novel's structure and functions as a coming-of-age story in which the protagonist is on a quest to resolve the conflicts— familial, amorous—that have divided him. The resolution leads Steve to accept the realities of life: he graduates, finds a new love interest, and connects with his father.

Richard Peck, writing in the *Horn Book*, made this observation about *Rats Saw God*: "Its protagonist represents a generation pressured to succeed without having to accept the necessary disciplines to achieve success. It's also a classic story about a defensive son moving in fits and starts toward the inarticulate father who has loved him all along. The book might be a reach even for high-school seniors who haven't yet perceived the need for this much self-awareness, but rewarding to those who reach for it."

Praise for *Rats Saw God* focused on Thomas's ability to portray Steven York as a believable adolescent. The true-life settings and dialogue add to the novel's realism. A *Publishers Weekly* critic stated, "The sharp descriptions of cliques, clubs and annoying authority figures will strike a familiar chord. The dialogue is fresh and Steve's intelligent banter and introspective musings never sound wiser than his years." "What will appeal here are the tone and the atmosphere: wisecracking Steven tells his story with an authentically adolescent shallow glibness, his camaraderie with his self-consciously offbeat friends is both warm and fragile . . . ," opined Deborah Stevenson in *Bulletin of the Center for Children's Books.* Lauren Adams, in *Horn Book,* concluded that "Steve's typically adolescent struggles are related with funny, self-mocking sarcasm and lots of one-liners . . . that make for an entertaining and engaging read."

Thomas noted that he didn't feel he "made a conscious decision" to write a young adult work as he worked on *Rats Saw God,* yet "in a way it is terrific: I like teenagers, and I taught high school for five years. The teen years are really a dramatic part of our lives, and I find I can do just about anything I want to" in the young adult genre, "so I am happy being there." He admitted that his book deal requires him to complete more YA novels, "but I don't regret that at all. It's not as though I am pining away to do an adult novel because it would make me feel more important. That's not the case at all. I have to say the television show I'm doing right now [*Cupid*] is actually about people my age. I'm glad I have an outlet for that, but it's not as if I feel like I'm writing in some fictional ghetto."

The idea for Thomas's second novel, *Slave Day,* came from a videotape he received from a high school student while working at Channel One, a Los Angeles-based teen news network. The videotape showed a student slave auction conducted for fund-raising purposes. In the book, Thomas uses eight points of view to bring a variety of voices to chronicle the events surrounding Slave Day at a high school in Texas. Using the high school as a microcosm of the larger society, Thomas explores racism as it stems from the tradition of students buying other students as slaves and then controlling them for the duration of the school day. Besides racism, other issues such as status and power are examined.

The conflict in the novel stems from the actions of Keene Davenport, who tries to organize a walkout by his fellow African American students to stop Slave Day but is greeted by indifference. He decides the best way to undermine Slave Day is from within. He "buys" Shawn Greeley, the first Black president of the student council and the school basketball star. Keene puts Shawn through a series of demeaning tasks ranging from picking up cotton balls to shining shoes.

Each student who purchases a classmate or teacher has personal reasons for doing so that the novel explores through its multiple narrators. Tiffany Delvoe, whose father is the mayor and owner of the local Ford dealership, "buys" a classmate, Brendan, to destroy her father's business records. "Know one? . . . I own one," Tiffany tells her father when he asks if she knows a computer hacker. Brendan, however, has ideas of his own as he copies the dealership's records instead of wiping them out. In addition to the Slave Day subplots, the novel explores ethical issues that arise during the school day; for example, a teacher accuses a student of cheating.

Still teaching while writing *Slave Day,* Thomas let some of his Black students read his manuscript. "I changed certain lines according to their suggestions. Also, a Black author named Trey Ellis (one of my faves) read the first fifty pages. He said it sounded on to him," Thomas told Shoemaker. Again, reviewers, although not as laudatory as they were with *Rats Saw God,* praised the novel's dialogue. A *Publishers Weekly* reviewer stated that "Thomas is so good at capturing teen language and responses that the book will be welcomed by readers looking for a reflection of their own struggles." The critic, however, also faulted the book for not always being hard hitting on race. Though the multiple narrators often sound too much alike, offered a contributor in *Kirkus Reviews,* "the headlong pace, rapid-fire wisecracking, and sustained intensity of mood twisting through subplots scary, sobering, hilarious, and triumphant keep the energy level high. . . ."

Doing Time: Notes from the Undergrad is a collection of short stories about students performing community service. "Pet Stories," one of the book's tales, first appeared in *Seventeen* magazine and involves a high school library volunteer who has a good laugh over a telephone inquiry about a "Loss of Pet" meeting. Fiona questions the need for such a group given all the "real" suffering in the world. When Tamara Reynolds arrives, Fiona can barely contain her glee. Tamara is pretty but not very smart—someone Fiona quickly dismisses.

On an assignment from the librarian, Fiona enters the meeting room, and from her position in the stacks overhears speakers talking of their loss, which Fiona, in her mind, ridicules. When it is Tamara's turn, Thomas adroitly lets her tell a poignant story of what her dog Blitzen meant to her. The story is a powerful one full of irony that stands in dramatic contrast to Fiona's earlier sarcasm.

Satellite Down is a novel that draws upon Thomas's experiences working for Channel One where two high school seniors—one male, one female—would be hired to work as reporters, relocating to Los Angeles from their hometowns and living on their own in an apartment. Thomas saw students being yanked out of their towns and set into the fantasy world of Hollywood: it was a situation he had to get on paper. In *Satellite Down*, a teenager named Patrick from west Texas arrives in Los Angeles naive and innocent, and his experience there strips him of that innocence. Later, Patrick is sent to Belfast to cover the peace talks and then disappears into the Republic of Ireland at the point where he has reached his nadir. "The last third of the novel is an attempt to recapture that innocence which I am not sure is possible," said Thomas to Saari. Thomas added that he wrote the book while traveling abroad: "The most fun I had writing was when I wrote *Satellite Down* in Ireland. I took my laptop and traveled from pub to coffee shop writing a couple of pages a day. That to me is why being a novelist is the greatest career you can have—that freedom to move around and be wherever you want."

Writing for Television

During the 1997-98 television season, Thomas wrote for *Dawson's Creek*, a show about four high school friends in the fictional town of Capeside, Massachusetts, which debuted midseason on January 20, 1998. A critical and popular success, *Dawson's Creek* appeared on the WB Network and garnered over one-third of the female teenage audience watching television during that timeslot. In addition, Thomas wrote the pilot for an ABC show called *Cupid*, a romantic comedy he compares to *Northern Exposure* and *Moonlighting*. If the network likes it, the show will be part of the 1998-99 television season; otherwise it will be what Thomas calls "a $2.5 million dollar science experiment."

If you enjoy the works of Rob Thomas, you may also want to check out the following books and films:

Theresa Nelson, *The Beggar's Ride*, 1992.
Stephen Roos, *You'll Miss Me When I'm Gone*, 1988.
Tres Seymour, *Life in the Desert*, 1992.
Ordinary People, directed by Robert Redford, 1980.

A career in television writing has resulted in new working conditions for Thomas. "The immediate difference for a novelist writing for television or for features is that it's a democracy. In fiction I am the king of this little world. My editor will make suggestions, but what I write appears in the book. In features and television you are one piece in a committee of people producing this thing and everyone has a voice. A lot of people who have a voice are your bosses. You are trying to please the producer, you are trying to please the director, and you are trying to please the studio. In the case of television, you are also trying to please the network.

"I write things here in Los Angeles, and I get edits from six different groups of people," he said in the *AAYA* interview. "I will go to a series of meetings where everyone has a voice. Frequently, those people differ in what they are looking for. It is a tough and frustrating process but a well-compensated process. You battle your way through it—you pick and choose your fights—and frequently the others do have good ideas that you incorporate in ways you would never have thought of. The key is getting to work with good people."

Thomas intends to honor his three-book contract with Simon & Schuster over the next four to five years, although a book due in the summer of 1998 has been postponed for a year. Thomas has yet to publish young adult novels about athletes and playing in a rock band, "the two things I did most as a teenager," though his next planned work is a "band on the road" story called *Seattle and Back*. "I played high school baseball, football, and basketball, and I ran track. I loved it." Thomas told Saari. He added, "I played college football, yet I never used any of that in a story. In fact, athletes have never fared terribly well in my books, which I also think is fairly odd. I will get around to a sports book, but I just haven't yet."

Thomas values young adult books as "the purest form of writing I get to do these days." Thomas has hired an assistant to help him answer his e-mail and support his Web site, which provides general information about him and his observations about writing. The assistant will draw upon Thomas's extensive file of e-mail answers, but Thomas promises to read all responses before they are sent out, and to answer personal messages. "There are some letters that kids will write me that are so heartfelt, and that they have put so much time and effort into, that I will make sure I answer them personally," said Thomas.

■ **Works Cited**

Adams, Lauren, review of *Rats Saw God*, *Horn Book*, July/August, 1996, pp. 468-70.

Peck, Richard, "Writing in a Straight Line," *Horn Book*, September/October, 1997, pp. 529-33.

Review of *Rats Saw God*, *Publishers Weekly*, June 10, 1996, pp. 100-1.

Review of *Slave Day*, *Kirkus Reviews*, February 15, 1997, p. 306.

Review of *Slave Day*, *Publishers Weekly*, February 17, 1997, p. 220.

Shoemaker, Joel, interview with Rob Thomas, *Voice of Youth Advocates*, June, 1997, pp. 88-91.

Stevenson, Deborah, review of *Rats Saw God*, *Bulletin of the Center for Children's Books*, May, 1996, p. 317.

Thomas, Rob, interview with Jon Saari for *Authors and Artists for Young Adults*, March 16, 1998.

■ **For More Information See**

PERIODICALS

Booklist, June 1 and 15, 1996, p. 1706.
Children Book Review Service, Spring, 1997, p. 143.
Emergency Library, Spring, 1997, p. 54.
Horn Book, May/June, 1998, p. 350.
Horn Book Guide, Fall, 1996, p. 306.
Journal of Adolescent and Adult Literacy, April, 1996, p. 599.
Kirkus Reviews, April 1, 1997, p. 538; October 15, 1997, p. 1590.
School Library Journal, December, 1996, p. 32.

WORLD WIDE WEB SITE

http://www.mediacomp.com/robt.*

—Sketch by Jon Saari

Edith Wharton

humanitarian work during World War I; Pulitzer Prize, 1921, for *The Age of Innocence*; honorary doctorate in literature, Yale University, 1923; Nobel Prize nomination, 1927; membership, American Academy of Arts and Letters, 1930; Gold Medal, National Institute of Arts and Letters; Motyon Prize, French Academy.

■ Personal

Born Edith Newbold Jones, January 24 (some sources say January 23), 1862 (some sources say 1861), in New York City, NY; died of cardiac arrest, August 11, 1937, in St. Brice-sous-Foret, France; buried in Versailles, France, next to Walter Berry; daughter of George Frederic (heir to merchant ship fortune) and Lucretia Stevens (Rhinelander) Jones; married Edward Robbins Wharton (a banker), April 29, 1885 (divorced, 1912). *Education:* Privately educated in New York and Europe.

■ Career

Novelist, poet, short story writer, and critic. *Wartime service:* Assisted in the organization of the American Hostel for Refugees, and the Children of Flanders Rescue Committee during World War I.

■ Awards, Honors

Legion of Honor, France, 1916, and Chevalier of the Order of Leopold, Belgium, 1919, both for

■ Writings

NOVELS

The Touchstone, Scribner, 1900, published as *A Gift from the Grave,* Murray, 1900.

The Valley of Decision, Scribner, 1902.

Sanctuary, Scribner, 1903.

The House of Mirth, Scribner, 1905, edited by Elizabeth Ammons, Norton, 1990, published as *The House of Mirth: A Critical Study in Contemporary Criticism,* edited by Shari Benstock, St. Martin's Press, 1993.

Madame de Treymes, Scribner, 1907, edited and with an introduction by Martha Banta, Oxford University Press, 1994.

The Fruit of the Tree, Scribner, 1907, reprinted, Virago, 1988.

Ethan Frome, Scribner, 1911, edited by Blake Nevius, 1968, published as *Ethan Frome: Authoritative Text, Backgrounds, Contexts, and Criticism,* edited by Kristin O. Lauer with an introduction by Cynthia G. Wolff, W. W. Norton and Co., 1994, edited and with an introduction by Elaine Showalter, Oxford University Press, 1996.

The Reef, Scribner, 1912, with an introduction by Louis Auchincloss, Scribner, 1995.

The Custom of the Country, Scribner, 1913, with an introduction by Stephen Orgel, Oxford University Press, 1995.

Summer, Appleton, 1917, with an introduction and notes by Elizabeth Ammons, Penguin, 1993.

The Marne: A Tale of the War, Appleton, 1918.

The Age of Innocence, Appleton, 1920, with an introduction by R. W. B. Lewis, Collier Books, 1993, edited and with an introduction by Cynthia G. Wolff, Viking Penguin, 1996.

The Glimpses of the Moon, Appleton, 1922.

A Son at the Front, Appleton, 1923, with an introduction by Shari Benstock, Northern Illinois University Press, 1995.

Old New York: False Dawn (The 'Forties), The Old Maid (The 'Fifties), The Spark (The 'Sixties), New Year's Day (The 'Seventies) (four short novels), Appleton, 1924, published as *Old New York: Four Novellas*, Scribner Paperback Fiction, 1995.

The Mother's Recompense, Appleton, 1925.

Twilight Sleep, Appleton, 1925.

The Children, Appleton, 1928, published as *The Marriage Playground*, Grosset and Dunlap, 1930.

Hudson River Bracketed, Appleton, 1929.

The Gods Arrive (sequel to *Hudson River Bracketed*), Appleton, 1932.

The Buccaneers (incomplete, published posthumously), Appleton, 1938, published with completion by Marion Mainwaring, Viking, 1993, published with *Fast and Loose*, edited by Viola Hopkins Winner, University Press of Virginia, 1993.

GENERAL COLLECTIONS

An Edith Wharton Treasury, edited by Arthur Hobson Quinn, Appleton, 1950.

The Edith Wharton Reader, compiled by Louis Auchincloss, Scribner, 1965.

The Edith Wharton Omnibus, with an introduction by Gore Vidal, Scribner, 1978.

Novellas and Other Writings, edited by Cynthia G. Wolff, Library of America, 1990.

(Under pseudonym David Olivieri) *Fast and Loose: A Novelette*, published with *The Buccaneers*, edited by Viola Hopkins Winner, University Press of Virginia, 1993.

Madame de Treymes and 3 Novellas, Simon and Schuster, 1995.

Ethan Frome and Other Stories, Courage Books, 1996.

The Age of Innocence and Two Other Complete Works of Love, Morals, and Manners (also includes *Summer*

and *Madame De Treymes*), Grammercy Books, 1996.

Four Novels, Library of America, 1996.

SHORT STORIES

The Greater Inclination, Scribner, 1899.

Crucial Instances, Scribner, 1901.

The Descent of Man and Other Stories, Scribner, 1904.

The Hermit and the Wild Woman, and Other Stories, Scribner, 1908.

Xingu and Other Stories, Scribner, 1908.

Tales of Men and Ghosts, Scribner, 1920.

Here and Beyond, Appleton, 1926.

Certain People, Appleton, 1930.

Human Nature, Appleton, 1933.

The World Over, Appleton, 1936.

Ghosts, Appleton, 1937.

Roman Fever and Other Stories, Scribner, 1964.

Collected Short Stories, edited by R. W. B. Lewis, Scribner, 1968.

The Ghost Stories of Edith Wharton, [New York], 1973.

Quartet: Four Stories, Allen Press, 1975.

The Stories of Edith Wharton, (2 volumes), edited by Anita Brookner, Simon and Schuster, 1988-89.

The Muse's Tragedy and Other Stories, edited by Candace Waid, Library of America, 1990.

Short Stories, Dover Publications, 1994.

Wharton's New England: Seven Stories and "Ethan Frome," University Press of New England, 1995.

The Ghost-Feeler: Stories of Terror and the Supernatural, edited and with an introduction by Peter Haining, Dufour Editions, 1996.

Afterward, Random House, 1996.

PLAYS AND POETRY

Verses, published anonymously, 1878.

(Adaptor) *The Joy of Living* (adapted from a play by Hermann Sudermann), produced 1902.

(With Clyde Fitch) *The House of Mirth* (based on the novel), produced 1906.

Artemis to Actaeon and Other Verse, Scribner, 1909.

Twelve Poems, Medici Society, 1926.

OTHER

(With Ogden Codman, Jr.) *The Decoration of Houses*, Batsford, 1897, Scribner, 1898.

(Translator) Hermann Sudermann, *The Joy of Living*, Scribner, 1902.

Italian Villas and Their Gardens (essays), Century, 1904.

Italian Backgrounds (memoirs), Scribner, 1905.

A Motor-Flight Through France, Scribner, 1908.

Fighting France: From Dunkerque to Belfort, Scribner, 1915.

(Editor) *Le Livre des sans-foyer*, 1915, published as *The Book of the Homeless: Original Articles in Verse and Prose*, Macmillan, 1916.

Wharton's War Charities in France, n.p., 1918.

L'Amérique en Guerre, n.p., 1918.

French Ways and Their Meaning (essays), Scribner, 1919.

In Morocco, Scribner, 1920.

The Writing of Fiction (criticism), Scribner, 1925.

A Background Glance (autobiography), Appleton, 1934.

(Editor with Robert Norton) *Eternal Passion in English Poetry*, n.p., 1939.

Letters of Edith Wharton, edited by R. W. B. Lewis and Nancy Lewis, Simon and Schuster, 1988.

Henry James and Edith Wharton Letters, 1900-15, Weidenfeld and Nicholson, 1990.

Edith Wharton Abroad: Selected Travel Writings, 1888-1920, edited by Sara Bird Wright, St. Martin's Press, 1995.

The Uncollected Critical Writings, edited by Frederick Wegener, Princeton University Press, 1997.

Contributor of poems and stories to literary journals including *Scribner's, Harper's, Century*, and *Atlantic*. Many of Wharton's diaries, letters, notebooks, and manuscripts are located in the Beinecke Library at Yale University.

■ Adaptations

The Old Maid was adapted by Zoe Akins and received the Pulitzer Prize for Drama in 1935; *Ethan Frome* was dramatized by Owen and Donald Davis and produced in New York in 1936; a version of *The Custom of the Country* by Jane Stanton Hitchcock was produced at the McGinn/Cazale Theater on Broadway in 1985; *Old New York* was adapted by Donald Sanders and produced in The Old Merchant's House Museum in New York in 1987; "The Other Two" and "Autres temps" were adapted by Dennis Krausnick and produced at Wharton's estate, The Mount, in Lenox, Massachusetts, in 1987; the story "Roman Fever" was adapted as an opera in one act with music by Robert Ward and text by Roger Brunyate, Vireo Press, 1993.

Films adapted from Wharton's work include the silent movies *The House of Mirth*, 1905; *The Glimpses of the Moon*, 1923; and *The Age of Innocence*, 1925. Other works adapted for film include *The Marriage Playground*, 1929, from *The Children; The Age of Innocence*, 1934, and by Martin Scorsese and Jay Cocks, 1993; *The Old Maid*, 1939; and *Ethan Frome*, 1992.

Several of Wharton's works have been adapted for audio cassette by Ingram, including *The Age of Innocence*, 1993, 1996; *Glimpses of the Moon*, 1994; *Summer*, 1994; *The Custom of the Country*, 1995; *Decoration of Houses*, 1995; *The Book of Homeless*, 1996; and *Ethan Frome*, 1997. Several works were adapted for audio cassette by Commuters Library, including "The Eyes," 1994; "The Mission of Jane," 1994; and "The Other Two," 1994. *The Buccaneers* was adapted for audio cassette by Penguin High Bridge Audio, 1993. *Ethan Frome* was published on CD by Ingram, 1995.

■ Sidelights

During the early decades of the twentieth century—at a time when New York City could ban women from smoking in public—one American woman published works which discussed love outside of marriage, scandal, class divisions, and poverty. Without apologies, she began to claim a place among the very best American novelists. Raised to disdain creative endeavors, this woman became an intellectual; cultivated for marriage, she divorced her husband; taught to obey the values of elite American society, she evaluated them. This woman, Edith Wharton, according to Gore Vidal, writing in *The Edith Wharton Omnibus*, "was never timid. Somehow in recent years a notion has got about that she was a stuffy grand old lady who wrote primly decorous novels about upper-class people of a sort that are no longer supposed to exist. She was indeed a grand lady, but she was not at all stuffy. Quite the contrary. She was witty. She was tough as nails."

Wharton, who published more than forty books, is best known for her novels, especially *The House of Mirth, The Age of Innocence* (for which she became the first woman to be awarded a Pulitzer Prize) and *Ethan Frome*. James W. Tuttleton explained in *Dictionary of Literary Biography* (*DLB*), "As a chronicler of the manners of New York society from the 1840s into the 1930s, an international novelist, and master of the short story, Wharton's principal focus, as indicated in her book *The Writing of Fiction* (1925), was the conflict between the desire of the individual and the authority of social convention. . . . Since the publication of R.W.B. Lewis's *Edith Wharton: A Biography* (1975), based on her private papers, it has become vividly clear the extent to which these intensely felt issues arose from her personal situation." Wharton herself was trapped by convention, and her own social status; she had to learn, throughout her life, how to balance her own desires and interests with the morals she internalized as a child.

In her fiction, as Cynthia Griffin Wolff suggested in her *DLB* entry, Wharton demonstrated "talents which were uniquely hers—an incomparable understanding of complex psychological motivation and perhaps the keenest satiric capacity in American fiction." Although, as Richard H. Lawson explained, Wharton was not an innovative short-story writer, her "style, above all her irony, from which her style is inseparable, is superb." According to Lawson, also writing in *DLB*, "quite aside from her reputation as a novelist," Edith Wharton "is among the most brilliant American short-story writers."

Yet Wharton did not just write fiction about elite New York society: her work took up topics—in a variety of forms—from interior decoration to the country of Morocco. In her nonfiction, Wharton's work was characterized by beautiful prose, an appreciation of fine artistry, and careful insight. While Wharton's literary legacy has suffered from the stuffy image Vidal has noted, and from constant comparisons of her work to that of Henry James, interest in Wharton's writings has ebbed and flowed for almost a century. Increasingly, casual readers, filmmakers, and scholars alike have come to appreciate the richness of Wharton's work in all its variations.

Wharton was born into New York society in 1862, to George Frederic Jones (from a notable family of merchant-ship owners) and his wife Lucretia (a beautiful, fashionable woman descended from a Boston tea party participant). Young Edith was educated privately by tutors and governesses, and traveled about Europe throughout her childhood. It was there that she met Henry James, who was to become a friend and mentor. Despite her acquaintance with James, Edith was not encouraged to engage in intellectual or artistic endeavors; however, she preferred her father's library to parties, and she wrote poems and stories as a teenager. Her works appeared in the *Atlantic*, *Scribner's*, *Harper's* and *Century* magazines. Under the pseudonym of David Olivieri she produced her first short novel (a romance entitled *Fast and Loose*) when she was still a teenager. In 1878, she published an anonymous volume of poetry called *Verses*. Edith was in her early twenties when she married Edward Wharton, a banker who was much older than she was and did not share many of her interests.

Writing Brings Fulfillment

Wharton was not happy in her role as a society wife, traveling and hosting parties. She had a nervous breakdown in 1894. Sent to a sanatorium to recover, Wharton was advised by her doctors to write to improve her condition. Soon afterward, she began her professional career as a writer. The first book she published under her name was *The Decoration of Houses*, a work of nonfiction which she co-authored with Ogden Codman, Jr. (the pair had redecorated the Wharton home in Newport, Rhode Island). *The Decoration of Houses* documented the project in Newport while advancing the notion that home decor should express the personalities of home owners, rather than what was fashionable in elite circles. Wharton's book sold well enough to encourage her to write some more. She moved to her estate in Lenox, Massachusetts, named The Mount, where she enjoyed the company of other writers.

Wharton published a collection of short stories, *The Greater Inclination*, in 1899, and her novel entitled *The Touchstone* appeared the next year. Critics introduced to Wharton's first books noted the similarity of her work to that of her friend, Henry James. "The stories in *The Greater Inclination*," wrote a reviewer in the *Critic*, "inevitably recall the work of Henry James" in "very substance" and "titular phrase" as well as method. Anna McClure Sholl, writing in *Gunton's* in 1903, noted the Jamesian quality of Wharton's work but also remarked on her "remarkable sensitiveness to the uses of words, her gift of condensing a volume in an epigram, her fondness for fleeting moods, delicately balanced situations" and "rare humor." Harry Thurston Peck exclaimed in an 1899 essay in the *Bookman* that Wharton was no mere imitator of James: "her stories . . . are superior in many ways to those of Mr. James's. . . . She deserves a wholly independent criticism."

Critics have also found much to appreciate in Wharton's early stories. Lawson noted that many critics find Wharton's initial efforts to be her best. According to Lawson, "The Lady's Maid's Bell," which first appeared in *Scribner's* in 1902, "is a highly successful ghost story." "The Eyes," which was published in the same magazine in 1910, "is a truly brilliant tale, a gripping ghost story in

This dramatic 1911 work, which portrays a doomed relationship between a man and his wife's young cousin, is set in a nineteenth-century rural New England community.

which the human relationship is all." Lawson also asserted that "*The Greater Inclination* is a remarkable effort for a first collection. As a whole the stories are characterized by complex and ambiguous personal relationships, generally well-tempered irony, and an elegant diction that only rarely succumbs to preciosity." "The Other Two," which first appeared in *Collier's* in 1904, "is one of Wharton's most engaging stories." According to Lawson, "Autres temps," written in 1911, "has been generally acclaimed as brilliant. While its structure may well deserve such praise, the further passage of time may well have dulled the sensitivity of today's reader to its narrative conflict."

The "first sensation of everybody" reading *The House of Mirth*, Wharton's fourth published novel, "was one of exultation," according to Henry Dwight Sedgwick in the *Atlantic*. *The House of Mirth* is the story of a beautiful, intelligent young woman, Lily Bart, who smokes and even gambles in public (to the dismay of conformists). Lily's father has died, leaving his small family poor. Without means of supporting herself in the manner in which she has grown up, Lily must decide between marrying for status and wealth (to a man she thinks vulgar) or for her own internal moral dignity (to a lawyer with much intelligence but few resources). As James W. Tuttleton noted in his *DLB* entry, before the novel's conclusion Lily "loses her tenuous position with the idle rich . . . falls in the social order and eventually drops out of it, only to die of an overdose of chloral in a cheap boarding house." Wolff asserted that "Wharton's intimate and sympathetic portrait of Lily Bart is perhaps the finest example anywhere in American fiction of the tragedy of a woman who has come to regard herself primarily as a decorative object."

Contemporary critics hailed *The House of Mirth*. Wharton's "mastery of the episode is as dashing as ever, and more delicate. The chapters are a succession of tableaux, all admirably posed," wrote Sedgwick. He continued, "The epigrams are as luminous as ever, but they are no longer firecrackers; they are brightened and softened to electric lights ensconced in Venetian glass, where they shed both illumination and color." *The House of Mirth* was also very popular and became a bestseller in the United States. According to William Lyon Phelps, writing in the *New York Times Book Review*, the novel "gave Mrs. Wharton an international reputation."

Wharton's success as a writer progressed rapidly for the remainder of the first decade of the twentieth century. The 1907 novel, *The Fruit of the Tree*, according to Tuttleton in *DLB*, "sought to capitalize on the then-current vogue of muckraking and reform literature," and concerned a group of textile workers in a small town in Massachusetts. In 1908, Wharton published a book about an automobile tour she took through France, and a book of short stories. By 1910, she had published another novel, a book of verse, and a book of stories, as well as the ghost tales "The Eyes" and "Afterward."

Despite her professional success, Wharton's personal life was troubled. Her relationship with her husband, who suffered from manic depression, deteriorated. In 1907, some sources say that she began an affair with Morton Fullerton, an American journalist. According to Tuttleton, "Wharton was filled with guilt, for she believed in the marriage commitment. . . . Besides that, Fullerton was an unstable scapegrace whose amorous escapades . . . scandalized their circle of friends. The affair was brief and intense." It ended around 1909.

Ethan Frome

Wharton published *Ethan Frome* in 1911. Although the book was set in New England, a place she knew well, it was about poor, rather than wealthy, characters. The book opens as a visiting engineer to the small town of Starkfield, Massachusetts, ponders the crippled figure of Ethan Frome. Frome was involved in a terrible accident that the townspeople are reluctant to discuss. Then, as the engineer is forced to spend the night at the Frome house during a blizzard, readers are given an account of the times leading up to the accident that maimed him.

Frome, intellectually frustrated and resigned to life on his barren farm, falls in love with the pretty, cheerful, and smart cousin of his sickly wife Zeena. While Frome keeps his love a secret, Zeena suspects Frome is in love with young Mattie. Once Frome and Mattie confess their love for one another, they find they cannot express it—on a pretext, Zeena wants to send Mattie away. Frome and Mattie share no more than a few kisses before their lives change forever. The lovers, in an attempt at suicide, survive only to suffer as never before.

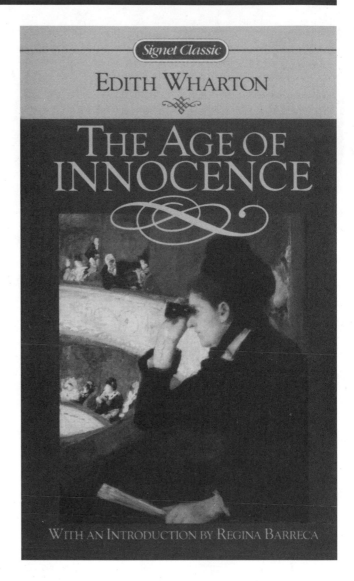

Wharton received the Pulitzer Prize for her 1920 novel exploring the struggle between love and social convention.

Full of tension and suspense due to its carefully composed structure, *Ethan Frome* was well received by the critics. "Few features of this remarkable book stand out more strikingly than its general design, by which the author has managed to satisfy at once our craving for surprise and our dislike of too much surprise," observed Edwin Björkman in his 1913 book *Voices of To-Morrow: Critical Studies of the New Spirit in Literature*. Today, *Ethan Frome* continues to be considered an American classic.

When Wharton and her husband divorced in 1912, she sold The Mount, traveled in Italy and Germany, and then moved to France. There, living in her estate on the Riviera or her home near Paris, Wharton consorted with American expatriate writers as well as English and French artists. (The latter group included Paul Valery, Paul Bourget, Charles du Bos, Auguste Rodin, and Jean Cocteau). Wharton, who socialized with the members of famous American families (including the Roosevelts, Tafts, and Vanderbilts), also entertained Americans traveling in France. Wharton herself traveled throughout England and Europe.

Only two of Wharton's novels are entirely set in France, *Madame de Treymes* and *The Reef*. In this latter work, published in 1912, "Wharton uses Jamesian stylistic devices to tell the story of . . . [an] American widow of a Frenchman," explained Margaret B. McDowell in *DLB*. The protagonist, Anna Leath, slowly learns that her fiance "has been the lover of her daughter's American governess. . . . Anna's resentment of the adventurous

American governess may foreshadow Wharton's moralistically negative view of American youth in the twenties." As McDowell pointed out, Henry James "regarded *The Reef* as a masterpiece, admiring Wharton's moral insight and aesthetic control."

Wharton's *The Custom of the Country*, published in 1913, is also regarded as one of her better works. This book, explained Tuttleton, provides "a long, rambling chronicle of manners, narrating the rise of a vulgar and aggressive girl to social prominence in the East and in Europe." The Midwestern girl, Undine Spragg, is relentless in her pursuit of wealth, and she seeks men who have it. Along with other "unscrupulous hucksters," as Cynthia Griffin Wolff has called them, Undine undermines the old order. Wolff deemed the book "a superb satirical novel," which seems to conclude that "the old order" of American society gave "way so utterly to the vulgar amorality of America's robber barons and their families" be-

Daniel Day-Lewis and Michelle Pfeiffer starred in the 1993 film version of *The Age of Innocence*.

cause of the culture's repression and lack of energy. "Poised on the brink of the future, *The Custom of the Country* records a period of momentous change," Wolff added.

Wharton did more than write, socialize, and travel in France. When World War I began, she devoted herself to relief work. Wharton worked to provide refugee facilities and to raise money for war relief from Americans. These efforts not only helped some thirty thousand refugees, but provided foster homes for orphans, communities for children and the elderly, and the treatment of military personal suffering from tuberculosis. As Wharton worked to gain aid for France, she wrote *Fighting France: From Dunkerque to Belfort*, which described the fighting she had witnessed. Wharton was awarded with an appointment by the French president as a chevalier of the Legion of Honor. She also received the Chevalier of the Order of Leopold from Belgium.

The Age of Innocence Hailed as a Classic

After publishing over ten novels and numerous short stories, Wharton was highly regarded in American literature. William Lyon Phelps remarked in a 1916 essay in *Bookman* that at the "moment Edith Wharton stands by common consent at the head of all living American women who write books; indeed there are many who say she is our foremost novelist." *The Age of Innocence*, published in 1920, furthered Wharton's reputation.

The Age of Innocence begins in New York in the 1870s as Newland Archer ponders his engagement to May Welland, a beautiful girl from a prominent family. May's cousin, Ellen Olenska, back in New York after years spent in Europe, has escaped from her husband, an unfaithful count. Countess Olenska's European attitudes, dress, and lifestyle, along with her scandalous separation from her husband, are not very welcome in high society. It takes the weight of Archer's family—linked as it is to Countess Olenska's by Archer's impending marriage—to provide her with a warm reception in the best parlors of the city. Yet Archer finds himself falling in love with the exotic Countess (whom he knew as a child); he rushes into a wedding with his fiance to end his dilemma. It is not long, however, before Archer finds his married life stifling, and his longing for the Countess growing. As Archer works to con-

ceal and contend with his feelings, his family conspires to keep him in his marriage. Writing in *DLB*, Margaret B. McDowell argued that *The Age of Innocence* "celebrates the worth of aristocratic values and rituals in the New York of the 1870s. Family responsibility and loyalty further self-development rather than deny it in this book."

Some contemporary critics were elated by the publication of *The Age of Innocence*. "Edith Wharton is a writer who brings glory on the name America, and this is her best book," asserted William Lyon Phelps in 1920 in the *New York Times Book Review*. "It is one of the best novels of the twentieth century and looks like a permanent addition to literature." Some critics applauded *The Age of Innocence* as a historical novel. Phelps, for example, remarked that "New York society and customs in the seventies are described with an accuracy that is almost uncanny; to read these pages is to live again." Others evidently agreed, for Wharton received the Pulitzer Prize in 1921 for *The Age of Innocence*.

While some critics contend that *The Age of Innocence* was the last great Wharton work, Wharton wrote many other notable pieces during the 1920s. *The Glimpses of the Moon*, a 1922 novel about poor lovers who have determined that they should find other, wealthier mates to support them as they continue their love affair, is one such work. Rebecca West, writing in *New Statesman* soon after the book was published, found *The Glimpses of the Moon* to be almost *too* perfect. "Nothing more competent than this book could be possibly imagined. . .," said West. Wharton published *A Son at the Front*, another novel, in 1923. The story follows a young American who, born in France, is called to serve in France during World War I. As his wealthy parents do what they can to keep him out of the battlefield, the young man himself transfers to the infantry. Although *A Son at the Front* was "criticized or ignored" at the time, as a *Publishers Weekly* critic wrote in 1995, the novel is "heartrending, tragic, powerful," and "not to be missed."

Wharton briefly returned to the United States in 1923 for the first time since she became a resident of France—to receive an honorary doctorate from Yale University. (It was the first such degree at Yale given to a woman). According to James W. Tuttleton, "Most of her old friends were long dead or unrecognizable, and New York itself was

If you enjoy the works of Edith Wharton, you may also want to check out the following books and films:

The works of E. M. Forster, including *A Room with a View*, 1908, and *Howard's End*, 1910.

The works of Henry James, including *The Europeans*, 1878, *The Potrait of a Lady*, 1881, and *The Ambassadors*, 1903.

The Wings of the Dove, starring Helena Bonham Carter, 1997.

measurably different from the pre-war city she had left almost two decades before. Her parents' world, old New York, was gone without a trace." *Old New York*, a work comprised of four short novels set in the New York that Wharton remembered, was not celebrated when it appeared in 1924. Edmund Wilson commented in *New Republic* that the stories "do not . . . follow life quite faithfully enough to be impressive as social studies and . . . are not quite dramatically enough developed to be satisfactory as conventional short stories."

During the remainder of the 1920s, Wharton continued her life in France, and met and counseled both F. Scott Fitzgerald and Sinclair Lewis. The year 1927 was a difficult one for Wharton. Her frequent companion (and some say lover) Walter Berry, the head of the American Chamber of Commerce in Paris, died. That same year, Wharton was nominated for a Nobel Prize but did not receive it.

Wharton died in 1937 of a heart attack at the age of seventy-five, with a novel, *The Buccaneers*, left unfinished. She was buried next to her beloved Walter Berry in Versailles, France. By that time Wharton's writings were out of vogue. Frances Theresa Russell, for example, stated in the *Sewanee Review* in 1932 that the substance of Wharton's work had been "static" for many years. "Mrs. Wharton's fictitious world is one in which total strangers sit aimlessly chatting on hotel verandahs. . . . She meditates a good deal over this and that: the evils of divorce, the aftermaths of deception, the individual versus society, the need and the danger of joy, the gulf between ambition

and ability; and she hatches a whole brood of concrete problems to serve for her themes and theses. But they turn out rather inconclusive."

In the words of Cynthia Griffin Wolff, Wharton "has been 'reclaimed'" many times since her death. Wolff's own efforts and those of R. W. B. Lewis, especially in his 1975 biography of Wharton, have allowed critics and readers to re-examine the life and literary career of Edith Wharton and to recognize her as one of the greatest American writers of the early decades of the twentieth century.

The 1990s saw a resurgence in interest in Wharton's work. *The Age of Innocence* was adapted as a highly acclaimed film in 1993. The Edith Wharton Restoration, Inc., worked to keep her titles in print. Tourists could visit the restored estate, The Mount, in Massachusetts. *Fast and Loose*, Wharton's first novel, was published along with her unfinished work, *The Buccaneers*, which was completed by Marion Mainwaring. Both books were edited by Viola Hopkins Winner.

In 1997, Frederick Wegener published a collection of Wharton's critical writings which includes book reviews, a biography, eulogies, introductions, evaluations, and explanations of her own work, along with other essays. About *The Uncollected Critical Writings*, a *Publishers Weekly* critic explained, "Wegener demonstrates that Wharton was a far better critic than she realized." Donna Seaman of *Booklist* agreed. "Everyone interested in literature will find much to savor here," she concluded. Whether or not Wharton's work is fashionable in the new millennium, Wharton's place among the great writers of America is secure.

■ Works Cited

Björkman, Edwin, "The Greater Edith Wharton," *Voices of To-Morrow: Critical Studies of the New Spirit in Literature*, Mitchell Kennerley, 1913, pp. 290-304.

Review of *The Greater Inclination*, *Critic*, August, 1899, pp. 746-47.

Lawson, Richard H., "Conclusion," *Edith Wharton*, Ungar, 1977, pp. 95-99.

Lawson, Richard H., "Edith Wharton," *Dictionary of Literary Biography*, Volume 78: *American Short-Story Writers*, Gale, 1989, pp. 308-23.

McDowell, Margaret B., "Edith Wharton," *Dictionary of Literary Biography*, Volume 4: *American Writers in Paris*, Gale, 1980, pp. 408-13.

Peck, Harry Thurston, "A New Writer Who Counts," *Bookman*, June, 1899, pp. 344-46.

Phelps, William Lyon, "The Advance of the English Novel," *Bookman*, July, 1916, pp. 515-24.

Phelps, William Lyon, "As Mrs. Wharton Sees Us," *New York Times Book Review*, October 17, 1920, pp. 1, 11.

Russell, Frances Theresa, "Melodramatic Mrs. Wharton," *Sewanee Review*, Autumn, 1932.

Seaman, Donna, review of *The Uncollected Critical Writings*, *Booklist*, February 1, 1997, p. 921.

Sedgwick, Henry Dwight, "The Novels of Mrs. Wharton," *Atlantic*, August, 1906, pp. 217-18.

Sholl, Anna McClure, "The Work of Edith Wharton," *Gunton's*, November, 1903, pp. 426-32.

Review of *A Son at the Front*, *Publishers Weekly*, November 6, 1995, p. 87.

Tuttleton, James W., "Edith Wharton," *Dictionary of Literary Biography*, Volume 12: *American Realists and Naturalists*, Gale, 1982, pp. 433-50.

Review of *The Uncollected Critical Writings*, *Publishers Weekly*, November 11, 1996.

Vidal, Gore, "Introduction," *The Edith Wharton Omnibus*, Scribner, 1978, pp. vii-xiii.

West, Rebecca, "Notes on Novels: 'The Glimpses of the Moon'," *New Statesman*, September 2, 1922, p. 588.

Wilson, Edmund, "Review of Books: 'Old New York,'" *New Republic*, June 11, 1924, p. 77.

Wolff, Cynthia Griffin, "Edith Wharton," *Dictionary of Literary Biography*, Volume 9: *American Novelists 1910-1945*, Gale, 1981, pp. 126-42.

■ For More Information See

BOOKS

Ammons, Elizabeth, *Wharton's Argument with America*, University of Georgia Press, 1980.

Bauer, Dale M., *Edith Wharton's Brave New Politics*, University of Wisconsin Press, 1994.

Bell, Millicent, editor, *The Cambridge Companion to Edith Wharton*, Cambridge University Press, 1995.

Bendixen, Alfred, and Annette Zilversmit, *Edith Wharton: New Critical Essays*, Garland, 1992.

Benstock, Shari, *No Gifts from Chance: A Biography of Edith Wharton*, Scribner, 1994.

Bentley, Nancy, *The Ethnography of Manners: Hawthorne, James, Wharton*, Cambridge University Press, 1995.

Brenni, Vito J., *Edith Wharton: A Bibliography*, West Virginia University Library, 1966.

Dwight, Eleanor, *Edith Wharton: An Extraordinary Life*, Abrams, 1994.

Dyman, Jenni, *Lurking Feminism: The Ghost Stories of Edith Wharton*, P. Lang, 1995.

Erlich, Gloria C., *The Sexual Education of Edith Wharton*, University of California Press, 1992.

Fedorko, Kathy A., *Gender and the Gothic in the Fiction of Edith Wharton*, University of Alabama Press, 1995.

Fracaso, Evelyn E., *Edith Wharton's Prisoners of Consciousness: A Study of Theme and Technique in the Tales*, Greenwood Press, 1994.

The Gilded Age: Edith Wharton and Her Contemporaries, Universe Publishing Company, 1996.

Goodman, Susan, *Edith Wharton's Inner Circle*, University of Texas Press, 1994.

Hadley, Kathy Miller, *In the Interstices of the Tale: Edith Wharton's Narrative Strategies*, P. Lange, 1993.

Howe, Irving, editor, *Edith Wharton: A Collection of Critical Essays*, Prentice-Hall, 1962.

Killoran, Helen, *Edith Wharton: Art and Allusion*, University of Alabama Press, 1996.

Lewis, R. W. B., *Edith Wharton: A Biography*, Harper and Row, 1975.

Nevius, Blake, *Wharton: A Study of Her Fiction*, University of California Press, 1953.

Price, Alan, *The End of the Age of Innocence: Edith Wharton and the First World War*, St. Martin's Press, 1996.

Singley, Carol J., *Edith Wharton: Matters of Mind and Spirit*, Cambridge University Press, 1995.

Springer, Marlene, *Ethan Frome: A Nightmare of Need*, Twayne, 1993.

Tuttleton, James W., Kristin O. Lauer, and Margaret Murray, editors, *Edith Wharton: The Contemporary Reviews*, Cambridge University Press, 1992.

Wagner-Martin, Linda, *The Age of Innocence: A Novel of Ironic Nostalgia*, Twayne Publishers, 1996.

Walton, Geoffrey, *Edith Wharton: A Critical Interpretation*, Fairleigh Dickinson University Press, 1970.

Wolff, Cynthia, *A Feat of Words: The Triumph of Edith Wharton*, Oxford University Press, 1977.

PERIODICALS

Americana, May-June, 1987, p. 6.
American History Illustrated, September, 1982, p. 10.
Architectural Digest, March, 1994, p. 78.

Atlantic, November, 1985, p. 115.
Choice, March, 1994.
Harper's Baazar, November, 1992, p. 136.
House Beautiful, July, 1990, p. 110.
New York, May 23, 1988, p. 25.
New York Times Book Review, January 2, 1994, p. 7.
Publishers Weekly, June 24, 1988, pp. 90, 92; September 20, 1993.
Vogue, June, 1988, p. 252.
Yale Review, Summer, 1988, pp. 560, 563.
Yankee, June, 1995, p. 82.

■ Obituaries

PERIODICALS

Commonweal, August 27, 1937, p. 412.
News Week, August 21, 1937, p. 5.
New York Times, August 13, 1937, p. 17.
Time, August 23, 1937, p. 53.
Publishers Weekly, August 21, 1937, pp. 575-76.*

—Sketch by R. Garcia-Johnson

Acknowledgments

Acknowledgments

Grateful acknowledgment is made to the following publishers, authors, and artists for their kind permission to reproduce copyrighted material.

JOAN AIKEN. Gorey, Edward, illustrator. From a cover of *The Wolves of Willoughby Chase*, by Joan Aiken. Yearling Books, 1987. Reproduced by permission of Bantam Doubleday Dell Books for Young Readers. / Berenzy, Alix, illustrator. From a jacket of *The Last Slice of Rainbow and Other Stories*, by Joan Aiken. Harper & Row, Publishers, 1988. Jacket art (c) 1988 by Alix Berenzy. Reproduced by permission of the illustrator. / Daniels, Beau, illustrator. From a jacket of *Give Yourself a Fright*, by Joan Aiken. Delacorte Press, 1989. Jacket illustration (c) 1989 by Beau Daniels. Reproduced by permission of Delacorte Press, a division of Bantam Double Dell Publishing Group, Inc. / Aiken, Joan, photograph. Reproduced by permission of Joan Aiken.

JULIA ALVAREZ. Munck, Paula, illustrator. From a cover of *How the Garcia Girls Lost Their Accents*, by Julia Alvarez. Plume Books, 1992. Reproduced by permission of the illustrator. / Perez, German, illustrator. From a cover of *In the Time of the Butterflies*, by Julia Alvarez. Plume Books, 1995. Reproduced by permission of the illustrator. / Perez, German, illustrator. From a cover of *Homecoming: New and Collected Poems*, by Julia Alvarez. Plume Books, 1996. Reproduced by permission of the illustrator. / Alvarez, Julia, photograph by Sara Eichner. Reproduced by permission of William Eichner.

ALLAN BAILLIE. Baillie, Allan, photograph. Reproduced by permission of Allan Baillie.

ANTHONY BURGESS. "Arena Brains II," by Robert Longo. From a cover of *A Clockwork Orange*, by Anthony Burgess. Norton, 1987. Reproduced by permission of Robert Longo. Cover typography by permission of W. W. Norton & Company, Inc. / Cover of *Earthly Powers*, by Anthony Burgess. Carroll & Graf Publishers, Inc., 1994. Reproduced by permission. / McDowell, Malcolm and others, in the film *A Clockwork Orange*, 1972, photograph. The Kobal Collection. Reproduced by permission. / Burgess, Anthony, photograph. AP/Wide World Photos, Inc. Reproduced by permission.

TIM CAHILL. Nichols, Michael, photographer. From a cover of *A Wolverine Is Eating My Leg*, by Tim Cahill. Vintage Books, 1989. Cover photograph (c) 1986 by Michael Nichols/Magnum Photos. Reproduced by permission of Random House, Inc. / Newman, Mark, photograph. From a cover of *Road Fever: A High-Speed Travelogue*, by Tim Cahill. Vintage Books, 1992. Reproduced by permission of Random House, Inc. / Erwitt, Elliot, photographer. From a cover of *Pecked to Death by Ducks*, by Tim Cahill. Vintage Books, 1994. Reproduced by permission of Random House, Inc. / Lynn, Renee, photograph. From a cover of *Jaguars Ripped My Flesh*, by Tim Cahill. Vintage Books, 1996. Cover photograph (c) Tony Stone Images. Reproduced by permission of Random House, Inc. / Cahill, Tim, photograph by Marion Ettlinger. Reproduced by permission of Tim Cahill.

ALEXANDER CALDER. Calder, Alexander, (standing with his sculpture "Le Guichet"), photograph. Archive Photos, Inc. Reproduced by permission. / Calder, Alexander (behind artwork), photograph. Archive Photos, Inc. Reproduced by permission. / Alexander Calder's 727-200, painted red, white, and blue, photograph. AP/Wide World Photos, Inc. Reproduced by permission. / Calder, Alexander, (looking up at mobile), photograph. Archive Photos, Inc. Reproduced by permission.

RAYMOND CHANDLER. Cover of *The Long Goodbye*, by Raymond Chandler. Ballantine Books, 1971. Reproduced by permission of Random House, Inc. / Cover of *Farewell, My Lovely*, by Raymond Chandler. Vintage Books, 1976. Reproduced by permission of Random House, Inc. / Amsel, illustrator. From a cover of *The Big Sleep*, by Raymond Chandler. Vintage Books, 1976. Reproduced by permission of Random House, Inc. / Cover of *The Lady in the Lake*, by Raymond Chandler. Vintage Books, 1976. Reproduced by permission of Random House, Inc. / Bogart, Humphrey, and Lauren Bacall, in the film *The Big Sleep*, 1946, photograph. The Kobal Collection. Reproduced by permission. / Chandler, Raymond, photograph. The Library of Congress.

WES CRAVEN. Englund, Robert, in the film *A Nightmare on Elm Street IV: The Dream Master*, 1988, photograph. The Kobal Collection. Reproduced by permission. / Langer, A. J., and Yan Birch, in the film *The People under the Stairs*, 1991, photograph by Carol Westwood. The Kobal Collection. Reproduced by permission. / Campbell, Neve, and Rose McGowan, in the film *Scream*, 1996, photograph by David M. Moir. The Kobal Collection. Reproduced by permission. / Craven, Wes, photograph by Richard Drew. AP/Wide World Photos, Inc. Reproduced by permission.

HELEN CRESSWELL. Hyman, Trina Schart, illustrator. From a cover of *Bagthorpes Liberated: Being the Seventh Part of The Bagthorpe Saga*, by Helen Cresswell. Macmillan, 1989. Cover (c) 1989 by Trina Schart Hyman. Reproduced by permission of the illustrator. / Lindberg, Jeffrey, illustrator. From a cover of *The Secret World of Polly Flint*, by Helen

Cresswell. Aladdin Books, 1991. Cover illustration (c) 1991 by Jeffrey Lindberg. Reproduced by permission of the illustrator. / Cresswell, Helen, photograph. Reproduced by permission of Helen Cresswell.

TOM FEELINGS. Feelings, Tom, illustrator. From an illustration in *Now Sheba Sings the Song,* by Maya Angelou. Dial Books, 1987. Illustrations copyright (c) 1987 by Tom Feelings. Reproduced by permission of Tom Feelings. In the U. S., Canada, and the Philippine Islands by permission of Dial Books for Young Readers, a division of Penguin Putnam Inc. / Feelings, Tom, illustrator. From an illustration in *The Middle Passage,* by Tom Feelings. Dial Books, 1995. Copyright (c) 1995 by Tom Feelings. Reproduced by permission of Dial Books for Young Readers, a division of Penguin Putnam Inc. / Feelings, Tom, photograph by Diane Johnson-Feelings. Reproduced by permission of Tom Feelings.

MEL GLENN. Glenn, Mel, photograph by Howard Wallach. Reproduced by permission.

LORRAINE HANSBERRY. Poitier, Sidney, and Claudia McNeil in the stage production of *A Raisin in the Sun,* 1959, photograph. AP/Wide World Photos, Inc. Reproduced by permission. / Hansberry, Lorraine, photograph. UPI/Corbis-Bettmann. Reproduced by permission.

OSCAR HIJUELOS. Estevez, Herman, photographer. From a cover of *The Fourteen Sisters of Emilio Montez O'Brien,* by Oscar Hijuelos. HarperPaperbacks, 1994. Reproduced by permission of HarperCollins Publishers, Inc. / Toelke, Cathleen, illustrator. From a cover of *The Mambo Kings Play Songs of Love,* by Oscar Hijuelos. HarperPerennial, 1994. Cover illustration (c) 1994 by Cathleen Toelke. Reproduced by permission of HarperCollins Publishers, Inc. / Banderas, Antonio, and Armand Assante, in the film *The Mambo Kings,* 1991, photograph. The Kobal Collection. Reproduced by permission. / Hijuelos, Oscar, photograph. AP/Wide World Photos, Inc. Reproduced by permission.

JACK KEROUAC. Kerouac, Jack, photograph. Archive Photos, Inc. Reproduced by permission.

KEN KESEY. Nicholson, Jack, in the film *One Flew Over the Cuckoo's Nest,* 1975, photograph. The Kobal Collection. Reproduced by permission. Kesey, Ken, Pleasant Hill, Oregon, 1990, photograph by Jeff Barnard. AP/Wide World Photos, Inc. Reproduced by permission. / Kesey, Ken, photograph. AP/Wide World Photos, Inc. Reproduced by permission.

BARRY LEVINSON. Redford, Robert, in the film *The Natural,* 1984, photograph. The Kobal Collection. Reproduced by permission. / Bacon, Kevin, Mickey Rourke, Daniel Stern and Timothy Daly, in the film *Diner,* 1982, photograph. The Kobal Collection. Reproduced by permission. / Williams, Robin, in the film *Good Morning, Vietnam,* 1987, photograph. AP/Wide World Photos, Inc. Reproduced by permission. / Cruise, Tom, and Dustin Hoffman, in the film *Rain Man,* 1988, photograph. The Kobal Collection. Reproduced by permission. / Levinson, Barry photograph. AP/Wide World Photos, Inc. Reproduced by permission.

HERMAN MELVILLE. Moser, Barry, illustrator. From a cover of *Moby-Dick; or, The Whale,* by Herman Melville. University of California Press, from the Arion Press edition, 1979. Reproduced by permission. / Joyner, Eric, illustrator. From a cover of *Billy Budd,* by Herman Melville. Tor Books, 1992. Reproduced by permission. / Peck, Gregory, as Captain Ahab in the film *Moby Dick,* 1954, photograph. UPI/Corbis-Bettmann. Reproduced by permission. / Melville, Herman, painting. Archive Photos, Inc. Reproduced by permission.

CLAUDE MONET. "Grainstack—Snow Effect," painting by Claude Monet. Gift of Misses Aimee and Rosamond Lamb in memory of Mr. and Mrs. Horatio A. Lamb. Museum of Fine Arts, Boston. (c) 1999 Artists Rights Society (ARS), New York / ADAGP, Paris. Reproduced by permission of the Artists Rights Society, Inc. and the Museum of Fine Arts, Boston. / "Impression Sunrise," painting by Claude Monet. (c) 1999 Artists Rights Society (ARS), New York / ADAGP, Paris. Reproduced by permission of the Artists Rights Society, Inc. / Monet, Claude, photograph by Nadar. Corbis-Bettmann. Reproduced by permission.

KYOKO MORI. Mazzella, Mary Jo, illustrator. From a jacket of *Shizuko's Daughter,* by Kyoko Mori. Holt, 1993. Jacket illustration (c) 1993 by Mary Jo Mazzella. Reproduced by permission of the illustrator. / Cover of *One Bird,* by Kyoko Mori. Fawcett Juniper Books, 1996. Reproduced by permission of Random House, Inc. / Mori, Kyoko, photograph by Katherine McCabe. Reproduced by permission of Kyoko Mori.

MARCIA MULLER. Singer, Phillip, illustrator. From a cover of *Edwin of the Iron Shoes,* by Marcia Muller. Mysterious Press, 1993. Reproduced by permission. / Singer, Phillip, illustrator. From a cover of *The Shape of Dread,* by Marcia Muller. Mysterious Press, 1993. Reproduced by permission. / Singer, Phillip, illustrator. From a cover of *Wolf in the Shadows,* by Marcia Muller. Mysterious Press, 1994. Reproduced by permission. / Singer, Phill, illustrator. From a cover of *Till the Butchers Cut Him Down,* by Marcia Muller. Warner Books, 1995. Reproduced by permission. / Muller, Marcia, photograph by Tom Graves. Reproduced by permission.

DONNA JO NAPOLI. Napoli, Donna Jo, photograph. Reproduced by permission of Donna Jo Napoli.

THERESA NELSON. Benson, Linda, illustrator. From a cover of *And One for All,* by Theresa Nelson. Yearling Books, 1991. Reproduced by permission of Bantam Doubleday Dell Books for Young Readers. / Cover of *Earthshine,* by Theresa Nelson. Laurel-Leaf Books, 1996. Reproduced by permission of Bantam Doubleday Dell Books for Young Readers. / Nelson, Theresa, photograph by Brian Cooney. Reproduced by permission of Theresa Nelson.

JAMES PATTERSON. Ovis, Joe, illustrator. From a cover of *The Thomas Berryman Number,* by James Patterson. Warner Books, 1996. Reproduced by permission. / Freeman, Morgan, and Ashley Judd, in the film *Kiss the Girls,* 1997, photograph by Kimberly Wright. The Kobal Collection. Reproduced by permission. / Patterson, James, photograph by Sue Solie Patterson. Little, Brown and Company. Reproduced by permission.

MARC TALBERT. Talbert, Marc, photograph by Jane Hill. Reproduced by permission of Marc Talbert.

ELEANORA E. TATE. Cover of *Front Porch Stories at the One-Room School,* by Eleanora E. Tate. Yearling Books, 1992. Reproduced by permission of Bantam Doubleday Dell Books for Young Readers. / Griffith, Gershom, illustrator. From a cover of *A Blessing in Disguise,* by Eleanora E. Tate. Yearling Books, 1996. Reproduced by permission of Bantam Doubleday Dell Books for Young Readers. / Tate, Eleanora, photograph by Zack E. Hamlett, III. Reproduced by permission.

ROB THOMAS. Raschka, Chris, illustrator. From a jacket of *Rats Saw God,* by Rob Thomas. Simon & Schuster Books for Young Readers, 1996. Jacket illustration copyright (c) 1996 by Simon & Schuster. Reproduced by permission of Simon & Schuster Books for Young Readers, a division of Simon & Schuster, Inc. / Thomas, Rob, photograph by Stanley W. Hensley. Reproduced by permission of Rob Thomas.

EDITH WHARTON. "Father's Home," painting by Grandma Moses. From a cover of *Ethan Frome,* by Edith Wharton. Signet Classics, 1987. Cover painting (c) 1987 Grandma Moses Properties Co., New York. Reproduced by permission of Grandma Moses Properties Co. / "In the Loge," painting by Mary Stevenson Cassatt. From a cover of *The Age of Innocence,* by Edith Wharton. Signet Classics, 1996. The Hayden Collection, Museum of Fine Arts, Boston. Reproduced by permission of Museum of Fine Arts Boston. / Pfeiffer, Michelle, and Daniel Day-Lewis, in the film *The Age of Innocence,* 1993, photograph by Phillip Caruso. The Kobal Collection. Reproduced by permission. / Wharton, Edith, photograph. The Library of Congress.

Cumulative Index

Author/Artist Index

The following index gives the number of the volume in which an author/artist's biographical sketch appears.